Democracy Derailed in Russia

Why has democracy failed to take root in Russia? After shedding the shackles of Soviet rule, some countries in the postcommunist region undertook lasting democratization. Yet Russia did not. Russia experienced dramatic political breakthroughs in the late 1980s and early 1990s, but it subsequently failed to maintain progress toward democracy. In this book, M. Steven Fish offers an explanation for the direction of regime change in post-Soviet Russia. Relying on cross-national comparative analysis and in-depth field research in Russia, Fish shows that Russia's failure to democratize has three causes: too much economic reliance on oil, too little economic liberalization, and too weak a national legislature. Fish's explanation challenges others that have attributed Russia's political travails to history, political culture, or "shock therapy" in economic policy. *Democracy Derailed in Russia* offers a theoretically original and empirically rigorous explanation for one of the most pressing political problems of our time.

M. Steven Fish is Associate Professor of Political Science at the University of California–Berkeley. In 2000–2001 he was a Fulbright Fellow and Visiting Professor of Political Science and Sociology at the European University at St. Petersburg. He is the author of *Democracy from Scratch: Opposition and Regime in the New Russian Revolution* (1995) and a coauthor of *Postcommunism and the Theory of Democracy* (2001). He has published articles in *Comparative Political Studies, East European Constitutional Review, East European Politics and Societies, Europe-Asia Studies, Journal of Democracy, Post-Soviet Affairs, Slavic Review, World Politics*, and numerous edited volumes.

Cambridge Studies in Comparative Politics

Other Books in the Series

Continues after the index

Democracy Derailed in Russia

THE FAILURE OF OPEN POLITICS

M. STEVEN FISH

University of California–Berkeley

CAMBRIDGE
UNIVERSITY PRESS

CAMBRIDGE UNIVERSITY PRESS
Cambridge, New York, Melbourne, Madrid, Cape Town, Singapore, São Paulo

Cambridge University Press
32 Avenue of the Americas, New York, NY 10013-2473, USA

www.cambridge.org
Information on this title: www.cambridge.org/9780521853613

First published 2005
Reprinted 2006 (twice), 2007

Printed in the United States of America

A catalog record for this publication is available from the British Library.

Library of Congress Cataloging in Publication Data

Fish, M. Steven (Michael Steven), 1962–
Democracy derailed in Russia : the failure of open politics / M. Steven Fish.
    p.   cm. – (Cambridge studies in comparative politics)
Includes bibliographical references and index.
ISBN 0-521-85361-3 (hardback) – ISBN 0-521-61896-7 (pbk.)
1. Russia (Federation) – Politics and government – 1991–   2. Democracy – Russia
(Federation).   3. Russia (Federation) – Economic policy – 1991–   I. Title.   II. Series.
JN6695.F57   2005
320.947–dc22   2004029359

ISBN   978-0-521-85361-3 hardback
ISBN   978-0-521-61896-0 paperback

For my wife,
Olga,
and
our magic munchkin,
Nathaniel

Contents

Figures and Tables

Figures

Tables

Acknowledgments

I owe an incalculable debt to many friends, colleagues, and family members. My research travels throughout Russia and other countries in the postcommunist region were made possible by the gracious hospitality and aid of many wonderful people, including Tsedendambyn Batbayar, Rustam Burnashev, Irina Chernykh, Ivana Djuric, Florin Fesnic, Manana Gnolidze, Alek Mamedov, Gustav Matijek, Peter Matijek, Ghia Nodia, Viktor Pestov, Corina Roman, Gheorghe Roman, Aleksandr Romash, Lev Shlosberg, Dorjiyn Shurkhuu, and Mikhail Suprun.

I have benefited greatly from being embedded in several extraordinarily stimulating intellectual environments. Over the past decade, I have learned a great deal from students I instructed in the International Summer School in Political Science and International Relations held in Mierki and Krynica, Poland, under the auspices of the Stefan Batory Foundation, and the Summer School in Social Science held in Almaty, Kazakhstan, sponsored by the Open Society Institute. I also profited from interchange with my students and colleagues at the European University at St. Petersburg, where I spent the 2000–2001 academic year as a Fulbright Fellow.

The intellectual arena that has made the greatest contribution to my work has been the University of California–Berkeley, where I have had the privilege of working since 1995. The Department of Political Science has been the most exciting place imaginable for a comparative social scientist to pursue research and teaching. I am grateful to the undergraduates I have taught in my courses on Russia (Political Science 129B) and on democratization (Political Science 137C) and the graduate students I have had in my seminar on comparative politics (Political Science 200). My students have challenged me year after year to think harder and more deeply about the big questions of political life. The Institute for Slavic, Eurasian, and East

European Studies (ISEEES) at Berkeley has also generated much intellectual electricity. ISEEES, under the masterful leadership of Victoria Bonnell and her successor, Yuri Slezkine, and the adroit administration of Barbara Voytek, furnishes a matchless milieu for scholars who specialize in the post-communist region. I owe a special debt of gratitude to Edward Walker, the director of ISEEES's Berkeley Program in Soviet and Post-Soviet Studies, for a decade of intellectual companionship and for his close reading of the manuscript that became this book.

Ned Walker was not alone in suffering through earlier drafts of this book; Neil Abrams, George Breslauer, Omar Choudhry, Stephen Hanson, Jeffrey Kopstein, Matthew Kroenig, Danielle Lussier, and Susanne Wengle read the manuscript in its entirety as well. Each provided a wealth of incisive criticism, and each reduced the number and egregiousness of the shortcomings in the final product. Nonna Gorilovskaya lent her formidable talents as a research assistant as well.

I am blessed with a wealth of close friends who sustain me with their intellectual guidance and personal support. They include Daniel Abbasi, Christopher Ansell, Boris Kapustin, Jonah Levy, Rose McDermott, and Kenneth Roberts.

Scholars do not always live by ideas and wits alone; some, including and especially me, need a great deal of spiritual as well as intellectual guidance. On this score I am particularly indebted to Mark Labberton, the senior pastor of the First Presbyterian Church of Berkeley, and Doug Bunnell, the pastor of the First Presbyterian Church of Bellingham, Washington.

I continue to labor happily under a profound debt of gratitude to my parents, Michael Fish and Cherrie Robinson, and my sister, Diana Fish.

My deepest debt is due my wife, Olga Fish, and our son, Nathaniel Fish. Olga has inspired this project and sustains me in every step I take; she has also deepened my understanding of the lands of the former Soviet Union. Nate has given my life fresh purpose and taught me to believe in magic. With gratitude, love, and joy I dedicate this book to them.

Abbreviations

(Where names and abbreviations are translated from Russian, their Russian equivalents are noted in parentheses and italics.)

ARCSPO   All-Russia Center for the Study of Public Opinion (*VTsIOM: Vse-Rossiiskii tsentr izucheniia obshchestvennogo mneniia*)
AUCCTU   All-Union Central Committee of Trade Unions (*VTsSPS: Vsesoiuznyi tsentral'nyi sovet profsoiuzov*)
CEC   Central Electoral Commission (*TsIK: Tsentral'naia izbiratel'naia komissiia*)
CELI   Cumulative Economic Liberalization Index
CPRF   Communist Party of the Russian Federation (*KPRF: Kommunisticheskaia Partiia Rossiiskoi Federatsii*)
DCR   Democratic Choice of Russia (*DVR: Demokraticheskii Vybor Rossii*)
EFI   Economic Freedom Index
ELI   Economic Liberalization Index
FH   Freedom House
FIG   Financial-Industrial Group (*FPG: Finansovo-promyshlennaia gruppa*)
FITUR   Federation of Independent Trade Unions of Russia (*FNPR: Federatsiia nezavisimykh profsoiuzov Rossii*)
FNS   Front for National Salvation (*FNS: Front natsional'nogo spaseniia*)
FR   Forward Russia (*VR: Vpered Rossiia*)
FSB   Federal Security Bureau (*FSB: Federal'naia sluzhba bezopasnosti*)
HDI   Human Development Index

IMF	International Monetary Fund
LDPR	Liberal Democratic Party of Russia (*LDPR: Liberal'naia Demokraticheskaia Partiia Rossii*)
LPS	Legislative Powers Survey
NTV	Independent Television Network (*NTV: Nezavisimoe televidenie*)
OECD	Organization for Economic Cooperation and Development
OHR	Our Home Is Russia (*NDR: Nash Dom Rossiia*)
OSCE	Organization for Security and Cooperation in Europe
PPI	Parliamentary Powers Index
RFE/RL	Radio Free Europe/Radio Liberty
RSFSR	Russian Soviet Federated Socialist Republic
RUIE	Russian Union of Industrialists and Entrepreneurs (*RSPP: Rossiiskii soiuz promyshlennikov i predprinimatelei*)
TI	Transparency International
UNDP	United Nations Development Programme
URF	Union of Right Forces (*SPS: Soiuz Pravykh Sil*)
VA	Voice and Accountability scores

1

<hr>

Introduction

A decade and a half after the collapse of the Soviet system, Russian democracy lies in tatters. After the spectacular political breakthroughs of the late 1980s and early 1990s, democratization slowly ground to a halt. As the 1990s wore on and the new century dawned, many of the gains of the late Soviet and early post-Soviet periods were in jeopardy. By the time of Vladimir Putin's reelection as president of Russia in 2004, Russia's experiment with open politics was over.

To be sure, Russian citizens live in a more open polity than they did during the Soviet era. They also live a freer political existence than do the inhabitants of some other lands of the former Soviet Union. Russia did undergo substantial democratization. Unlike Uzbekistan and Turkmenistan, Russia did not merely slide from one form of autocratic police state to another. In contrast with Belarus and Kazakhstan, it did not swiftly revert to full-blown dictatorship after a brief opening.

Yet unlike many of its other postcommunist neighbors, Russia failed to advance to democracy. This book seeks to explain why.

The Study and Its Arguments in Context

Russia was the central entity of the Russian Empire and then the Soviet bloc. Its course of political change after the demise of communism could not be dictated by foreign powers or be driven by mechanical emulation of foreign models. Russia had the economic, bureaucratic, military, and cultural resources to make its own choices. Thus, for social scientists, Russia is the big "independent" case in the postcommunist world. It had to chart, and has charted, its own course. What is more, the fate of regime change in Russia is of immense practical significance. Russia is the core power in

1

the postcommunist area, and its politics affect all other countries in the region. Russia is also a major player in Europe, the Middle East, and East Asia. It is one of the world's two great nuclear powers and one of its top three producers of oil and natural gas. What happens in Russia has been, and remains, central to international politics and security.

It is therefore unsurprising that Russia has been the subject of great attention in the West. Recent books have furnished penetrating accounts of post-Soviet Russian politics. Michael McFaul (2001) has published an exhaustive story of the transformation of elite politics and situated it in an original theoretical framework. George Breslauer (2002) has written an incisive study of top leaders. Timothy Colton (2000), Timothy Colton and Michael McFaul (2003), Richard Rose and Neil Munro (2002), and Stephen White, Richard Rose, and Ian McAllister (1997) have written illuminating books on Russian elections and voters. Thomas Remington (2001) has constructed a masterful examination of the national legislature, and Eugene Huskey (1999) has laid bare the anatomy and inner workings of the presidency. Jeffrey Kahn (2002) has explored the legal aspects of post-Soviet decentralization and relations between the central and regional governments. Debra Javeline (2003) has written an impressive study of labor politics. Timothy Frye (2000), Andrei Shleifer and Daniel Treisman (2000), Daniel Treisman (2001), and David Woodruff (2000) have plumbed the politics of economic policymaking. William Zimmerman (2002) has unearthed the connections between public opinion and foreign policy. During the 1990s and first half of the current decade, Russia was arguably the subject of more extensive and sophisticated treatment in Anglo-American comparative political science than any other country.

This book differs in focus, argument, and method from other available studies on postcommunist Russia. First, the phenomenon I intend to explain – the dependent variable – is the failure to democratize. McFaul's (2001) and Remington's (2001) studies consider democratization, but they focus more on the emergence of stable rules than on democratization per se. Both McFaul and Remington argue that the institutions that structure political competition stabilized during the 1990s. Both explain how this process occurred. The focus of the present study is different. I am concerned with democratization rather than stabilization.

Several studies besides the present one have focused on regime change, and this one is not the first to argue that democracy has failed in Russia. Yet my argument differs from others in the way it accounts for this failure. Some works that have addressed Russia's democratic deficit hold that Russian culture is incompatible with democracy (Duncan, 2000; Huntington, 1996; McDaniel, 1998). Others argue that Russia is no less democratic than one would expect, given its level of economic development (Shleifer and Treisman, 2004). Many authors fault excessively rapid economic liberalization or, in a similar vein, the imposition of inappropriate economic reform models on Russia by external powers (Cohen, 2000; Klein and Pomer, eds., 2001; Medvedev, 2000; Reddaway and Glinski, 2001).

My explanation differs from these. I do not find that cultural or historical factors provide compelling explanations for the failure of democratization. Nor is Russia's level of economic development decisive. I find that economic policy has influenced democratization. In contrast with many other studies, however, I hold that a deficit, rather than a surfeit, of economic liberalization has undermined democratization. I find, too, that Russia's extraordinary endowment of natural resources has inhibited democratization, but in ways that differ from what one finds in other resource-abundant countries. I further argue that the choice of a particular institution – the constitutional provision for a powerful presidency and a weak legislature – has compromised democratization.

None of these three variables has heretofore received adequate treatment in the literature on regime change in Russia. In my account, they explain Russia's failure to democratize.

This book also differs from others in its method. Most books on a single country rely on within-country analysis. Comparisons are often made between stages of the country's development. Both McFaul and Remington, for example, divide recent Russian history into three periods, and these serve as the authors' cases. Both authors use cross-temporal comparison to good effect. In some works on single countries, territorial entities within the country serve as the units for comparison. Kathryn Stoner-Weiss's (1997) investigation of regional politics in Russia, Barry Ames's (2001) inquiry into the causes of dysfunction in Brazilian democracy, and Ashutosh Varshney's (2003[a]) study of the causes of intercommunal violence in India are examples. The present book differs from these studies. It tests hypotheses in the context of large-N, cross-national analysis.

This book, in some respects, is a sequel to *Democracy from Scratch: Opposition and Regime in the New Russian Revolution*, which was published in 1995. In that book I sought to explain why, despite the dramatic political openings of the period of Mikhail Gorbachev's tenure as Soviet leader, a robust civil society did not emerge in Russia. I conceived of civil society broadly to include political parties, interest associations, labor unions, and

3

social movement organizations. The dependent variable was the extent of the development of civil society.

I set off for Russia in 1989 as a graduate student in search of a blossoming civil society. At home in the United States, I had read that Russia was teeming with new nonstate groups and that these groups were spawning a civil society. In the field, I encountered something different. I found not a civil society in the making but rather something I came to label a "movement society" – a realm of energetic but fragile and ephemeral political campaigns.

I attributed the failure of civil society to three factors. The first was the sequencing of political reforms. The timing of the first competitive elections, and especially the decision to hold elections before political parties were legalized, was of particular importance. The electoral openings of 1989 and 1990 were at once too sudden and too partial. Elections without bona fide parties reduced incentives for anti-regime leaders to invest in parties. The timing of the reforms encouraged a highly individualistic – almost antiorganizational – form of political entrepreneurship.

The second causal factor was the peculiar character of state agencies during the Gorbachev period. State agencies retained their potential for coercion, or at least disruption, but lost their positive capacities to make things happen. So the new autonomous organizations experienced crippling interference, yet when they nonetheless overcame it and managed to articulate demands, they found that the state agencies responsible for policy were in disarray and incapable of responding. Just as effective intermediation requires that societal groups have some influence over the state, so too must state agencies be able to deliver something of value. Yet by the end of the 1980s, state power in Russia had been reduced to negative power, meaning that the state could prevent things from happening but could not really make things happen. It could harass, obstruct, and repress, but it could not negotiate, entice, or deliver. The combination of intransigence and weakness on the part of the state circumscribed incentives for individuals to participate in the new politics of independent association. It checked the emergence of the institutions of bargaining, balancing, denying, and delivering that normally govern state–society relations.

The third cause of civil society's travails was communist-era property relations and the social conditions they created. The state's near monopoly on property, production, distribution, and employment stymied autonomous groups' efforts to establish resource bases and represent interests outside the confines of state organizations.

The tenuous development of societal organizations dimmed democracy's prospects. I held that Russia was headed either for "democracy by default" or "moderate authoritarianism." The former would combine a fairly open political regime with weak institutions for translating popular preferences into policy; the latter would spell a mostly closed political regime, albeit one that included some channels for the expression of public voice. Writing in 1992 and 1993, I held that Russia was a democracy by default, but that the weakness of political-societal development presaged descent into moderate authoritarianism.

The present study extends the previous one, though what I seek to explain has changed. *Democracy from Scratch* tried to explain the development (or underdevelopment) of civil society. The prediction just cited was merely a closing rumination on the likely effects of civil society's underdevelopment on the future of regime change. *Democracy Derailed in Russia* attempts to explain the fate of regime change itself, and specifically the failure to democratize, through the middle of the current decade.

Russian civil society remains poorly developed, but I now focus on it only insofar as its development (or underdevelopment) has affected democratization. The present book discusses the weakness of civil society, but as just one of several factors that are embedded in a chain of causation that culminates in the failure of democratization.

Just as the dependent variable of this study is different from that of the earlier book, the determinants of the phenomenon to be explained differ as well. Some factors that I ignored in my earlier study on civil society are of central importance in postcommunist regime change. Russia's superabundance of raw materials is one such factor. Some political institutions that did not exist or whose effects were uncertain in the early 1990s also must be considered closely in any explanation of subsequent political change. The distribution of power between the president and the legislature is especially important.

Yet some of the factors in *Democracy from Scratch* that were used to explain society's weakness left a legacy that helps account for the failure of democratization. The choice of constitution in 1993 was influenced by conditions whose roots lie in the reforms of the Gorbachev period. Furthermore, continuities between the Soviet and post-Soviet periods in the operation of state agencies and the nature of property relations shape latter-day politics. An urge to repress on the part of state agencies continues to check the development of autonomous organizations, which in turn impairs democratization. The endurance of economic statism has reproduced

Soviet-era conditions and retarded socioeconomic change that would bolster open rule.

Method and Logic of Causal Inference

The methods used in this book have a much stronger cross-national thrust
than those used in *Democracy from Scratch*. The empirics in the earlier book
were based on ethnographic work in a single country. I have continued to
conduct in-depth research in Russia during the past decade, and I draw heavily on my findings from the field in this book. But the wealth of quantitative
data that has become available in recent years furnishes fresh opportunities
for examining Russia in broad comparative perspective, and I use these data
extensively.

The logic of causal inference is straightforward. To test hypotheses that
are amenable to quantification, I use simple descriptive statistics, as well
as regression analysis. In much of the analysis, I first examine the hypothesis by analyzing all countries of the world with populations of one-half
million or more, and then narrow the universe to the postcommunist region alone. The postcommunist region is defined as the 28 countries of the
former Soviet Union, East Europe (including the countries of the former
Yugoslavia), and Mongolia. Due to a shortage of data, Bosnia is excluded
entirely from this study, bringing the number of countries to 27. In testing
some hypotheses, data are missing for several countries, and these countries will be excluded in the relevant analyses. If a given variable is not a
determinant of regime type in cross-national analysis, it will be discarded
as a potential determinant of political regime in Russia. If the variable is
significant in cross-national analysis, Russia's place in the world and the region will be examined. If Russia is an outlier and is atypical in a manner that
reveals that the variable is not of consequence in Russia, the variable will be
discarded. If Russia is not an outlier, the variable will be considered a potentially important determinant, and its effects will be investigated further
with in-depth focus on Russia.

For example, consider the claim that Russia's failure to democratize stems
from Russians' fondness for alcohol (a hypothesis that I have yet to encounter in the literature and that will not be tested, accordingly). I would
begin by considering whether there is any logical reason to regard drinking
a determinant of political regime. If there is any basis for a positive answer,
I would test empirically whether alcohol consumption per capita is a good
predictor of the extent of democratization in the world as a whole and in the

postcommunist region in particular. If the empirical analysis showed that alcohol consumption per capita is not a good predictor of political regime, I would rule it out as an explanation for Russia's political condition, regardless of how much Russians drink. If drinking proved to be a good predictor of regime type, however, I would examine Russia's place in comparative perspective. If heavier drinking was associated with less-democratic politics but the data showed that Russians, contrary to popular wisdom, were comparatively light drinkers, drinking would be ruled out as a determinant of Russia's democracy deficit. If Russians were indeed heavy drinkers and Russia's political condition was roughly what one would expect, given how much Russians drink, the drinking hypothesis would gain credibility and be further investigated with specific attention to Russia. If I could establish a convincing causal account of how drinking undercuts democracy, I would conclude that drinking is the enemy not only of personal health but also of political openness in Russia.

Quantitative measures are unavailable for some potentially important variables. These variables' effects must still be tested. The same logic of causal inference obtains as in quantitative analysis. Suppose that some observers argue that Russia's failure to democratize is due to the fact that the Russian people are pessimists (again, I have yet to encounter this hypothesis, but let it suffice for the purpose of illustration). Unlike drinking, pessimism cannot be easily measured using a quantitative indicator. Investigating the pessimism hypothesis would require, first, an assessment of whether pessimism theoretically could affect political regime. If an argument could be made that it might, qualitative comparison of pessimism in Russia and other countries would be undertaken. If there were good theoretical reasons to believe that pessimism countervails democracy and compelling evidence that pessimism is worse in Russia, I would further investigate the argument. If I could unearth a solid causal connection in Russia, I would conclude that the pessimism hypothesis is sound.

While the logic of causal inference used here is simple, it is also unusual in single-country studies. One of the few that does adopt such a logic is Seymour Martin Lipset and Gary Marks's *It Didn't Happen Here: Why Socialism Failed in the United States* (2001). In order to explain why socialism never took hold, Lipset and Marks compare the United States to other advanced industrialized countries. They locate several ways in which the United States differed from countries where socialist movements did make inroads. The authors do not engage in large-N, cross-national statistical analysis. They rely on historical accounts. But their logic of causal inference is largely the same as mine. What is more, like the present book, Lipset and Marks's work explains why something that might have happened did not. In their study, that something was the emergence of socialism in America; in this book, it is the emergence of democracy in Russia.

This approach to causal inference is vulnerable to criticism. Circumstances that are specific to the country under investigation may be important for understanding outcomes, and cross-national analysis may not uncover certain variables that are crucial to political change in Russia itself. Different causal paths to – and away from – democracy may exist at different times in different parts of the world, and broad global analysis might obscure factors that are central to a single country's experience.

The approach undertaken in this book addresses this legitimate concern. By testing hypotheses in the context of the postcommunist region in particular as well as in the world as a whole, I can at least detect distinctions that may be specific to countries that emerged from communist-party rule in the late 1980s and early 1990s. There may well be a discrete causal path of regime change in the postcommunist region that differs from that of, say, interwar Europe, southern Europe in the 1970s, or Latin America in the 1980s, and Russia might partake of a distinct experience by virtue of being a postcommunist country. The analyses conducted here, by alternating between a global sample of cases and postcommunist countries alone, should be able to account for regional specificities that may be of importance to the Russian experience.

Yet one might further argue that the approach may still overlook an influential factor that is unique to Russia and that cannot be uncovered even in within-region analysis. Such a possibility cannot be excluded entirely, but several precautions taken here mitigate the danger. First, I test the influence of a large number and wide range of candidate causal variables, including all those that appear prominently in the literature on regime change in post-Soviet Russia. Second, the risk of overlooking uniquely Russian conditions is also mitigated by my time in the field in Russia, which amounts to a total of almost three years following the demise of the Soviet Union at the end of 1991. This experience included not only work in Moscow, where I usually resided, but also intensive field research involving several hundred interviews with a broad range of politicians, political activists, scholars, and journalists in northwest Russia (St. Petersburg and Pskov), far northern Russia (Arkhangelsk), south-central Russia (Saratov), and the Urals region (Ekaterinburg, Cheliabinsk, and Perm). I also spent about one year conducting field work in 11 postcommunist countries besides Russia between

1992 and 2003. Together with the year and a half I spent in a broad range of Russian sites during the late Soviet period, this experience may reduce – though of course still not eliminate – the hazard of overlooking the importance of distinctly Russian conditions.

The overarching approach to method and causation taken here is inspired by Emile Durkheim. According to Durkheim, the investigator "must systematically discard all preconceptions" at the beginning of inquiry; doing so was "the basis of all scientific method" (1982, p. 72). To "discard all preconceptions" may sound like a grandiose and unattainable goal, but Durkheim had in mind simply eschewing controlling assumptions that were self-reinforcing and treated a priori as beyond methodical doubt, or that were subjected only to such tests as they were bound to pass, given the prior commitments of the investigator. Contemporary political science has spawned a robust industry of sparring over methods and theoretical approaches. Such debates have their place, but when showing the superiority of a given methodology or theoretical approach takes precedence over understanding the cases at hand, as it sometimes does in political science, the result may be an exercise in cramming facts into preestablished theoretical frameworks. I aim better to understand regime change in Russia and, in the best case, regime change in general in the contemporary world. I am not concerned with whether the findings demonstrate the virtues of rational choice, historical institutionalism, or some other political-scientific approach. I am interested in using theory to gain knowledge about the case, not using the case to illustrate the superiority of a particular approach to political science. I embrace Durkheim's view, expressed in his assertion: "We do not start by postulating a certain conception of human nature, in order to deduce a sociology from it; it is rather the case that we demand from sociology an increasing understanding of humanity" (1982, p. 236). Discarding preconceptions, in practical terms, means placing substantive gains in knowledge about the subject matter above vindicating this or that scholarly paradigm.

This also means allowing the evidence to lead to the conclusions, rather than the opposite. Such an imperative does not require shunning deduction entirely, since deduction is necessary to generate a hypothesis. It does, however, mean eschewing the pretensions of a strong form of deductivism. Durkheim embraced a method advocated by J. S. Mill known as eliminative induction, in which putative causal hypotheses are systematically eliminated by comparing them with facts. While favoring induction, Durkheim also assumed that a hypothesis was needed to engage in meaningful observation. Just as a hypothesis cannot materialize out of thin air (contra the logic of pure deductivism), neither could one imagine an "observation" in the absence of some more general understanding that made sense of the thing (contra the logic of pure inductivism). Durkheim regarded inductivism and hypothesis testing as the mutually dependent elements that constituted the core of the effort to advance scientific knowledge. In this respect, he was a methodological centrist. He formulated and worked with hypotheses, which required some deduction. Yet he spurned the exercises in making-the-facts-fit-the-theory that he saw in some works that meticulously strove to maintain the appearance of adhering to deductive thinking. He conceded that deductively based approaches were capable of generating elegant theoretical constructs. But he held that beauty was not necessarily truth, and that aesthetics furnished flimsy criteria for evaluating scientific theories or modes of inquiry (1982, pp. 67–8). The present study embraces Durkheim's outlook and method.

This study also places comparison at the core of the effort to show causation. Durkheim held: "We have one way of demonstrating that one phenomenon is the cause of another. This is to compare the cases where they are both simultaneously present and absent, so as to discover whether the variations they display in these different combinations of circumstances provide evidence that one depends on the other." In the absence of the ability to conduct controlled experiments, "the comparative method is the sole one suitable for sociology" (1982, p. 147).

Not just any comparative method promises sound findings, however. Durkheim argued:

Nothing is proved when, as happens so often, one is content to demonstrate by a greater or lesser number of examples that in isolated cases the facts have varied according to the hypothesis. From these sporadic and fragmentary correlations no general conclusion can be drawn. To illustrate an idea is not to prove it. What must be done is not to compare isolated variations, but series of variations, systematically constituted, whose terms are correlated with each other in as continuous a gradation as possible and which moreover cover an adequate range. For the variations of a phenomenon only allow a law to be induced if they express clearly the way in which the phenomenon develops in any given circumstances. (1982, p. 155)

This statement implies that covering the broadest universe of cases possible is desirable. Analyzing a large number of cases bolsters the possibility for displaying the "series of variations" that Durkheim found necessary to demonstrate causation. It also increases the opportunities for exhibiting the full range of variation on the variables under analysis, such that the data units "are correlated with each other in as continuous a gradation as possible" and "cover an adequate range."

If the number of potential cases is unmanageably large, then proper case selection, informed by attention to locating a representative sample, is crucial. But if the whole universe is reasonably small, one can examine it in its entirety. The opportunity to do so obviates the problem of case selection. It also enables – and forces – one to elude the trap of selecting cases to fit the theory, which Durkheim warned against and which is an ever-present hazard in scientific inquiry.

In the present study, examining the whole universe is possible. The universe is countries with populations over one-half million for which adequate data are available, which number only 147 cases. Furthermore, the scope of the analysis is confined to a discrete, limited stretch of time, specifically the 1990s and the early 2000s. The claims that arise from the findings are limited to this period. I do not hold that the arguments are necessarily valid for other times, still less for all history.

Further insight into causal relationships can be gained by also zeroing in on a subset of cases that share essential features. Durkheim held that the most fruitful comparisons were among societies that were "varieties of the same species" (1995, p. 91). In the present study, the postcommunist region of which Russia is a part composes a natural family of cases. Countries of the region share a common history of Leninist political regimes and command economies, and they underwent regime change at virtually the same time. As noted, after examining hypotheses in light of global data, I will proceed to evaluate them in the context of postcommunist countries alone. The analysis of this subset provides additional purchase on unearthing causal relationships.

Yet however amenable the cases may be to rigorous and multifaceted analysis, investigation of the type undertaken here cannot establish hard and fast covering laws. Both determinism and probabilism have distinguished careers in social science, and each has its exponents among contemporary scholars. Karl Marx believed that he had discovered the principles that guide all of history. He was a determinist. Sigmund Freud thought that he had unearthed the master key to explaining human behavior; while less strictly deterministic than Marx's, his thinking tended toward determinism rather than probabilism. Durkheim, like Max Weber, in contrast, strove for a high level of generalization but held that the scientific enterprise was the art of the probable. Durkheim expressed the matter succinctly: "Science progresses slowly and never establishes more than probabilities" (1982, p. 218). The ambitions of the present work are probabilistic.

Cross-national statistical approaches, such as the one adopted here, have been the subject of criticism in recent years. Prominent scholars have argued that political regimes are deeply embedded in historical circumstances, that the dynamics of much social interaction are nonlinear, and that linear regression analysis is not optimal for comparative study (Abbott, 2001; Mahoney and Rueschemeyer, eds., 2003; Pierson, 2004). An especially acute presentation of such a view is made in a recent article by Peter Hall (2003). Hall argues that scholars know from the past several decades of research that history often unfolds unevenly; some periods of time are clearly more important than others. What is more, some events may place a system on a distinct path that dramatically narrows the range of possible future outcomes. Such formative moments may hold the keys to understanding outcomes. Hall also asserts that we know well that feedback mechanisms are often at work in politics. In real life, causal relationships are very often reciprocal. Thus, the notion that we may clearly distinguish between variables that are "independent" and those that are "dependent" is at odds with what we know to be true about history. He therefore holds that linear regression analysis, which requires that the scholar label some variables independent and others dependent, is not the best way to grasp cause and effect in large-scale social and political change. Instead, he recommends that scholars who are interested in demonstrating causal relationships focus on tracing historical processes.

Hall and other writers have made important contributions to understanding social and political phenomena, and they have successfully drawn attention to the shortcomings of large-N studies that rely on regression analysis. They are undoubtedly right to suggest that feedback mechanisms are often in play in real life, and that modeling some factors as causal (independent) and others as caused (dependent), as linear regression analysis requires, risks distorting reality and overlooking complex causal relationships.

Still, critics such as Hall have not always furnished a satisfactory set of alternative methods. They propose carefully examining how history unfolds as the alternative to regression analysis. While historical process tracing may be of great value, it is not necessarily superior to regression analysis as a means for testing the empirical validity of theoretical hypotheses. Linear regression analysis does, as critics note, require making simplifying assumptions about the direction of effects in causal relationships, and it often fails to detect nonlinear relationships and critical moments. But even the most careful effort at historical process tracing is also vulnerable to the charge; no matter how painstaking one's efforts to include all relevant facts in the analysis, some potentially important moments will go undetected or need to be suppressed for the sake of concision. If one is concerned primarily with testing hypotheses about causation, working with some simplifying assumptions is unavoidable, and statistical approaches that encompass a large number of observations may provide at least as good a source of leverage for testing hypotheses as historical process tracing does (Gerring, 2001; Goldthorpe, 1997; Jackman, 1985; King, Keohane, and Verba, 1994).

The present study may help show how the basic methodological principles articulated by Durkheim and other founders of social science retain their value for comparative political research. It may show that despite its limitations, analysis that focuses on comparison across a large number of cases, rather than on unpacking the history of a single case or a small number of cases, provides a good way of gauging the validity of alternative hypotheses in the study of large-scale political change.

While this book is full of tables and figures, the statistical methods used are uncomplicated. The reader who is familiar with basic regression analysis will have no problem understanding the quantitative analysis. The statistical findings, moreover, are discussed in the prose. The reader who lacks statistical training and feels a surge of somnolence at the sight of regression coefficients need not abandon this book. All of the findings shown in the tables are also presented in the text. The reader can skip the tables and still fully comprehend the book's arguments and the evidence used to support them.

Overview of the Book

Before testing hypotheses and grappling with causal explanation, I discuss conceptual issues as well as the phenomenon that is to be explained. Chapter 2 presents a concept of and measures for democracy. It also includes a preliminary look at how Russia rates in terms of democratic attainment. Chapter 3 specifies the dependent variable, the extent of democratization in Russia. It shows that Russia has not achieved democracy, even according to a spare, minimalist definition of the concept. Chapter 4 tests a variety of hypotheses about why democracy has not taken hold. Some plausible and widely embraced explanations for Russia's democratic deficit do not survive scrutiny.

13

Chapters 5–7 examine in depth the three factors that do explain the travails of democratization, with one chapter devoted to each. Chapter 5 addresses the resource curse. It presents evidence that the Russian economy's dependence on raw materials has compromised democratization. It also shows that resources undermine democracy in Russia by different means than they do in other resource-abundant countries, such as those of the Persian Gulf.

Chapter 6 investigates the influence of economic policy. It shows that thoroughgoing economic liberalization facilitates democratization. While many scholars claim that "shock therapy" jeopardizes open politics, the evidence presented in Chapter 6 shows precisely the opposite. It also demonstrates that Russia did not carry out shock therapy. Russia actually pursued policies that reproduced economic statism, and these policies in turn stymied democratization.

Chapter 7 examines the third determinant of the failure of democratization: the adoption of a "superpresidential" constitution. The constitution's provision for a formidable president and a relatively ineffectual legislature bestowed an inauspicious institutional framework. It facilitated backsliding to closed rule.

Chapter 8 summarizes and discusses the book's central arguments and considers the arguments' limitations. It further examines recent trends in Russian politics in light of the book's causal arguments. It concludes that natural resource dependency is not abating, Putin's plans for economic liberalization have collided with his interest in political control, and empowerment of the legislature is not in the works. I therefore predict that Russia's experiment with open politics will not resume for the foreseeable future.

As a preliminary caveat, it is important to note that the drama of Russian politics continues. Change is the order of the day. It would be premature to conclude that Russia has firmly consolidated a distinct form of regime. The outcomes examined here do not represent genuine "endpoints." Political regimes are always in flux. To say that democratization has failed so far is not to deny the possibility of political opening in the future.

But nearly two decades have passed since Gorbachev cracked open the Soviet system. Sovereign, postcommunist Russia has been in existence for two-thirds as long. It is not too early to assess the direction of change and to hazard an explanation for why democracy has proven so elusive.

2

Some Concepts and Their Application to Russia

A Definition of Democracy

Characterizing the political regime depends not only on one's interpretation of facts and understanding of conditions but also upon the standards of measurement, concepts, and expectations that one brings to the task of evaluation. Put another way, the characterization of cases depends upon the criteria for classification as well as the comparative referent. If one's definition of "revolution" contains violent overthrow of the regime as a diagnostic feature, then even Hungary's and South Africa's transformations of the early 1990s would fail to qualify as revolutions, whereas Congo-Zaire's regime change in the late 1990s would meet the standard. If one's definition is based on the distance between the old and new regimes in the extent of popular control over the state, the Hungarian and South African transformations were revolutions and the change of regime in Congo-Zaire was not.

Similarly, depending upon one's criteria, one could classify virtually any polity – or no polities at all – as democratic. During the Brezhnev period, Soviet ideologists claimed not only that the USSR was a democracy but also that it was one "of a higher type." The rulers' self-professed commitment to the welfare of the people and the people's supposedly extraordinary – if elusive and mysterious – control over the state qualified the polity for such status. Few analysts would now take seriously such a conception of democracy, but even within mainstream Western political science, a multiplicity of definitions and conceptions of democracy is available. Choice of definitions and conceptions, whether or not made explicit, shapes characterization of real cases.

Many definitions and conceptions of democracy are found in comparative politics and political philosophy. Among the most widely embraced is Joseph Schumpeter's celebrated concept. Schumpeter understood democracy in terms of free elections. He defined "the democratic method" as "that institutional arrangement for arriving at political decisions in which individuals acquire the power to decide by means of a competitive struggle for the people's vote" (1950, p. 269). Schumpeter is often accused of stopping there and defining democracy simply as the presence of elections. I too have made the mistake (Fish, 2001[a]). But he is not guilty of the charge, as Guillermo O'Donnell (2001) has reminded us in a penetrating article on democratic theory. In fact, Schumpeter suggested that open communication and the universal right to compete for elective office were also diagnostic features of democracy. Without these rights, elections would not necessarily reveal the public will. He states: "If, on principle at least, everyone is free to compete for political leadership by presenting himself to the electorate, this will in most cases though not in all mean a considerable amount of freedom of discussion *for all*. In particular it will mean a considerable amount of freedom of the press" (1950, pp. 271–2; italics in the original). Schumpeter did see the interdependence between political rights (by which I mean the right to vote and to run for office) and civil liberties (by which I mean freedoms needed to make elections meaningful and to maintain citizens' ability to monitor the rulers).

Schumpeter's conception has been borrowed and sharpened by many political scientists. Juan Linz summarizes the "criteria for democracy" as

[l]egal freedom to formulate and advocate political alternatives with the concomitant rights to free association, free speech, and other basic freedoms of person; free and nonviolent competition among leaders with periodic validation of their claim to rule; inclusion of all effective political offices in the democratic process; and provision for the participation of all members of the political community, whatever their political preferences. (1978, p. 5)

Samuel Huntington, who claims to follow in the "Schumpeterian tradition," holds that a regime is democratic "to the extent that its most powerful collective decision makers are selected through fair, honest, and periodic elections in which candidates freely compete for votes and in which virtually all the adult population is eligible to vote." According to Huntington, the presence of elections is not sufficient; democracy also requires "those civil and political freedoms to speak, publish, assemble, and organize that are necessary to political debate and the conduct of electoral campaigns"

(1991, p. 7). Giuseppe Di Palma offers an especially spare version of essentially the same definition: "[f]ree and universal suffrage in the context of civil liberties" (1990, p. 16). Norberto Bobbio provides an elegant summary of the logical and historical basis for what he calls the "double interdependence" of political rights and civil liberties. He states: "The concession of political rights has been a natural consequence of the concession of basic liberties; the only guarantee that the right to liberties will be respected consists in the right to control in the last instance the power that underwrites this guarantee" (1987, pp. 32–3). Many other contemporary theorists of democracy, including Giovanni Sartori (1987) and Ian Shapiro (1996), also embrace such conceptions.

Perhaps the best known and most widely used contemporary definition of democracy that is located in the Schumpeterian tradition is Robert Dahl's. His definition, which he labeled "polyarchy" since he regarded "democracy" as an unachievable ideal type, has the advantage of providing a short list of specific criteria. In Dahl's conception (and in his words, 1982, p. 11), the defining conditions of democracy are the following:

1) [C]ontrol over government decisions about policy is constitutionally vested in elected officials; 2) elected officials are chosen in frequently and fairly conducted elections in which coercion is comparatively uncommon; 3) practically all adults have the right to vote in the election of officials; 4) practically all adults have the right to run for elective offices in the government; 5) citizens have the right to express themselves without the danger of severe punishment on political matters broadly defined; 6) citizens have the right to seek out alternative sources of information. Moreover, alternative sources of information exist and are protected by law; and 7) citizens . . . have the right to form relatively independent associations or organizations, including independent political parties and interest groups.

Dahl's definition, by emphasizing citizenship – meaning the franchise and the rights needed to make it meaningful – casts democracy as a relationship between rulers and the ruled. The definition specifies the procedural conditions that enable people to govern themselves – that is, that empower the ruled to control the rulers.

The definitions offered by Schumpeter and elaborated and clarified by Linz, Huntington, Di Palma, Bobbio, Sartori, Shapiro, and Dahl, among other theorists, share several traits. First, they focus on free elections and the communicative and associational rights necessary for the electors to be informed and capable of organizing themselves for political participation, and thus for elections to represent public opinion faithfully. They avoid the error of defining democracy as elections alone. As such, they are not overly

17

permissive (or "minimalist"). Such excessive minimalism is found in the definition offered by Adam Przeworski and colleagues, who have argued that the presence of elections alone, provided that the outcome is uncertain and irreversible and that the elections are repeatable, is a sufficient condition for the presence of democracy (1996[a], 1996[b]). Thus, Przeworski and colleagues (2000) classify Brazil during 1979–84 as a democracy, though the head of government was selected by the armed forces and imprisonment or worse was often the price of participation in an organization that the military rulers regarded as leftist. Even Guatemala between 1966 and 1981 is labeled a democracy by Przeworski and colleagues, though systematic and atrocious human rights violations carried out by the government and government-backed paramilitaries were ordinary aspects of political life, while leftist political forces were effectively banned. By leaving out of their definition basic liberties and control of the state by elected officials, Przeworski and colleagues end up labeling as democracies polities in which elections neither revealed public opinion nor even decided who governed. As Scott Mainwaring and colleagues have argued, the definition offered by Przeworski and colleagues is "subminimal," since it allows for the classification of polities in which elections are shams as democracies (2001, p. 43).

While steering clear of the error of subminimalism, so do Schumpeter, Linz, Huntington, Di Palma, Bobbio, Sartori, Shapiro, and Dahl also avoid the problem of maximalism. Maximalist definitions are overly restrictive and demanding because they are laden with conditions that are not aspects of political regime, such as socioeconomic equalities. Maximalist conceptions are rooted in the socialist tradition and are popular among Marxist scholars. They often emphasize what they call "substantive" or "real" – as opposed to strictly "procedural" or "formal" – properties and regard democratization as requiring the extension of citizenship rights from political to economic and social relationships (Huber, Rueschemeyer, and Stephens, 1999; Macpherson, 1973; Marshall, 1965; Rueschemeyer, Stephens, and Stephens, 1992). Such conceptions are vulnerable to the charge of utopianism and are of limited utility. Democracy by its terminological nature refers to *political regime*. Maximalist definitions run the risk of failing to distinguish between *diagnostic features*, on the one hand, and *sustaining conditions* or *desirable outcomes*, on the other. Democracy may well promote socioeconomic equality; so too may socioeconomic equality help sustain democracy. But to confuse either what may help sustain a phenomenon or a sought-after product of a phenomenon with the phenomenon itself is conceptually unsound. While

18

such definitions may still be found in the literature, they do not predominate in writings on democracy. As Larry Diamond has noted with approval: "The incorporation of social and economic desiderata into the definition of democracy – an approach fashionable in the 1960s and 1970s – has waned considerably in the past two decades. By and large, most scholarly and policy uses of the term *democracy* today refer to a purely political conception of the term" (1999, p. 8; italics in the original; see also Collier and Levitsky, 1997; Karl, 1990; Schmitter and Karl, 1996).

While I embrace the definition of democracy offered by Schumpeter and his followers and in this respect stand in the conceptual mainstream, on several other matters my concepts and terminology differ from those that predominate in comparative politics. First, I discuss differences among political regimes in terms of degrees of openness and closure; I use openness/closure as the metric to assess regime type. Typically, discussion of differences in regime types is worded in terms of the "degree of democracy" or "how democratic" or "how authoritarian" a regime is. But these terms do not function well as a descriptive metric for characterizing degrees along a spectrum. The terms "democraticness" and "authoritarianness" are more satisfactory but are awkward. Rather than refer to regimes in terms of how democratic or how authoritarian they are, I prefer to consider how open/closed they are. Dahl's definition essentially establishes the conditions that make for an *open* political regime: Political participation is open to everyone (or almost everyone), competition is open, political communication flows openly, people associate openly for political ends, government operations are open to scrutiny, and so on. A political regime may be considered more or less open/closed given the extent to which it meets Dahl's criteria.

Second, in depicting nondemocracy, I will not rely on the term "authoritarianism." The concept has a long and distinguished history in political science and still figures prominently in leading works on political regimes (Levitsky and Way, 2002). But "democracy" and "authoritarianism" do not make good opposites, since they are located on different conceptual planes.

Democracy refers to rule by the people – or, in practical terms in the contemporary world, popular control over the state; "-cracy," like "-archy," simply means rule or government. The prefixes that may be appended refer to the part of the people that rules. In a democracy, the rulers are the people as a whole; in an oligarchy, a part of the people; in an aristocracy, the best; in an ochlocracy, the rabble; and so on.

Authoritarianism, in contrast, is not a "-cracy" or an "-archy." It is an "-ism." Like many other "-isms," authoritarianism refers to a style, a manner, or a cast. Authoritarianism implies harsh rule, but unlike democracy, it does not specify who rules. Authoritarianism is not conceptually compatible with democracy; it makes for an awkward and unworthy opposite. I therefore use other terms that are commensurable with democracy: "oligarchy" and "monocracy."

Oligarchy refers to rule by a part, monocracy to rule by one. Both are types of what are usually referred to as authoritarian regimes, though a monocracy is more closed than an oligarchy. In an oligarchy, the right to hold high office and to communicate and associate with others as one pleases is open to multiple actors, but these actors constitute only a part of the people. In a monocracy, a single actor alone, be it an individual or a party, may rule and act freely according to his/her/its preferences; political life is closed to everyone else. I prefer the term monocracy to "autocracy" because the latter carries the connotation of rule by a single individual, whereas monocracy leaves open the possibility of total control by a unified collective actor. Democracy, oligarchy, and monocracy all refer to who rules and who may participate, rather than to a style of rule.

Measuring Political Openness

Even if a single, uncontroversial conception of democracy completely dominated discourse on political regimes, which it does not, measuring political openness would be difficult. Assessing the extent of a polity's openness/closure necessarily involves judgment calls about which criteria to include, how to weigh criteria, how to observe political conditions, who is qualified to observe political conditions, and so on. Nothing is gained by arguing simply that political regime type really cannot be measured precisely. Everyone – and particularly the analyst who has tried to measure it – knows that.

The inevitability of question marks and controversy should not and does not halt efforts. Material living standards cannot be measured precisely either, though we often accept figures on economic matters without question. Sources differ on product per capita figures. This is hardly surprising; entire sectors are necessarily left out of any assessments of national income, and only bits of the sectors whose activities are included are actually observed and calculated. As Richard Rose aptly notes: "Macroeconomic measures are intellectual constructs; no one has ever seen a gross national product" (2002/2003, p. 64). Estimates do and must involve a great many educated guesses about the unknown based on the tips of the icebergs that are visible.

Even assessing the actual value of what can be seen is problematic. Social scientists continue to debate how to measure purchasing power parity and whether figures adjusted for purchasing power do a better or worse job of capturing relative differences in living standards than do figures that are not so adjusted.

Measuring the openness/closure of a political regime is similarly complicated. But there have been numerous serious efforts to do so. A sophisticated and ambitious attempt is found in the "Voice and Accountability" indicators devised by Daniel Kaufmann, Aart Kraay, and Massimo Mastruzzi (2003). The scores are available for 1996, 1998, 2000, and 2002. The Voice and Accountability indicators (hereafter "VA scores") are one of the six "Governance Indicators" that Kaufmann and colleagues have created. Scores range between about −2.5 (least open polity) and +2.5 (most open polity).

My understanding of democracy, which is essentially popular control over the state, coupled with the basic rights that are essential to ensure the possibility of such popular control, is well represented by the VA scores. According to Kaufmann, Kraay, and Mastruzzi, the VA scores "measure the extent to which citizens of a country are able to participate in the selection of governments." The authors note that they "also include in this category indicators measuring the independence of the media, which serves an important role in monitoring those in authority and holding them accountable for their actions" (p. 3). Given my definition of democracy, the VA scores provide a good source of measurement. The scores are consonant with Dahl's criteria for polyarchy. In the quantitative analyses, I measure the dependent variable (the extent of political openness/closure) using the VA scores for 2002, which is the most recent year for which the data are available.

The scores are based on extensive, multiple surveys and are available for all major countries. The components of the VA scores for 2002 were drawn from seven main sources: The State Failure Task Force's *State Capacity Survey*; *The Economist Intelligence Unit*; Freedom House's *Freedom in the World* and *Nations in Transit*; the Human Rights Database, which is based on Amnesty International's *Annual Report* and the U.S. Department of State's *Country Reports on Human Rights Practices*; Political Risk Services; Reporters sans frontières (Reporters Without Borders); and the World Markets Online database.

Each of these sources furnishes some information that Kaufmann and colleagues drew upon to create the VA scores (for details, Kaufmann, Kraay, and Mastruzzi, 2003, p. 91). The part of the State Failure Task Force's survey that was used for the creation of VA scores was that on state repression of citizens. *The Economist Intelligence Unit* furnished information on the accountability of public officials, freedom of association, the possibility for orderly transfer of power, and human rights. Freedom House provided data on political rights and civil liberties. From the Human Rights Database, Kaufmann and colleagues extracted information on freedom of political participation, travel freedom, and the risk of imprisonment for reasons of ethnicity, race, or political or religious beliefs. The information drawn from Political Risk Services was on military involvement in politics and the likelihood that a popularly elected government would be able to retain power. That drawn from Reporters Without Borders, a Paris-based organization, was the group's "Press Freedom Index." World Markets Online supplied information on the representativeness of government.

The VA scores are not the only available measure for the dependent variable. Some scholars who engage in cross-national analysis assess political openness/closure using the "freedom ratings" issued by Freedom House in its annual reports, *Freedom in the World* (Karatnycky, Piano, and Puddington, eds., 2003). The VA scores draw on this source, as mentioned. The Freedom House data are neither as finely differentiated nor based on as many sources as the VA scores, and I therefore prefer using the latter. Still, VA scores are available only for several years (1996, 1998, 2000, and 2002) and thus do not provide a good measure for assessing change over time. Where data that do capture change over time are needed, I rely on Freedom House's freedom ratings (hereafter referred to as "FH scores"), which have been issued annually for each country in the world since 1972. Scores range from 1 ("most free") to 7 ("least free"). Freedom House provides separate scores on "political rights" and "civil liberties"; the FH score is the average of the two. Discussion of the methodology of the survey is available in the appendices of each of the annual editions of *Freedom in the World* (see Karatnycky, Piano, and Puddington, 2003). The political rights score, for the most part, operationalizes the extent to which Dahl's points 1–4 are met; the civil liberties score to the extent to which Dahl's points 5–7 are fulfilled. Countries that score between 1 and 2.5 are classified as "free"; between 3 and 5, "partly free"; and between 5.5 and 7, "not free." When using and referring to FH scores, I invert them to provide a more intuitive presentation, meaning that 7 stands for greatest openness and 1 for least openness. Thus, with both the VA scores and the FH scores, higher numbers stand for greater political openness. Many scholars have tested and evaluated the scores (for example, Hadenius and Teorell, 2004; Munck and Verkuilen, 2002). Whatever their possible shortcomings, however, FH scores are the most widely used measure of the openness/closure of political regimes in American comparative political science. A rough consensus appears to exist that supports Peter Smith and Scott Bailey's (2004) statement that the scores "provide useful and usable indicators of the prevalence of democratic practices" (also Coppedge, 2004).

Other measures of political openness are available as well. The "Polity scores," published as part of the Polity IV Project, provide yet another source (Gurr, Marshall, and Jaggers, 2004). They, like the FH scores, are based on less wide-ranging and less numerous sources than are the VA scores.

Scores are highly correlated across sources. For 2002, the correlation between VA scores and FH scores for the 147 countries under examination in this book is .95. The correlation between VA scores and Polity scores for these countries, minus Lebanon (for which the Polity dataset lacks a score), is .81. FH scores and Polity scores are correlated at .90 (for each correlation, $p < .001$). For the 27 countries of the postcommunist region analyzed in this book (all but Bosnia), the correlation between VA and FH scores is .97; between VA and Polity scores, .86; and between FH and Polity scores, .90 (again, for each correlation, $p < .001$). While the VA scores provide an especially fine-grained indicator, all of these sources aim to measure roughly the same thing, and the correlations among their data are high.

Rating Russia's Regime

The average VA score for 2002 for countries with populations over one-half million is -0.10. For the postcommunist region, the average is -0.06. Russia's score is -0.52, which puts it in a tie for 93rd place with Qatar and Nepal. Russia ranks below Malaysia, Morocco, Zambia, and Gabon. Within the postcommunist region, Russia ranks 20th, ahead of only Ukraine, Azerbaijan, Belarus, and the five countries of Central Asia. Table 2.1 shows the VA scores of the postcommunist countries. It presents the average FH score for the 1999–2003 surveys (the five-year average) for each country as well.

A reasonable standard for candidacy as a democracy is inclusion in the top half of countries in the VA survey. Of these 73 countries, 54 also received scores in the five most recent FH surveys that average 5.5 or better, meaning that they were generally classified as "free" polities. All countries that average 5.5 or better in the FH score also rank in the top 73 countries

Table 2.1. *Voice and Accountability (VA) Scores (2002) and Freedom House Freedom Scores (1999–2003, five-year average), Postcommunist Countries*

Country	VA score	FH score
Hungary	1.17	6.5
Poland	1.11	6.5
Slovenia	1.10	6.6
Estonia	1.05	6.5
Slovakia	0.92	6.4
Latvia	0.91	6.5
Czech Republic	0.90	6.5
Lithuania	0.89	6.5
Bulgaria	0.56	5.8
Croatia	0.46	5.0
Mongolia	0.44	5.6
Romania	0.38	6.0
Albania	−0.04	4.0
Yugoslavia (Serbia and Montenegro)	−0.20	3.9
Macedonia	−0.29	4.7
Moldova	−0.30	4.9
Georgia	−0.30	4.2
Armenia	−0.42	4.0
Russia	**−0.52**	**3.3**
Ukraine	−0.59	4.2
Tajikistan	−0.95	2.1
Kyrgyzstan	−0.96	2.7
Azerbaijan	−0.97	2.7
Kazakhstan	−1.05	2.5
Belarus	−1.45	2.0
Uzbekistan	−1.66	1.5
Turkmenistan	−1.85	1.0

on VA scores. The countries that fall in the top half of countries in the VA survey but score below 5.5 in their average FH score are Argentina (FH average score 5.4), Ghana (5.3), Mali (5.3), Ecuador and Mexico (both 5.2), Honduras and Nicaragua (both 5.1), Croatia (5.0), Brazil and Madagascar (both 4.9), Peru (4.7), Fiji, Senegal, and Sri Lanka (all 4.5), Lesotho (4.3), Albania (4.0), Yugoslavia/Serbia and Montenegro (3.9), Niger (3.4), and Singapore (3.1). There is room for disagreement over whether members of this group of 19 countries are democracies. In general, however, most of the countries that fall into the top half (that is, 73 countries) in VA scores *and* that averaged 5.5 or better on FH scores satisfy most of Dahl's criteria for polyarchy most of the time. Polities that rank between, say, 30th and 50th on

VA scores and that consistently place in the "free" category in FH scores include Botswana, Bulgaria, Mongolia, and South Korea. Few observers would quarrel with characterizing them as democracies as of the first half of the current decade.

Similarly, however, most observers *would* quarrel with characterizing Malaysia, Morocco, Zambia, Gabon, and Lebanon as democracies. The first four rank ahead of Russia on VA scores, the last one immediately behind. This is the group of polities in which Russia finds itself in the first decade of the twentieth century. These countries rank in the bottom half of the world on VA scores. In all of them, including Russia, elections are held for at least some offices that wield power, and multiple candidates compete for the same position. But in all of these countries, coercion and/or fraud in elections are common; in none do most citizens have untrammeled access to diverse sources of information and opinion in the media; and in none do people enjoy the right to express themselves and associate freely without fear of monitoring, harassment, and punishment. In Malaysia, a hegemonic party controlled by a dominant figure regularly engages in extralegal repression of challengers. In Morocco, a monarch continues to enjoy vast powers, and the public lacks access to information about the actions of the rulers. In Zambia, elections are riddled with fraud, and the government throttles critical reporting. In Gabon, an elite rigs elections and relies upon a foreign army (namely, the French marines stationed in Gabon) to maintain power. In Lebanon, the government is controlled by a foreign power, Syria, and arbitrary arrest and detention are commonplace.

These polities and others like them are oligarchies. Only a small circle enjoys real voice in politics and the ability to say and do what it pleases on matters political. The ability of the people to dismiss peacefully those who control the polity's commanding heights is severely circumscribed or entirely absent. Most people are effectively shut out of political life most of the time.

One can, of course, argue that all polities are oligarchies, insofar as all have an elite and nowhere is the "voice of the people" ever either consistently decisive or, for that matter, even possible to discern with precision. In the United States, some citizens lack the material and educational wherewithal to participate in political life. In fact, the United States does not rank at the top of the world on VA scores; it places 15th, behind most West European countries and just slightly ahead of Hungary, Costa Rica, and Chile. Money corrupts American elections. Personal wealth or fundraising clout is a prerequisite for standing for elective office. In Chile, the military retains considerable autonomy. In Japan, corporate and political interests merge in a manner that limits popular control over the state. Yet in the United States, Chile, and Japan, as in Botswana, Bulgaria, Mongolia, South Korea, Hungary, and Costa Rica, mass electorates can throw the top rulers out of office in favor of others; powerful politicians are often humbled and upstarts replace them as the result of shifts in public opinion; vast majorities have access to diverse sources of information and opinion; and citizens say and write what they wish and organize for political ends without fear of retaliation. The exclusion of citizens, such as it is, is irregular and indirect and cannot be enforced systematically by agents of the state. As a result, most citizens are not entirely excluded. They have some voice, and politicians' actions are indeed shaped by public opinion – according to some critical voices, all too readily and reflexively so.

Oligarchies are different. In oligarchies, electoral fraud, control over public communication and the suppression of criticism, and monitoring and repression of opponents are not aberrations, and they regularly, directly, and systematically exclude people from political life. They reduce the politically relevant portion of the population to a circumscribed elite.

In monocracies, the extent of closure is still greater. A wall of coercion and closure insulates rulers, who have little need to heed popular preferences so long as the coercive apparatus remains intact. Elections are not held at all or they are held with a single candidate for each office (which, from the standpoint of democratic theory and elementary common sense, are the same thing), or manipulation and fraud are so pervasive and systematic that the results of all significant electoral contests are foreordained. The state controls association and communication so tightly that neither the organizational rights nor the information citizens need to make informed choices are present in adequate measure for elections to be meaningful, even if some choice is formally available.

Russia and the other mentioned countries that rank near Russia in political openness are oligarchies. They are more open than monocracies. For example, the lower house of the Moroccan parliament is elected relatively freely, though its powers are sharply circumscribed by the monarch and by the upper house of parliament, which is largely subservient to the royal palace. In Zambia, there is no such unelected power standing above elected officials, but elections are typically marred by serious irregularities and the government dominates broadcasting. In monocracies, in contrast, there is no (or practically no) pluralism. Some monocracies take the form of single-party dictatorships, such as the Soviet Union, Cuba, Laos, and

Nazi Germany. In other monocracies, a single individual, his family, and his entourage dominate politics entirely. In some monocracies, all major media are little more than mouthpieces of the supreme leader, and communicative life, at least in the political realm, is reduced to a celebration of the leader's indispensability and innumerable virtues. North Korea, Mobutu-era Zaire, Saddam-era Iraq, and present-day Turkmenistan are examples. Some of the countries that populate the bottom quintile of the rankings on VA scores would qualify as monocracies. In addition to the countries just mentioned, this group includes Uzbekistan, Belarus, Saudi Arabia, Libya, Syria, and Myanmar. Some other countries in the bottom quintile on VA scores have shredded states that are incapable of engaging in even the rudiments of government. What makes them highly unaccountable and the people's voice inaudible is their weakness, rather than their closure per se. Angola is an example. States in some countries, such as Sudan, combine a high level of closure in some realms (and regions) with stark incapacity in others.

Post-Soviet Russia is by no means a monocracy. It is far more open than was the Soviet system until the late 1980s. Sovietism was monocracy par excellence. Few if any political regimes in history have been as thoroughly *closed* – to popular participation in the selection of rulers, the expression of preferences, autonomous popular organization, and the flow of information – as the Soviet regime was. A single party – and, in practice, a single person or a small circle within that party – held absolute power. Rulers were entirely unaccountable to the people; no meaningful elections were ever held. Citizens enjoyed scant rights and freedoms even during the least repressive times. This monocratic partocracy is now gone. Multiple-candidate contests have replaced charades in which but a single candidate appeared on the ballot for each office. The president, members of the lower house of parliament, governors, and mayors are popularly elected. The agencies of coercion are less intrusive than they were during the Soviet period. Public political discourse has changed from the argot of Soviet-era *Pravda* to less surreal and more open discussion.

But while the breakthroughs of the late 1980s and early 1990s destroyed the monocracy, they were not followed by advancement to democracy. Explaining why Russia has taken the road to oligarchy, rather than to democracy, is the main purpose of this book. Before examining the determinants of Russia's post-Soviet path of regime change, however, it is necessary to pursue in greater depth the argument that Russia has not achieved democracy. The cross-national surveys adduced earlier provide some evidence, but a complete picture requires closer examination of actual conditions in Russia in light of the definition of democracy explicated in this chapter.

The necessity of making the case that Russia is not a democracy is all the greater given that many leading scholars do regard Russia as a democracy, even if an imperfect one. Philip Roeder (2001) divides the countries of the former USSR into "autocracies," "oligarchies," "exclusive republics," and "democracies," and he places Russia in the last of these categories. Daniel Treisman holds that Western observers have acquired the habit of holding Russia to a higher standard than other countries in terms of democratization. He argues that "democracy, for all its flaws, still exists" in Russia (2000, p. 154). At the time of Vladimir Putin's reelection as Russia's president, Treisman and coauthor Andrei Shleifer (Shleifer and Treisman 2004, p. 20) argued that Russia "has changed from a communist dictatorship to a multiparty democracy in which officials are chosen in regular elections." They saw Russia as a place in which "political leaders were being chosen in generally free – if flawed – elections, citizens could express their views without fear, and more than 700 political parties had been registered" (2004, p. 22). Michael McFaul devotes *Russia's Unfinished Revolution* – arguably the richest and best-informed study of post-Soviet Russian politics published to date – to explaining how Russia managed to stabilize a regime that, for all of its shortcomings, is still best characterized as "a highly imperfect democratic order" (2001, p. 17). Valerie Bunce (2003, pp. 182–83) states: "Since independence, Russia has held five elections at the national level – and hundreds more at the local and regional levels. These elections have by and large been free and fair." Bunce further argues that "the court system has functioned reasonably well." She concludes: "Gloomy predictions to the contrary, Russian democracy has lasted."

Each of these authors adopts more or less the same definition of democracy that I do. Despite some differences in outlook, all embrace the mainstream definition of democracy propagated by Schumpeter, Huntington, Linz, Di Palma, Bobbio, and Dahl discussed and endorsed earlier. None makes the mistake of adopting a subminimal or maximalist definition of democracy; all define democracy in terms of free elections and the rights required to ensure that voters have what they need in order to form and express their preferences freely.

But these authors are wrong in their assessments of the Russian condition. They are wrong to regard Russia's elections as free. Russian elections are riddled with too much fraud and coercion to call them free. So too are these scholars wrong to assume that Russians enjoy the communicative and associational rights needed to express their views without fear, to make informed political choices, and to monitor government agencies. Russians do not and for some time have not enjoyed such rights. My quarrel with these leading scholars, therefore, is not about the definition of democracy. It is about the facts of the Russian situation.

At stake is not merely whether the glass is half full or half empty. All the authors cited here regard the glass as at least a bit more than half full. In my judgment, it is about three-quarters empty. It is not dry. Russia is a more open polity than the Soviet Union was or than Uzbekistan and Belarus and Vietnam now are. But falsification, coercion, and the arbitrary disqualification of candidates in elections, as well as constriction of communicative interaction and associational life, have prevented democracy from taking hold. They have kept control of politics out of the hands of the electorate as a whole and vested it in a slim stratum of officials who control and manipulate the process for their own ends. The resulting regime is an oligarchy. It is not an oligarchy in the same sense that, say, Great Britain in the nineteenth century or South Africa under the pre-1994 apartheid regime were oligarchies. In each of these cases, a minority of the population influenced the government, while a majority was entirely disenfranchised. In Great Britain, property and class determined whether one was included in the enfranchised minority; in South Africa, race did so. In postcommunist Russia, everyone has the right to vote. But a host of mechanisms empties suffrage of content and severs the tie between citizens' preferences, on the one hand, and who holds power and to what ends, on the other. Meaningful political participation is therefore limited to circumscribed circles of rulers. This type of oligarchy is common in the modern world.

Showing that Russia is not a democracy requires looking at Russia much more closely and establishing the factual bases for the argument presented here. The following chapter takes up this task.

3

Symptoms of the Failure of Democracy

> Our local electronic media here are completely under the sway of the administration. The government controls what's aired. And the electoral commission – that's under the administration's control too. We're on the Putin model here.
>
> > – Viktor Ostrenko, staff director, Center for Social Development "Vozrozhdenie" (an NGO dedicated to democracy promotion), Pskov, July 11, 2001

> Putin is no enemy of free speech. He simply finds absurd the idea that somebody has the right to criticize him publicly.
>
> > – Ksenia Ponomareva, deputy chief of Vladimir Putin's presidential campaign staff in 1999–2000, March 26, 2001 (reported in the *St. Petersburg Times*, March 27, 2001)

Russia held four elections for parliament and three elections for president between 1993 and 2004. Elections have been carried out on a regular basis for officials at subnational levels. Control over government is constitutionally vested in elected officials, which means that Russia satisfies Robert Dahl's first criterion for polyarchy.

Dahl's other six criteria specify the conditions that ensure that election results express popular preferences. None of these other conditions is met in Russia. Dahl's second and third criteria specify that "elected officials are chosen in frequently and fairly conducted elections in which coercion is comparatively uncommon" and that "practically all adults have the right to vote in the election of officials." In practice, elections are carried out frequently and at regular intervals, but they are not conducted fairly and coercion is common. Furthermore, while all adults have the right to vote, this right is hollowed out by practices that prevent votes from counting

30

equally – or from being counted at all. The regularity of fraud and coercion in elections prevents Russia from fulfilling Dahl's second and third criteria for an open polity. His fourth criterion, which requires that "practically all adults have the right to run for elective offices in the government," is met in strictly legal terms. No portion of the population is de jure disenfranchised. In practice, however, an important segment of adults – namely, those who pose a serious challenge to incumbents – often find themselves barred from seeking office. Thus, Dahl's fourth criterion, while met on paper, is not fulfilled in practice. Finally, the communicative and associational rights that he specifies in his fifth, sixth, and seventh conditions for democracy are sharply circumscribed.

This chapter examines Russia in light of each of Dahl's criteria. On each condition, with the exception of the first one, Russia comes up short.

Electoral Fraud

Problems and Logics of Detection

Detecting and measuring electoral fraud in any polity is difficult (Lehoucq, 2003). One source of evidence is anecdotes produced by one's own investigation or by other observers or participants. The second source is deductive inference that compares the official results with what one knows about popular preferences before the vote or what one can glean about voter preferences after the vote from exit polls. In some fully closed polities, assessing the extent of fraud by means of anecdotal evidence is simply impossible, since the government disallows any independent observation and investigation of elections. This problem produces a paradox: The more closed the polity, the harder it is to demonstrate fraud. In fully closed polities, one must rely exclusively on deductive inference.

Compare two examples. In the 2000 presidential election in the United States, every vote really mattered, at least in Florida. The election result hinged on the returns from that state alone, and the results there amounted to a virtual dead heat. A plethora of investigations were launched after the election, and a consensus developed among the agencies conducting the investigation that George W. Bush had won the state by a few thousand votes, though some investigators argued the opposite. Other issues, such as whether voters in some districts were confused by a ballot that may have been poorly designed, clouded the question of whether the final tally represented all voters' true preferences. But there was no shortage of investigation. The ballots were recounted by hand, both parties to the conflict were represented during the recount of ballots, and media coverage was, to understate the matter, extensive. Perhaps some fraud went undetected, and since the difference between the candidates' vote totals was so small, that fraud might even have been decisive. But the chances that fraud in any given presidential election in the United States is extensive enough to taint the result is reasonably small, and the fraud that does occur is normally detected in a recount of ballots or in an independent investigation conducted by journalists and scholars. There is rarely a need to rely on a comparison of the official results with what one had expected before the vote. Had the official results shown that Al Gore swept Wyoming and Utah or that George W. Bush romped in the District of Columbia, and were Wyoming, Utah, and the District of Columbia inaccessible to outside observers, the need to engage in deduction would have kicked in, and one may have been justified in deducing that something was amiss. One knows that Wyoming and Utah are strongly Republican and the District of Columbia is overwhelmingly Democratic; from these priors one may have inferred that the particulars reported in the official results were erroneous. But the need to rely on such deduction rarely arises in open polities. The inductive enterprise of recounts and investigation – at least usually – does the job.

On the other hand, deductive reasoning is all one has when assessing the accuracy of official reporting on Iraq's 2003 referendum on Saddam Hussein. What percentage of Iraqis actually endorsed Saddam? There was no opportunity for independent investigation. Common sense, however, may lead one to question the government's claim that 11,445,938 voters endorsed Saddam and zero voted against him. But in what many would regard as this most egregious electoral sham, the observer must rely on deductive reasoning alone to assess the fairness of the vote, since there is no other way to know whether the officially reported result was accurate. In the absence of evidence garnered through observation, one cannot know – even remotely – what the final tally "really" was.

In Russia, unlike in Iraq, one need not rely entirely on deduction to assess the extent of fraud. There is just enough media coverage and other investigation to make induction based on actual observation possible. Unlike in an open polity, however, some reliance on deduction is necessary, since the capacity of independent observers to investigate is severely limited. Such capacity, moreover, has declined over time. By the beginning of the current decade, thoroughgoing independent investigation of elections results was carried out only by foreign or foreign-owned media. The most serious and extensive investigation of the 2000 presidential election was conducted by and published in the *Moscow Times*, an English-language newspaper whose readership and circulation are limited largely to intellectuals and English-speaking expatriates residing in Moscow and St. Petersburg. The vast majority of other papers, as well as the main electronic media outlets, were by then either controlled or intimidated by the government and therefore disinclined to report any fraud that favored incumbents. In short, when investigating fraud in Russian elections, one must rely on a combination of induction, using what evidence is gathered by independent sources, and deductive reasoning that compares official results with reasonable prior expectations.

Funny Numbers

If deduction is all one has to detect foul play in some cases, it is sometimes also all one needs. The result in the Iraqi referendum of 2003 provides an example. Another is provided by balloting in Tatarstan in the 1996 presidential election. According to the official results, in the first round of voting, Boris Yeltsin received 38.3 percent to Gennadii Ziuganov's 38.1 percent, though this result transpired only after initial press reports announced that Ziuganov had won a plurality in the republic. Then, in the second round, when the field was narrowed to only two candidates, Ziuganov's vote declined in *absolute* terms, from 38.1 percent to 32.3 percent, while Yeltsin received 61.5 percent. In the first round, Ziuganov won absolute majorities in 19 rural districts; in the second round, he lost every one of these to Yeltsin. In Bavlinskii district, Ziuganov's vote total went from 45.3 percent in the first round to 5.9 percent in the second. In some districts, turnout exceeded 99 percent (McFaul and Petrov, eds., 1998, pp. 229, 241–2). Mintimer Shaimiev, Tatarstan's president and an election-day ally of whoever controls the executive branch in Moscow, clearly managed to deliver the proper result for Yeltsin. As the numbers suggest, he overdid things a bit.

How can such obvious mischief occur in a supremely important national election that involves open competition among multiple viable candidates and no marauding goons stealing ballot boxes or blocking roadways leading to polling places? How can it happen, moreover, in a major country that is under the scrutiny of the whole world? Some answers are to be found in a few arcane but consequential matters of electoral procedure. Examination of the 2000 presidential vote, which Vladimir Putin won with 52.9 percent in the only round of balloting, sheds some light on these problems.

In this contest, as in all national elections in Russia, each of the country's 94,864 voting precincts writes an official document, called a protocol, which records the results. The precincts tally the votes immediately after the polls close (usually at 8 pm), record them in the form of the protocols, and send their protocols up to the territorial electoral commissions, which number several hundred. Territorial commissions send their tallies to the regional electoral commissions, one of which is located in each of Russia's 89 provinces. The regional commissions then report their results to the federal Central Electoral Commission (CEC) in Moscow.

By law, the protocols are supposed to be made public at each precinct immediately after votes are tallied. This measure is meant, in principle, to check abuses higher up the chain. Each precinct's results, in theory, also can be looked up in the vote count of the territorial commissions and compared to the results recorded in the protocol. Crucially, however, the precinct captains usually do not make the protocols available to the public after the vote. Independent efforts to obtain them from the CEC in the days and months after the vote normally meet only official stonewalling. Usually the CEC claims that there is no need for it to publicize the protocols since the latter were – despite actual practice – freely available to all interested parties at the precincts on election night.

Reporters from the *Moscow Times*, who conducted a major investigation of the 2000 election, managed to obtain 245 of Dagestan's 1,550 protocols. By law, obtaining all the protocols should have been easy, but getting a hold of just one-sixth of them was an investigative coup. Comparing the protocols that they were able to obtain with the territorial commission's reported totals, the *Times* found 87,139 fewer votes for Putin in the former than appeared in the latter (Borisova, Peach, Chernyakova, and Nunayev, 2000[c] and 2000[d]).

The votes cast in these 245 precincts accounted for 16 percent of Dagestan's precincts. If the rate of overreporting for Putin in the 84 percent of the precincts that the investigators did not have access to was the same as it was in the 16 percent on which they did manage to gather data, 551,287 votes of the 877,853 that Putin officially won in Dagestan would have been attributed to him wrongly. These extra votes alone would equal one-quarter of the 2.2 million votes that stood between the 52.94 percent that Putin officially received and the 50 percent-plus-one that he had to receive to avoid a second round. Such an extrapolation may not be accurate;

the actual number of votes falsely attributed to Putin in Dagestan might have been much lower than this. So too might it have been much higher.

Table 3.1 shows the numbers for ten precincts in Dagestan that the *Times* published in its report on the 2000 election. As just mentioned, the *Times* found gross disparities between the results as reported locally – that is, in the protocols – and the results as subsequently reported by the territorial commissions. The results are from Makhachkala, the capital of Dagestan and a city of 300,000 people. The finding belies the notion that falsification, while perhaps easy to pull off in the countryside, is difficult to engineer in the cities. If the fraud occurs as the votes move up the chain of reporting of results, especially if local election officials refuse to release the protocols to journalists or other investigators, it may be difficult to detect even if there is no mischief at all at the polling place.

The *Times* investigators found discrepancies in other places in which it was able to obtain protocols as well. In Saratov's polling precinct number 1,617, the original precinct results as recorded in the protocols gave Putin 666 votes; the results reported by the territorial commission gave him 1,086. In precinct number 1,797, the analogous figures were 667 and 995; in precinct number 1,591, they were 822 and 1,012 (Borisova et al., 2000[e]). The numbers suggest that the voting data in Saratov, like in Dagestan, underwent creative processing between the precinct and territorial levels. What happened at higher levels can only be a matter of speculation. The data also show why electoral commissions usually do not pressure the precincts to publicize their protocols and why protocols are so hard for investigators to obtain. They may contain information that does not jibe with the numbers that the electoral commissions subsequently report.

The CEC's reporting of results on election night provides grounds for further speculation about what happens to votes as they move up the hierarchy of electoral commissions. According to the CEC, as of 6 pm, 59.2 percent of Dagestan's registered voters had cast their ballots. By the close of voting at 8 pm, however, that number had surged to 83.6 percent. A skeptical Russian sociologist who examined the data noted of the reporting: "Normally most people come in the morning, then attendance decreases slowly and in the end, there is a small rise, but not a vertical skyrocket of visitors" (Borisova et al., 2000[a]). Indeed, a rise of a few percentage points would have been expected, and an increase of up to 10 percent would have been plausible. But the surge recorded by the CEC contradicts normal voting behavior. Election days are holidays in Russia; no voters must rush to the polling place from their workplaces to cast their ballots before the polls

Table 3.1. *Mischief in Makhachkala: Discrepancies Between Vote Totals as Counted and Reported Locally (Protocol Copies) and the Official Results Reported by Territorial Electoral Commissions in Ten Districts in Makhachkala, Dagestan, 2000*

Polling precinct number	842			852			855		
	Protocol copies	Official results	Difference	Protocol copies	Official results	Difference	Protocol copies	Official results	Difference
# of valid ballots	1215	1655	440	1344	1344	0	2198	2518	320
# of invalid ballots	8	0	−8	1	1	0	0	0	0
Votes for:									
Govorukhin	0	0	0	0	0	0	0	0	0
Dzhabrailov	5	0	−5	3	0	−3	0	0	0
Zhirinovskii	3	0	−3	6	0	−6	0	0	0
Ziuganov	384	84	−300	516	116	−400	626	126	−500
Pamfilova	4	0	−4	2	0	−2	0	0	0
Podberezkin	4	0	−4	2	0	−2	0	0	0
Putin	777	1569	792	749	1228	479	1572	2372	800
Skuratov	1	0	−1	0	0	0	0	0	0
Titov	4	0	−4	3	0	−3	20	0	−20
Tuleev	6	0	−6	20	0	−20	0	0	0
Iavlinskii	19	2	−17	10	0	−10	0	0	0
Against all	8	0	−8	22	0	−22	22	0	−22

	858			876			889		
Polling precinct number	Protocol copies	Official results	Difference	Protocol copies	Official results	Difference	Protocol copies	Official results	Difference
# of valid ballots	1859	3121	1262	1847	3793	1946	no data	1980	—
# of invalid ballots	5	5	0	13	13	0	no data	0	
Votes for:									
Govorukhin	3	3	0	2	0	−2	0	0	0
Dzhabrailov	4	4	0	4	0	−4	0	0	0
Zhirinovskii	7	7	0	11	0	−11	4	0	−4
Ziuganov	989	239	−750	689	258	−440	423	191	−232
Pamfilova	3	3	0	1	0	−1	0	0	0
Podberezkin	1	1	0	0	0	0	0	0	0
Putin	732	2752	2020	1070	3535	2465	928	1782	756
Skuratov	3	0	−3	1	0	1	6	2	−4
Titov	2	108	106	3	0	−3	0	0	0
Tuleev	13	0	−13	17	0	−17	0	0	0
Iavlinskii	98	0	−98	29	0	−29	0	3	3
Against all	4	4	0	11	0	−11	9	2	−7

(*continued*)

37

Table 3.1 (*continued*)

Polling precinct number	896			899			900			903		
	Protocol copies	Official results	Difference	Protocol copies	Official results	Difference	Protocol copies	Official results	Difference	Protocol copies	Official results	Difference
# of valid ballots	1823	2560	737	1423	2074	651	318	491	173	913	1914	1001
# of invalid ballots	18	3	−15	29	0	−29	2	0	−2	1	0	−1
Votes for:												
Govorukhin	1	0	−1	1	0	−1	0	0	0	0	0	0
Dzhabrailov	4	0	−4	4	0	−4	4	2	−2	2	0	−2
Zhirinovskii	7	0	−7	6	0	−6	3	2	−1	0	0	0
Ziuganov	634	244	−390	631	204	−427	111	40	−71	401	80	−321
Pamfilova	2	0	−2	7	0	−7	0	0	0	3	0	−3
Podberezkin	2	0	−2	4	0	−4	1	0	−1	2	0	−2
Putin	1110	2312	1202	728	1870	1142	197	447	250	480	1830	1350
Skuratov	2	0	−2	6	0	−6	0	2	−2	3	0	−3
Titov	2	0	−2	1	0	−1	0	0	0	2	0	−2
Tuleev	12	0	−12	9	0	−9	1	0	−1	7	0	−7
Iavlinskii	21	0	−21	14	0	−14	1	0	−1	7	0	−7
Against all	24	4	−20	11	0	−11	9	0	−9	8	4	−4

Source: Borisova et al., 2000[c] and [d].

38

close in the evening. At any rate, the lion's share of these latecomers must have weighed in for Putin, since the then-acting president, according to the final official tally, captured a whopping 81 percent of the republic's vote.

According to the analyst just cited, "'ghost voters' or 'dead souls' created by electoral commissions" almost certainly accounted for a large portion of the voters in Dagestan who allegedly rushed to the polls in the closing two hours of voting. Such apparitions appear to have played a substantial role in the government's efforts in 2000. The country's voting rolls, according to the CEC, expanded by 1.3 million voters between the parliamentary elections of December 19, 1999, and the presidential vote of March 26, 2000. The number grew from 108,073,956 to 109,392,046. Unlike the United States, Russia does not have a system of voluntary voter registration. By law, all people are added to the voting register when they turn 18 years of age – and, of course, are supposed to be removed when they die. The official numbers suggest a major surge in the size of the voting-age population over the course of 14 weeks. The remarkable demographic phenomenon caught the attention of some observers. The explanation that the CEC offered after the election included some interesting statements. In a written response on the question, Aleksandr Veshniakov, the head of the CEC, said that 550,000 Russians had turned 18 between the elections. One of his spokespersons, Taisiia Nechiporenko, said in a separate statement that immigration into Russia from other former Soviet republics had augmented the rolls (Borisova et al., 2000[a]).

The numbers are intriguing. The birth rate has lagged behind the death rate in Russia for many years, yielding a decline in population that has averaged about 800,000 people per year over the past decade. Numbers from Goskomstat (the State Statistics Committee) show that consistent with this long-term national trend, Russia lost 235,100 people to the differential between the birth rate and the death rate during the first three months of 2000, which was offset by 53,000 immigrants from abroad. Thus, in the period between the elections, Russia experienced a net loss of 182,100 people, most of them presumably of voting age. It is conceivable, albeit not likely, that even while the population contracted, the pool of voters expanded due to a dramatic spike in births in 1981 and 1982 that would have flooded the rolls with many hundreds of thousands of people who turned 18 between December 19 and March 26. The CEC, as just noted, claimed that 550,000 new 18-year-olds joined the ranks of voters during the 14-week interval. Yet in separate statements, Murray Feshbach, an American demographer, Evgenii Andreev, a demographer at Russia's Institute of National

Economic Forecasting, and Irina Rakhmaninova, head of the Goskomstat's department that tracks national trends in population change, noted that there was no baby boom in the early 1980s. All three concluded that the CEC's claims do not stand up to any reasonable demographic assessments (Borisova et al., 2000[a]).

Indeed, the CEC's behavior after the vote left room for question about the integrity of even the highest-level and highest-profile electoral commission. After the 2000 election, the CEC publicized every aspect of the results – except the protocols. That is to say, the CEC published everything but the one set of documents that would make possible a systematic investigation of falsification. The CEC often sang the virtues of transparency and posted the election results on its website (www.fci.ru) shortly after it announced the final tally. The protocols data, however, were not published; nor did the CEC help observers denied protocols at the precincts to gain access to them. Furthermore, in August 2000, soon after some observers began publicly questioning the unexpected expansion of the voting rolls just discussed, all data on the presidential election vanished from the CEC's website (*St. Petersburg Times*, editorial of November 17, 2000, p. 8).

In Chechnya, whether use of "dead souls," some other means of fraud, or the actual mass expression of highly counterintuitive preferences stood behind the result must be left to question. There, Putin captured 50.6 percent. The outcome, if accurate, represented either a magnificent spirit of forgiveness or an intriguing display of masochism on the part of people whose homes had been decimated by a military campaign associated closely with Putin himself. Similarly peculiar sentiments were even more strongly evident in the Ingush Republic, which has been sorely affected by the war in neighboring Chechnya. In the Ingush Republic, 85.4 percent cast their votes for Putin. By analogy, one must imagine George W. Bush winning smashing victories in the District of Columbia and Massachusetts.

In these cases, suspicions arise due to a clash between commonsense reasoning and official results. Yet evidence on fraud comes not only from such deductive inference but also from direct observation. Though most fraud is invisible, many naked eyes have witnessed abuses that corroborate what can be inferred through extrapolation. Yet monitors in Russian elections are often hobbled by powerlessness and timidity. Powerlessness is commonly experienced by domestic observers and stems from official intransigence and manipulation. Timidity is often found among foreign observers and arises from counterproductive habits of thinking, fear of the consequences of candor, and lack of self-confidence bred by ignorance.

Spectacles of Mischief and Failures of Monitoring

A half-dozen mundane but telling anecdotes culled from recent elections illustrate the difficulties that monitors face. They show that if electoral officials and incumbent politicians are resolved to rig the results and unwilling to provide redress, election monitors may find themselves in the place of United Nations peacekeeping troops – acutely aware of the disorder and utterly unable to cure it.

As mentioned, while the law calls for making protocols publicly available at each precinct immediately after the votes are counted, in practice, precinct captains often ignore this rule. In fact, precinct officials may go well beyond simply failing to provide information; they may also shunt observers aside. Doing so obviously eliminates any possibility of effective parallel tabulation of votes by observers. One observer in 2000, a teacher at a local school of agriculture, recounted such an experience in Makhachkala's Kirovskii district. Her story puts the flesh of real experience on the bones of the curious numerical results discussed earlier. The observer, who called herself "Natalia," recalled: "When they turned the ballot boxes upside down, there were two big packets of ballots there on top. Clearly they had been inserted altogether – and one even had a sheet of paper around it. I rushed on them, grabbed both packets and saw they were all filled in for Putin. I pressed them tightly to my chest. The [other observers] were astonished. I said, 'Each person must vote separately, these are fake.'" The hapless teacher quickly found that some observers had more authority than others. Observers representing Putin's campaign took the packets of ballots from her and, she recalled, "spread them over the pile. They all got mixed together." Not only did Putin's observers prove to be highly effective advocates whose authority apparently transcended mere observation, but the precinct election commission also proved unequal to the rigors of counting all the ballots. Once ballots cast for each candidate had been divided into separate piles, members of the electoral commission took the stack of votes for Ziuganov, which Natalia estimated to be about 15 centimeters thick, into a separate room. The officials emerged a short time later with a much smaller stack (Borisova et al., 2000[b]).

An election observer from the village of Priiutovo in Bashkortostan, Klavdiia Grigorieva, recounted how things worked in the same elections at her polling station, No. 514. Unlike in the case from Makhachkala just recounted, apparently no stuffing or robbing of ballot boxes took place. Like in Makhachkala, however, electoral officials themselves perpetrated fraud. In Bashkortostan, precinct officials doctored the protocol. Grigorieva watched the vote count and recorded the results: 862 votes for Putin, 356 for Ziuganov, 24 for Vladimir Zhirinovskii, 21 for Konstantin Titov, and 12 for Grigorii Iavlinskii. But the precinct's protocol, which the precinct chief wrote up, listed 1,092 votes for Putin, 177 for Ziuganov, and no votes for anyone else. Grigorieva lodged a formal complaint with the CEC, but never received a response (Borisova et al., 2000[e]).

Grigorieva's account is especially interesting because it reveals precisely the type of vote counting illustrated in Table 3.1, which provides data on Dagestan, though the fraud was perpetrated by electoral officials at different levels in the two cases. In the Dagestani results shown in Table 3.1, precinct officials may have been honest, but electoral officials at the territorial level cooked the results. In Bashkortostan, the results were fixed at the precinct level. In both cases, however, cheating took the form of inflating Putin's total, reducing Ziuganov's – and discarding the votes for the other candidates. In most of the Dagestani precincts shown in Table 3.1, as well as in Grigorieva's precinct in Bashkortostan, artlessness – indeed, laziness – is evident in the work of the election officials, who simply threw out the odd votes for candidates other than Putin and his main challenger. Results that show zero totals for Zhirinovskii and/or Iavlinskii are especially suspect. Each is a household name in Russia, a long-standing standard-bearer of a major political camp (nationalism and liberalism, respectively), and the head of a major political party (the Liberal Democratic Party of Russia [LDPR] and Iabloko, respectively). Doctoring the numbers in a way that took account of these facts and thereby presented more plausible-looking totals, however, apparently was not worth the effort for some of the numbers fixers.

One need not rely exclusively on abused observers and intrepid journalists for accounts of falsification. Officials themselves will sometimes gladly recount their own exploits. In Tatarstan, whose president, Mintimer Shaimiev, supported Putin in 2000 with the same resolve that he supported Yeltsin in 1996, officials added a sophisticated methodological twist to the oldest form of falsification. Voters and officials alike in Tatarstan called their creative form of ballot-box stuffing "the caterpillar." Vladimir Shevchuk, head of the Tatarstan Elections-2000 Press Center, whose pride in fulfilling Shaimiev's wishes exceeded his concern for covering up abuses, explained to journalists how the system worked. According to Shevchuk: "There are people standing near the elections precincts and when they see a voter coming up, they offer him or her 50 rubles or a 100 rubles so that he or she takes a pre filled in ballot to drop in the box, and then returns with a blank ballot. Then [the fraudsters] fill in the new clean ballot and offer it to the next voter." After the election, Shaimiev's personal spokesman, Irek Murtazin, confirmed the existence of the caterpillar with a chuckle and without embarrassment. The method seems to have worked nicely. In the Drozhzhanovskii district, a traditional stronghold of the Communist Party of the Russian Federation (CPRF; KPRF in Russian) inhabited mostly by collective farmers, Putin won 86.2 percent to Ziuganov's 8.1 percent. In some places, the trouble of organizing the caterpillar was not necessary. Many voters in Tatarskii Saplyk, a village in the Drozhzhanovskii district, reported that the heads of their collective farm simply took their ballots from them at the polling place and filled them out for them (and for Putin) (Borisova et al., 2000[d]).

In the republican capital of Kazan, however, seizing ballots from voters or running a caterpillar operation might not have suited local conditions. Some of the 1.3 million "new voters" that appeared on the CEC's voting rolls on election eve might well have "resided" in Kazan. All manner of people and places that did not exist showed up on the rolls. Alkhat Zaripov, a pensioner who resides in Kazan, noted in an interview after the election that the form he signed at the polling place where he voted listed 209 apartments in his building. Zaripov knew, however, that the building houses only 180 apartments. Twenty-nine apartments – each of course full of "voters" – had been imagined onto the registration list by the precinct officials. The list for the apartment building next door, which held 108 dwellings, underwent election day expansion to accommodate 125 units. Zaripov, a longtime resident, raised the matter on the spot and asked for an explanation, but the precinct official he addressed picked up the list of residences and voters and walked away. Zaripov reported: "I decided to tell Putin's election headquarters, but I could not find it. I then asked for Iabloko's headquarters, but no one knew where it was. Someone told me where the Communist Party office was. I went there and filed a complaint. I am not a Communist, I only wanted justice" (Borisova et al., 2000[a]). Unsurprisingly, Putin picked up a handsome 68.8 percent of the vote in Tatarstan.

If fraud cannot be perpetrated on the spot, it can be carried out on the hoof. In Volgograd's most recent mayoral elections, the vehicle delivering ballots from the city's most populous district to the station where the ballots were to be tabulated disappeared for five hours en route to a location that was located less than an hour away, driving slowly. The representative of the local government body responsible for delivery claimed that the vehicle had hit some rough traffic. Unsurprisingly, these ballots that temporarily lost their way ended up providing a mighty lift to the incumbent mayor, despite preelection polls that showed his main opponent far ahead in the district (Tsygankov, 2002).

Denying citizens access to protocols, cooking numbers during tabulation, stuffing ballot boxes, drawing on reservoirs of "dead souls," and disappearing with carloads of ballots en route to delivery might not be the stuff of elections in Russia if electoral commissions were immune from the blandishments that the presidential, governmental, and gubernatorial apparatuses might offer them. But in practice, electoral commissions are often under the sway of incumbent executives. In many cases where the opposition insists on a seat at the table, the incumbents simply exclude it with impunity. In the fall of 2001, as Moscow prepared for its elections for the municipal Duma, local electoral authorities under the sway of the mayor, Iurii Luzhkov, denied representatives from the leading liberal parties their places on the city's electoral commissions. By law, the representatives of all major parties had the right to sit on the commissions. But Arkadii Murashev and Natalia Borodina, leaders of the Moscow organizations of the liberal Union of Right Forces (URF; SPS in Russian) and Iabloko, respectively, reported that their parties' representatives were barred from participation (Abakumova, 2001).

If any doubt about the politicization of electoral commissions persisted after the national elections of 1999 and 2000, the CEC's decision of November 2000 on the proposed referendum on nuclear waste dispelled them. During 2000, a grassroots movement in Russia organized a petition drive to reverse a law that allowed importation of spent nuclear fuel into Russia for long-term storage. The Putin government planned to import several tens of thousands of tons of spent nuclear fuel from around the world. It saw the usage of Russian land for the purpose as a cash cow that promised to generate billions of dollars, but popular opposition was stiff. Environmental groups, led by the Russian chapter of Greenpeace, gathered about 2.5 million signatures – about a half million more than the 2 million needed by law to trigger a referendum on the issue. But the CEC recognized the legitimacy of slightly fewer than 2 million – 1,873,216 to be exact. The rest of the signatures the CEC rejected on the basis of technicalities. As Thomas Nilsen, a researcher at a major Norwegian environmental group that supported the referendum drive, noted of the chairman of the CEC and his relationship with the Putin government: "Veshniakov did as he was told" (Badkhen, 2000).

The probity of the officials in charge of elections is, in any polity, the first and best check on electoral fraud. It is also a necessary condition for free elections. If electoral commissions are corrupt, meaningful elections are unlikely. Those who run the electoral machinery need not be professionals, intellectuals, experts, or even nice people; but if they are not shielded from politicians' pressures and inducements and committed to preserving the integrity of the vote, the prospects for free and fair elections are slight.

Lack of autonomy and honesty on the part of electoral commissions might not completely undermine efforts to deter falsification if election observers, investigators, and candidates themselves could obtain a serious hearing with high-level electoral commissions, such as the CEC, or other bodies. But redress is rare. The individuals named in the preceding few paragraphs – "Natalia," Grigorieva, Zaripov, Borodina, and Murashev – did complain. In fact, more than 2,000 complaints and 200 lawsuits were filed in connection with the 2000 election alone. But, true to the norm, few complaints received any meaningful response (*St. Petersburg Times*, November 17, 2000, p. 8). Inquiries lodged by prominent citizens at high levels are sometimes answered, but in the form of logically indefensible or even ludicrous claims, such as those that Veshniakov and Nechiporenko offered the demographers who questioned the startling growth in the voting-age population between December 1999 and March 2000. Observers may report suspected fraud, but when their complaints disappear into a morass of official stonewalling, their influence amounts to naught.

The courts would seem to provide an alternative forum for redress. But the executive branch's control of the courts, combined with the nature of the prosecutorial process, virtually excludes the courts as agencies of redress in electoral affairs. In Russia, the public prosecutor must agree to take up the case of the aggrieved party and prosecute it against a given electoral commission in order for the case to have a chance of receiving a hearing in court. The probability of such an event is so small that when it actually happened recently, following an election for the regional legislature in Samara oblast (province), it received national attention. In the case, observers at a precinct in the city of Samara noted that approximately a quarter of eligible voters participated in the election. Those observers were then surprised to see the final results, which reported that nearly fourth-fifths of eligible voters in the precinct had fulfilled their civic duty. Aleksandr Efremov, the public prosecutor of Samara oblast, acknowledged that for someone in his position to take up such a case was virtually unheard of. He said "I understand my colleagues" – that is, the prosecutors who normally would not touch such a case – and noted that resources are so tight that just handling violent crime in a single city in his oblast was enough to keep his office busy. But Efremov nevertheless concluded that the fraud had gone way too far to ignore and that "dirty voting technologies merit [prosecutors'] attention no less than major criminal cases" (Ivanov, 2002).

As of this writing, the outcome of the case is not known. Regardless of the result, the case does not carry the potential to alter the way elections are conducted. Indeed, it received attention because it was perhaps the first time that a public prosecutor in Russia had ever seriously taken up a case of alleged electoral falsification (Ivanov, 2002). The norm is better reflected by Dmitrii Fomin, who campaigned for Grigorii Iavlinskii in Tatarstan's Naberezhnye Chelny district in 2000. Fomin remarked that "undoubtedly there was large-scale forgery here," but he did not bother to prepare a formal complaint. According to Fomin, "Here we expect better results from publications in the media than from court decisions" (Borisova et al., 2000[c]).

Fomin's comment says more about the inaccessibility of the courts than about the power of the media. Here is another obstacle in the phalanx of barriers to redress: the inability or unwillingness of the press to uncover – or even cover – falsification. By 2000, much of the press on both the national and provincial levels was under state control. As of this writing in 2004, even fewer media outlets are independent and capable of vigorous investigation than in 2000. The fact that the most thoroughgoing journalistic investigation of the 2000 elections was carried out by an English-language newspaper, staffed mostly by Russian reporters but under the sponsorship of foreigners, speaks volumes. As Fomin suggested, the press may be more open to complaints of forgery than the courts. But its effectiveness as a check on fraud is insubstantial. The conundrum illustrates and substantiates Norberto Bobbio's (1987) contention that in modern politics, maintaining popular control over the state depends vitally on basic civil liberties, and above all, the rights to communicate freely and to probe government operations. Free expression and its link to political voice will be taken up again later in the chapter.

Even if domestic actors are hobbled by official intransigence, can't international organizations and foreign governments blow the whistle? The question raises a delicate and complicated set of problems. In general, international observers of Russia's post-Soviet elections have routinely noted violations, including serious ones, but then concluded that the elections nevertheless advanced Russian democracy.

The Organization for Security and Cooperation in Europe (OSCE) is the largest and most influential organization that monitors elections in Russia. The OSCE sent a team of about 400 observers to Russia's 1999 parliamentary and 2000 presidential elections. As is customary in the OSCE's delegations, about one-tenth were "long-term" observers who know the language and arrive several months before the elections to assess the situation. Whatever the contents of the OSCE's final report, which is issued several months after the election, the press conference held by the head of the delegation the day after the vote gets the most attention. If the OSCE then pronounces that the elections seemed fair enough to count as valid, the victors bear this mark of international approval forever after. Little of the detail that may appear in the final report ever attracts the attention of an audience wider than a handful of scholars and journalists. In its initial public statements following both the parliamentary elections of December 1999 and the presidential elections of March 2000, the OSCE gave the contests an essentially clean bill of health.

Following the presidential elections, the *Moscow Times* reported that long-term OSCE observers in Russia, speaking on condition of anonymity, "expressed disgust for the cheery tone of the day-after OSCE commentary – and dissatisfaction that the more thorough, official OSCE report on the elections – which was published two months later and was harsher and more informed – got no attention" (Borisova et al., 2000[d]). Indeed, the final report, issued on May 19, listed a catalogue of abuses, including some of those mentioned here. The final report noted that some allegations were "serious and deserve the full weight of investigation. They involve charges that protocols were falsified, in some instances by reversing or increasing the vote totals recorded for Putin over Zyuganov." The report also mentioned "inclusion of deceased persons on voter lists" and "improper influence of administrative authorities seen to be directing the work of polling station commissions [and] expulsion of individual observers from some sites." Yet the report concluded that the elections nevertheless "represented a benchmark in the ongoing evolution of the Russian Federation's emergence as a representative democracy." So too did it state that "it is a tribute to Russia's political development that the elections took place in a politically stable environment" and that "the presidential election was conducted under a constitutional and legislative framework that is consistent with internationally recognized democratic standards, including those formulated in the OSCE Copenhagen Document of 1990." As for the allegations that were "serious and deserve the full weight of investigation," the report claimed that the

OSCE is "not in a position to judge . . . and can draw no conclusions as to the proficiency and seriousness with which [the allegations] were reviewed by competent election commissions or the courts" (Organization for Security and Cooperation in Europe, 2000).

It is interesting to note that an OSCE representative responded to the investigation conducted and published by the *Moscow Times*. In a long, tortuous letter to the *Times* that showed that he indeed felt stung by the newspaper's investigation, Hrair Balian, head of the OSCE's election section, defended his organization. In the only major substantive discussion in the letter, Balian tried to grapple with the remarkable growth of the electorate between the December 1999 and March 2000 elections by citing "routine demographic changes," "the accounting method used for voters abroad," and "inclusion of supplementary voter lists." He offered no compelling details on any of these possible sources of the sudden expansion of the electorate, and the numbers and causes he mentioned do not begin to explain how the rolls increased by 1.3 million between the elections. Most of Balian's letter was devoted to rehashing the long list of violations reported by the *Times* and insisting that OSCE's final report itself also noted many such violations. So too did Balian take pains to reiterate that the OSCE's report held that some allegations of fraud made by Russian observers were "serious and deserve the full weight of investigation" (Balian, 2000).

Yet as I mentioned, the *Times* itself reported that the OSCE had mentioned fraud and labeled it serious in its final report. Balian's defense amounted to little more than repetition of what the *Times* itself had already reported. The criticism that the *Times* made of the OSCE, and the charge that I am also making here, is not that the OSCE refused to see or hear any evil. It is, rather, that despite seeing and hearing plenty of evil, the OSCE claimed for itself *both* incompetence to make judgments about the evil *and* the competence to issue the judgment that the elections were free and fair. So too am I criticizing the OSCE's practice of issuing up-or-down judgments on the legitimacy of elections at press conferences *fewer than 24 hours after the polls close* – long before monitors' findings can possibly be aggregated and analyzed. Perhaps morning-after evaluations are innocuous when assessing Norwegian elections. But in countries where competitive elections are novel and where the state controls most of what the public hears about politics, the practice of snap judgment risks giving flawed elections the stamp of international approval and legitimating political forces that benefited from or even perpetrated fraud.

Why did the OSCE endorse the elections at all? Specifically, how could a body that proclaimed itself "not in a position to judge" whether allegations of gross violations were "reviewed by competent election commissions or the courts" nevertheless feel itself competent to issue the judgment that the "the presidential election represented a benchmark in the ongoing evolution of the Russian Federation's emergence as a representative democracy"? Three factors offer some explanation. They are not necessarily specific to the OSCE; they may be evident in other international organizations as well. The factors are 1) the presumption of fairness; 2) the anticipated consequences of *not* endorsing the elections; and 3) monitors' justified lack of confidence in their own ability to read the situation on the ground.

The prior assumption of fairness is common to most international observers and certainly characterizes the culture of the OSCE. Edouard Brunner, head of the OSCE's long-term election observation mission in 1999, told the *Moscow Times* a week *before* the Duma vote in December 1999: "One expects that at the end of the process, international observers will come up with a statement that the elections were conducted in a democratic way" ("'And They Call This Elections?'" 1999). This is the gentlemanly thing to assume. But does the courteous presumption of innocence – and the public announcement of innocence the day after the election, long before investigation and analysis can possibly be completed – promote good electoral hygiene? The question may be particularly pressing for Russia and other polities that lack long-standing traditions and institutions of open electoral competition.

Second, international observers must and do weigh the consequences of *not* blessing elections. Had the OSCE not declared the elections valid, it would have been admitting that it had failed to deter fraud. Such a statement would have amounted to an admission of malfunction. The OSCE is a large, authoritative body whose very presence is supposed to minimize the risk of falsification. It sometimes refuses to engage in observation in countries whose leaders are well known to hold sham elections. Once it has invested the time and resources in a country and observed the elections, the monitors' hopes are intended to be self-reinforcing. Elections officials are supposed to have played fair because the observers were on the premises.

Although the consequences of such thinking can be extremely unfortunate, the mentality is found in many areas of human interaction that involve judgment and monitoring. Consider grade inflation in universities. If a student has taken a course with me, been advised by me, and taken my exams, his or her failure is my failure and his or her success is my success. The

49

more I have invested in a student, moreover, the more I am loath to fail him or her.

And my motivations, like those of the OSCE, may be shaped at least in part by benevolent intentions. What will become of the student if he or she fails? My instinct is to assume that the student might be in even worse shape than if I allow him or her to slide by. In response to failure, the student might lose motivation. He or she might even give up altogether and drop out of school. I doubt that the student will respond by reenrolling in the same class with me the next time I offer it and attempt to rectify the failing grade.

In election monitoring, more is at stake but the same mentality is at work. A thumbs-down means that a government has failed to carry out the most rudimentary and important of all democratic practices. How might the government react? If the fraud favored the incumbents, will they really step down? Will they repeat the elections? Or will the failing grade only arouse defensiveness and even prompt the government to abandon any pretense of open politics?

In a country whose experience of regime change is universally regarded as affecting the peace of the entire world, international organizations cannot help but fear the consequences of issuing a failing grade. Nor could they or should they reasonably expect that the Russian government under either Yeltsin or Putin would respond to failure by admitting its folly and mending its behavior. To deny elections a passing grade would be, in effect, to admit that democratization had failed – and to risk provoking yet greater political closure. International organizations such as the OSCE and the governments that constitute them understandably do not savor such prospects.

An analogous mentality is evident in international lending institutions, which continued to emit enormous credits to Russia long after most economists knew that the government was not coming close to meeting the conditions for dispersal of the loans – indeed, right up to the moment when the government's ill-guided schemes for covering its debt brought the Russian economy crashing down in August 1998. Just weeks before a collapse that had been in the works for years, the International Monetary Fund, with some prodding from the U.S. government, announced that Russia would receive nearly $23 billion over the next two years. The international community could not "allow" the Russian economy to fail. Even after bankers, businesspeople, and government officials inside and outside Russia realized that the government's policies were leading the economy to the precipice, international lending agencies continued to dole out the funds. In fact, the funds continued to flow in part *because* the government's policies were bringing the economy to ruin (Freeland, 2000; Rutland, 1999). Just as the international community was unable to fathom losing the Russian economy (at least not until market forces brought the crash of 1998), so too did it shrink from acknowledging that democracy had failed in Russia. And nothing would send a clearer signal that Russian democracy had failed than pronouncing that elections did not pass the test of credibility. The existence of sophisticated reporting by knowledgeable observers that counsels skepticism is often not enough to sway actors who wish to see the situation as auspicious or at least salvageable. There exists a substantial scholarly literature that reveals the glaring shortcomings found in many Russian regions in meeting minimal standards for democratic practice (for example, Alexander, Degtyarev, and Gelman, 2002; Gelman, 1999; Kirkow, 1995 and 1998; Lallemand, 1999; Mendras, 1999; Ross, ed., 2002). The ready availability of such studies, however, is often not enough to induce wariness in organizations such as the OSCE, anymore than the obviousness of Russia's impending financial collapse gave pause to the IMF.

In addition to the presumption of fairness and anxieties over the consequences of not endorsing elections, a third factor encourages overly sanguine assessments: observers' justifiable doubts about their own ability to grasp the meaning of what they see. The spectacle of armed goons stuffing ballot boxes presents a nicely unambiguous picture. But post-Soviet Russia is not the Philippines of the Marcos era. Falsification does not take such comfortably detectable forms. And perpetrators of fraud rarely act when the foreigners with the inquiring looks and the colorful badges are on the scene, peering over shoulders and chatting (usually through interpreters) with precinct officials. Observers simply cannot usually assess whether what *may indicate* fraud *necessarily spells* fraud; and it is always easier to err on the side of optimism than to kick up a fuss without hard proof.

I was present in Russia during every major national election during the 1990s and encountered the problem myself. An example may provide illustration.

I served as an international observer in the 1995 parliamentary elections. I was part of a small group headed by a prominent scholar whose observational acumen and knowledge of Russian politics and society (not to mention language) far outstrip my own. One of our stops included a polling place at an army base just outside Moscow. We arrived at midday, four hours after voting commenced and eight hours before polling places were to close.

Merely gaining access to the precinct was difficult. We were held up for 15 minutes by an army officer who disputed our right to enter the polling place even after we presented our credentials, which entitled us to inspect any polling place at any time during the vote. After gaining entry, we saw that no voting was taking place at all. Several men in army uniform stood by a large container, which, we were told, held the ballots already cast. The precinct head told us that the polling place had already closed – though by law all polling places were to remain open until 8 pm – and that all eligible voters had already cast their ballots. He informed us that people around the place were early risers. In fact, everyone had already voted by 9 am.

It is impossible to establish whether the circumstances we observed were evidence of fraud. We knew that closing the polling station early constituted an infraction, but was it hard evidence of falsification? I felt discouraged by my own inability to tell. I could take comfort only in my much better informed colleague telling me during our drive back to central Moscow that he did not know what to make of the situation either. He promised to make a note of the (very) early closing of the polling station in our report (which he wrote). Still, we could not assert confidently that we had witnessed fraud.

Yet the experience helped prepare me for a result that otherwise would have left me stunned. Several days after the election, the Defense Ministry announced that throughout Russia as a whole, fully three-fifths of all officers and enlisted personnel who voted in the election chose Our Home Is Russia (OHR; NDR in Russian), the party that then-President Boris Yeltsin supported and that then-Prime Minister Viktor Chernomyrdin led. The party's stellar performance among the military contrasted with the one-tenth of the vote it received overall. The figures were so extravagant that they would be suspect even had OHR been especially attractive to military personnel. But the party had no such special allure. What is more, independent surveys conducted after the elections contradicted the official results. They found that the CPRF and the nationalist LDPR each far outdistanced OHR in support among the military (Khripunov, 1996).

Does Falsification Really Matter?

These examples raise several issues that are sometimes overlooked, glossed over, or misunderstood. The first regards the impact of falsification on electoral outcomes. It may be natural to assume that despite falsification, things roughly even out in the end. According to such logic, perhaps the military's vote for OHR was greatly inflated in the 1995 parliamentary elections; but surely the CPRF "compensated" for such abuses elsewhere. The CPRF, after all, has its own stalwarts among regional elites. Does falsification really matter if "everyone does it"? A leading Russian social scientist quipped in personal conversation on the eve of the 1999 parliamentary elections that he anticipated "full pluralism of falsification." This meant that "every conceivable technology of falsification and hiding falsification will be used" and that "every party that has any support among those holding power anywhere will engage in it."

As it turned out, this analyst's prediction was almost certainly on target. But it is important to bear in mind something that is not always well understood: Pluralism of falsification does not wash out the effects of falsification. Perhaps both OHR and the CPRF benefited from fraud in 1995. But the chances that they benefited equally are remote. And parties that do not wield great clout among regional leaders, such as Iabloko, will always lose from it.

In some elections, moreover, small numbers make a great difference. In 1995, fully six parties received more than 3.75 percent on party-list balloting but still failed to reach the 5 percent threshold required for representation in the Duma. These included the ultraorthodox Communists-Working Russia, the liberal Democratic Choice of Russia (DCR), and the centrist Women of Russia. The presence of one or more of these parties in the Duma would have affected the legislature's complexion between 1996 and 1999.

Not only does "pluralism" not necessarily neutralize the effects of falsification; it also does not wash out the stain of falsification, meaning the blot of illegitimacy that fraud leaves on the political process. Putin was the most popular candidate for president in 2000. Even if he did rely on fraud to put him over the 50 percent-plus-one mark needed to avoid a second round, he probably would have beaten Ziuganov in the second round had the event taken place – even had it been a squeaky clean affair. Putin did not need fraud to win. But the presence of widespread mischief in the first round – on a scale that may well have been decisive in eliminating the need for a second – damaged the legitimacy of the electoral system. Establishing procedures for selecting rulers that are respected and regarded as fair by the citizenry as a whole is no mean problem, particularly where institutionalized humiliation of the people by the powerful has long marred political life. Even when it is not "decisive," electoral fraud perpetuates the overlordship, hoodwinking, and injustice that characterized political life under the Soviet monocracy.

The consequences are hard to measure precisely, but may nevertheless be significant. In a study of eight African countries, Jørgen Elklit and Andrew Reynolds (2002) found that individuals' perceptions of the conduct of elections directly affected their sense of political efficacy and the legitimacy of the political regime. The matter is of great importance in Russia. In a major public opinion survey carried out in Russia in late 1996, shortly after Yeltsin's reelection, 87 percent of respondents said that it is "important" that "honest elections are held regularly," but only 36 percent said that their country actually holds "honest elections" (United States Information Agency, 1998). There is little evidence that opinion has since turned toward greater faith. In another major survey carried out in 2002, two-thirds of respondents said that they regarded elections as window dressing (*Nations in Transit*, 2003; Petrov, 2003[b]; Weir, 2002; also Moses, 2003). Such surveys must be taken as just one bit of evidence. But it merits note that an overwhelming majority of Russians consistently say that their country's elections are not honest or even determinative of who rules.

Falsification in Russia is not as severe as it is in countries, such as Azerbaijan and Belarus, where elections are charades. Still, it occurs on a scale that gravely compromises the elections' "fair conduct," Dahl's second criterion for an open polity.

Election-Related Coercion

Soft Coercion and Abuse of "Administrative Resources"

A second problem that violates Dahl's requirement for meaningful elections and thus open politics, election-related coercion, is rife in Russia. Like falsification, coercion is often difficult to observe and measure. But as with falsification, neglecting or glossing over the problem for that reason would be a mistake.

Some forms of coercion are "soft," insofar as they do not involve the commission of violence. In Russian electoral politics, soft coercion often takes the form of playing on individuals' and communities' economic dependence, threatening dissenters with loss of employment, intimidating people with threats of violence, and using voting schemes that do not necessarily qualify as falsification but that nevertheless ensure powerholders' control over blocs of votes.

People who depend on the state for their subsistence in Russia frequently hear from their bosses, who in turn are under the influence of government officials, that their sustenance depends on their vote. A secretary of the CPRF in Mordovia, Valentina Liukzaeva, recounted after the 2000 elections: "In the village of Permievo, where I am from, the head of the collective farm told villagers that if they vote for Ziuganov, he would find out – and they would not get tractors for sowing, or wood, or food. The villagers, most of whom are old women, of course got frightened and voted for Putin." Rinat Gabidullin, a secretary of the CPRF in Bashkortostan, reported that observers as well as voters came under similar pressure: "In many polling stations our [the CPRF's] observers were threatened that they would not receive food and fodder packages." Gabidullin has argued that such pressure is so extensive in small towns and rural areas that villagers as a class have effectively been cut out of the electoral process (Borisova et al., 2000[d]). Communists are not the only source of such complaints and sentiment. Viktor Sheinis, a prominent academic, parliamentarian, and leader of Iabloko, argued after the 2000 vote: "I think this [bullying] has affected the final results of the presidential elections more than even direct falsification of votes." Particularly outside the large cities, the influence of the ballot is readily annulled by local and regional powerholders. According to Sheinis: "If some babushka comes to vote, and she is completely dependent on the administration chief for getting wood and fodder for her animals, she will of course vote the way he tells her to" (Borisova et al., 2000[d]). Indeed, as one elderly woman resident of Mesker-Yurt, Chechnya, remarked of her village after the October 2003 election for the president of that republic: "Only pensioners went [to vote], and those who are getting children's or unemployment allowances, because they were told by our administration that if they didn't go and support [Akhmad] Kadyrov [the Kremlin's favored candidate], they would stop getting their money" (Borisova and Aliev, 2003).

During the first post-Soviet decade, I frequently heard such stories from people from every major region. For example, several weeks after the December 1999 parliamentary elections, I interviewed four prominent political activists from the city of Tiumen. Two were from the liberal URF and two from the CPRF. I spoke with them as a group in a lengthy conversation in Moscow. Each insisted upon anonymity. Each worked in the parliamentary campaign for their respective parties, as well as for candidates for single-member district seats. Both the liberals from the URF and the communists from the CPRF reported that local officials in Tiumen raion, one of the four districts in the city of Tiumen, informed large groups of people in workplace meetings that if they did not support Gennadii Raikov in his reelection bid for the Duma, wages in arrears would be withheld indefinitely and local budgets would be revised to the detriment of the district's workers. Threats were not always economic in nature, nor were they always delivered to large collectives. Several of the activists also recounted that they had received ominous personal warnings during the election campaign, delivered anonymously over the telephone or on the street, including threats against their children.

Those who challenge incumbents may find their jobs as well as their persons and families in jeopardy. One of the interviewees from Tiumen was a teacher at a local institute whose boss told her that her political activism would cost her her job. On this score, officials often do little to mask their actions. Displaying fealty to higher-ups is usually more important than demonstrating loyalty to fair process. In the run-up to the 2000 elections, Tatarstan's President Shaimiev made clear to his subordinates that their jobs depended on delivery of the proper result. Rashid Khamadeev, mayor of Naberezhnye Chelny, recounted after the vote (Borisova et al., 2000[d]):

Mintimer Sharipovich [Shaimiev] collected us, the heads of local governments, and said approximately this: "If [Evgenii] Primakov had put forward his candidacy, we would call on Tatarstan's people to vote for him. But as he has declined to do so, today the republic urges its citizens to vote for Putin. Today I earnestly urge our leaders to create initiative groups headed by heads [of enterprises], and to organize public receptions at every enterprise to support Putin's candidacy. Of course if [a local leader] does not desire to do so, he may refuse. But after the elections, I have a great desire to analyze the quality of work of each [enterprise director or local leader]. We will take the results of each polling station and see how many people came and how they voted. And we will see how each local leader worked – and in whose favor? And is it worth it to keep him in his post?"

No one ever accused Shaimiev of political ineffectiveness; as noted earlier, Putin racked up 68.8 percent in Tatarstan. Placing the jobs of local officials, enterprise directors, and sundry others on the line was, unsurprisingly, a good way of ensuring that the "caterpillars" functioned properly and that turnout was extraordinarily high – and even included many nonexistent residents who occupied nonexistent apartments.

Such behavior is hardly limited to Shaimiev, who has a well-established reputation for running his republic of 3.8 million like his personal estate. The day after the 2000 elections, the governor of Nizhnii Novgorod, Ivan Skliarov, delivered a speech to an assembly of officials from the province that included a blustering tirade against those from districts where Ziuganov had done well. The speech, which was partially televised, could not have revealed more plainly that Skliarov had ordered his subordinates to deliver the proper result – that is, an overwhelming endorsement of Putin – in advance of the election (Borisova et al., 2000[d]).

The president of Bashkortostan, Murtaza Rakhimov, similarly saw to it that underperforming administrators paid with their jobs. Like Shaimiev and Skliarov, Rakhimov was concerned that his bailiwick not falter in its support for the acting president. Ravil Khudaiberdin, head of the local government in the Uchaly district of Bashkortostan, where Ziuganov outpolled Putin, explained his postelection resignation (or dismissal) using a precious logic that could only make his boss proud. According to Khudaiberdin (Borisova et al., 2000[d]):

It's no secret that a major propaganda campaign was part of the run-up to the elections. A personality was defined who could lead our country by the way of democratization of our society – Vladimir Vladimirovich Putin. Our local government, like others, was explaining who all must vote for, but our appeals were not heard. This means that I and my team were not supported by the residents of the city and district. Such a result in the elections is a vote of no confidence in my administration, and that is why I decided to resign.

Rakhimov himself could not have said it better. But in most places in his republic, such disappointing "votes of no confidence" in local administrators did not take place, or at least did not come to light. While Rakhimov was bested by his neighbor and kindred spirit, Shaimiev, who delivered 68.8 percent of Tatarstan's vote to Putin, Rakhimov's performance (and that of his underlings) was not shabby: 60.3 percent of Bashkortostan's voters, according to the official tally, chose Putin.

Does what I am calling soft coercion really qualify as coercion? Don't high-ranking provincial politicians in democracies often pressure their subordinates to line up behind the superior's candidate of choice in national elections? In fact, such pressure does amount to coercion, and provincial politicians cannot normally apply it in democracies the way that they do in Russia. Gray Davis, the Democratic former governor of California, may well have urged his aides – who, at any rate, probably did not need much urging – to support the Democratic candidate for president of the United States. He certainly could dismiss or exert pressures to dismiss any personnel in his state's Democratic Party apparatus if the Republicans or the Greens did better than expected in this or that county or city. But the governor cannot threaten the jobs of civil servants, mayors, employees of state universities, managers of companies run by the state government, or principals and teachers in public schools if voters in their place of work or residence fail to support him or his choice for president to his satisfaction. Were a Russian-style system in place in the United States, Republican candidates for national and statewide office might have swept Berkeley while Pete Wilson, a Republican, ran the statehouse in the 1990s. Democrats might have made spectacular inroads in Orange County during the 2000 elections, when Davis was governor. If the students at my university voted in a single precinct near the university's premises, and if my own job depended on the performance of a particular candidate in that precinct, I might have been sorely tempted to organize a "caterpillar" on behalf of the candidate whose performance would determine whether I kept my job. If I were an observer at the precinct polling place, I certainly would have felt the urge to avert my eyes if faced with the fuzzy creature.

In some democracies in which parties' influence permeates (or used to permeate) state-owned companies or institutions of higher education, such as Italy and Japan, high-ranking administrators are (or were) often tied closely to a political party. That party may well demand loyalty and even labor on behalf of the party in the administrator's workplace during election campaigns. But university personnel, civil servants, and the managers of public enterprises normally need not fear for their jobs if the provincial governor or head of administration is dissatisfied with the electoral tally in precincts where those personnel, civil servants, and managers work. Nor need public school teachers fear for their jobs if they support a party or individual that is out of favor with the provincial head of administration. Still less must they fear that their political activity will imperil the physical safety of themselves and their families.

In sum, "soft" coercion does amount to coercion, and it is not a normal part of politics in democracies. The soft coercion that permeates post-Soviet politics, moreover, bears a striking resemblance to what some democratic-movement activists suffered during the elections of the late Soviet period. The stories activists now tell hardly differ from those I heard in the Russian provinces at the end of the Soviet period. The manipulation of people's dependence on the state for employment and access to the material means of survival, as well as threats of violence delivered by anonymous callers, were commonplace during 1989–91 (Fish, 1995).

Another form of manipulation that may sway elections without violence is government-managed absentee voting. I learned about this practice only during field research in several provinces in 2001. I knew of the provision that allowed people who are physically unable to make it to polling places to vote at home but had been unaware of the bonanza that incumbents were reaping from abuse of the law. For example, the governor of Pskov oblast, Evgenii Mikhailov, relied on his administration's control of at-home voting to secure his narrow victory in his reelection bid in November 2000. Employees of the government administration went door-to-door before the elections, especially in rural areas, armed with ballots. Voters who stated their intention – or willingness – to make the "right" choice received ballots, while those who did not support the incumbent did not. After the individuals who intended to vote for the incumbent did so – usually under the watch of those who had supplied the ballots – the magnanimous suppliers of the ballots carted them back to headquarters. It is little wonder that fully one-fifth of voters – 60,000 of the 300,000 who participated in the election – cast their ballots from the comfort of their own homes. What is more, ballots cast at home – or supposedly cast at home – could easily be altered, destroyed, or manufactured by those who supplied the ballots and then returned them to headquarters. No monitoring system, not even a faulty one, was in place to protect against fraud in at-home voting. Since Mikhailov won reelection with only 28 percent of the vote (about 84,000 of the 300,000 votes cast), and 25 percent plus one vote was the minimum winning number, it is not unreasonable to surmise that at-home voting decided the election's outcome. Asked whether the electoral commission knew about the practice, Viktor Ostrenko, an analyst at Pskov's leading nongovernmental organization devoted to fighting corruption and promoting open media, noted: "Of course. The electoral commission here is all part of the [Mikhailov] administration" (Ostrenko and Maxim Kostikov, personal interviews, July 11, 2001, Pskov; also EastWest Institute, 2000).

This practice represents a form of the "abuse of administrative resources" that Russians often cite as one of the most formidable barriers to meaningful elections. Russians apply this concept to a wide range of ethically dubious practices that involve incumbents using the powers of office to advance their own political fortunes. Still, one must distinguish between abuses that violate the free conduct of elections and those that do not necessarily do so. Many people I have interviewed in recent years regard advancing one's reelection by changing the electoral laws, timing the scheduling of public works and other spending projects to coincide with elections, and doling out state funds to enterprises located in a politically important district as abuses of administrative resources. Such practices may be unethical but they do not, in my own conception, constitute fraud. In fact, in many open polities, politicians constantly change electoral laws to enhance their own chances in future elections, and the timing of public spending is often driven by political concerns.

But the manipulation of at-home voting discussed here crosses the line. It breaks Russian law on the secrecy of the ballot. So too does it clearly violate Dahl's requirement that elections be "fairly conducted," which he specifies in his second requirement for democracy.

Hard Coercion

While soft coercion and manipulation are staples of Russian elections, so too is hard coercion. Politically motivated assault and murder are ordinary occurrences in Russia, even if they are rarer than violence motivated by conflict over commercial affairs and even if they seldom draw major international attention. What is more, politically motivated violent crimes are almost never solved, and only very rarely are perpetrators brought to justice.

Journalists are particularly vulnerable. Beginning at the time that he came to power as head of Primorskii krai in 1993, Evgenii Nazdratenko regularly deployed both the police and private thugs to pummel any journalist who irritated him. By the time of his highly dubious reelection in 1999, what at the beginning of the decade had been a freewheeling regional press had been quite literally beaten into submission (Kirkow, 1995; Working, 1999[b]).

Primorskii krai was by no means unique or exceptional. To cite just a few other examples: In late November 1999, during the closing weeks of the election campaign, a leading journalist in Kaliningrad, Igor Rostov, who took a critical stance toward the governor, Leonid Gorbenko, was badly beaten by a band of thugs. Igor Rudnikov, a Kaliningrad city legislator and editor of a local newspaper that had also criticized the governor, was beaten nearly to death in an attack in 1998. One of Rudnikov's associates had earlier been attacked as well, and the newspaper's offices finally moved to Lithuania after being bombed twice. Just a few days before Rudnikov was savaged in Kaliningrad, Sergei Bachinin, the editor of a newspaper critical of local and regional officials in Kirov and in 1996 the main opponent of the city's mayor in municipal elections, was assaulted, sustaining extensive skull and brain injuries ("Editor Attacked," 1998; "News Editor Beaten," 1998; Peach, 1999; "Zashchita Iliumzhinova," 1998).

Candidates for office themselves, along with their staffs, are often in danger as well. Challengers to incumbents are usually in the greatest danger. In some cases, incumbents who run against Moscow's – that is, the president's – favored candidates or against candidates who control the agencies of coercion are also vulnerable. In the run-up to the election for the governor of Smolensk oblast in May 2002, a large portion of the staff of Aleksandr Prokhorov, then governor, suffered attack. Prokhorov was challenged and defeated in the election by Viktor Maslov, the head of the regional Federal Security Bureau (the successor agency to the KGB). Although the source of the violence was – unsurprisingly – never authoritatively identified, Maslov appears to have made effective use of his offices in his election bid. In the period before the election, the dachas of two members of Prokhorov's election staff were burned, the son of Prokhorov's lawyer was attacked and beaten, and Prokhorov's election headquarters was bombed. Days before the election, the car of Anatolii Makarenko, Prokhorov's deputy, was attacked by gunmen. Makarenko's bodyguard was wounded and his driver killed in the attack (Satter, 2002).

The cases discussed here are not isolated incidents. They are frequent, entirely normal events in Russia (Committee to Protect Journalists, 2001; Pacific Media Watch, 2002; Radio Free Europe/Radio Liberty, 2002). In many places they are an integral part of the conditions under which elections are held. Coercion of many types, as well as some types of what is often called "abuse of administrative resources," violate Dahl's second condition for an open polity, which posits that "elected officials are chosen in frequently and fairly conducted elections in which coercion is comparatively uncommon."

Arbitrary Exclusion from Electoral Participation

Dahl's fourth criterion for polyarchy, which stipulates that "practically all adults have the right to run for elective offices in the government," is also regularly violated. Unless by including "practically" Dahl meant to provide a loophole to excuse the exclusion of candidates who threaten the reelection of incumbents, which is doubtful, then the arbitrary disqualification of such people constitutes a violation.

Russia is not Iran; candidates are not screened for their political or religious views. By law, anyone has the right to run for office. But the law and actual practice are two very different things. A few examples will illustrate the problem.

Evgenii Nazdratenko's campaign for reelection as governor of Primorskii krai in late 1999 provides one. Using his powers as incumbent and his grip on regional courts, Nazdratenko disqualified a leading opponent, Svetlana Orlova. Orlova was removed from contention just two days before the vote after it became clear that she threatened to attract substantial support. According to the court, Orlova had failed to list a plot of land she possessed on her declaration of personal property, a document that candidates are required to furnish. The same court that announced Orlova's disqualification also banned Nazdratenko's political archenemy, the former mayor of Vladivostok, Viktor Cherepkov, from running for the Duma. Cherepkov was scratched from ballots on the grounds that he had supposedly failed to provide campaign spending information in time. In a final touch of absurdity, the court also canceled mayoral elections in Vladivostok, thereby leaving a close Nazdratenko ally in office, on the grounds that the city did not yet have a charter. That elections had been held previously in the city despite the absence of a "charter" did not figure in the court's reasoning ("Court Cancels Far East Race," 1999; Medetsky, 1999; Working, 1999[a]).

The courts' disqualification of candidates does not always favor the incumbent. If the incumbent has fallen afoul of the president, the former may attract the zealous gaze of the judiciary or electoral commissions and fall prey to disqualification. In October 2000, one day before the gubernatorial elections in Kursk oblast, a regional court barred Governor Aleksandr Rutskoi from seeking reelection. The court was responding to complaints lodged by Viktor Surzhikov, a KGB officer and Putin's main federal inspector in the oblast. The violation that prompted Rutskoi's disqualification: In his declaration of personal property, the governor had failed to mention his sale of a six-year-old Volga automobile. He no longer owned the vehicle, but he had neglected to de-register it and had simply transferred the ownership papers to the new owner. Alas, the roadster was still registered in his name. In comments to the press about the case, the CEC's Veshniakov intoned that a candidate "should not give erroneous information about income and property." Georgii Poltavchenko, the presidential representative to the Central District (which includes Kursk oblast), weighed in on the side of virtue as well. According to Poltavchenko, Ruskoi "should have known the law." Rutskoi had long been an antagonist of the Kremlin. He had broken with Yeltsin, whom he served as vice president, in 1993, and had angered Putin in 2000 by launching a program to help the families of the seamen who were killed in the disaster that befell the *Kursk* submarine (*RFE/RL Russian Federation Report*, October 25, 2000).

In the elections for president of North Ossetia in January 2002, the incumbent was a Putin ally and it was his challenger who faced exquisitely penetrating legal scrutiny. The president, Aleksandr Dzasokhov, won reelection after his main rival, Sergei Khetagurov, was disqualified by the Supreme Court of the Republic of North Ossetia for an infraction nearly as grave as the one that cost Rutskoi his candidacy in Kursk: Khetagurov's domicile was registered in both Vladikavkaz, the capital of North Ossetia, and Moscow. During the 1990s Khetagurov had served as a deputy minister in the federal government. He had neglected to cancel his registration of residence in Moscow when he moved back to Vladikavkaz after his stint in the national government. According to the court, Khetagurov had violated Russia's residence registration laws. The court issued its verdict 10 days before the election, when polls showed Khetagurov poised to win an absolute majority of the vote. Putin strongly favored Dzasokhov, whose loyalty was not in question, to the less manageable – and more popular – Khetagurov (Fuller, 2002[b]; Globachev, 2003).

Three months after Khetagurov was removed from contention in North Ossetia, the most popular candidate in the contest for president of the neighboring Ingush republic, Khamzat Gutseriev, was scratched from the ballot. In a ruling issued on April 5, 2002, two days before the election, the Russian Supreme Court invalidated Gutseriev's registration on the grounds that the candidate, who served as interior minister of the Ingush Republic, had failed to take the required leave of absence from his government job within three days of registering as a candidate for republican president. The Supreme Court enjoyed some vigorous investigative assistance in the Ingush Republic itself. On April 3, armed men representing Viktor Kazantsev, the presidential representative to the Southern federal district, which includes North Ossetia, forced their way into the Ingush Supreme Court hearing that was considering an appeal to disqualify Gutseriev and demanded that all documents pertaining to the case be transferred to the Russian Supreme Court. As the chronology shows, not only did the Supreme Court have some forceful support on the ground; it also benefited from having justices who enjoyed formidable talents as quick studies. The documents were seized from the Supreme Court of the Ingush Republic on April 3, and already on April 5, the Supreme Court of Russia issued its ruling disqualifying Gutseriev.

Even with Gutseriev out of the race, however, the first round of balloting did not go as the presidential administration planned. Alikhan Amirkhanov, who enjoyed the support of Ruslan Aushev, the republic's popular former president and a prominent critic of the war in Chechnya, faced Murat Ziazikov, the Moscow-backed candidate who was a general in the FSB and Kazantsev's deputy. In the first round, Amirkhanov won a plurality, receiving 32 percent to Ziazikov's 19 percent. In the second round, authorities in Moscow placed polling places under strict FSB control and dismissed all observers. The Kremlin's candidate then staged a truly remarkable rally; Ziazikov vanquished Amirkhanov in the second round with 53 percent of the vote. As this case shows, sometimes disqualification of an undesirable candidate is not enough. If another undesirable candidate who was not disqualified before the election performs well in the first round, extra measures may be needed in the second round of voting to ensure the proper outcome (Fuller, 2002[a] and [b]; Satter, 2002).

The fate of Leonid Ivanchenko, a challenger to the incumbent governor, Vladimir Chub, in Rostov oblast's fall 2001 gubernatorial contest provides another instance of creative exclusion. Here, the electoral commission rather than the courts took care of business. Ivanchenko, a Duma deputy from the CPRF and Chub's main challenger, was charged by the oblast electoral commission with submitting bogus signatures endorsing his run for governor. Candidates must submit lists of signatures of voters endorsing their candidacy in order to run for office, and electoral commissions sometimes closely investigate the lists of signatures gathered on behalf of challengers to the incumbent or challengers to the Kremlin's favored candidate. In this instance, the electoral commission found the signatures of some individuals on Ivanchenko's petitions who, upon questioning, denied that they had signed. The electoral commission disqualified Ivanchenko as a result. Polls showed that Ivanchenko was running neck and neck with Chub at the time of the electoral commission's ruling. The commission also disqualified another challenger, a well-known local entrepreneur, Valentin Chistiakov, leaving Chub to face a single, virtually unknown, opponent. From this enviable position, Chub romped to reelection with over three-quarters of the vote (Andrusenko and Shapovalov, 2001; Zueva, 2001).

Not all instances of disqualification necessarily violate democracy. Recent elections provide examples of what may be regarded as legitimate exclusion as well. In the January 2002 elections for the president of Sakha (formerly Yakutia), the federal Constitutional Court ruled against Mikhail Nikolaev's attempt to run for a third term, a decision that was endorsed by the CEC's Veshniakov. The legal basis for the ruling was vague, since at the time, Putin and the legislature were in the middle of a complicated discussion over changes in the law on term limits for governors and republican presidents. But some legal basis for the decision did exist. To be sure, the Putin administration's campaign against Nikolaev was not motivated by concern for the integrity of the law. Rather, Nikolaev had fallen out of grace with Putin for his independent behavior. Putin considered an alternative candidate, Viacheslav Shtyrov, the head of Almazy Rossii-Sakha, Sakha's giant diamond production company, to be friendly to the idea of Moscow's obtaining control of the firm. Such a move would give Putin untrammeled access to the revenues from gems that theretofore had resided in part with republican-level authorities. Many of the 1 million residents of the vast province credited Nikolaev for Sakha's impressive economic development during the first post-Soviet decade. Polls taken a month before the election showed that Nikolaev stood to capture 80 percent of the vote. Getting people to show up at the polls after Nikolaev's disqualification therefore required some imagination. Local authorities hit on a novel plan, which included offering voters a rebate on their monthly housing payments, a reduction in their arrears on electricity payments, and participation in a lottery for a Volga automobile. The enticements helped get out the vote, and Shtyrov beat his rival, Fedot Tumusov, a businessman with little political following or stature (Radio Free Europe/Radio Liberty Reports, various issues, November 2001–February 2002).

In the April 2002 gubernatorial elections in Lipetsk oblast, the Kremlin sided with the incumbent, Oleg Korolev, against a popular challenger and enterprise director, Vladimir Lisin. Georgii Poltavchenko, the presidential representative to the Central District, brokered an agreement on the eve of the election that secured Lisin's withdrawal from the race. Left without a credible challenger, Korolev was handily reelected; his closest competitor received 5 percent. In the absence of the most popular alternative to the incumbent and of enticements such as local authorities used in Sakha, however, turnout was under a third, and 13 percent voted against all candidates (Radio Free Europe/Radio Liberty Reports, various issues, January–April 2002).

The Kremlin's approach to the elections in Sakha and Lipetsk hardly inspires confidence in its commitment to local and regional self-rule. Both examples show heavy-handed intervention by Moscow that subverted the expression of popular preferences. Yet these were not blatant violations of democratic norms. In Sakha, some legal grounds for excluding Nikolaev did exist. In Lipetsk, Lisin was not, to the best of my knowledge, intimidated into withdrawing; nor was he disqualified on a bogus technicality. He may have been bribed to withdraw but, in the event, he could have refused the offer.

But the cases of Primorskii krai, Kursk, North Ossetia, the Ingush Republic, and Rostov discussed here do amount to arbitrary exclusion and manifest violations of Dahl's fourth criterion for an open polity, which stipulates that running for election be a universal right. Leading contenders were disqualified for purely political reasons in the waning hours of election campaigns on the basis of absurdly trivial or fabricated technicalities. The exclusion of challengers to the incumbent or the Kremlin's favorite in regional elections is as much a part of political life in Russia as are electoral fraud and election-related coercion. As Liubov Tsukanova (2002), a reporter for *Novoe Vremia*, remarked in an article published in June 2002: "No one is surprised when significant rivals are kicked out of the race through the use of the courts." In the Central Asian republics of the former Soviet Union, challengers to the dictator in "elections" who cannot be bought off or intimidated are simply disqualified by the courts during the "campaign." Much the same obtains in some regions of Russia.

The perpetrators of politically motivated disqualification are often the same as the agents of election-time fraud and coercion: electoral commissions working on behalf of the president of Russia or heads of provinces (meaning governors of oblasts or presidents of autonomous republics). In the arbitrary disqualification of candidates, the courts – which are often controlled by those same incumbent executives – also play an active role (Newburg, 2000).

While the courts are often part of the problem, they are never part of a solution. One of the most problematic aspects of arbitrary disqualification is that its victims lack legal recourse. Machinations such as one sees in Russia are also common in many other polities that hold elections but that regularly suffer official abuse of power. In many other such polities, however, candidates who are treated like Orlova, Cherepkov, Rutskoi, Khetagurov, Gutseriev, Amirkhanov, and Ivanchenko have recourse to the courts. In mass surveys carried out in both Russia and India in the mid-1990s, people were asked whether it is important that the judicial system "punishes the guilty no matter who they are" and whether such a condition obtains in their country. Ninety-four percent of Indians and 96 percent of Russians said that such a condition is important; 53 percent of Indians and 15 percent of Russians said that the condition actually exists in their country (United States Information Agency, 1998). Such data must be regarded as provisional and illustrative rather than definitive, but it is not difficult to see why Russians do not view their courts as evenhanded. One problem, as noted in an incisive report, is that judges in Russia live in fear of the FSB. Even those who may be personally committed to upholding the law still must consider how the state security services will react to decisions that countervail the will of the executives to whom the security services answer, and especially the president. It is therefore unsurprising that the courts in Russia never reverse elections results. Vladimir Tumanov, the former chairman of the Constitutional Court, recently complained that in his country, unlike in most others that hold competitive elections, legal action after the vote is futile. Tumanov noted that courts never invalidate elections, regardless of the strength of the evidence that a candidate was disqualified on legally dubious grounds. Once the elections commissions speak – typically, immediately after the vote – the case is closed. For their own part, electoral commissions have proven as unable to block arbitrary disqualification as they have been unwilling to investigate falsification. Like the courts, the electoral commissions not only engage in arbitrary disqualification before elections but also fail to provide a forum for redress after elections (Tsukanova, 2002).

In sum, severe irregularities – falsification, coercion, and the arbitrary disqualification of candidates – characterize elections. Russia holds elections, but they regularly include abuses that prevent the contests from revealing public opinion and determining who governs. Russia fulfills point one in Dahl's list of procedural minima, since elected officials control (at least a substantial portion of) state power and the franchise is universal. But pervasive fraud and extensive election-related coercion twice violate Dahl's point two, which requires that elections be fairly conducted and that coercion be rare. Dahl's point three is fulfilled in principle, since practically all adults have the right to vote. But the right is compromised in practice by the fraudulent counting of ballots. The arbitrary disqualification of candidates contravenes Dahl's point four, which requires that practically all adults have the right to run for elective office.

Constriction of Civil Liberties

Restrictions on Communication

In terms of Dahl's fifth, sixth, and seventh criteria, which enumerate several basic rights, Russia again comes up short. First, many citizens do not "have

67

the right to express themselves without the danger of severe punishment on political matters broadly defined" (Dahl's point five). Journalists – the very individuals who supply and interpret public information – are often deprived of this right, as reviewed earlier. Here, the problems of political coercion and freedom of expression are joined, underlining the intimate interdependence of political voice and civil liberties. The harsh pressures faced by many journalists who oppose or expose officials violate Dahl's points two (on freedom from coercion) and five (on rights of expression). Election-related coercion of journalists was discussed in a previous section. Such violence and intimidation is not, however, limited to election time; it occurs regardless of the political season.

Several cases of official repression of journalists in Russia have received attention in the West. The abuse of Anna Politkovskaia, Andrei Babitskii, and other journalists who attempted to continue covering Chechnya after the resumption of hostilities in the summer of 1999 has been reported in some Western media. So too was the sensational case of Grigorii Pasko, who was imprisoned for treason for reporting on radioactive pollution. The Putin government has made no secret of its intentions to shut down press coverage of the war in Chechnya and anything else that it determines to be a matter of national security. Politkovskaia, Babitskii, and Pasko broke no laws, but they ran afoul of the central government's policy. From reading the Western press alone – or for that matter, the increasingly closed Russian press – one might think official abuse of journalists is limited to matters that involve national security.

But these high-profile cases represent a trifling portion of the coercion that journalists endure. Far more typical are the innumerable instances of abuse that happen away from the gaze of Western press agencies and that have nothing to do with national security. In February 2001, Rashid Khatuev and Vladimir Panov, the editors of *Vozrozhdenie*, a newspaper in Cherkessk, the capital of the Karachaevo-Cherkes region, were badly beaten in their workplace by attackers armed with guns and rubber truncheons. Khatuev and Panov's paper had been critical of the republic's president, Vladimir Semenov. The assailants, who were dressed in special police force uniforms, destroyed computers and broke journalists' bones. Criticism of local officials ended even more tragically in Reftinskii, a town in Sverdlovsk oblast. Eduard Markevich, the editor and publisher of *Novyi Reft*, which exposed malfeasance among local officials, was severely beaten at home in front of his family in 1998 and detained for 10 days in 2000 by the local prosecutor's office for defamation. The defamation charge stemmed from an article he

68

had published that questioned the propriety of a large government contract that the former deputy prosecutor of the town had received. In May 2001, Markevich's treatment prompted Vladimir Ustinov, the federal prosecutor general, to reprimand the local prosecutor in Reftinskii for violating Markevich's constitutional rights. Faced with the prospect of drawing more unwanted attention, local authorities decided to do away with the problem altogether: In September 2001, Markevich was found dead after having been shot in the back. A series of threatening phone calls had foretold his death, but true to what had become his courageous style, Markevich had not heeded the warnings to cease his investigation of local officials (Committee to Protect Journalists, 2001).

As Markevich's story shows, reporting on public prosecutors can be especially dangerous. In another such case, Olga Kitova, a reporter in Belgorod who wrote for *Belgorodskaia Pravda* as well as for the Moscow-based national newspaper, *Obshaia gazeta*, was repeatedly assaulted, threatened, and finally prosecuted for her writings that raised questions about the legitimacy of the Belgorod prosecutor's case against several university students. In March 2001, 10 police officers surrounded Kitova outside her home, forced her into a police car, and beat her unconscious. The local prosecutor's office then launched an investigation against Kitova for insulting and using force against the police officers who had abducted her. In May she was arrested again, and in December convicted of insulting an individual's honor, obstructing justice, using force against state officials, and insulting state officials (Committee to Protect Journalists, 2001).

In April 2003, Dmitrii Shvets, deputy to the general director of a television station in Murmansk, was shot to death near the headquarters of the television company. Shvets's colleagues said that he had been subject to death threats and that his car had been torched shortly before his death. The station at which Shvets worked had been critical of the mayor ("Sluchai gibeli zhurnalistov, 2003," 2003).

Journalists who air their work on the Internet rather than traditional media are also vulnerable. In January 2003, Dmitrii Motrich and Lada Motrich of the Internet publication *kandidat.ru*, which is associated with the group Democratic Russia, were attacked by a group that beat them and seized a bag of documents. The editor in chief of *kandidat.ru* remarked after the attack that the publication had experienced pressure since its inception, and that the violence was probably backed by politicians that the publication had criticized ("Napadeniia na zhurnalistov i redaktsii, 2003," 2003).

69

Such events are not at all unusual. On average, between late 1991 and 1998 one journalist was murdered for political reasons every 10 weeks in Russia. In 1996, Reporters Without Borders named Russia and Algeria as the most dangerous countries for journalists (Saradzhyan, 1998). The pace doubled during the current decade: In the first three years of the 2000s, 40 Russian journalists were murdered for political reasons and 4 others disappeared. Many times more were subjected to crippling assaults but survived. The Paris-based World Association of Newspapers reported in 2001 that after Colombia, Russia was the world's most dangerous place for journalists. The report highlights the enormity of the problem in Russia, though the judgment that Russia is less dangerous than Colombia is open to dispute, since on a per capita basis, slightly more journalists have been killed in Russia over the past decade than in Colombia (Dolgov, 2001; Rosenberg, 2003). Most coercion occurs not over matters of national significance, such as the war in Chechnya, but in response to reporting that power holders do not like, as in the cases of Khatuev, Panov, Markevich, Kitova, Shvets, Motrich, and Motrich recounted here. Crimes against journalists are almost never solved in Russia; the powerful act against those who criticize or embarrass them with impunity. Thomas Dine, the president of Radio Free Europe/Radio Liberty (RFE/RL), remarked in January 2003: "Russian authorities have shown little interest in solving these crimes, perhaps because the trail of culpability too often leads back to the boardroom, the police station, or the city hall" (Dine, 2003, p. 44).

The courts often do come into play in conflicts between power holders and journalists, but the latter nearly always find themselves in the role of defendants. Suits for libel and criminal proceedings against journalists for defamation were common during the 1990s, but the first three years of the Putin presidency witnessed the initiation of more criminal cases against journalists than were seen during the entire Yeltsin era. The 1992 Law on the Mass Media and the 1991 Law on the Protection of Citizens' Honor, Dignity, and Business Reputation make libel a criminal offense, and power holders can usually rely on the courts to deliver verdicts that define unflattering commentary, revelations, or allusions as insults to dignity and honor. Kitova's prosecution in Belgorod represents an example. So too does the sentencing to a year of corrective labor of Iiulia Shelamydova, the editor of *Simbirskie izvestiia*, for publishing an article that criticized some associates of the governor of Ulyanovsk, Vladimir Shamanov (*Nations in Transit 2003*, 2003).

As one might expect, the combination of violence, harassment, and the threat of legal action severely restricts the flow of political communication. Dine notes: "In a climate such as this, when independent journalists face everything from lawsuits to jail to death, it is almost a miracle that anyone is willing to do journalism at all. In fact, fewer and fewer are willing" (Dine, 2003, p. 44). Uncommon bravery and integrity are requirements for those who seek to provide the public with unprejudiced information about politics. Russia does not lack such journalists. Eduard Markevich, the publisher from Sverdlovsk oblast who published *Novyi Reft*, continued to displease the authorities despite threats on his life, beatings, and detentions. After Markevich was shot dead, his widow took up the task of publishing the paper. Such extraordinary individuals enjoy some organizational support in society. The Society for the Defense of Glasnost, a union of journalists, teachers, and lawyers, organizes training programs to foster professional ethics and help journalists resist the bribes and the blows of officials and private interests. The organization, however, obviously finds itself in a lop-sided battle that favors those who control the agencies of administration, prosecution, and coercion (Rosa Burkutbaeva and Liudmila Shevchenko, personal interviews, February 28, 2001, Ekaterinburg).

When embarrassing publications make it to the newsstands despite all good efforts to stop their dissemination, officials can take other actions. One popular technique is seizing the newspapers. During 2001 and 2002, Governors Sergei Darkin of Primorskii krai and Boris Govorin of Irkutsk oblast and President Valerii Kokov of Kabardino-Balkar autonomous republic, to name three examples, regularly sent the police to the vendors to confiscate and destroy runs of the one or handful of newspapers left in their bailiwicks that published unflattering articles (Committee to Protect Journalists, 2001; Radio Free Europe/Radio Liberty, 2002).

These practices by provincial officials obviously violate Dahl's point six, which requires that "citizens have the right to seek out alternative sources of information. Moreover, alternative sources of information exist and are protected by law." They amount to trivial harassment, however, compared to the national government's policy toward the media since the onset of the Putin era. During his first three years in office, Putin shut down or took over all private television networks with national reach. By the middle of 2003, serious criticism or scrutiny of the president in the electronic media had become as scarce in Russia as in the dictatorships of Central Asia. Anything resembling thorough or balanced coverage of the war in

Chechnya had disappeared. Parliament was fully complicit in the statization of the airwaves, even though the president, and not the legislature, assumed control of the flow and content of information. Provincial officials took their cue from the chief executive (Sakwa, 2003). Local television stations and newspapers that previously enjoyed some autonomy increasingly came under the control of provincial executives. Aleksandr Prokofev, the mayor of Pskov between 1996 and 2000, noted shortly after leaving office: "The national leadership sets the tone in Russia, as it always has, including in the treatment of opposition. The provincial leaders take their cues from the center. They mimic it even when they don't obey it" (Prokofev, personal interview, July 11, 2001, Pskov). Based on his in-depth research in Iaroslavl' oblast, Sakhalin oblast, Primorskii krai, Khabarovsk krai, and the city of St. Petersburg, Jeffrey Hahn (2004) concluded that only in the last of these five regions did a trace of meaningful freedom in the local media survive into the third year of the current decade. Even in St. Petersburg, the local electronic media are in the governor's hands and, through the president's sway over the governor, under the control of the central government.

Television was not the only medium to undergo statization. While some nonstate newspapers continued to publish, the most incisive independent print media, notably the daily newspaper *Segodnia* and the weekly news magazine *Itogi* (which was copublished with the U.S. magazine *Newsweek*), were taken over by the government. Putin has wrapped his every move against the media in a web of pretense about the outlet's financial insolvency, inadmissible business practices, or illicit dealings or connections. He has relied on state-owned corporations, the courts, and the police to do the dirty work, always coyly denying personal interest and involvement. Ann Cooper, the executive director of the Committee to Protect Journalists, a leading international press watchdog organization, remarked in May 2001: "President Putin pays lip service to press freedom in Russia, but then maneuvers in the shadows to centralize control of the media, stifle criticism, and destroy the independent press" (Kovalyev, 2001). To use Dahl's formulation, "citizens have the right to seek out alternative sources of information" in Russia; the problem is that the chances of actually finding such sources, not to mention enjoying regular, reliable access to them, became increasingly slim during the first half of the 2000s. "Alternative sources of information exist and are protected by law": This portion of Dahl's sixth point is met in Article 29 of the Constitution, which explicitly guarantees freedom of speech and information. The catch is that the Putin government simply ignores Article 29 in practice (Albats, 2001; Committee to Protect Journalists, 2001; Dewhirst,

2002; Mendelson, 2000; *Nations in Transit, 2003*, 2003; Oates, 2000; Pacific Media Watch, 2002).

Some sources of political information are still difficult for the state to control. The Internet is one potentially important source; others include the *Moscow Times* (and its sister paper, the *St. Petersburg Times*) and Radio Free Europe/Radio Liberty (RFE/RL). Such sources have become increasingly important as the government has methodically eliminated independent outlets. Indeed, researchers such as this author, as my citations make clear, must rely on them, as well as on personal interviews and on international agencies, such as the Committee to Protect Journalists, the World Association of Newspaper Journalists, and Journalists Without Borders. Valuable as they are for the researcher, however, such sources are not readily accessible to most people in Russia, and they certainly cannot be as influential as conventional media outlets. The *Moscow Times* is accessible only to people who read English and is difficult to obtain outside Moscow, St. Petersburg, and a handful of other large cities. The number of Russians who have a computer at home is rising rapidly, but in 2003 it was still only 7 percent of the population. By contrast, 97 percent of Russian households have a television. As in most of the world, people get their political information from TV. It is little wonder that the government has focused on it with particular intensity. RFE/RL broadcasts its radio programs in Russian and is widely accessible. This fact has not been lost on the government: In October 2002, Putin cancelled an August 1991 decree that guaranteed the legal rights of RFE/RL to operate in Moscow. At the time of the 1991 revolution, Yeltsin regarded the outlet as a valuable source of independent information. He issued the decree to protect RFE/RL from governmental or commercial manipulation. True to form, the Putin government claimed that the move was a strictly technical measure designed to give equal status to all foreign media outlets in Russia (*Nations in Transit, 2003*, 2003). The ruling's ultimate consequences are, as of this writing, still unsettled. But one need not be a rocket scientist – or even a political scientist – to predict them.

Putin's policies have degraded freedom of expression in Russia, but the downward trend was already evident during the second half of the 1990s. During the Yeltsin period, Article 29 was not a dead letter. Some pluralism in mass communications obtained at the national level and in many regions. Critical scrutiny of officials, including the president, was common. But the growth of the national electronic media's slant toward Yeltsin was palpable in the 1990s. In 1996, the chief of NTV, then the main private television station with national reach, also served as the director of media operations in Yeltsin's presidential campaign. The presidential administration probably had to do little beyond allowing Ziuganov, Yeltsin's communist opponent, to serve up his warm accounts of Soviet life to ensure that most journalists would rally behind the incumbent. Still, even granting a great deal of leeway for the possibility that bias did not result from official pressure, it is hard to escape the conclusion that the national electronic media severely distorted the political process during the second half of the 1990s. It is impossible to establish a clear threshold beyond which systematic media bias undermines fair competition, but for the observer who lived in Russia during election campaigns, it was obvious that some such threshold was habitually crossed.

While all political parties are allowed to buy television advertisements, most discussion relevant to campaigns takes the form of coverage on political news reports and talk shows. Such programs occupy a larger portion of total air time in Russia than they do on the major commercial networks in the United States. By the middle of the 1990s, pro-government candidates and parties received an abundance of flattering coverage, while opposition parties and candidates encountered virtual embargoes. In the presidential election of 2000, television coverage of Putin reached Soviet levels of sycophancy, with tender reporting on the acting president's recreational activities crowding out coverage of politics. One could easily have surmised that one was watching television during "normal" times in Belarus, Azerbaijan or Kazakhstan, where the chief executive's virtues are slavishly extolled as a matter of course.

Thus, even before Putin's victory in March 2000, the medium in which the vast majority of voters get their political information was so thoroughly preferential that alternative voices were often drowned out or not represented. Putin's full-blown assault on the independent media represented a new level of state-led constriction of communication, but state interference in the free formation of popular political preferences was evident during the Yeltsin period as well.

Figure 3.1 illustrates Russia's press freedom scores between 1994, when Freedom House began publishing its analyses of press openness around the world, and 2003. The numbers capture the deterioration in openness during the second half of the 1990s, as well as the continuation of closure in the 2000s. Countries are scored on a 100 point scale. In the ratings as published by Freedom House, lower scores represent greater freedom. Here, I reverse the scale for more intuitive presentation. As the figure shows, press openness has declined substantially. In 1994, Russia received a score of 60, which placed it in the "partially free" category. A decade later, Russia's

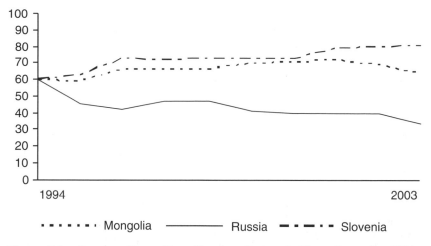

Figure 3.1. Freedom House Press Freedom Ratings in Three Countries, 1994–2003.

score had fallen to 34, leaving it in the "not free" category. For comparative purposes, the figure also includes graphs for Slovenia and Mongolia. These two countries (and, in the postcommunist region, only these two countries) received scores in 1994 that were identical to Russia's in the same year. The graphs show the divergence between Russia and the other two countries. Press freedom in Mongolia improved moderately in the late 1990s and the beginning of the 2000s but then fell back a bit. In 2003 it received a score of 64. In Slovenia, press freedoms improved steadily and markedly; in 2003 it received a score of 81. While Russia began the period on the same level of openness as Slovenia and Mongolia, in 2003 its score was the same as Singapore's, 8 points worse than Pakistan's, and just 3 points better than Kazakhstan's (Karlekar, ed., 2003).

Limitations on Association

Control, manipulation, and repression are not limited to communicative interaction. Restrictions on associational freedoms also characterize official action and policy.

In conformity with Dahl's point seven, free formation of political parties and interest groups is possible in Russia. During the early post-Soviet years, restrictions on associational rights were fairly light. But some types of organizations have come under increasing, systematic official pressure since the mid-1990s. These include most religious associations other than the Russian Orthodox Church. Since the mid- and late 1990s, the Orthodox Church has enjoyed official "protection" and has been used ever more frequently by political leaders as a tool for enhancing their own legitimacy and for building a new Russian nationalism (Gvosdev, 2000[b]). "Protection" for Orthodoxy has included new laws that restrict "alien" religious associations. Rights of organizations other than the Orthodox Church to hold bank accounts, publicize activities, and hold meetings have eroded. Restrictions hem in not only evangelists from abroad but also organizations made up of Russian citizens if those groups are deemed "alien" – that is, not Russian Orthodox. Strictures on religious organizations have not returned to the wholesale persecution of the Soviet period. But the trend has clearly run in the direction of less, rather than more, associational freedom. By the end of the 1990s, it was impossible to speak of full freedom of association for religious purposes in Russia (Brown, 1998; Knox, 2003; Krasikov, 1998; Uzzell, 1997; Zolotov, 2002).

During the Putin era, restrictions on association have grown more acute and have been tethered to the constriction of communication. During the 1990s, surveillance of private citizens' communications and lives – a hallmark of the Soviet regime – fell off dramatically. But since 2000, the monitoring of those whom officials consider opponents – be they Committees of Soldiers' Mothers, the nationwide network that fights official mendacity on casualty counts in Chechnya, or opponents of incumbents in regional elections – has returned with a vengeance. Proving such activity is always difficult, but the behavior of political actors themselves is instructive. As the *Nations in Transit* (2003, p. 513) report for 2003 notes: "Many environmental and political activists ... now eschew e-mail for sensitive communications in favor of faxes and face-to-face meetings." Under such circumstances, associational life is cramped at best. The report concludes that "whether the authorities have the resources to monitor the burgeoning flow of information is unclear."

In my own experience and that of many political activists in Russia with whom I have contact, the state indeed has the necessary resources, or at least enough to chill associational life. At the beginning of the 2000–2001 academic year during my stay as a visiting professor at the European University at St. Petersburg, little state presence was visible, with the occasional exception of the uniformed police officer who stopped by the next-door café for a cup of tea and a snack. By the end of the academic year, 10 months later, FSB agents were prowling the halls and squeezing administrators for information on foreign students and Russians who associated with them. Such activity is as socially degrading as it was during the Soviet period. So too is it as wasteful and useless – unless the intended effect is again to draw a blanket of quiet intimidation over associational life, a cover that has a familiar feel to anyone raised in Soviet times.

The Putin government's push to bring "order" to political party competition also threatens free association. In mid-2001, the Duma passed a Kremlin-sponsored bill that required a political party to have 10,000 members and a substantial presence in at least half of Russia's 89 provinces in order to maintain the legal right to exist. As of this writing, the effects of this provision are still unclear, but several parties have already been denied registration on dubious grounds, and it is obvious that only a handful of parties will pull through. The measure is pure and typical Putinism. First, target an arena of political life for takeover. Second, justify takeover by claiming that it is needed to rectify a pathology that most reasonable people do, in fact, regard as a pathology. In this case, the pathology is the whole realm of diminutive, short-lived parties that crowd the political arena during elections but that represent no one's interests and contribute nothing to structuring political competition. Third, redress the apparent pathology by issuing a rule that prima facie makes good sense but that in practice opens limitless possibilities for abuse by officials who answer to the president alone. In the case of the law on parties, the Putin government claims only to seek the consolidation of small, weightless parties and the formation of larger, stronger organizations that are better able to structure political competition. But the law essentially gives the state – in practice, the executive – the right to decide who gets to compete. If Putin intends to establish state control over political competition and participation, the new law will enable him to do so. It would not be surprising if Putin's intentions run in such a direction. According to Vladimir Pribylovskii, the director of the Panorama think tank in Moscow: "The law on political parties potentially gives the authorities the power to decide who will be allowed to participate. The Kremlin wants to have a stable of tame parties that cover the spectrum – including tame communists, tame democrats, and tame patriots" (Weir, 2002; see also Balzer, 2003).

Coda: The 2003–2004 Elections

Discussion to this point has focused on elections that preceded the December 2003 parliamentary and March 2004 presidential contests. Even before these contests, the conditions under which elections were held fell far short of a minimal standard for open politics. In the 2003–4 national elections, each of the pathologies discussed in this chapter was evident in full color. Indeed, the elections so obviously lacked the rudiments of free competition that even international observers who were loath to criticize earlier contests refused to endorse them.

In the December 2003 vote for the Duma, Putin's United Russia party scored a major victory, winning 37.1 percent in the party-lists portion of balloting. It was followed by the CPRF (12.7 percent), the LDPR (11.6 percent), and Motherland (9.1 percent). Neither major liberal party crossed the 5 percent threshold for parliamentary representation: Iabloko received 4.3 percent and the URF 4.0 percent. The LDPR serves any master who resides in the Kremlin and has become slavishly pro-Putin. The Motherland party, a new nationalist group, also is pro-Putin. The elections therefore handed Putin an overwhelmingly friendly majority in the Duma.

The results were due in part to Putin's popularity at the time of the vote. But this alone was not responsible for the result that suited the president so well. Media coverage was even more blatantly lopsided in favor of the Kremlin's favorites than in previous contests. What is more, falsification may have pushed the liberals under the 5 percent barrier. Within the confines of a difficult situation that was shaped by the hostility of the CEC, the CPRF launched an alternative count. According to the party's data, its own performance was essentially what the official figures stated it to be. But the alternative count found that United Russia's total was actually 33.1 percent and that Iabloko received 6.0 percent (rather than the official tally of 4.3 percent) and the URF 5.1 percent (compared to 4.0 percent in the official count). The numbers correspond approximately to those of an exit poll sponsored by the *Moscow Times*, the Soros Foundation, and Renaissance Capital. In the exit poll, Iabloko received 5.8 percent and the URF 6.1 percent (Medetsky and Mereu, 2003).

Knowing how much actual fraud took place is impossible. Two hours before the polls closed, only 47 percent of eligible voters had turned up. At that point, the CEC, inexplicably, ceased announcing turnout. Until then it had been reporting on turnout regularly throughout the day (Myers, 2003). After the polls closed, the CEC announced turnout of 55 percent. With the organization that controlled the machinery of vote tabulation and publicity engaging in such behavior, the fog covering the results had grown quite thick.

The curious cessation of reporting results resembled the actions of the CEC's Mexican counterpart in the 1988 presidential election. In that contest, the Mexican electoral authorities suddenly quit reporting results as it became clear that Carlos Salinas, the candidate of the then-hegemonic Institutional Revolutionary Party, was headed for defeat. When they reemerged from under the cover of silence, the authorities announced a narrow victory for Salinas. In that election, falsification determined the result. Cuauhtémoc Cárdenas, Salinas's leftist challenger, would have won decisively had the votes been counted properly, a fact that Miguel de la Madrid, the outgoing president who presided over the fraud, later admitted in his autobiography (Thompson, 2004).

Fraud in Russia in 2003 was not as consequential as it was in Mexico in 1988. But Russia in 2003 nevertheless illustrates how a "little" fraud can make a big difference. Had Iabloko and the URF passed the 5 percent threshold in the official results, liberals would have maintained a foothold in the legislature and a platform from which to articulate their views. Pro-Putin parties would still predominate, but not as unequivocally as they do in fact. Had Iabloko and the URF crossed the threshold, they could, if they were so inclined, sometimes ally with the CPRF and make at least a little trouble for Putin, particularly on matters such as changing the constitution to scrap the two-term limit for the president.

So too did the election again demonstrate the complete absence of recourse for aggrieved parties. Rather than support the recount carried out by the CPRF, the CEC's Veshniakov reacted by declaring: "This [the alternative count] is a swindle! We will severely punish falsification and slander" (Litvinovich, 2003). Given the famous elasticity of the concept of "slander" in Russia, or, more precisely, the regularity with which it is defined as impugning the judgment of officials, the communists conducted their study under the shadow of a threat of prosecution. The courts promised little more help than the CEC. Iabloko's Iavlinskii declared soon after the vote that disputing the outcome in court would be useless. Irina Khakamada, co-chair of the URF, shared Iavlinskii's view. Of the possibility of challenging the result in court, she said: "We realize perfectly well that all this would make no sense" (Medetsky and Mereu, 2003).

The presidential contest of March 2004, in which Putin took 72 percent of the vote, accelerated the drift toward expunging uncertainty from electoral competition. Sergei Mironov, the head of the Federation Council, the upper chamber of parliament, threw his hat into the ring with a stirring speech – in which he endorsed Putin. The LDPR's candidate was Oleg

Malyshkin, Zhirinovskii's former bodyguard known to the public mainly for his antics in parliament. The second-place finisher in the election was the CPRF candidate, Nikolai Kharitonov, who was virtually unknown to the public. Kharitonov received 14 percent. Most candidates who really intended to contest the election and who might have reduced the margin of Putin's victory were disqualified on trivial technicalities. The lack of a notary's stamp on the nomination papers of German Sterligov, a radical nationalist businessman, prompted his disqualification by the CEC. The CEC disqualified Viktor Gerashchenko, former governor of the Central Bank, after resolving that the party he represented, the Party of Russian Regions, was not really a party but rather a "bloc" ("Postanovlenie Tsentral'noi izbiratel'noi komissii," 2004; Shishkunova, 2004).

The presidential administration's major concern was voter turnout. By law, turnout must exceed 50 percent to validate the election, and after the parliamentary election of the previous December, officials had reason for concern. But local and provincial administrators did their work. In Vladivostok, where turnout was low in December, students were warned that their right to dormitory housing depended on their showing up to vote. But all was not vinegar: The honey of free theater tickets awaited students who did go to the polls. Stores offered discounts on election day to draw impecunious voters out of their homes (Nezhdanova, 2004). Hospitals in Moscow provided patients with ballots. To avoid taxing patients with the stress of decision making, election officials distributed ballots that were premarked for Putin (Samigullina and Rumiantsev, 2004). In Voronezh and Khabarovsk, during the weeks before the vote, health officials showed an urgent sense of civic duty, ordering hospitals not to admit patients who had failed to apply for absentee ballots prior to hospitalization (Yegorov, 2004). In some cases, good old-fashioned inflation of vote totals was the preferred method. In Chechnya, the overwhelming majority participated, according to the official results, though foreign journalists on the scene witnessed only deserted streets and empty polling stations (Meyer, 2004). The CEC showed great vigilance in its effort to ensure high turnout. In response to a call by Sergei Kovalev, a well-known human rights activist, for a boycott of the vote, Veshniakov actually warned that those calling for a boycott could be prosecuted under a law that forbids anyone to stop citizens from voting (Borisov, 2004).

International observers appear finally to have grasped the reality of political competition in Russia. The OSCE, in a departure from its acquiescent posture in 1999 and 2000, refused to bless the 2003 and 2004 elections. It concluded that the parliamentary contest was "overwhelmingly distorted" by pro-government bias ("U.S. Shares Russian Poll Concerns," 2003). After the presidential election in March 2004, the chief of the OSCE's observer mission, Julian Peel Yates, declared that "[e]ssential elements of the OSCE commitments and the Council of Europe standards for democratic elections, such as a vibrant political discourse and meaningful pluralism, were lacking" (Myers, 2004[c]). Whether the observers became sterner or the violations too egregious to discount, or both, must be left to question. Whatever the reason, international observers finally stopped dispensing the salve of external validation in 2003.

Summary

The monocracy that Russians endured during most of the Soviet era is gone. Not all elections in Russia are predetermined charades. Nor do Russian citizens live in a rights-free polity that walls them off from all politically relevant information and bans association for political ends. Russia has not merely traded one form of monocracy for another since the Soviet demise. Unlike, say, Belarus, Uzbekistan, and Turkmenistan, Russian politics has some elements of pluralism and competition.

But falsification, coercion, and the arbitrary disqualification of candidates are frequent and pervasive – not merely occasional and deviant – features of elections in post-Soviet Russia. Communicative and associational rights – the crucial requirements for the free formation and expression of popular political preferences – are cramped and restricted. These conditions have kept control of political life out of the hands of the electorate as a whole and vested it in a circumscribed stratum of officials who manipulate the process for their own ends. Thus, oligarchy, rather than democracy, has emerged in Russia. Russia's place in the comparative rankings on political openness reviewed in the previous chapter, which put it in league with Morocco, Malaysia, and Lebanon, is justified by the evidence. In terms of both electoral practice and the liberties needed to make elections meaningful, Russia does not satisfy Dahl's criteria for an open polity. The antiauthoritarian breakthroughs of the late 1980s and early 1990s were not subsequently sustained. As of mid-decade since 2000, democratization has failed in Russia.

4

The Russian Condition in Global Perspective

The previous chapter established that Russia has failed to democratize; the current one begins to address why. It grapples with the problem by examining the determinants of political regime on a global scale. The major hypotheses found in the literature on democracy's determinants are considered. The simple logic of causal inference introduced in the first chapter obtains here and throughout the book. If the cross-national analysis shows that a given variable does not affect political regime in global perspective, that variable's status as a determinant of political regime in Russia will be placed in doubt. If additional investigation that focuses on Russia suggests that the variable probably has little impact in that country as well, the hypothesis that the variable is responsible for Russia's democratic deficit will be discarded. If a variable has causal force on a global scale, I assume that it might be important in Russia. If Russia is an outlier in the larger global picture, and is atypical in a manner that suggests that the variable is not important in Russia, the variable will not be considered an important determinant of political regime in Russia. If the variable is a good predictor of regime type and Russia is not an outlier, it will be considered a potentially important determinant of conditions in Russia. It will then be subjected to further scrutiny with specific attention to Russia.

After examining the causal power of alternative hypotheses, I examine more closely those variables that do *not* explain Russia's failure to democratize. Those that do carry causal force are examined at length in Chapters 5, 6, and 7.

I include in the analysis several variables – most notably, a postcommunist heritage and an Orthodox Christian religious tradition – that are not always tested in other cross-national studies of democracy's determinants but that are potentially important for assessing Russia. I examine countries with populations that exceeded one-half million as of 2000. There are 158 such countries. Data are missing for one or more variables for 11 of them: Afghanistan, Bhutan, Bosnia, Cambodia, Djibouti, Eritrea, Liberia, North Korea, Somalia, Swaziland, and Taiwan. These countries are excluded, leaving 147 available for analysis. They constitute the universe of cases examined here and in the rest of the book.

A few caveats are in order. Although an examination of the whole world (or almost all of it) has substantial advantages, the analysis is not free of selection bias. I do not use a random sample of countries from all of history. I seek to cast light on the determinants of regime change in contemporary politics only. Whether or not an examination of some other time in history would show similar results is an important question, but I do not pursue it here. The analysis is therefore temporally limited. A second caveat regards the quality and quantity of the data. Compared to data generated by public opinion surveys that query thousands of people, my data are of modest quantity and quality. Countries, not people, serve as my cases. Some of the variables, moreover, are inherently difficult to measure precisely.

The dependent variable is the extent of political openness. As in the previous chapter, I rely upon Daniel Kaufmann and colleagues' Voice and Accountability (VA) scores for 2002 to measure political openness. The actual empirical range extends from Denmark (1.72) to Iraq (−2.12); the mean score is −0.10. The task at hand is to uncover the factors that explain cross-national variation in the extent of political openness.

Determinants of Political Regime: Cross-National Analysis

Hypotheses

The most widely embraced causal hypothesis in the study of political regimes holds that a positive relationship obtains between *economic development* and democratic attainment. Scholars associate higher economic development with less social conflict, more sophisticated populations, larger middle classes, less desperate lower classes, and greater social pressure for popular rule, all of which may favor more open government (Boix and Stokes, 2003; Bunce, 2000; Janos, 2000; Lipset, 1960; Schedler, 2001). The most commonly used measure of economic development is gross domestic product (GDP) per capita. Here I use log GDP per capita in 1990.

A second potentially important variable is *natural resource endowment*. Politicians and mass publics alike covet natural resources, but social scientists have sometimes found abundance to act as a hindrance to democratization. Copious endowment of raw materials may enable the state to buy off society with low taxation and high social spending and thereby allay popular demand for political accountability. It may also finance a large and powerful internal security apparatus capable of repressing challengers – an apparatus that would be unaffordable in the absence of abundant rents from raw materials exports. Resource abundance may also distort modernization, spurring increase in national income without inducing the socioeconomic transformations that normally accompany growing prosperity and that favor democracy (Ross, 2001). I measure natural resource endowment as the percentage of merchandise export income accounted for by fuels and ores, which include oil, gas, metals, and precious stones (International Monetary Fund, 2003; World Bank, 2002[a]).

An alternative measure would be the percentage of GDP accounted for by these goods. The numbers on exports, however, may produce more accurate statistics. In Russia, for example, the practice of "transfer pricing" has the effect of greatly underestimating the place of hydrocarbons in Russia's national accounts. The practice is not limited to Russia. With transfer pricing, a firm's production subsidiary sells output cheaply to the same firm's trading subsidiary. The trading subsidiary then sells at market prices to customers. On paper, the trading company is responsible for most of the value added. Companies use this accounting trick to reduce tax burden, since trading subsidiaries can often pay a lower effective tax rate than the production subsidiary would have to without the "transfer" of value added. The practice produces odd numbers. For example, according to official data, the production of oil and gas in Russia accounts for about 9 percent of GDP – while exports from oil and gas account for more than 20 percent of GDP. Figures on exports, which lend themselves to correcting trade margins and to international comparisons, produce a much more realistic picture of the place of oil and gas in the economy. When the proper adjustments are made, between one-quarter and one-third of Russia's GDP – rather than 9 percent – is accounted for by oil and gas (World Bank, Russia Country Department, 2004). Studies that use raw materials as a percentage of GDP, rather than as a percentage of exports, may be of value, but figures on exports are more open to external scrutiny and may be more accurate. They may provide a superior basis for cross-national analysis.

Economic variables may influence political regime, but they are by no means the only possible determinants. Sociocultural and historical factors might matter. One such variable that is widely assumed to affect regime type is degree of *ethnic fractionalization*. In his report on the 2001–2 Freedom House survey, Adrian Karatnycky, the president of Freedom House, claimed that high fractionalization vexes open politics. Reviewing the findings of the survey, Karatnycky concluded that "democracy has been significantly more successful in monoethnic societies than in ethnically divided and multiethnic societies" (Karatnycky, 2002, pp. 109–10). Writing in the wake of the demise of Communist Party regimes in Europe, Donald Horowitz expressed a similar view: "Democracy has progressed furthest in those East European countries that have the fewest serious ethnic cleavages (Hungary, the Czech Republic, and Poland) and progressed more slowly or not at all in those that are deeply divided (Slovakia, Bulgaria, Romania, and of course the former Yugoslavia)" (Horowitz, 1993, p. 19). According to Horowitz, while countries in the first group might have had other advantages as well, the ethnic factor strongly influenced political regime change.

The claim that heterogeneous societies are disadvantaged and homogeneous ones are fortunate is common in social science (Dahl, 1971; Lijphart, 1977; Rabushka and Shepsle, 1972; Welsh, 1993). According to many observers, diversity makes compromise and consensus – the stuff of democratic practice – difficult. Social conflict is often believed to be more frequent and intense in heterogeneous societies. Some scholars even use fractionalization as a proxy for the degree of conflict in society, operating on the assumption that higher fractionalization automatically spells more conflict (Arnett, 2001). Political parties and other organizations may coalesce more readily around ethnic than other identities. Political entrepreneurs, therefore, have an incentive to play on ethnic divisions and neglect civil rights and class concerns (Horowitz, 1985; Karatnycky, 2002). Even well-intentioned efforts by elites to avert ethnic conflict may engender arrangements during periods of political opening that subsequently check further democratization (Jung and Shapiro, 1995). Thus, when democracy succeeds in heterogeneous polities, extraordinary conditions must obtain; and even in the presence of auspicious circumstances and institutions, heterogeneity is seen as a challenge. Not all scholars are pessimistic about the viability of democracy under conditions of social heterogeneity. The vast literature on ethnicity and nationalism includes arguments and evidence that peace rather than conflict is the norm in interethnic relations. Such studies at least imply that high ethnic fractionalization does not necessarily countervail open politics (Fearon and Laitin, 1996 and 2003).

Measuring diversity is notoriously difficult. Any attempt to assess ethnic composition collides with the thorny matter of determining the criteria for defining ethnicity itself (Varshney, 2003[b]). Individual and group identities are themselves complex and contested, and so it is unsurprising that quantifying identities is a highly inexact endeavor. Until recently, scholars have relied largely on one of three or four sources of data, none of which has been widely accepted as providing adequate measures (Grimes, 2000; Gunnemark, 1991; Krain, 2001; Laitin and Posner, 2001; Taylor and Hudson, 1972). Recently, Alberto Alesina and colleagues (2002) have provided new measures that represent a breakthrough in the effort to assess ethnic diversity. The measures are comprehensive and highly differentiated. The Alesina ethnic fractionalization index will be used here.

British colonial heritage has long been considered an advantage for popular rule's prospects. Myron Weiner held that the most important determinant of democracy in the developing world was a legacy of British tutelage. According to Weiner: "The British tradition of imposing limits on government, of establishing norms for the conduct of those who exercise power, and of creating procedures for the management of conflict has had a powerful influence on the creation of democratic systems in the Third World" (Weiner, 1987, p. 20). The British built a tradition of civil service in some of their colonies. Some scholars have argued that the British penetrated societies in their colonies more deeply than other colonists, thereby weakening the forces of traditionalism that often stand in the way of effective state building in the postcolonial setting (Herbst, 2000). Scholars have also credited the British with leaving behind the Westminster model of parliamentarism, which some regard as a strong constitutional basis for democracy (Lardeyret, 1996; Lipset, 1996; Payne, 1993). Here, a dummy variable is used for former British colonies, which number 30 countries.

Recently, another type of legacy has also come to be regarded as a potentially important determinant of political regime: *a communist heritage*. If a history of British tutelage is usually seen as an advantage, a legacy of Sovietism is usually regarded as a liability. According to many scholars, Communist Party rule bequeathed a profoundly illiberal political culture (Jowitt, 1992). To a greater extent than other types of authoritarianism, Soviet-type regimes quashed political and civil society (Fish, 1995; Howard, 2003; Linz and Stepan, 1996). The 28 countries of the former USSR, Mongolia, and postcommunist Eastern Europe fall into this category. Bosnia is excluded for lack of data, leaving 27 countries, which are represented by a dummy variable in the analysis.

Islam is also sometimes regarded as an impediment to political openness. Observers have noted what appears to be an especially high incidence of authoritarianism in the Islamic world (Karatnycky, 2002). The proximity of temporal and divine authority and the subordination of women, among other phenomena, are sometimes seen as creating an affinity between Islam and political closure (Fish, 2002; Goodwin, 1995; Miller, 1997). Contrariwise, some other scholars have held that Islam is not necessarily antithetical to open politics and may hold advantages for democracy (Beinin and Stork, eds., 1997; Esposito and Voll, 1996; Hefner, 2000; Stepan, 2001). Here I include a variable for the percentage of the population of each country made up of Muslims.

Islam is not the only religious tradition that has been regarded as incompatible with democracy. Some forms of Christianity are also seen as a liability. For decades, scholars argued that Catholicism encouraged popular acceptance of hierarchy and intolerance, thereby undermining the prospects for open politics (Huntington, 1984; Lipset, 1960). The democratization of much of Southern Europe, Latin America, and the Philippines in the 1970s and 1980s reduced the appeal of such arguments. In recent years, however, *Orthodoxy* has emerged as the antagonist of democracy in some writings. Since Orthodox Christianity is Russia's predominant religious tradition, its possible influence is of particular relevance. Samuel Huntington (1996) asserts that Orthodox churches are invariably fused with and subordinate to state power and that Orthodoxy therefore cannot play a creative or counterhegemonic role in politics (also Clark, 2000). Some other authors hold, in contrast, that Orthodoxy includes practices and teachings that are conducive to open government (Gvosdev, 2000[a] and [b]; Petro, 1995). To test the hypothesis, a variable for the percentage of the population of each country made up of Orthodox Christians is included.

In addition to the seven variables discussed so far, three others will be examined. They concern public attitudes and orientations. Data for them are drawn from public opinion surveys and are available for fewer than half of the world's polities. What is more, many analysts regard them as effects as well as causes of political regime. They are therefore analyzed separately and not included in the main multiple regression analysis. Data for all three variables are drawn from the World Values Surveys for the 1990s (Inglehart, 2002).

The first of these factors is *trust*. Ronald Inglehart (1999) has found a positive relationship between the percentage of respondents who say that they generally trust other people, on the one hand, and political openness, on the other. Interpersonal trust is widely regarded as a boon for open politics. It is associated with lower social tension, greater ease in undertaking tasks collectively, and other conditions that may be conducive to democracy. Many scholars have investigated the relationship between trust and open government and found a positive link (Putnam, 1993; Rose and Shin, 1998; Rose-Ackerman, 2001). Data on trust are available for 63 countries.

The second attitudinal factor is *tolerance*. It is a bit harder to measure than trust. Asking someone in a survey whether he or she is tolerant is obviously not the best way to get to the bottom of the matter. In the World Values Surveys, people are asked whether they agree with the statement that "homosexuality is never justifiable." According to Inglehart, the percentage agreeing is assumed to be a reasonably good indicator of social intolerance (Inglehart, 2002). The logic of Inglehart's supposition may well be sound, all the more since opposition to *homosexuality* – in contrast to opposition to given racial or ethnic groups, immigrants, or even to *homosexuals* – is still socially acceptable outside a few cities in a handful of countries. People are more likely to be honest about their intolerance if expressing it seems socially acceptable. Lower tolerance, one may hypothesize, is conducive to less open politics. Data are available for 46 countries.

The third factor is *orientation toward political regime*. The World Values Surveys include a question that asks people how they evaluate "authoritarian leadership." The percentage saying that they regard it as "very good" or "good" may be used to assess popular orientations toward political regime. One would expect higher support for authoritarian leadership to encourage less open politics. Data are available for 68 countries.

Analysis

I use ordinary least squares (OLS) regressions. Table 4.1 shows the results of simple bivariate regressions of VA scores on each hypothesized determinant. Economic development is highly and positively correlated with political openness, as one would expect. Natural resource endowment, ethnic fractionalization, and Islam are negatively correlated with VA scores. The signs are all in the expected directions. British colonial heritage, communist heritage, and Orthodoxy are uncorrelated with political openness.

Determinants of Political Regime

Table 4.1. *Bivariate Regressions of Voice and Accountability Scores on Hypothesized Determinants*

Variable	Coefficient	Adj. R^2
Economic development (log GDP p/c$_{1990}$)	0.98***	.43
Natural resource endowment (natural resources as percentage of exports)	−0.01***	.15
Ethnic fractionalization (Alesina et al. fractionalization scores; 0 = lowest, 1 = highest fractionalization)	−1.54***	.15
British colonial heritage (dummy variable)	0.07	.00
Communist heritage (dummy variable)	0.05	.00
Islam (Muslims as percentage of population)	−0.01***	.24
Orthodoxy (Orthodox Christians as percentage of population)	0.0002	.00

$N = 147$ countries.
*p < 0.05; **p < 0.01; ***p < 0.001
Sources: For VA scores, Kaufmann et al., 2003. For economic development, UNDP, 2000; except data for Cuba, Germany, Iraq, Kuwait, Libya, Macedonia, Myanmar, and Qatar, which are from United Nations Statistics Division, 2002. For natural resource endowment, World Bank, 2002[a], and International Monetary Fund 2002. For ethnic fractionalization, Alesina et al., 2002. For Islam, *Muslim Population Worldwide*, 2003. For Orthodoxy, United States Department of State, 2001.

Table 4.2 shows the multiple regression models. The findings are clear and straightforward. Economic development, natural resource endowment, and Islam are good predictors of the extent of political openness. Higher economic development, in accordance with long-standing social-scientific wisdom, strongly favors political openness. Natural resource endowment is indeed the curse for democracy that some writers have supposed it to be. Larger Muslim populations are associated with less political openness.

The negative findings are as interesting as the positive ones. A Soviet-type past is not an insuperable obstacle to democratization. Status as a former British colony is also unrelated to political openness. The size of the Orthodox Christian population has no appreciable effect. Neither is ethnic fractionalization shown to be a substantial hindrance to democracy. While greater ethnic homogeneity is associated with more open politics in the bivariate regression presented in Table 4.1, this effect does not hold up when other causal variables are included in the model, as is evident in Table 4.2 (see Fish and Brooks, 2004).

The limited number of cases and the possible sensitivity of the results to the choice of indicators recommend the presentation of multiple models,

Table 4.2. *Multiple Regressions of Voice and Accountability Scores on Hypothesized Determinants*

Variable	Model 1	Model 2	Model 3	Model 4	Model 5	Model 6
Constant	−2.42***	−2.49***	−2.83***	−2.49***	−2.58***	−2.51***
	(0.36)	(0.28)	(0.37)	(0.28)	(0.30)	(0.28)
Economic	0.86***	0.87***	0.94***	0.87***	0.85***	0.87***
development	(0.09)	(0.08)	(0.09)	(0.08)	(0.09)	(0.08)
Natural resource	−0.008***	−0.009***	−0.011***	−0.009***		−0.009***
endowment	(0.002)	(0.002)	(0.002)	(0.002)		(0.002)
Ethnic	−0.20		−0.18			
fractionalization	(0.24)		(0.25)			
British colonial	0.21		0.23			
heritage	(0.13)		(0.14)			
Communist	0.09	0.05	0.11			
heritage	(0.16)	(0.16)	(0.17)			
Islam	−0.006***	−0.006***		−0.006***	−0.009***	−0.006***
	(0.002)	(0.002)		(0.001)	(0.001)	(0.001)
Orthodoxy	−0.004	−0.004	−0.003	−0.003	−0.003	
	(0.003)	(0.003)	(0.003)	(0.002)	(0.003)	
Adj. R^2	.61	.61	.56	.61	.55	.61

$N = 147$ countries. Entries are unstandardized regression coefficients with standard errors in parentheses.
*p < 0.05; **p < 0.01; ***p < 0.001

as is done here. So too do these potential problems suggest that checking the results using alternative indicators is of some value. In alternative regressions (results not shown), I substituted percentage of the workforce occupied in agriculture for GDP per capita to control for economic development. A larger agrarian workforce indicates a lower level of development. I also tried alternative indicators for religious tradition. In the analyses presented in these tables I used ratio variables for Islam and Orthodox Christianity, measuring each in terms of the proportion of its adherents in the national population. In alternative specifications, I coded countries that were predominately Muslim and predominantly Orthodox using dummy variables instead of ratio variables. Finally, I used alternative indicators for fractionalization. The data on fractionalization used in the analyses shown are on ethnicity. In their data set, Alesina and colleagues present data not only on what they term "ethnic" fractionalization but also on "linguistic" and "religious" fractionalization. One of the advantages of the data set is that the authors disaggregate "ethnic" (by which they mean, for the most part, racial), linguistic, and religious difference. The data facilitate more thorough and differentiated analysis of the possible effects of sociocultural diversity than was heretofore possible. In alternative models, I substituted the statistics for linguistic and religious fractionalization for ethnic fractionalization.

Use of the alternative indicators does not change the results. However one measures it, economic development is a good predictor of VA scores. Whether Islam is represented by a ratio or a dummy variable, it is a powerful predictor of VA scores. Predominantly Muslim countries are dramatic underachievers in terms of political openness. Predominantly Orthodox countries are neither better nor worse than other countries in terms of political openness. Nor is either linguistic or religious fractionalization any better a predictor of VA scores than is ethnic fractionalization. Use of percentage of the workforce in agriculture rather than GDP per capita to control for economic development, moreover, changes none of the findings for the other variables. Natural resources and Islam are consistent foes of political openness. Sociocultural fractionalization, British colonial heritage, a post-communist heritage, and Orthodox Christianity are not predictors of the extent of political openness.

What effects do mass attitudes have on political regime? Table 4.3 shows the analysis. Models 1, 3, and 5 show bivariate regressions of VA scores on trust, tolerance, and orientation toward political regime, respectively. Models 2, 4, and 6 add the control for economic development. In the bivariate regressions, each of the attitudinal variables is statistically significant, though the goodness of fit in the analyses of the effects of trust and orientation toward political regime is not impressive. The effect of tolerance on political regime appears potentially to be substantial. Yet none of the three attitudinal factors holds up as a statistically significant predictor when the control for economic development is added. None of the three factors may be confidently considered an important determinant of the level of political openness.

What do these findings tell us about Russia? The rest of this chapter focuses on what the preceding analysis tells us about what *does not* explain Russia's condition. It examines the factors that are not good predictors of political regime in the cross-national analysis, as well as those that are important globally but that cannot, in light of circumstances in Russia, explain the failure of democratization in that country. Subsequent chapters investigate the variables that *do* explain the Russian condition.

Table 4.3. *Regressions of Voice and Accountability Scores on Variables for Trust, Tolerance, and Orientation Toward Political Regime*

Variable	Model 1	Model 2	Model 3	Model 4	Model 5	Model 6
Constant	−0.22	−3.96***	2.15***	−2.79**	0.99***	−3.73***
	(0.25)	(0.38)	(0.29)	(0.90)	(0.22)	(0.43)
Trust (people can be	0.02**	0.001				
trusted)	(0.01)	(0.005)				
(In)tolerance			−0.02***	−0.005		
(homosexuality is			(0.005)	(0.005)		
never justifiable)						
Orientation toward					−0.018**	−0.004
political regime					(0.006)	(0.003)
(approve of						
authoritarianism)						
Economic development		1.21***		1.02***		1.20***
		(0.12)		(0.18)		(0.10)
Adj. R^2	.11	.68	.37	.63	.12	.71
N	63	63	46	46	68	68

*p < 0.05; **p < 0.01; ***p < 0.001

What Is Not to Blame for Russia's Quandary

The Irrelevance of What Russia Is Not: Islamic Tradition and British Colonial Heritage

Islam is highly significant in substantive and statistical terms in the cross-national analysis. Does Islam therefore account for Russia's democratic deficit? It probably does not. Muslims make up 19 percent of Russia's population. The predicted value of Russia's VA score given the size of its Muslim population would be roughly 0.10. Russia would therefore be situated in the company of Thailand (0.20), Argentina (0.12), and Bolivia (0.01). Such a place would be markedly superior to that which Russia occupies in fact, with its score of −0.52.

Now, if one could show that Muslims have thwarted democratization in Russia, the variable would have explanatory power. But there is little evidence that this has occurred. Some parts of Russia that have large Muslim populations – most notably Tatarstan and Bashkortostan – do have high-handed leaders and autocratic provincial politics (Alexander and Grävingholt, 2002; Hale, 1998). Yet we lack good cross-regional measures for the extent of political openness in Russia, and in their absence, it is exceedingly difficult to assess whether the size of a given region's Muslim population influences its politics. Certainly Tatarstan and Bashkortostan – or for that matter, these regions plus all others that have substantial Muslim populations – do not account for Russia's democratic deficit. The democracy-undermining practices discussed in the previous chapter are by no means limited to largely Muslim areas. They are common in areas with small or nonexistent Muslim populations (Drobizheva, 1999; Gelman, Ryzhenkov, and Semenov, 2000; Hale, 2003; Kirkow, 1995; Lallemand, 1999). Some of the practices that have thwarted democratization in Russia have been perpetrated by holders of the highest offices in the national government – and there are few Muslims there. Russian culture has been influenced by Islam but is in no way predominantly Islamic. The problems that Islam may pose for democracy – most notably the oppression of women and the religious domination of the political – are not features of Russian culture or politics. The unusually large difference between male and female literacy rates evident in the Muslim world is not found in Russia; even among Muslims, near-universal female literacy obtains. Islamic religious institutions certainly do not dominate the state, nor is there any evidence that many Muslims living in Russia believe that they should. In broader global perspective, Islam is, for whatever reasons, strongly associated with less open politics, but there is little reason to believe that it explains Russia's failure to democratize (Kishkovsky, 2000; Menon and Fuller, 2000; Treisman, 1997; Yarlykapov, 1999).

Russia is not, of course, a former British colony. Unlike Muslim countries, however, former British colonies are neither more nor less politically open than other countries. During the 1960s and 1970s, the notion that a history of British tutelage provided big advantages for democracy might have made sense. But three decades after the onset of the third wave of democratization in the mid-1970s, the claim has the musty smell of damp old English leather. For every (relatively open) Botswana, India, and Jamaica, there is also a (relatively closed) Zimbabwe, Pakistan, and Nigeria. A British colonial heritage is not sufficient to ensure subsequent political openness in developing countries; nor is it remotely necessary. Although many scholars and observers of politics continue to see a history of British overlordship as an advantage, cross-national analysis provides no support for the idea. The main point here is that nondemocratization in Russia cannot have much to do with the fact that Russian elites never knew the rigors of British public school, imbibed the ethos of the British civil service system, or adopted English as their national (or second) language.

The Insignificance of Autocracy, Orthodoxy, and Nationality

"Autocracy, orthodoxy, and nationality," the watchwords that the tsars invoked to define the core values of the Russian Empire in the nineteenth century, changed their stripes during the Soviet period, but the trinity persisted. The Soviet regime was nothing if not autocratic. The spirit of religion, though repressed and mangled, remained Orthodox. Nationality arguably grew even more salient under Soviet rule than it had been during the time of the Russian Empire. Yet the hyperautocratic communist legacy, the tradition of Orthodox Christianity, and the national composition of society do not explain Russia's failure to democratize.

In the analysis presented in Tables 4.1 and 4.2, the variable representing a communist past was not a predictor of regime type. In fact, postcommunist countries, taken as a whole, have done reasonably well in terms of democratization. The mean VA score for the 27 postcommunist countries is −0.06, which is very close to the global mean of −0.10. The respectable mean score for postcommunist countries is remarkable, given how closed political life was from Prague to Vladivostok just 15 years ago.

The evidence shows that many writers who earlier anticipated that the communist past left insuperable barriers to democratization overestimated the enormity – or at least the uniformity – of the legacy. Ken Jowitt argued that Leninism bequeathed a culture and forms of social organization that made democratization unlikely. By the time Soviet-type regimes came apart, suspicion outweighed trust, charisma and demagoguery were more attractive than rational administration, and contempt for the public realm exceeded the desire to engage in public life. In a celebrated essay written at the beginning of the 1990s, Jowitt predicted: "It will be demagogues, priests, and colonels more than democrats and capitalists who will shape Eastern Europe's general institutional identity" (1992, p. 220). By the end of the first postcommunist decade, however, democrats and capitalists were enjoying ascendancy over colonels and priests in shaping East Europe's political institutions. Demagogues are indeed present and influential in East Europe, but usually they must at least pretend to be democrats in order to survive. The aftereffects of Leninist culture did not vanish, but in many countries they were not sufficiently corrosive to prevent rapid and thoroughgoing democratization, an outcome that at least provisionally confirms the sanguine predictions that some observers issued at the beginning of the 1990s (Di Palma, 1991[a] and [b]).

Indeed, many countries have authored success stories since the end of Communist Party hegemony. Poland, Hungary, the Czech Republic, Lithuania, Latvia, Estonia, and Slovenia rapidly established open political regimes in the early 1990s. These countries' VA scores for 2002 are higher than those of all Latin American polities except Costa Rica and Uruguay. Success has not been limited to the westernmost edge of the region. Mongolia, Bulgaria, and Romania underwent dramatic political openings in the early or mid-1990s and subsequently maintained open regimes. Since the late 1990s, regime change in Croatia, Slovakia, and Yugoslavia/Serbia and Montenegro has moved toward greater openness. Mongolia, Bulgaria, and Slovakia rank in the top third of all countries on VA scores, Romania and Croatia in the top several places of the next third. Impoverished Albania and Moldova both score higher than the global mean. Yet, since Russia gets far more attention than any of these countries, a communist heritage is sometimes associated with aborted democratization.

The results do not prove that the communist past is irrelevant in Russia. But they do suggest that Russia's failure to democratize cannot be attributed wholly to its communist heritage. The legacy has not stymied the emergence of open politics everywhere it is present, or even in most places. The cross-national analysis leaves little room for regarding a communist past as an insurmountable obstacle.

So too does the evidence provide little basis for judging Orthodox Christianity as a culprit. The proportion of the population accounted for by Orthodox Christians is not a good predictor of regime type. Using a dummy variable, rather than a ratio variable, similarly shows no tie between Orthodoxy and closed politics. The world's 12 Orthodox countries (or, more precisely, its 11 Orthodox polities plus Armenia, which has its own Eastern rite church that does not embrace the "Orthodox" label) do not fare badly in the empirical analysis. Primarily Orthodox societies are not significantly less prone to democracy than other countries. Their average VA score is −0.10, which is identical to the global mean. Cyprus, Greece, Bulgaria, and Romania score in the top third of all countries on VA scores. Yugoslavia/Serbia and Montenegro, whose dictators helped maintain Orthodoxy's bad reputation during the 1990s, began the 2000s as a partially open polity. Among countries whose predominant religious tradition is Orthodoxy, only Belarus has a monocratic regime. The argument that Orthodoxy countervails democracy does not enjoy strong empirical support.

Orthodox churches do have a tradition of subordination to the state that may prevent them from playing the creative oppositional role that, say, the Catholic Church assumed in Poland and Lithuania during the time of Communist Party domination. Max Weber (1978, p. 1174) was undoubtedly right to term Orthodoxy's structure "caesaropapist." The degree of subordination of the church to the state is generally greater in Orthodox societies than in Catholic and Protestant ones. The leaders of some contemporary Orthodox churches certainly do their fair share of genuflecting to temporal authority. Belarus's Metropolitan Filaret ostentatiously speaks of President Aleksandr Lukashenko, the very embodiment of nostalgia for the Soviet regime, in mystical terms. Filaret vaunts Lukashenko, a self-avowed "Orthodox atheist" (by which Lukashenko means not that he is a conventional atheist, but rather that he is an adherent of atheism *and* Christian Orthodoxy), as the great potential unifier of all Slavic peoples. The two men have warm personal relations. The frequent spectacle of Aleksei II, the patriarch of the Russian Orthodox Church, blaming sinister Western conspiracies for Russia's social ills and cozying up to politicians who lack a shred of religious sensibility but who adore public association with that most "national" of Russian institutions, provides a striking contrast with Pope John Paul II's subversive visit to his native Poland in 1979 (International League for Human Rights, 2000; United Civil Party, 2002).

Still, the behavior of the patriarch does not fully determine a confession's influence on political culture. What is more, Orthodoxy, including and especially Russian Orthodoxy, does have a history of resistance to overweening secular authority, even if it is not as pronounced as the tradition of the Catholic Church's independence. The faithful and some segment of the priesthood even during the Soviet period challenged the monocracy. The appeals written by the bishops at Solovki monastery in 1927, which challenged the Moscow Patriarchate's collaborationist policy, serve as particularly poignant examples (Uzzell, 2000 and 2001). In the post-Soviet context, the Orthodox Church is beginning to establish its own schools for children whose education has been compromised by their families' poverty and, in some places, a decline in the quality of public schools. Such a development represents not an example of state domination of the Church but, rather, of the Church, on its priests' own initiative, filling a gap created by state incapacity (Karush, 2001).

Statistical and anecdotal evidence supports Alfred Stepan's assertion that Orthodox Christianity in general is neither ally nor enemy of democracy (Stepan, 2001; also Prodromou, 2004; Veniamin, 2001). Stepan rightly notes that while Orthodox church authorities are normally more subservient to – and replaceable by – state officials than are Catholic and Protestant church leaders, Orthodox churches typically neither hinder democratization nor undermine democratic institutions once they are in place. He points out that this has been the case in Greece since the mid-1970s; one may now add that the same is true of Bulgaria. The Church has scarcely been a mouthpiece for the expression of democratic values in Romania, but nor has it really impeded democratization (Mungiu-Pippidi, 1998; Stan and Turcescu, 2001).

All we may conclude with confidence from the preceding analysis is that Orthodox Christianity does not normally undermine democracy and that Russia's democratic deficit cannot readily be blamed on its Orthodox tradition.

A more unequivocal statement may be made about the influence of ethnic composition. There is no basis whatsoever for attributing Russia's democratic underachievement to ethnic fractionalization. As shown in Table 4.2, there is no robust relationship between ethnic fractionalization and democracy in the world in general. The finding countervails much conventional thinking about the snares that diversity supposedly places in the path of democratization.

Even if a high degree of fractionalization hinders democracy, this factor probably could not explain Russia's postcommunist political quandary because Russia is not, in comparative perspective, especially diverse. The Russian Federation is indeed a multinational entity with more than 100 ethnolinguistic groups, some of which are geographically concentrated. Dagestan alone, with its 2 million inhabitants, has some 20 ethnolinguistic groups, making it one of the world's most multichrome territories. The conflict in Chechnya, whose roots may be traced to the Chechens' protracted struggle for independence from the Russian Empire in the nineteenth century, only adds to Russia's reputation for multiethnicity. Yet Russia is still a relatively homogeneous society. Its fractionalization score is .25, compared to the global mean of .45 and the postcommunist mean of .38. In the postcommunist region, only Poland, Armenia, Hungary, Azerbaijan, Albania, and Slovenia have lower ethnic fractionalization scores than Russia. For all its diversity, Russia is dominated by a single (ethnic Russian) group. Almost everyone speaks Russian, and even many members of the largest non-Russian groups speak Russian as their first language. The difference between the Russian spoken in Vladivostok and that spoken in Pskov, 10 time zones away, is minimal.

In sum, neither Russia's legacy of Communist Party domination nor its Orthodox religious tradition necessarily threaten political openness. Ethnic diversity does not harm democracy's prospects at all in global perspective. Even if it did, it could not explain Russia's failure to democratize because Russia is actually relatively homogeneous.

Socioeconomic Conditions: The Myth of Russian Destitution

In contrast with the sociocultural and historical variables discussed thus far, economic factors seem to hold promise for explaining Russia's postcommunist politics. The statistical analysis shows that higher economic development is democracy's ally and lower development its antagonist. This hoary proposition weathers scrutiny well.

But Russia is not poor and its level of economic development does not explain its shortcoming in democratization. This statement clashes with a great deal of conventional wisdom. Some scholars hold that Soviet Russia had a formidable economy but that post-Soviet Russia has undergone pauperization (Cohen, 2000; Reddaway and Glinski, 2001). The evidence for such a thesis, however, is tenuous at best. Russia is backward by the standards of most OECD countries, but in the context of the rest of the world, Russians enjoy a reasonably high material standard of living.

If GDP per capita in 1990 is used as the measure of economic development, as it is here, Russia ranks 47th out of 147 countries, just ahead of Venezuela, Lithuania, Malaysia, Botswana, Chile, Mauritius, and Poland. Russia is an underachiever in democratization given its economic status at the beginning of the 1990s. Figure 4.1 illustrates the point. Russia is well below the regression line.

Do more recent numbers tell a different story? The Russian economy suffered during the 1990s. Even if the country was rich enough to democratize at the beginning of the postcommunist period, perhaps its chances of political opening dimmed rapidly during the 1990s. Figure 4.2 illustrates the relationship between political openness and economic development in 2000. Russia again falls below the regression line, showing that it is a laggard in democratization given its economic status, even if the latter is measured in terms of data for the year 2000. In 2000, Russia ranked 46th in the world in income per capita – virtually the same position that it occupied a decade earlier.

A look at the postcommunist region alone provides another (and less cluttered) illustration. Figures 4.3 and 4.4 reproduce Figures 4.1 and 4.2,

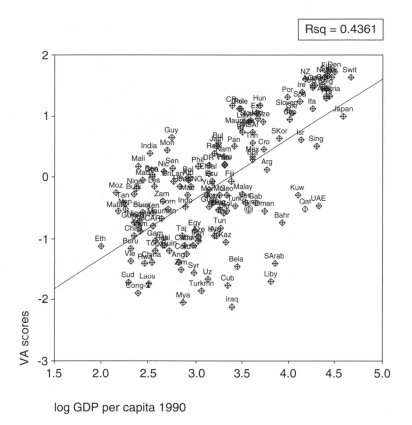

Figure 4.1. Political Openness and Economic Development in 1990

respectively, but include only the postcommunist world. Russia is much less politically open than one would expect given its level of economic development. In terms of income per capita, it is roughly in line with Poland, Lithuania, Latvia, and Croatia; but in terms of VA scores, it is in league with Kyrgyzstan, Armenia, and Ukraine.

Product or income per capita measures do not, of course, capture the entirety of socioeconomic development. Indicators on social conditions are also helpful for understanding overall level of development. Table 4.4 provides relevant information on socioeconomic well-being in the world's 20 most populous countries, which together account for about 70 percent of the world's inhabitants. Countries are listed in the order of their national income per capita in 2000.

99

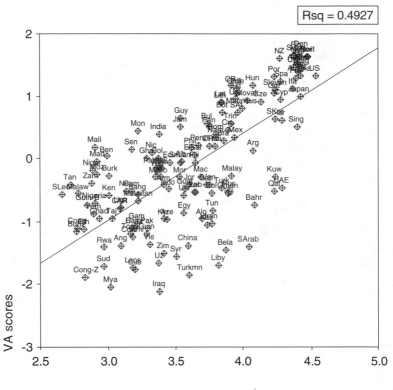

Figure 4.2. Political Openness and Economic Development in 2000

The data help put to rest two misconceptions about Russia's socio-economic situation. The first is that Russia is destitute. In terms of conventional indicators of socioeconomic well-being, Russia lags behind most OECD countries but fares reasonably well compared to all others. The second misconception is that regional variation in Russia is so extreme that while the glittering capital city might look good to visiting foreigners, the rest of the country is mired in penury. Such a conception is held by Stephen Cohen, who characterizes Moscow as a "den of thieves" embedded in "provincial wastelands" that make up the rest of the country (2000, p. 151). If this characterization were sound, the numbers for Russia would not be as uncatastrophic as they are in fact, since only about 6 percent of Russia's inhabitants live in the city of Moscow.

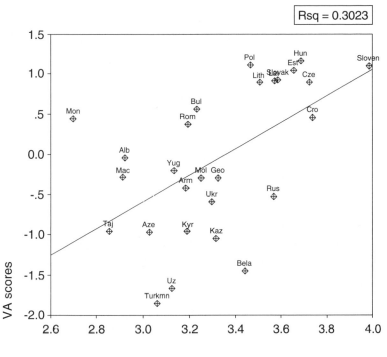

Figure 4.3. Political Openness and Economic Development in 1990, Postcommunist Region

The thesis merits closer examination, all the more since so many Western scholars uncritically accept the image of Moscow versus Everywhere Else without seeing Russia's provinces or even examining available data on them. Table 4.5 provides information on income in Russia's richest and poorest regions, drawn from a study conducted by the United Nations Development Programme (UNDP). The table summarizes information for each region with income above $7,000 per capita and each below $4,000 per capita in 1998. There are 16 regions in each category. In the top regions, incomes are roughly analogous to those found in Greece, Uruguay, and the Czech Republic. In Russia's poorest regions, incomes resemble those of the poorer countries of Latin America and the Middle East, such as Bolivia and Egypt. Cross-regional diversity is marked. But the evidence is not consistent with the image of Moscow versus Everywhere Else. Leaving aside oil-rich Tiumen oblast, Moscow tops the list. Yet seven other provinces – two in

101

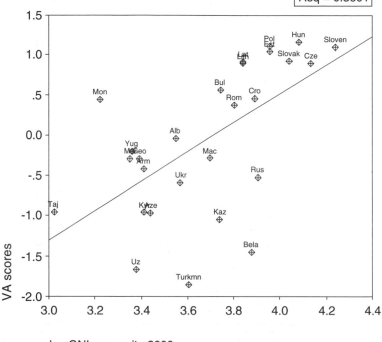

log GNI per capita 2000

Figure 4.4. Political Openness and Economic Development in 2000, Postcommunist Region

the Volga region, two in the Urals, two in Siberia, and one in the European North – have per capita incomes greater than two-thirds that of the city of Moscow. These seven provinces are home to roughly 20 million people. They, in addition to the other provinces that had average incomes over $7,000, account for 30 percent of Russia's population. This group does not include the city of St. Petersburg, whose 5 million inhabitants enjoy a high level of educational attainment and a rich cultural setting but who have incomes that are slightly below the national average.

None of this is to deny the existence of a gap between the capital and other cities in terms of economic dynamism. Moscow has indeed been the site of a disproportionate amount of investment, including foreign direct investment, and the disparity in living standards between Moscow and other regions, according to some sources, has grown during the 2000s (Ickes, 2004). But the notion that Muscovites alone have kept their heads above

Table 4.4. *Indicators of Economic Development and Socioeconomic Well-Being in the World's 20 Most Populous Countries*

	GNI per capita (PPP US$), 2000	Agrarian workforce (percentage of workforce in agriculture, animal husbandry, fishing, and forestry), mid-1990s	Life expectancy at birth (years), 2000	Infant mortality rate (per 1,000 live births), 2000	Daily per capita supply of protein (grams), 1997	Literacy rate (% of people 15 years old and above)
United States	34,260	3	76.6	7	112	97
Japan	26,460	6	80.6	3	96	99
Germany	25,010	3	78.1	4	96	99
UK	23,550	1	77.8	5	95	99
Mexico	8,810	22	71.5	26	83	90
Russia	**8,030**	**16**	**67.2**	**20**	**90**	**98**
Brazil	7,320	31	70.3	35	76	83
Turkey	7,030	43	71.0	49	98	82
Thailand	6,330	54	70.7	24	54	94
Iran	5,900	33	68.4	48	75	72
Philippines	4,220	40	68.3	27	56	95
China	3,940	50	71.4	29	78	82
Egypt	3,690	40	69.5	40	89	51
Indonesia	2,840	41	68.0	42	67	84
India	2,390	67	62.5	65	59	52
Vietnam	2,030	65	69.1	34	57	94
Pakistan	1,960	47	61.1	82	61	38
Bangladesh	1,650	65	60.2	72	45	38
Nigeria	790	54	52.3	74	62	57
Ethiopia	660	80	42.2	107	54	36

Sources: For GNI per capita, World Bank, 2002[b]. For percentage of the workforce in agriculture and literacy rates, Central Intelligence Agency, 2000. For life expectancy and infant mortality, United States Census Bureau, 2003. For daily per capita supply of protein, UNDP, 2000.

water while the rest of Russia has gone under is not supported by the evidence.

In sum, Russia is not steeped in privation. Its failure to democratize cannot be interpreted as the inexorable consequence of poverty. Russia is an underachiever in democratization for its level of economic development. Excluding members of the OECD, Russia ranks at the top of the world's

Table 4.5. *Levels of Income in Russia, by Region*

	GDP per capita (PPP US$), 2000	Population (in millions)	Regional location
Richest areas:			
Tiumen oblast	19,350	1.4	West Siberia
City of Moscow	12,050	8.6	Central
Republic of Tatarstan	10,140	3.8	Volga
Krasnoiarsk krai	9,870	3.0	East Siberia
Samara oblast	9,750	3.3	Volga
Republic of Komi	9,090	1.2	European North
Perm' oblast	8,620	2.9	Urals
Republic of Bashkortostan	8,190	4.1	Urals
Tomsk oblast	8,040	1.1	West Siberia
Lipetsk oblast	7,670	1.2	Central Black Earth
Nizhnii Novgorod oblast	7,630	3.7	Volga Viatka
Vologda oblast	7,420	1.3	European North
Irkutsk oblast	7,400	2.7	East Siberia
Ulianovsk oblast	7,150	1.5	Volga
Iaroslavl' oblast	7,130	1.4	Central
Belgorod oblast	7,130	1.5	Central Black Earth
Poorest areas:			
Republic of Marii El	3,900	0.8	Volga Viatka
Ivanovo oblast	3,870	1.3	Central
Pskov oblast	3,860	0.8	North West
Altai krai	3,790	2.7	West Siberia
Kabardino-Balkarian Republic	3,750	0.8	North Caucasus
Chukotka autonomous okrug	3,690	0.1	Far East
Republic of Gorno-Altai	3,590	0.2	West Siberia
Karachaevo-Cherkes Republic	3,460	0.4	North Caucasus
Jewish autonomous oblast	3,340	0.2	Far East
Chita oblast	3,330	1.2	East Siberia
Penza oblast	3,310	1.6	Volga
Republic of North Ossetia	2,740	0.7	North Caucasus
Republic of Kalmykia	2,650	0.3	Volga
Republic of Dagestan	2,330	2.1	North Caucasus
Republic of Tuva	1,880	0.3	East Siberia
Ingush Republic	1,510	0.3	North Caucasus

PPP, purchasing power parity.
Source: UNDP, 2001.

20 largest polities in terms of socioeconomic conditions, but places only 6th in VA scores. Brazil, India, Indonesia, the Philippines, and Thailand, as well as all of the OECD countries including Mexico and Turkey, score higher than Russia in terms of political openness.

The finding is important in part because leading scholars have claimed that Russia's level of political openness is what one would expect it to be given the country's level of economic development. Andrei Shleifer and Daniel Treisman, while rightly arguing that reports of Russia's pauperization are grossly exaggerated, wrongly claim that the shortcomings that are found in Russia's political system can be attributed to the country's level of development. They exaggerate Russia's level of political openness, and hold that whatever defects persist in the political system are due to – and typical of – Russia's level of economic development. They hold that "Russia has become a typical middle-income democracy" (Shleifer and Treisman, 2004, p. 37). The cross-national data do not support this thesis. In terms of political openness, Russia is well behind where one would expect it to be given its income level.

Excursus: Life Expectancy in Russia

Yet one aspect of socioeconomic conditions in Russia is peculiar and deserves special attention. As Table 4.4 shows, life expectancy is briefer than in countries that rank lower than Russia on other measures. Russia's high mortality rate has rightly alarmed observers.

Table 4.6 shows data on life expectancy in Russia. The numbers reveal several facts. First, low life expectancy is not a specifically post-Soviet phenomenon. Life expectancy in the Russian Federation/RSFSR was virtually identical in the late Yeltsin era (1998) and at the culmination of Brezhnevism (in 1980), and it was lower in both of those years than in 1965. Second, there have been two periods of deterioration and two periods of improvement. The entire Brezhnev era was one of decline. The numbers were so embarrassing that the Soviet government stopped furnishing data for a time. The UNDP notes: "In contrast to Western countries, where the alarming changes in mortality have been widely discussed and given rise to dynamic countermeasures, the Soviet government's response to the negative mortality trends was to stop publishing any statistics apart from crude mortality rates" (United Nations Development Programme [UNDP], 2001, p. 71). The mid- to late 1980s, however, witnessed an upturn in life expectancy.

Table 4.6. *Life Expectancy in Russia*
(in Years)

	Males	Females
1965	64.6	73.4
1970	63.1	73.4
1975	62.5	73.2
1980	61.4	72.9
1985	62.8	73.3
1990	63.8	74.3
1995	58.3	71.7
1998	61.3	72.9
2003	62.3	73.0

Sources: For 2003, Central Intelligence Agency, 2003; for all other years, UNDP, 2001.

The early 1990s were marked by a sharp deterioration; but after mid-decade, life expectancy again improved.

How can these fluctuations be explained? The UNDP reports that the increase in mortality between the mid-1960s and the beginning of the 1980s "occurred mainly because of death at a younger age from diseases of the circulatory system and a rise in mortality from accidents, poisoning, and injuries" (UNDP, 2001, p. 72). The reduction in mortality during the mid-1980s was due primarily to a single factor: "The anti-alcohol campaign, whatever might have been said about it, delayed the deaths of millions of people exposed to risk of dying from accidents, alcohol poisoning, suicide and other such causes" (UNDP, 1999, p. 73). Thus, while some tragic cases of poisoning from homemade substitutes were trumpeted in the press, both in the West and in Russia, these incidents were few in number and small in influence compared to the benefits of the policy. The government cut vodka production in half and wine production by two-thirds in 1985 and 1986. It backed away from slashing supply in 1988, but the policies' effects lingered for several years. The reduction in supply (and consumption) lowered mortality mainly by reducing deaths from what specialists call "external causes," which include road accidents, alcohol poisoning, drowning, homicide, and suicide. The subsequent rise in mortality after the effects of the anti-alcohol policies faded was caused mainly by an increase in deaths among the working age population from external causes, with a rise in ischemic heart diseases among middle-aged men aggravating the retrogression. After the mid-1990s, when mortality peaked, life expectancy rose again, with the improvement attributable in equal measure to a reduction in external causes and cardiovascular diseases (UNDP, 1999, pp. 71–4, and 2001, pp. 70–80).

The upheavals that political and economic change induced may have played a part. As the UNDP notes, the trials of adaptation to rapidly changing (and deteriorating) economic conditions almost certainly contributed to the dramatic losses of the early 1990s. Furthermore, the "gradual adaptation of the population to the market economy most likely played a role in mortality falling in 1994–98" (UNDP, 2001, pp. 72–3). Problems in the health care system, moreover, may account for some of the decline during the early 1990s. Even though public spending on health in Russia actually grew from 2.7 percent to 4.5 percent of GDP between 1990 and the mid- to late 1990s, deterioration in health care delivery in many regions may have exacerbated mortality (UNDP, 2000, p. 215, and 2001, pp. 72–3). Nevertheless, the UNDP concluded: "The idea popular among politicians and in the mass media that the growth in mortality was caused by mass impoverishment of the Russian population has not been directly confirmed. Indeed, had absolute poverty been the cause of rising mortality, the most vulnerable and economically dependent groups of the population would have been the primary victims – children and old people (as it happened many times in the past in other countries and in Russia itself)." In fact, the increase in mortality was greatest "among the able-bodied population segments (the most active and economically affluent), whereas child mortality and mortality among the elderly changed little." The report added that while alcohol was scarcely the only factor, "it is safe to say that the fall and, then, rise in alcohol consumption created the main conditions leading to the colossal fluctuations in mortality after 1984" (UNDP, 2001, p. 72). The UNDP report's conclusions are consistent with the findings of studies conducted by physicians and demographers (Shkolnikov, McKee, and Leon, 2001; Wasserman and Vdmik, 2001).

Discussion of life expectancy has merited this brief excursus for two reasons. First, the numbers themselves are alarming and indicate a serious problem. This alone makes the matter worth discussing. Second, consideration of the data casts some doubt on the notion that economic reform is the main culprit for Russia's post-Soviet demographic travails. Many analysts have attributed Russia's post-Soviet demographic distress to the travails of "shock therapy" (Cohen, 2000; Rosefielde, 2001). Yet examination of

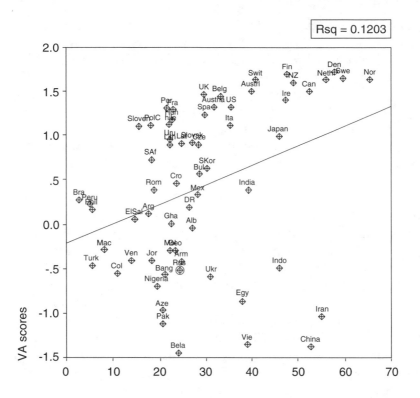

Figure 4.5. Political Openness and Interpersonal Trust

the numbers reveals a steep rise in morality during the Brezhnev period, which was hardly a time of radical economic reform. Matters of economic reform, social welfare, and political regime will be pursued further in Chapter 6.

Mass Attitudes: (Dis)trust, (In)tolerance, and Orientation Toward Political Regime

The main multiple regression analysis did not include mass attitudes as independent variables. Separate analyses showed that interpersonal trust, personal tolerance, and orientation toward political regime are correlated with political regime type and that the relationships are all in the expected direction. Higher trust, higher tolerance, and lower esteem for authoritarian

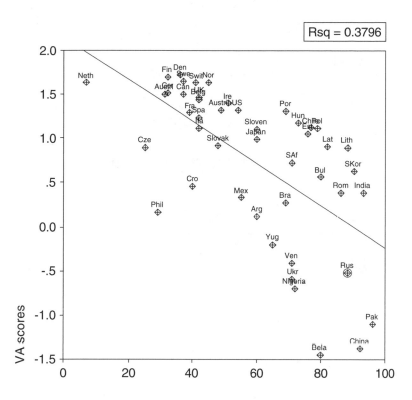

Percentage saying that homosexuality is "never justifiable"

Figure 4.6. Political Openness and Personal Tolerance

leadership are each associated with greater political openness. Although the relationships are not robust to the inclusion of a control for economic development, they merit brief reexamination with special attention to Russia.

Figures 4.5, 4.6, and 4.7 illustrate the simple bivariate relationships, and Table 4.7 presents relevant data. In each case, Russia is located below the regression line; in each case it is an underachiever in democracy given its score on the independent variable. The level of interpersonal trust in Russia is not especially low. In fact, Russia's VA score is very low given its level of interpersonal trust. A deficit of trust cannot help explain Russia's democratic deficit, just as even more obviously, it cannot account for the absence of democracy in China or Iran.

Table 4.7. *Mean Scores on Trust, Tolerance, and Orientation Toward Political Regime*

	All countries	Postcommunist countries	Russia
Trust: Respondents saying that "people in general can be trusted"	29% (N = 63)	23% (N = 19)	24%
(In)tolerance: Respondents saying "homosexuality is never justifiable"	59% (N = 46)	69% (N = 15)	88%
Orientation toward political regime: Respondents saying that "authoritarian leadership" is "very good" or "good"	35% (N = 68)	38% (N = 21)	49%

Source: Inglehart, 2002.

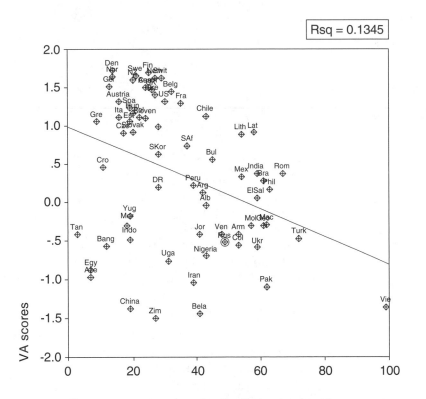

Figure 4.7. Political Openness and Orientation to Political Regime

Intolerance of homosexuality in Russia is very high, though so too is it astronomical in most other postcommunist countries and in Asia. In each of the three Baltic states, as well as in Poland, Hungary, Bulgaria, and Romania, 73 percent or more held that homosexuality is never justifiable. Eighty-eight percent of Russians affirmed their intolerance; but so too did an identical percentage of Lithuanians and nearly as many Poles (79 percent), Latvians (82 percent), and Romanians (86 percent). Sixty percent of even the famously cosmopolitan Slovenes weigh in against tolerance. Intolerance did not prevent extensive and thoroughgoing democratization in the region. It might contribute to Russia's deficit of democracy, but the data do not provide strong evidence in favor of this hypothesis.

These cross-national findings on mass attitudes are consistent with some major studies that have focused specifically on Russia. In the multiple surveys that he carried out over the 1990s, James Gibson (2002) found that most Russians express intolerance for their political enemies and readiness to ban or curtail the rights of elements they consider threatening. At the same time, however, Gibson found considerable fluctuation in the numbers over short periods and instability in respondents' answers from survey to survey.

The cross-national evidence also fails to bear out the notion that Russians are especially fond of authoritarianism and that popular support for political closure explains Russia's nondemocratization. Russians are not greatly more inclined to endorse authoritarianism than are people in other postcommunist countries. The evidence lends support to in-depth studies that have found that Russian public opinion is not hostile to open politics (Bahry, Boaz, and Gordon, 1997; Bashkirova and Melville, 1995; Colton and McFaul, 2002; Gibson, 1997 and 2001; Kullberg and Zimmerman, 1999; Reisinger, Miller, Hesli, and Maher, 1994). At any rate, the relationship between the size of the proauthoritarian population and actual regime type is modest in cross-national perspective. The cross-national data do not show a strong link between whether people say they like democracy and whether or not they get it, as is shown in Table 4.3 above and Figure 4.7. The weakness of the link between the opinions individuals express about democracy in surveys, on the one hand, and the political regime they actually have, on the other, has been noted recently by several leading specialists on political culture and democracy (Inglehart and Welzel, 2003).

The findings do not rule out the possibility that a generally favorable orientation toward open politics on the part of the population might facilitate democratization in some cases. John Dryzek and Leslie Holmes (2000) argue that democratization has been especially robust in Poland and the Czech Republic in part because Poles and Czechs hold a deep-seated, positive attitude toward open politics – a "civic republicanism" – that transcends instrumental calculation and immediate material interest. Dryzek and Holmes may well be right about Poland and the Czech Republic, and their inquiry probes more deeply than the survey data presented here into the content of public orientations toward politics. But the cross-national survey data do not show that the general orientation of the people toward democracy in the abstract strongly affects whether they have it in practice.

Summary

This chapter has investigated hypothesized determinants of political regime with an eye to understanding what might have derailed democratization in Russia. The evidence suggests that Russia is none the worse because it is not a former British colony; British colonial heritage is not a reliable ally of democracy. Nor does Russia's communist heritage in itself provide an explanation; postcommunist countries, as a group, have not done badly in democratization. Russia's Orthodox tradition probably is not decisive; the evidence does not show that Orthodoxy countervails democracy. Russia's ethnic composition does not explain its democratic deficit, since ethnic diversity is not necessarily bad for democracy and Russia, at any rate, is not especially heterogeneous. Nor does economic underdevelopment provide a good explanation. Level of economic development does affect political regime in global perspective, but Russia is not especially poor, and it is a striking underachiever in political openness given its level of development. Level of popular trust cannot explain Russia's nondemocratization. Trust is not a good predictor of political regime and trust is not, at any rate, unusually low in Russia. Popular intolerance is, in accordance with common sense, associated with more closed politics, and Russia shows signs of intolerance. Yet intolerance is not a robust predictor of regime type; in a regression that adds a control for economic development, intolerance is not statistically significant. Popular attitudes toward political regime are not decisive either. How people evaluate authoritarianism and whether they actually have it are not strongly linked. Russians do not, at any rate, profess overwhelmingly proauthoritarian preferences.

Summary

One variable is both important globally and relevant to Russian conditions. Natural resource endowment is a powerful predictor of political regime in the cross-national analysis, and Russia is one of the world's main sources of fossil fuels and ores. The next chapter investigates the problem in greater depth.

5

The Structural Problem

GREASE AND GLITTER

> We live so badly, though we are in the richest country in the world.
>   – A lament very commonly heard in Russia

Anyone who has never heard the dirge in this epigram has not spent much time in Russia. It rings out in dinner conversations, classrooms, and political campaigns. The reference to riches is an allusion to Russia's matchless endowment of oil, gas, metals, and precious stones. In the minds of most, the superabundance of grease and glitter found in the ground only adds to the shame of the persistent gap in living standards and freedom between Russia and the advanced industrialized West. Few regard their country's extraordinary fossil and mineral endowment as a problem. Most consider it a solution – even if an ever-elusive one – to the country's problems. Rulers must *really* mismanage the state in order for things to be unidyllic as they are. If Russia were a "poor" country, perhaps the hardships would be understandable. But how can the inhabitants of such an exorbitantly rich land continue to lack control over their own fates and fortunes?

Such sentiment is hardly surprising. Rich natural endowment appeals to people everywhere. Some may be aware of the hazards of superabundance. But has striking oil ever been met with a groan? Natural riches often appear to provide enormous advantages. Under some conditions and in some places perhaps they actually do. But natural superabundance is usually one of democracy's worst antagonists. This chapter explores the link between the glow of fuels and gold, on the one hand, and the blight of unfreedom, on the other.

114

Does Resource Abundance Undermine Democracy? Empirical Evidence

Although oil and minerals are highly coveted, social scientists have noted that their abundance may cause mischief. A lively debate surrounds the effect of resource abundance on economic performance (Mehlum, Moene, and Torvik, 2002; Sachs and Warner, 2001). So too do authors debate the effect of resources on the institutional development of the state apparatus (Auty, 1990; Chaudhry, 1997; Karl, 1997; Vandewalle, 1998). Recently, Pauline Jones Luong and Erika Weinthal launched an effort to extend research on the effects of resource superabundance to the study of postcommunist countries. Luong and Weinthal have focused mostly on the effects of resources on state building and have advanced evidence that privatization of energy sectors can alter – sometimes for the better – the often pernicious effects of resource superabundance on state capacity (Luong and Weinthal, 2001 and 2004; Weinthal and Luong, 2001). Robert Ebel, Rajan Menon (2000) and their collaborators have also extended the comparative study of resources and politics to post-Soviet space. They have focused largely on the relationship between security and natural resources.

I am concerned with the effect of natural resources on democracy. Until recently, the literature has lacked systematic, cross-national analyses on the subject. Some cross-national studies on democracy's determinants have omitted "oil states" completely (Przeworski, Alvarez, Cheibub, and Limongi, 2000). Other writings have placed "oil states" in a separate category using a dummy variable (Barro, 1999). Some studies that focus on one or a small number of countries have provided insights (Clark, 1997; Lewis, 1996; Yates, 1996). But they have not established whether an empirical link exists in cross-national perspective, or whether such a link, if it does exist, is specific to the Middle East.

A recent article by Michael Ross (2001) advances the debate. Ross examines the relationship between natural resource endowment and political regime in global perspective. He finds a substantial negative relationship between oil and mineral exports, on the one hand, and political openness, on the other. He investigates the basis of the causal link. Writings that focus on one or several countries provide a rich store of insights, and Ross finds in the literature three main mechanisms that may link oil and political closure: the rentier effect, the repression effect, and the modernization effect. The rentier effect refers to a government's ability to provide popular social services and patronage while taxing populations lightly or not at all. The windfall from oil appeases the people and preempts or diminishes pressure for democracy. The repression effect operates when governments maintain large coercive apparatuses that would be unafford-able in the absence of large profits from resource exports (also Bellin, 2004). The modernization effect is at work when resource wealth boosts income but does not induce the ensemble of social, economic, and cul-tural transformations that normally accompany rising income in economies whose growth is driven by something other than fuel. Oil-driven mod-ernization is peculiar, and its pro-democratic, developmental effects are severely limited. In cross-national analysis, Ross finds empirical support for all three effects, though the evidence in favor of the modernization effect is equivocal.

Ross provides a useful point of departure. Here I reexamine each major idea with attention to understanding Russia. I then consider several other candidate causal mechanisms as well. Before I investigate causal mecha-nisms, a brief review of the evidence on the link between raw materials and political regime is in order.

The previous chapter showed a strong relationship between raw mate-rials and political regime (see Table 4.2). In all models in which the vari-able for natural resources was included, it was statistically and substantively significant, and its effect on democracy was negative. Natural resource en-dowment is statistically significant at a demanding level in all specifications. Its effect is substantial as well. A change of 1 percent in the total value of exports accounted for by fuels and ores is associated with a change of about 0.01 in the VA score. Thus, the difference between a country whose exports are made up entirely of raw materials and one that exports none of them is associated with a difference of one point, or between a quarter and a third of the actual empirical range, in the VA score.

Figure 5.1 illustrates the relationship between raw materials and polit-ical openness. Some countries defy the general rule. Norway's prodigious endowment of grease (oil) and Botswana's enormous dependence on glitter (diamonds) do not prevent either country from enjoying open politics. On the other side of the regression line, Laos exports no grease or glitter and has a closed polity. Raw materials abundance obviously is neither a sufficient nor a necessary condition for political closure. Still, there is a substantial negative correlation between the openness of political regime and raw ma-terials endowment and, as Table 4.2 shows, the relationship holds up in the presence of other independent variables.

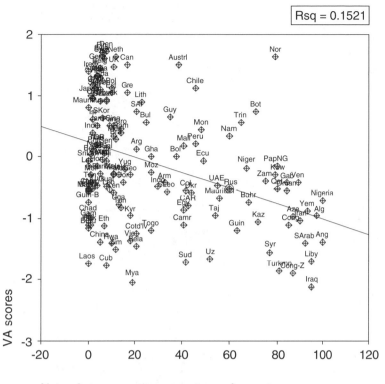

Figure 5.1. Political Openness and Natural Resources

What is more, Russia is on the regression line. Its level of political openness is what one would expect given the composition of its exports. In 2000, fuels accounted for 51 percent and ores and metals 9 percent of the value of Russia's exports, and so raw materials made up three-fifths of export income. Russia shared 28th place (with Namibia), meaning that only 27 of 147 countries had export profiles that were more heavily dominated by raw materials than Russia.

The relationship between raw materials and political regime is even stronger in the postcommunist region than in the world as a whole. Figure 5.2 illustrates the correlation. As in the analysis of the whole world, Russia is again close to the regression line, suggesting that it is no exception. As in the global analysis, one could predict Russia's level of political openness well if one only knew what percentage of its exports are accounted

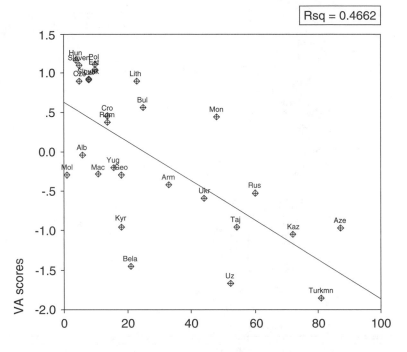

Figure 5.2. Political Openness and Natural Resources, Postcommunist Region

for by natural resources. The relationship between raw materials and political regime in the region holds when controlling for economic development. In a partial correlation that controls for economic development, the link between natural resources and VA scores is substantial (r = −.59; p < .01).

In short, natural resources do seem to pose a problem for democracy, in the postcommunist region as well as in the world as a whole. Do they undermine open politics in Russia? If so, how do they exert their pernicious influence in that country?

How Resources Curse Democracy: Russia in Light of Standard Arguments

The Rentier Effect

If there is a causal link between oil and nondemocratization in Russia and if a rentier effect is to blame, two conditions should obtain. First, Ross

118

must be right in his argument that a rentier effect links oil and democratic shortfall on a global scale. Second, Russia must fit the profile of the rentier state. In fact, the first condition holds but the second does not.

Ross uses multiple measures of rentierism. One is the percentage of government revenue that is collected through taxes on goods, services, incomes, profits, and capital gains. The relationship between this indicator and political openness should be positive, since governments that fund themselves by taxing their citizens should be less capable of buying them off with low taxation and high benefits. He also measures rentierism in terms of government consumption and, separately, the share of GDP accounted for by government activity. He hypothesizes that higher government spending and a higher share of GDP accounted for by government should be negatively associated with democracy.

Ross finds support for the rentier hypothesis, meaning that rentierism accounts for part of how resource abundance undermines democracy. His method is sound and straightforward. Here I adopt it, though I use somewhat different indicators of rentierism. A simpler and more direct measure of governmental reliance on the population for revenues is nontax revenue as a percentage of total current central government revenues. The predicted relationship between this variable and political openness is negative. Data on nontax revenues are available for 112 countries. Another good indicator of rentierism is the ratio of tax revenue to government expenditures. I devised this measure by dividing central government tax revenue as a percentage of GDP by central government expenditure as a percentage of GDP. The data needed to construct the measure are available for 91 countries. An exceptionally low tax-revenues-to-government-expenditures ratio indicates that the government may extract a little and provide a lot. The lower the tax-revenues-to-government-expenditures ratio, the greater the extent of rentierism. Providing services without requiring payment is what rentier states are capable of doing and what may enable them to co-opt or preempt popular demands for open government. This indicator provides an alternative to Ross's government consumption and government spending variables.

Use of the indicators adopted here produces results that are consistent with Ross's. Model 1A in Table 5.1 shows a regression of VA scores on economic development and natural resources. Model 1B adds nontax revenue as a percentage of total revenues. Nontax revenue is statistically significant and reduces the regression coefficient for natural resources. Similarly, Models 2A and 2B show that the taxes-to-government-expenditures indicator

119

Table 5.1. *Rentier Effects (Dependent Variable Is Voice and Accountability Scores)*

Variable	Model 1A	Model 1B	Model 2A	Model 2B
Constant	−3.35***	−3.25***	−3.37***	−3.75***
	(0.29)	(0.29)	(0.35)	(0.38)
Economic	1.09***	1.09***	1.10***	1.03***
development	(0.08)	(0.08)	(0.10)	(0.10)
Natural resource	−0.010***	−0.008***	−0.011***	−0.009***
endowment	(0.002)	(0.002)	(0.002)	(0.002)
Nontax		−0.009***		
revenue		(0.004)		
Government tax-revenue-				0.79***
to-expenditure ratio				(0.35)
Adj. R²	.66	.67	.66	.68
N		112		91

*p < 0.05; **p < 0.01; ***p < 0.001

is statistically significant and that its inclusion reduces modestly the regression coefficient of the natural resources variable. The findings support the hypothesis that rentierism helps explain part of how natural resources hinder political openness.

Yet Russia does not fit the profile of the rentier state. The Russian government is not disproportionately dependent on nontax revenues. Fourteen percent of its revenues come from nontax sources, compared to the global mean of 16 percent. Nontax revenue is indeed very large in proportional terms in some major oil producers, but not in Russia. The first column of numbers in Table 5.2 shows the magnitude of nontax revenue in what I will call the oil-based economies, which are the members of OPEC, the non-OPEC countries that Ross counts as among the world's 10 most "oil-reliant states" (Bahrain, Congo-Zaire, Oman, and Yemen), and Russia. Data are missing for many countries, but the available numbers show that some oil producers do survive on nontax revenues. Russia, however, is not one of those countries.

The data on the ratio of central government tax revenue to central government expenditure, presented in the right-hand column in Table 5.2, tell the same story. Some governments are capable of spending without taxing, or at least without taxing much. The governments of Bahrain, Congo-Zaire, Iran, Kuwait, Oman, the United Arab Emirates (UAE), and Yemen collect less than half as much revenue in taxes as they spend. In Kuwait, the

Table 5.2. *Symptoms of Rentierism in the Oil-Based Economies*

	Nontax revenue as % of total current central government revenue, 1999	Central government tax revenue (as % of GDP) as percentage of central government expenditure (as % of GDP), 1998
Algeria	8	105
Angola	NA	NA
Bahrain	NA	32
Congo-Zaire	12	41
Indonesia	8	87
Iran	34	42
Iraq	NA	NA
Kuwait	90	3
Libya	NA	NA
Nigeria	NA	NA
Oman	71	20
Qatar	NA	NA
Saudi Arabia	NA	NA
UAE	48	6
Venezuela	26	65
Yemen	61	36
Russia	**14**	**72**

Sources: For nontax revenue as percentage of total current central government revenue, World Bank, 2002[a]. For ratio of central government expenditure as percentage of GDP to central government tax revenue as percentage of GDP, UNDP, 2000.

government must rely on taxes to finance only 3 percent of its expenditures; the analogous figure in the UAE is 6 percent. These governments can, if they are so inclined, lavish services on their people while requiring little material sacrifice. But the Russian government cannot spend without taxing; central government tax revenues are equivalent to 72 percent of central government expenditures, which is virtually identical to the global mean.

In sum, while some countries, most notably those of the Persian Gulf region, can afford to spend a great deal without extracting resources from their citizens and companies, other countries, including Russia, do not enjoy such a luxury. Perhaps Kuwait's government can maintain political quiescence with a combination of high spending and low taxation. Like the Algerian, Indonesian, and Venezuelan governments, the Russian government cannot afford to do so. The revenues they realize from resources exports are substantial but insufficient to sponsor a policy of perpetual popular pacification. The rentier effect may be real, but Russia is not a rentier state.

The Repression Effect

Does the income that raw materials generate enable the Russian state to maintain a coercive apparatus that inhibits democratization? The question is difficult to answer. Reliable numbers on government expenditures on the secret police and other internal security organs are, unsurprisingly, unavailable for most countries. Ross measures the size of coercive apparatuses using military expenditures as a fraction of national income and, alternatively, military personnel as a fraction of the labor force. Yet figures on military spending usually do not include expenditures on the organs of internal security and are not necessarily good measures of the magnitude of the repressive apparatus. Still, the size of the military might provide a glimpse of the state's capacity for maintaining its coercive apparatus. Ross finds that oil wealth is linked to military spending and that military spending, in turn, is negatively associated with democracy, as the repression effect hypothesis suggests. He does not find a link between resource wealth and the proportion of the workforce accounted for by military personnel.

I find that both military spending and military personnel, in separate analyses, are good predictors of political openness, and that the relationship, as expected, is negative. The results are shown in Table 5.3.

The proportion of the workforce in the armed forces in Russia is 1.2 percent, which is identical to the global mean. The fraction of gross national income (GNI) taken by the military in Russia, however, is relatively high. In 1999, the year used here, the global mean was 3 percent; the figure for Russia was 5.6 percent. In the postcommunist region, only Armenia and Azerbaijan exceed Russia in military spending as a proportion of GNI. Russia ranks 18th of 147 countries. It devotes a bit less of its national income to the military than Pakistan and a bit more than Turkey (World Bank, 2002[a]).

The evidence provides some support for the possibility of a repression effect in Russia. Perhaps the income from raw materials exports helps Russia sustain a coercive apparatus that is larger than would be feasible in the absence of resource superabundance. Indeed, the sprawling apparatus of coercion that the Soviet Union maintained may have depended in part on earnings from raw materials exports. But political repression in Russia, during Soviet times as well as after, has almost always been handled by the secret police, now formally called the FSB and during the Soviet period (and

Table 5.3. *Repression Effects (Dependent Variable Is Voice and Accountability Scores)*

Variable	Model 1A	Model 1B	Model 2A	Model 2B
Constant	−2.87***	−2.73***	−2.99***	−3.18***
	(0.28)	(0.27)	(0.28)	(0.26)
Economic	0.95***	0.95***	0.98***	1.09***
development	(0.08)	(0.08)	(0.08)	(0.08)
Natural resource	−0.012***	−0.008***	−0.011***	−0.009***
endowment	(0.002)	(0.002)	(0.002)	(0.002)
Military		−0.08***		
expenditures		(0.02)		
Armed forces				−0.18***
personnel				(0.04)
Adj. R^2	.56	.60	.58	.63
N		146		141

$*p < 0.05; **p < 0.01; ***p < 0.001$
Source: World Bank, 2002[a]. Military expenditures are measured as military spending as percentage of GNI in 1999. Armed forces personnel is measured as the percentage of the labor force accounted for by armed forces personnel in 1999.

to the present day in popular parlance) called the KGB. In the post-Soviet setting, monitoring, harassment, violence, and other tasks associated with repression are carried out not only by the FSB but also by local officials, ordinary police, and hired goons. So too is such dirty work done by private security and strong-arm agencies, which are staffed largely by former police and KGB personnel (Knight, 2000; Shelley, 2000). Some officials may draw on the proceeds from raw materials extraction that occurs in the territories that they control in order to fund repression, though hard evidence on this matter is scarce (Le Huérou, 1999).

Similarly, drawing conclusions on the more general matter of a repression effect in Russia is difficult. If military spending is a good measure of the size and strength of the coercive apparatus, as Ross assumes it is, then there is some evidence for a repression effect in Russia. But military spending may not be a good indicator. The military, at least in Russia, is not responsible for internal political control. In short, we do not have data that allow for a firm conclusion on a repression effect in Russia.

The Modernization Effect

According to some scholars, natural resource abundance may boost income without inducing the social, cultural, and economic changes that often accompany rising wealth in places where economic expansion is spurred by other means. In short, oil may produce growth without modernization. To assess modernization, Ross uses 11 indicators, including urbanization, telephones per capita, televisions per capita, school enrollment rates, and occupational specialization. His findings lead him to conclude that a modernization effect may be part of the resource curse, though his evidence is ambiguous.

Modernization is indeed a complex and multifaceted phenomenon, which might explain why Ross uses a multitude of indicators. Here I use four that may capture modernization reasonably efficiently: televisions, telephones, fertility rates, and literacy rates. A larger number of televisions and telephones per capita, higher literacy, and lower fertility indicate greater modernity.

Table 5.4 presents the results of the regressions. Televisions and telephones are both statistically significant predictors of VA scores, and the inclusion of each reduces the regression coefficient for natural resources. Neither literacy rate nor fertility rate is statistically significant, probably due to the problem of collinearity that arises from the high correlation between each of these variables and GDP per capita, the measure for economic development. The analysis lends a bit of support to the hypothesis that a modernization effect accounts for part of how resource abundance countervails open politics. How, then, does Russia fit in?

According to these indicators, Russia is actually a fairly modern country. Television ownership is nearly twice the international mean of 241 per 1,000 inhabitants. There is slightly more than one telephone mainline per five inhabitants, which is a bit higher than the global average, about twice as many mainlines as in Mexico, and about half as many as in Spain. Literacy is 98 percent – 1 percentage point higher than the rate in the United States and 20 percentage points higher than the international average. Russia's fertility rate stands at 1.4 – the same as Portugal's, a bit higher than Italy's (1.3) and a bit lower than Japan's (1.5). The global mean is 3.6.

Table 5.5 presents the numbers for the oil-intensive economies. The table provides striking illustration of the modernization effect. Saudi Arabia and Libya, which rank in the top third of the world in income per capita, place in the bottom 40 percent in literacy, and fertility in each country is almost twice the international mean. In most of the countries in the table, real underdevelopment – that is, lack of modernization – is manifest. The

Table 5.4. *Modernization Effects (Dependent Variable Is Voice and Accountability Scores)*

Variable	Model 1	Model 2	Model 3	Model 4	Model 5
Constant	−2.88***	−2.19***	−0.92***	−2.88***	−2.17***
	(0.27)	(0.39)	(0.44)	(0.28)	(0.49)
Economic development	0.95***	0.65***	0.15	0.94***	0.80***
	(0.08)	(0.15)	(0.17)	(0.11)	(0.12)
Natural resource	−0.012***	−0.011***	−0.007***	−0.012***	−0.010***
endowment	(0.002)	(0.002)	(0.002)	(0.002)	(0.002)
Televisions (sets per		0.001*			
1,000 people)		(0.0005)			
Telephones (mainlines per			0.003***		
1,000 people)			(0.001)		
Literacy rate				0.0003	
				(0.003)	
Fertility rate					−0.07
					(0.04)
Adj. R^2	.56	.58	.63	.56	.57

$N = 147$ countries.
$*p < 0.05$; $**p < 0.01$; $***p < 0.001$
Sources: For televisions per 1,000 people, which are for 1999, World Bank, 2001: except data for Bahrain, Comoros, Cyprus, Fiji, and Qatar, which are from Central Intelligence Agency, 2000; and for Guinea-Bissau, which are from World Bank, 2003. For telephones per 1,000 people, which are for 1999, World Bank, 2001: except data for Bahrain, Comoros, Congo, Cyprus, Fiji, Guyana, and Qatar, which are from CIA, 2000. For literacy rate, which are for 1995, CIA, 2000; except data for Yugoslavia/Serbia and Montenegro, which are from World Bank, 1995. For fertility rate, United States Census Bureau, 2003.

numbers for Russia, however, are entirely atypical for this group. They are closer to the norm for other European countries.

Of course, Russia suffers from forms of backwardness relative to the West, such as the obsolescence of much of its industrial technology outside the military sector, its relatively low per capita income, and the marginalization of many of its rural inhabitants. But such problems are more obviously rooted in the logic of Soviet-style planning than they are in an abundance of raw materials. Russia did undergo a distinctive form of modernization, but the sources of peculiarity are found more surely in aspects of Sovietism – collectivization and neglect of agriculture, the supremacy of military industry, plan-and-command economic administration, and the elimination of private property – than in the effects of natural resource superabundance. Russia is a high-culture, highly educated, highly industrialized society. The

Table 5.5. *Indicators of Modernization in the Oil-Based Economies*

	Television sets per 1,000 inhabitants, 1999	Telephone mainlines per 1,000 inhabitants, 1999	Literacy rate (percentage over age 15 who read and write), 1995	Fertility rate (average number of live births per woman), 1995
Algeria	107	52	62	3.7
Angola	15	8	42	6.4
Bahrain	429	117	85	3.1
Congo-Zaire	2	0	77	6.7
Indonesia	143	29	84	2.7
Iran	157	125	72	4.9
Iraq	83	30	58	6.6
Kuwait	480	240	79	2.9
Libya	136	101	76	6.3
Nigeria	68	4	57	6.3
Oman	575	90	53	6.2
Qatar	283	222	79	4.6
Saudi Arabia	263	129	63	6.5
UAE	252	332	79	4.5
Venezuela	185	109	91	3.0
Yemen	286	17	38	7.4
Russia	**421**	**210**	**98**	**1.4**

Sources: See Table 5.4.

patently antidevelopmental – or at least nondevelopmental – effects of oil visible in some other countries in Table 5.5 are conspicuous by their absence in Russia.

In sum, theories that attribute the pernicious influence of resource abundance for democracy to rentier, repression, and modernization effects are essentially sound. But the first and third of these effects cannot explain the link between resources and nondemocratization in Russia since Russia is neither a rentier state nor an underdeveloped country. The causal force of the repression effect is unclear; it cannot really be gleaned from available data. Russian spending on the military is indeed high, and high military spending does appear to link raw materials endowment and political regime in global perspective. Perhaps grease and glitter help sustain coercive institutions and practices in Russia. But the military has not typically been the main organ of political repression in Russia. The KGB and its successor bureau have traditionally fulfilled this function, and data on their share of national income are, unsurprisingly, unavailable.

How the Resource Curse Works in Russia: Extending the Analysis

The Corruption Effect

Several other factors may link natural resource endowment and political regime. One is corruption. It has not received as much attention as the rentier, repression, and modernization effects, though some authors do see a link between resource abundance and corruption (Leite and Weidmann, 1999; Okonta and Douglas, 2003). The logic is not difficult to envision. The dominance in the economy of a product or products that can be controlled by one or a handful of state agencies may reduce politics to a struggle over control of those agencies. Holding office can afford access to enormous funds and make one fabulously rich overnight. As Marshall Goldman (1999, p. 74) notes: "Russia's immense supply of valuable natural resources almost guaranteed the enormous corruption and theft that resulted from the privatization of state industry. Too much was up for grabs and the rewards for unethical behavior were too high."

There is nothing uniquely Russian about such a situation. In any resource-abundant country that does not have a highly developed, long-standing system of laws and effective agencies of law enforcement in place prior to the discovery and exploitation of the resources, the very reason for holding office may be nothing more (or less) than robbery. In Norway and Britain, which struck oil long after mass publics had secured control over the levers of state power, resources have not fueled an explosion of corruption. But most countries do not have sturdy democratic regimes in place prior to striking oil. In these less fortunate places, resources may indeed corrupt. Resource wealth may influence the incentives to enter politics. It encourages the greediest, nastiest, and most unscrupulous to seek high office. In resource-poor economies, such people may stay away from politics and leave government office to individuals who are motivated more by a thirst for fame, responsibility, or the achievement of cherished ideals. In Nigeria, holding a high position in a ministry connected to the oil industry for a month can be a ticket to fabulous riches. In neighboring Benin, corruption may well be present at high levels, but becoming an instant multimillionaire by virtue of occupying a ministerial position for a brief spell is not an option; there is not enough to steal.

127

The corrupting influence of natural resources may inhere in the products themselves. Oil, gas, gold, and diamonds (to name a few of the most popular items) are extracted from the ground, often in sparsely populated, remote areas. The process of extraction, particularly of hydrocarbons, is capital intensive, and the workers who engage in it are skilled, well paid, and fairly small in number; they do not usually have an interest in exposing malfeasance related to their companies' work. The products may be marketed and sold abroad entirely without publicity; there is no need for advertising. The governments of the countries that import the resources have little interest in ensuring probity in the exporters' governments. These conditions may spell a deficit of transparency – indeed, much more opacity than normally obtains in the production and marketing of automobiles, children's toys, or wheat, which must in some respects occur out in the open.

The hypothetical link between corruption and political regime is even easier to envisage than that between natural resources and corruption. The causal arrow may run in either or both directions. Political openness may countervail corruption. More media freedom facilitates greater transparency of government operations, and greater transparency invests the ruled with more power to monitor the rulers and punish them for corrupt behavior. One would therefore expect greater political openness to favor lower corruption.

Yet the causal arrow also might run the other way. Corruption may undercut open government (Geremek, 2002). Corruption may damage the legitimacy of any type of political regime. In a closed polity, it may lead to greater popular pressure for political openness. But in a polity that is at least partially open, greater corruption may increase the attractiveness of political closure. High corruption, especially in a fledgling neodemocracy where the status of the political regime is still unsettled, might reduce popular enthusiasm for an open polity or even erode citizens' beliefs that the regime provides open politics at all. Public opinion survey data from major projects show that the extent of corruption may play a weighty role in citizens' evaluations of the political regime, especially in new democracies. His extensive work on mass political orientations in Africa has led Michael Bratton to conclude: "The more widely state officials are seen to engage in illegal rent seeking, the lower are public assessments of democratic supply.... In this regard, Africa's prospects for democracy depend critically on whether state elites can establish a reputation for probity and honesty in the eyes of ordinary citizens" (Bratton, 2004; see also Afrobarometer Network, 2004; Bratton, Mattes, and Gyimah-Boadi, 2004). In a major empirical study of the link between corruption and citizens' political behavior in Latin America, Charles Davis, Roderic Camp, and Kenneth Coleman (2004) found that public perceptions of high official corruption undermined the legitimacy of the political regime and bred political alienation among citizens. These findings are intuitively sensible. Voters who are more thoroughly and regularly victimized by the diversion of public funds from the provision of services to the consumption wants of officials may be more open to the appeals of politicians who promise to reduce corruption by any means necessary.

But high corruption may not only raise popular demand for nondemocratic practices; it may also enhance political elites' interest in political closure. Officials who engage in corrupt practices normally prefer less public scrutiny to more, and less popular control over the political arena to more. Stealing state assets and/or accepting bribes from private actors heightens an official's interest in reducing public information about, and control over, officialdom.

In practice, of course, the causal arrow in the relationship between corruption and political regime probably points in both directions. For the purposes of our discussion, the possibility that corruption undermines political openness is of greater interest than the reverse. We are also concerned with whether natural resource endowment affects the level of corruption. If countries that are more resource rich are also more corrupt, and if those that are more corrupt are less politically open, a causal link between resources and political regime might be found in resources' corrupting influence.

To measure corruption, I use the "control of corruption" scores that make up one of Kaufmann and colleagues' "Governance Indicators." Scores are scaled like the VA scores that serve as the dependent variable, with higher numbers indicating less corruption.

Table 5.6 shows that corruption may reduce political openness. Control of corruption is highly correlated with economic development, as is suggested by the decline of the regression coefficient for the latter in Model 2. Poorer countries are more corrupt. Of greater interest for the present discussion is that the inclusion of the corruption variable also diminishes the regression coefficient for natural resources. The findings suggest the merit of stepping back and examining the link between natural resources and corruption scores.

There is, in fact, a link. In the world, the partial correlation between natural resources and control of corruption score, controlling for economic development, is notable ($r = -.40$; $p < .001$). In the postcommunist region

Table 5.6. *Corruption Effects (Dependent Variable Is Voice and Accountability Scores)*

Variable	Model 1	Model 2
Constant	−2.88***	−0.83*
	(0.28)	(0.39)
Economic development	0.95***	0.29*
	(0.08)	(0.12)
Natural resource endowment	−0.012***	−0.007***
	(0.002)	(0.002)
Control of corruption score		0.55***
		(0.08)
Adj. R^2	.56	.67

$N = 147$ countries.
*p < 0.05; **p < 0.01; ***p < 0.001
Source: Data for control of corruption score, which are for 2000, Kaufmann et al., 2003.

alone, the partial correlation is also substantial ($r = -.50$; $p < .01$). Russia is no outlier, as Figure 5.3 shows. It is just as corrupt as one would expect it to be, given the prominence of natural resources in its exports.

The findings support the possibility that natural resources corrupt, and that corruption in turn discourages political openness. If these relationships indeed obtain, it is not surprising that democratization in Russia has hit a rough patch. Russia's superabundance of natural resources has already been mentioned. Its corruption, and the possible relationship between corruption and failed democratization, merits further discussion.

How corrupt is Russia? It is filthy. According to the INDEM Center for Applied Political Studies, Russia's leading think tank devoted to studying corruption, Russians spend $37 billion per year on bribes and kickbacks. The sum is roughly equivalent to the $40 billion that the Russian government collects in legal revenue (INDEM, 2002; also Bransten, 2002).

As always, such information makes more sense in a comparative context. In global perspective, Russia indeed fares abysmally. It ranks 132d of 147 countries in control-of-corruption scores – a bit lower than Haiti and slightly higher than Nigeria. No other country that is anywhere near Russia in terms of economic development, with the exception of Yugoslavia/Serbia and Montenegro, scores nearly as badly on corruption. Almost all of the other countries that rank near Russia on control of corruption are among the world's poorest. In the postcommunist world, only Yugoslavia/Serbia and Montenegro, Azerbaijan, Turkmenistan, and Tajikistan rank below Russia.

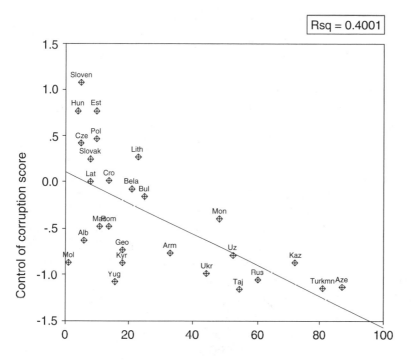

Natural resources as percentage of exports

Figure 5.3. Control of Corruption and Natural Resources, Postcommunist Region

Pakistan, the Philippines, China, and Vietnam rank far ahead of Russia on control of corruption.

Anecdotal evidence is legion. The literature on Russia includes an industry dedicated to recounting the scope of the rot. Such books as *Casino Moscow* (Brzezinski, 2001), *Darkness at Dawn: The Rise of the Russian Criminal State* (Satter, 2003), *Violent Entrepreneurs* (Volkov, 2002), *Bandits, Gangsters, and the Mafia* (McCauley, 2001), and *The Russian Mafia* (Varese, 2001) tell an increasingly familiar story. It is a tale of corruption so pervasive that even when credible reports of acts by high officials that would land them in prison almost anywhere else do make it to the Russian newspapers, few readers are surprised enough to react with more than a cynical sigh.

But that does not mean that people do not notice or do not care. The World Values Surveys ask respondents whether they believe that "someone accepting a bribe in the course of his/her duties" can be justified. In the survey for 2000, 70 percent of Russians answered that taking a bribe is "never

131

justifiable." The proportion who offered the same answer in the 81 countries included in the survey averaged 76 percent; for the 21 postcommunist countries in the survey, the average was 66 percent. For comparison, one may note that the proportion of the population that is unconditionally opposed to bribery in Russia is roughly the same as it is in Spain (72 percent) and Sweden (69 percent), somewhat lower than in the United States (80 percent) and Japan (83 percent), and considerably higher than in Hungary (53 percent) and Brazil (49 percent). The data provide no evidence that a culture of tolerance for graft prevails in Russia and that Russians are insensitive to corruption; just the opposite. While some citizens may be resigned to living under predatory authorities, most cannot accept it (Inglehart et al., eds., 2004; also INDEM, 2002).

Given the Soviet regime's extreme closure, the low visibility of high-level corruption during Soviet times, and the occurrence of a political opening since the end of the Soviet regime, many Russians naturally associate more corruption with greater political openness. Unsurprisingly, even though most opinion polls and elections show that Russians are not hostile to democracy or enamored with reviving the police state, so too do the polls and the ballots show that popular demand for political openness has waned since the late 1980s. Putin's popularity certainly has never indicated nostalgia for the economic certainties of the Soviet era. Putin and the political party he uses as his organizational weapon refuse even to speak of "social justice" or anything else that smacks of state-imposed economic equality. At the same time, Putin has consistently put reducing the influence of bribe payers in politics near the top of his agenda. His election in 2000 showed that corruption had already taken a toll on public demand for democracy; no electorate that put open politics above reducing sleaze would ever have opted for Putin. The remarkable public support for his moves against the highest-rolling bribe payers of the 1990s (the "oligarchs," such as Vladimir Gusinskii, Boris Berezovskii, and Mikhail Khodorkovskii), and the feebleness of public opposition to his methods, which include trampling on individual rights and constricting public access to information, provide further evidence that the corruption of the 1990s seriously eroded public demand for open politics (Gudkov, 2004; White and McAllister, 2003).

Such a dynamic is visible in other countries as well. The success of Hugo Chavez, who was elected president of Venezuela in 1998, was based largely on his promise to humble the high fliers who made their fortunes through corrupt practices. Many of Chavez's supporters stuck with him even as he turned despotic and undermined the institutions of open rule. Venezuela's export profile, like Russia's, is dominated by oil. Venezuela, like Russia, is extraordinarily corrupt given its level of economic development. In Venezuela, as in Russia, oil fuels corruption. By the late 1990s, Venezuelan voters had had enough, and opted for a politician who promised to take on the injustices of corruption by whatever means necessary. Voters' actions did not necessarily signal mass contempt for democracy. They did reveal that disgust with corruption had grown so intense and widespread that it trumped other concerns (Gott, 2001).

So too has corruption diminished elite demand for open politics. As argued here, not only may massive official malfeasance reduce popular demand for democracy; it also undermines elites' interest in democracy. The more corrupt the public official, the greater his or her interest in avoiding public scrutiny and thwarting popular control of politics. Nothing illustrates the point better than the experience of post-Soviet Russian political elites. Champions of political openness turned more conservative as they – of apparent necessity or Faustian choice – soiled their records and ideals. Stephen Holmes (1997[a], p. 69) notes of one former idealist:

When a liberal reformer like Anatoly Chubais scanned Russian society to rally support for Yeltsin's 1996 presidential campaign, whom did he address? Was he able to turn to honest businessmen, who had gained their riches without use of force or fraud? Could he draw support from a new Russian middle class, eager to protect its legal earnings from possible confiscation after a communist comeback? No. To help re-elect Yeltsin, Chubais had to rely on a clutch of robber tycoons, who had waxed rich on asset-stripping, export licenses, rigged privatizations, and control of the pet banks where public tax revenues, federal and local, are deposited even to this day.

Unsurprisingly, by the time that Chubais successfully completed his fundraising task, there was little of the "liberal reformer" left in him, at least in the political sense. Chubais could not possibly have been as enthusiastic about an open polity by the late 1990s as he was at the beginning of the post-Soviet period; by late in the decade he had too much to hide. Much the same may be said of many other politicians who began the 1990s as "liberal reformers." Thus, not only did official corruption reduce the demand for open government on the part of a public that came to associate openness with official impunity, but it also erased the enthusiasm that many former champions of democracy had earlier had in advancing the cause of an open polity.

Why, though, did officials such as Chubais have to rely on the shady characters Holmes mentions? The answer is simple: They had the big money. Where did they get it? The question brings us back to the structure of Russia's exports. They got it in the fuels and minerals businesses. Some held diversified assets by the late 1990s, but most relied for their fortunes on oil, gas, nickel, diamonds, and gold. The most important of the "rigged privatizations" to which Holmes refers were auctions of oil, gas, and metals companies, and the export licenses that Holmes mentions were mostly permits to ship those same fuels, ores, and minerals abroad. The existence of raw materials industries that could reap not merely millions but rather hundreds of millions of dollars for their owners and governmental protectors, combined with the technological obsolescence of most Soviet manufacturing industry, meant that the gold rush in the early post-Soviet period was indeed for gold – both yellow and black. Tiumen Tea (known in the United States as Texas Tea) was where the capital was; it was therefore where the capitalists were made. Given the Soviet legacy, the masters of the tea ceremony were government officials, most of whom in the post-Soviet setting could not resist the temptation to exploit their positions to join the ranks of the world's wealthiest individuals virtually overnight (see Freeland, 2000).

The outcome was not improbable. Ten of the 15 countries that rank below even Russia in Kaufmann's corruption scores also place in the top third of all countries in the percentage of exports accounted for by raw materials. None of these countries really fits the profile of the rentier state. There is not enough oil revenue per capita to turn Russia – or, for that matter, Indonesia or Nigeria, both of which score even worse than Russia on corruption – into a "rentier state." Even if they were so inclined, none of these countries' governments could play the role of the Kuwaiti rulers, showering the people with services without taxing them. But in each of these countries, as in Russia, there is more than enough oil to corrupt the state apparatus.

The Economic Policy Effect

If the state was so readily corruptible by resource superabundance, state agencies had to have some control over the proceeds from the extraction and export of the resources. The problem raises the matter of economic policy doctrine and, in particular, the extent of state control over the economy. Does natural resource wealth affect the extent of the state's control over the economy? Samuel Huntington (1991, pp. 31–2) has raised the possibility that the Middle East has been especially resistant to democratization because so many countries in that region "depend heavily on oil exports, which enhances the control of the state bureaucracy." Implicit in Huntington's statement are two notions: first, that oil wealth may be conducive to economic statism, and second, that state control over the economy may inhibit democratization.

Does resource abundance encourage economic statism? Assessing overall economic policy doctrine is complicated, but several sources of data are available. Perhaps the best and most comprehensive is the "Economic Freedom Index" (hereafter EFI) compiled annually by Gerald O'Driscoll and colleagues (2002). The scores run from 1 (most free) to 5 (least free). I reverse the scale so that higher scores stand for more freedom. The O'Driscoll project began publishing annual scores for most of the world's major countries in 1995. I use an average of scores from 1995 to 2001. The scores are an index that consists of ratings on trade policy, fiscal burden, government intervention, monetary policy, foreign investment, banking and finance, wages and prices, property rights, regulation, and the black market. Economic freedom is understood in purely classical terms and is defined as the opposite of economic statism. Greater economic freedom is understood as less protectionism, lower government expenditure and lower taxation, less government intervention in the economy, tighter monetary policies, lower barriers to foreign investment and capital flows, smaller government presence in the banking sector, less government involvement in the determination of wages and prices, greater protection for property rights, less intrusive government regulation, and less black market activity.

Whether greater economic freedom is, in turn, associated with more open politics is the source of a vigorous, long-standing debate. Many scholars hold that market forces stand in tension with democracy. Others regard the market as a close and consistent ally of open politics.

The empirical evidence supports the second view. As Table 5.7 shows, economic freedom is strongly and positively related to political openness in cross-national perspective. What is more, in the regression analysis, the inclusion of the measure of economic freedom reduces the coefficient for natural resources, suggesting that natural resources may hinder democracy in part by promoting statism in the economy. Correlational analysis provides further evidence. The partial correlation between natural resources and economic freedom scores, controlling for economic development, is sizable ($r = -.38$; $p < .001$). In the postcommunist region alone, the partial correlation between resource endowment and economic freedom is also

Table 5.7. *Economic Freedom Effects (Dependent Variable Is Voice and Accountability Scores)*

Variable	Model 1	Model 2
Constant	−2.87***	−3.32***
	(0.28)	(0.25)
Economic development	0.95***	0.43***
	(0.08)	(0.10)
Natural resource endowment	−0.012***	−0.007***
	(0.002)	(0.002)
Economic Freedom Index		0.70***
		(0.10)
Adj. R^2	.56	.68

$N = 143$ countries.
*p < 0.05; **p < 0.01; ***p < 0.001
Source: For economic freedom scores, O'Driscoll et al., 2002.

strong (r = −.55; p <.01). Russia is not an outlier, as Figure 5.4 shows. Russia's EFI is roughly what one would predict, given the composition of the country's exports.

When considering the effects of natural resources on corruption and economic liberalization in Russia, an important question arises: Wouldn't the businessmen who reaped fortunes from privatization subsequently favor economic liberalization? Perhaps some of the corrupted government officials who profited from the privatization schemes might support the continuation of economic statism, but one might expect the private actors – in particular, the newly minted oil and mineral barons who now enjoyed ownership rights – to form a constituency for economic opening. Liberalization would improve access to investment capital and especially foreign investment, as well as access to lucrative foreign markets.

Yet those who benefited most handsomely from the deals of the mid-1990s did not, for the most part, turn out to be champions of economic liberalization. In a celebrated article, Joel Hellman (1998) showed that in postcommunist countries that undertook piecemeal reform, the big winners from early reform become more of a hindrance than a help to subsequent economic liberalization. In the "partial reformers," Hellman found that the biggest winners were groups that gained substantial rents from the distortions of a "partially reformed economy," and that these groups subsequently retained a stake in "maintaining a partial reform equilibrium" that restricted competition.

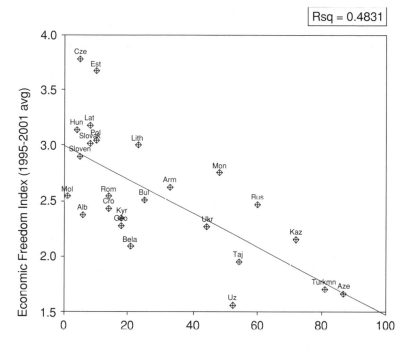

Rsq = 0.4831

Natural resources as percentage of exports

Figure 5.4. Economic Freedom and Natural Resources, Postcommunist Region

Hellman only mentioned in passing the possible effects of natural resources on economic policies, though what little he said on the matter suggested that countries with economies that rely on a superabundance of raw materials may have been particularly vulnerable to the politics of partial economic reform. While this possible extension of Hellman's argument cannot be pursued at length, it merits note that two of his clearest cases of "partial reform" are Russia and Kazakhstan, both of whose economies are based largely on the export of hydrocarbons.

Summary

The superabundance of raw materials counteracts democratization. It typically does so via three mechanisms. The first is a rentier effect, in which rulers buy popular quiescence with a combination of low taxes and high social spending. The second is a repression effect, in which the state maintains a formidable security apparatus that would be unaffordable in the absence of large-scale rents from raw materials. The third is a modernization effect, which refers to the tendency of raw materials superabundance to spur a growth in income without inducing real industrialization and the social transformations that typically accompany it and that may promote democratization. In global perspective, the data suggest that all of these effects indeed obtain.

Yet these effects do not explain how raw materials stymied democratization in Russia. First, Russia does not fit the profile of the rentier state; the government cannot lavish services on the citizens without demanding sacrifice. Second, Russia does have a large internal security apparatus, but it is unclear how large it is or whether the state is dependent on raw materials to finance it. Third, Russia did not experience the pseudomodernization that many "oil states" did. It underwent thoroughgoing industrialization, and its basic socioeconomic indicators, including rates of literacy and fertility, approximate the European norm, rather than the norm in most other oil-rich countries.

In Russia, hydrocarbons and precious metals hindered political opening by other means. First, they contributed to runaway corruption, which in turn undermined public and elite support for open politics. Second, they circumscribed and distorted economic liberalization and encouraged policies that reproduced economic statism. Precisely how economic statism, in turn, hampered political opening requires closer investigation. In fact, it deserves a chapter of its own. That chapter follows.

6

The Policy Problem

ECONOMIC STATISM

One of the most contentious and politically significant debates in social science focuses on the relationship between economic policy and political regime. Social scientists and others continue to differ starkly over even the most fundamental issues.

An especially vigorous polemic swirls around whether measures that enhance the freedom of private economic actors do or do not promote democracy. This debate is immediately relevant to Russia's postcommunist experience. Like other postcommunist countries, Russia has undergone shifts in economic policy that may have shaped its trajectory of political regime change.

The closing pages of the previous chapter presented some evidence that economic freedom and democracy go together. But the matter requires more extensive consideration. The difficulty of measuring economic policy orientation, along with the possibility that the relationship between economic and political liberalism is different in established democracies from what it is elsewhere, suggest the need for closer analysis.

This chapter examines the influence of economic policy orientation on democracy and democratization. The first section reviews the theoretical debate. The second examines the empirical evidence in cross-national perspective. The third addresses potential limitations in the analysis. The fourth considers the logic of the link between liberal economic policy and political regime. The fifth and sixth sections focus on how economic policy has influenced political regime change in Russia. The chapter's main finding is that economic and political liberalism are closely linked and that economic liberalization facilitates democratization in Russia as in the world as a whole. A shortage, rather than surplus, of economic liberalization has contributed to Russia's deficit of democracy.

139

The Great Debate over Market and Political Regime

How does economic freedom affect political regime? Some social scientists have decided that the question is too broad and unmanageable to merit addressing. According to such thinking, the causal link between economic liberalism/liberalization and political liberalism/liberalization is not straightforward. The answer depends on the country, the region, the institutions, the policymakers, external circumstances, culture, historical circumstances, popular opinion, or something else.

Still, many analysts who suspect that economic policy doctrine systematically affects political regime cannot steer clear of the big, unwieldy question that engages our philosophies and our politics as much as it does the philosophies and politics of the people we study. Despite protests and caveats about the complexity of it all, moreover, most scholars do hold a position on the relationship between economic and political liberalism. There is nothing wrong with that. The problem is that our inclinations are too often based on the one or handful of countries or policies we know well or on deeply ingrained normative inclinations that we rarely question or subject to empirical test.

The controversy is most salient and interesting in the realm of policy. In roughest outline, it pits "shock therapy" against "gradualism." Differences in outlook are often evident even in our language. Frequent resort to the term *neoliberalism* usually signals gradualist sympathies and skepticism about the influence of markets on democracy. How often does one see neoliberalism *lauded* in the scholarly literature? "Neoliberalism" is usually bad; "liberalism" (plain and simple, unsullied by the prefix that updates it) is usually good or at least neutral.

Many scholars regard economic liberalism (or neoliberalism) as a threat to democracy. According to them, neoliberal economic policies depress popular living standards and undercut the legitimacy of open government, especially in fledgling democracies. Economic liberalization requires state officials to ignore popular demands, contain popular participation, deceive the electorate, and generally act undemocratically (Borón, 1998; Callaghy, 1993 and 1994; Chua, 2003; Huber, Rueschemeyer, and Stephens, 1999; Oxhorn and Ducantenzeiler, eds., 1998). This picture of the relationship between economic liberalism and popular rule is consistent with a philosophical position that emphasizes the areas of dissimilarity in the principles on which democracy and capitalism are based. Democracy demands equality before the law and the practice of one person, one vote. In capitalism's marketplace, "votes" – economic resources – are distributed inequitably. What is more, equality per se is not an important part of the theory of capitalism (Dahl, 1992; Lindblom, 1977; Miliband, 1992). The viewpoint of those who question the compatibility of economic and political liberalism is also consonant with the historically grounded argument that the dictates of deep economic transformation, or even of proximate changes such as economic stabilization and adjustment, often require the rise of formidable state apparatuses to repress popular consumption and demobilize opponents of economic policy change (Gerschenkron, 1962; Malloy, 1987; Skidmore, 1977).

Other writers regard the market as an ally of open politics. They see an expansive realm of autonomous economic activity as a bulwark against despotism (Bobbio, 1990; Diamond, 1995). This perspective is consistent with the notion that both capitalism and democracy are based on free choice, and that capitalism separates economic power from political power and thereby enables the two to balance one another. So too is it consonant with the proposition that the market encourages personal and group independence and strengthens the ability of people to resist the encroachments of an overweening state (Friedman, 1962; Hirschman, 1977).

Contention is no less salient among analysts who study the postcommunist region than it is among those who specialize in other regions or in pure theory. Many students of the former Soviet Union and East Europe hold that rapid economic liberalization derails democratization or at least creates social circumstances that jeopardize popular rule (Amsden, Kochanowicz, and Taylor, 1998; Burawoy, 1996[a] and [b]; Cohen, 2000; Fairbanks, 1999; Herrera, 2001; Kollontai, 1999; Maravall, 1997; Millar, 1995; Murrell, 1995; Nelson, 1996; Orenstein, 1998; Ost, 2000; Poznanski, 2002; Przeworski, 1993 and 1996; Reddaway and Glinski, 2001; Sapir, 2000; Stavrakis, 1993; Urban, 1997; Vassilev, 2003; Verdery, 2000). Other writers claim that fast and thoroughgoing economic reform buttresses democratization (Åslund, 2000; Bunce, 1999; Frye, 2000; McFaul, 2001; Murphy, Shleifer, and Vishney, 1992; Sachs, 1995).

Debate between the liberals and the gradualists is often vigorous, even acrimonious, but it usually remains stuck in the realm of pure theory or takes the form of sparring over interpretation of the experience of a single country or a handful of countries. Hypothesis testing that uses cross-national data is surprisingly rare. The following section offers cross-national analysis of the possible effect of economic policy doctrine on political regime.

Table 6.1. *Multiple Regressions of Voice and Accountability Scores on Hypothesized Determinants, Including Economic Freedom Index (EFI)*

Variable	Model 1	Model 2	Model 3	Model 4	Model 5	Model 6
Constant	−2.81***	−3.03***	−3.15***	−2.97***	−3.06***	−3.04***
	(0.31)	(0.24)	(0.32)	(0.25)	(0.25)	(0.24)
Economic	0.28**	0.32***	0.33**	0.36***	0.30**	0.31***
development	(0.11)	(0.10)	(0.11)	(0.10)	(0.09)	(0.09)
Natural	−0.003	−0.004*	−0.006***	−0.004*		−0.004*
resource	(0.002)	(0.002)	(0.002)	(0.002)		(0.002)
endowment						
Ethnic	−0.25		−0.27			
fractionalization	(0.21)		(0.22)			
British	0.04		0.06			
colonial	(0.11)		(0.12)			
heritage						
Communist	0.31*	0.32*	0.33*			0.27*
heritage	(0.14)	(0.14)	(0.15)			(0.12)
Islam	−0.006***	−0.006***		−0.006***	−0.007***	−0.006***
	(0.001)	(0.002)		(0.001)	(0.001)	(0.001)
Orthodoxy	−0.002	−0.002	−0.001	−0.001	−0.001	
	(0.003)	(0.003)	(0.003)	(0.002)	(0.002)	
Economic	0.75***	0.75***	0.77***	0.70***	0.77***	0.76***
Freedom	(0.09)	(0.09)	(0.10)	(0.09)	(0.09)	(0.09)
Index (EFI)						
Adj. R^2	.73	.73	.69	.72	.71	.73

$N = 143$ countries. Entries are unstandardized regression coefficients with standard errors in parentheses.
*$p < 0.05$; **$p < 0.01$; ***$p < 0.001$

Empirical Evidence

Table 5.7, shown at the end of the previous chapter, presented some evidence that economic liberalism, measured in terms of the Economic Freedom Index (EFI), is associated with political openness. In a regression of VA scores on economic development, natural resource endowment, and the EFI, the EFI was substantively and statistically significant. The inclusion of the EFI in the analysis, moreover, lowered the regression coefficient for the natural resources variable, showing that resource abundance may exercise its pernicious effect on political openness in part by promoting lower levels of economic freedom.

Here we are concerned with the effects of economic freedom itself on political openness. In order to test the importance of economic freedom, I return to a more fully specified model that also includes other variables whose effects were tested in Chapter 4. Results are shown in Table 6.1. Like Table 4.2, Table 6.1 furnishes a variety of specifications. The main difference is that in the analyses presented in Table 6.1, the EFI is added as an independent variable. Data are missing on the EFI for the Central African Republic, Comoros, Macedonia, and Yugoslavia/Serbia and Montenegro, and so the number of cases is four fewer in the regressions in Table 6.1. In all specifications, the EFI is a good predictor of political openness. The regression coefficient for the EFI is very large. An increase of one point in the EFI, which ranges from 1 to 5, is associated with an improvement of about three-quarters of a point in the VA score. In comparison with the regressions presented in Table 4.2, which do not include the EFI, the regression coefficients for economic development and natural resource endowment are smaller, and the dummy variable for postcommunist countries is statistically significant and positive, indicating that postcommunist countries actually do better on VA scores than others when the EFI is included in the analysis.

A scatterplot reveals a close correlation between economic freedom and political openness. Figure 6.1 illustrates it.

Measuring economic freedom is not simple, and the EFI, created by Gerald O'Driscoll and colleagues, is only one of several available measures. The use of an alternative measure provides a check on the results. The Fraser Institute's Economic Freedom Ratings (Gwartney and Lawson, 2003), which have been issued every five years since 1970, provides the other source of cross-national measures, though Fraser evaluates fewer countries than do O'Driscoll and colleagues. The Fraser project, headed by James Gwartney and Robert Lawson, also seeks to measure economic freedom. The Fraser Institute's self-proclaimed mission is to promote economic freedom. Like O'Driscoll and colleagues, Gwartney and Lawson conceive of economic freedom as the opposite of economic statism. Smaller government, lower taxes, more secure property rights, more open trade policies, less regulation of the right to own foreign currency, less government regulation of credit and labor markets, and less government regulation of business serve as the main criteria for scoring countries. I will refer here to Gwartney and Lawson's Economic Freedom Ratings as "Fraser scores." Countries are scored on a 1–10 scale, with higher scores representing more economic freedom. Table 6.2 substitutes the Fraser scores for the EFI. For the sake of brevity, fewer models are presented than in Table 6.1. The results are

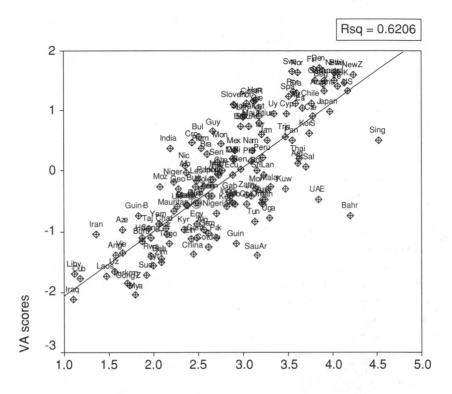

Figure 6.1. Political Openness and Economic Freedom (Economic Freedom Index)

virtually identical to those obtained using the EFI. Economic freedom is a good predictor of political openness. An increase of one point in the Fraser score is associated with an improvement of roughly one-third of a point in the VA score. The relationship is depicted in the scatterplot shown in Figure 6.2.

The results are unambiguous. Are they sound and are they relevant to the postcommunist region?

Are the Results Irrelevant or Misleading?

The Danger of Regional Specificity

The first and perhaps most relevant potential problem is that the results may be driven by conditions in the advanced industrialized world. Economic

144

Table 6.2. *Multiple Regressions of Voice and Accountability Scores on Hypothesized Determinants, Including Fraser Economic Freedom Scores*

Variable	Model 1	Model 2	Model 3	Model 4
Constant	−3.77***	−3.85***	−3.80***	−4.20***
	(0.38)	(0.40)	(0.32)	(0.31)
Economic	0.47***	0.57***	0.65***	0.60***
development	(0.11)	(0.12)	(0.11)	(0.11)
Natural	−0.003	−0.006**	−0.006***	
resource	(0.002)	(0.002)	(0.002)	
endowment				
Ethnic	−0.04	−0.08		
fractionalization	(0.22)	(0.24)		
British	0.08			
colonial	(0.11)			
heritage				
Communist	0.49**			
heritage	(0.16)			
Islam	−0.005***			
	(0.001)			
Orthodoxy	0.002	0.006		
	(0.003)	(0.003)		
Fraser	0.39***	0.35***	0.30***	0.37***
Economic	(0.07)	(0.07)	(0.07)	(0.07)
Freedom Score				
Adj. R^2	.74	.68	.68	.65

$N = 115$ countries.
*$p < 0.05$; **$p < 0.01$; ***$p < 0.001$

freedom and political openness comfortably coexist in Australia, Canada, and the Netherlands. Most scholars agree that economic and political liberalism are compatible in the very long run – meaning in long-standing democracies with prosperous market economies. The main controversy is over the Second (communist/postcommunist) and Third Worlds, where political regimes are often in flux and where majorities do not generally enjoy material security. To examine the matter, it is useful to conduct the analysis excluding high-income OECD countries. Table 6.3 presents results of regressions that exclude these countries. The results resemble those presented in Table 6.1, which analyzed all countries. The coefficient for the EFI is similarly large and statistically significant at a demanding level. Substituting Fraser scores for the EFI, the results for which are not shown here, yields virtually identical results. Figure 6.3 plots the relationship between

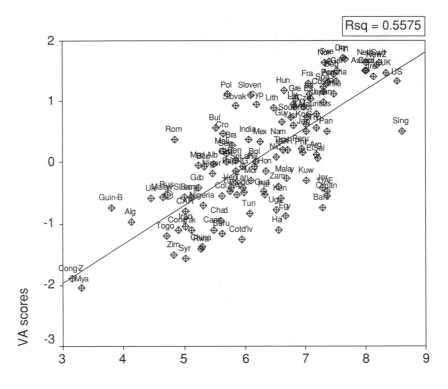

Fraser Economic Freedom Score, 2000

Figure 6.2. Political Openness and Economic Freedom (Fraser Scores)

VA scores and the EFI for all countries except the high-income members of the OECD. Economic freedom remains a powerful predictor, even with the advanced industrialized countries removed from the analysis.

Is the postcommunist region exceptional? Students of postcommunist countries have penned some of the writings that most strongly condemn the effects of neoliberal economics on democracy. Figure 6.4 suggests that there may be a gap between such claims and the evidence. The correlation between economic freedom and political openness is even stronger in the region than in the world as a whole.

Use of still another source of data provides another check. Martha De Melo, Cebdet Denizer, and Alan Gelb (1996 and updates) constructed a widely used economic liberalization index for countries of the postcommunist world. The index scored each country, except Bosnia and Mongolia,

Table 6.3. *Multiple Regressions of Voice and Accountability Scores on Hypothesized Determinants, Excluding High-Income OECD Countries*

Variable	Model 1	Model 2	Model 3
Constant	−2.35***	−2.58***	−2.76***
	(0.35)	(0.36)	(0.32)
Economic	0.06	0.07	0.25*
development	(0.12)	(0.13)	(0.12)
Natural resource	−0.003	−0.005**	−0.006***
endowment	(0.002)	(0.002)	(0.002)
Ethnic	−0.13	−0.11	
fractionalization	(0.22)	(0.23)	
British	0.05		
colonial heritage	(0.12)		
Communist	0.51***	0.46***	
heritage	(0.15)	(0.14)	
Islam	−0.005***		
	(0.001)		
Orthodoxy	−0.004		
	(0.003)		
Economic Freedom	0.76***	0.79***	0.68***
Index (EFI)	(0.10)	(0.10)	(0.10)
Adj. R^2	.60	.55	.51

$N = 122$ countries.
*$p < 0.05$; **$p < 0.01$; ***$p < 0.001$

for every year from 1989 to 1997. Scores for each country for each year range between 0 and 1. Country totals for all nine years are dubbed the Cumulative Economic Liberalization Index (CELI). Figure 6.5 plots the relationship between VA scores and the CELI. Again, the picture could hardly be less ambiguous.

In sum, the evidence provides no support for the notion that the strong link between economic freedom and political openness is specific to the advanced industrialized world. The correlation is strong even among non-wealthy countries, and is even greater in the postcommunist region than in the world as a whole.

Potential Problems of Measurement

Another legitimate but, upon inspection, unfounded concern is the danger of extensive overlap in the criteria for measuring the dependent and

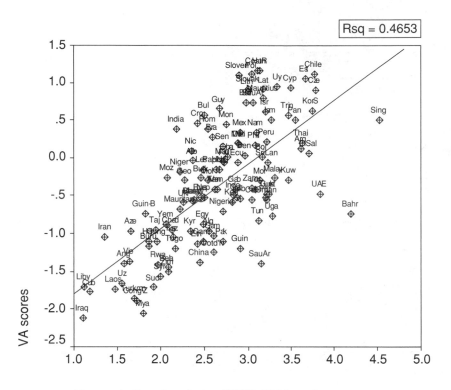

Figure 6.3. Political Openness and Economic Freedom, Excluding High-Income OECD Countries

independent variables. If the Kaufmann measure of voice and accountability (the VA scores) places substantial weight on *economic* freedom, and/or if O'Driscoll surveys that create the EFI give points for *political* freedom, the correlation between VA scores and the EFI may be artificially inflated. It may not accurately reflect the true relationship between political regime and economic policy doctrine.

The hazard of such a problem is minimal. The Kaufmann surveys measure the voice of the governed and the accountability of the government alone. Countries do not get points for economic liberalism. Furthermore, the danger that O'Driscoll and colleagues grant more favorable EFI scores to countries that have more open political regimes is remote. The descriptive portion of the evaluation of Chile includes a thinly veiled

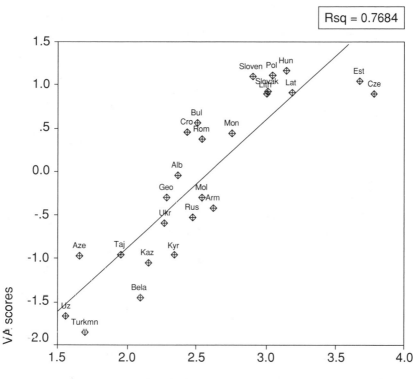

Figure 6.4. Political Openness and Economic Freedom, Postcommunist Region

laudatory word for the former Chilean dictator, Augusto Pinochet. Qatar's and Bahrain's ruling sheikhs, economic liberalizers who are hardly democratic idealists, receive praise. O'Driscoll and colleagues and their sponsors, the Heritage Foundation and the *Wall Street Journal,* are neoliberal true believers who do not allow free elections and human rights to influence their assessment of property and commerce. Countries get no points for democracy. Similarly, the Fraser scores are issued by a think tank that has an unabashedly libertarian, pro-market orientation. The authors of the EFI and the Fraser scores may be criticized for their disregard of the freedom of anything but the market, but their ideological purity makes their assessments of economic freedom all the more useful for the present analysis.

149

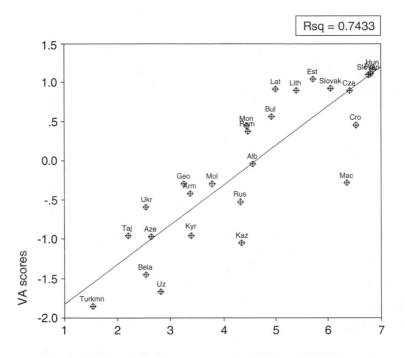

Figure 6.5. Political Openness and Economic Liberalization, Postcommunist Region

The Logic of the Link

The Logic of the Case for Gradualism

The evidence should be regarded as suggestive rather than definitive. Some potential problems cannot be fully addressed. Establishing the direction of the causal arrow in the relationship between economic liberalization and democratization is difficult. Some scholars who have attempted to do so have concluded that economic liberalization has a stronger effect on democratization than the other way around (Burkhart and de Soysa, 2003). That said, the matter is still open to debate, and the relationship between economic liberalization and democratization may well be a two-way street. Still, the evidence presented here does suggest strongly that economic liberalization is no foe of democratization.

Yet "neoliberalism" is one of the bogeymen of Western social science. As noted earlier, many who write on the postcommunist region have characterized it as a mighty foe of democratization and other good things as well (Hout and Gerber, 1998; Kurtz and Barnes, 2002; Nelson, 1996; Orenstein, 1998; Przeworski, 1993; Reddaway and Glinski, 2001; Stark and Bruszt, 1998; Stavrakis, 2002). None of the studies cited here, or those available elsewhere, actually demonstrates that a rush to the market undermines democratization. Still, many scholars continue to insist that rapid economic reform is a disaster for popular welfare and popular rule, and their arguments are worthy of closer consideration.

Many scholars believe that neoliberalism is driven by blind ideological zeal. Adam Przeworski, for example, calls the attempt to transform postcommunist economies "the greatest ideologically inspired experiment since Josef Stalin initiated the forced industrialization of the Soviet Union in 1929" (1992, p. 45). In an esteemed and influential work, Przeworski (1991, pp. 183, 186–7) makes a forceful case:

Market-oriented economic reforms are an application of a technical economic blueprint based on theories developed inside the walls of North American universities and often forced on governments by the international lending agencies.... The particular measures implement technicians' ideas; they are adopted without consultation and sometimes announced by surprise.... Once confidence in reforms is eroded, each new government tries to make a clean break with the past by doing something that people have not yet learned to distrust. Reforms are addictive; a stronger dosage is needed each time to soothe the accumulated desperation. Market-oriented reforms may be based on sound economics. But they breed voodoo politics. The effect of this style is to undermine representative institutions.... Democracy is thus weakened.... Technocracy hurls itself against democracy.

Przeworski's argument summarizes the case against shock therapy. Market-oriented reforms are antidemocratic because they are forced on the people. In order to implement reforms, governments must emasculate representative institutions. If mass publics were enthusiastic about reforms, governments could implement them without hurling technocracy against democracy. But, states Przeworski, "The main obstacle to reforms is the people" (1993, p. 185). The people, after all, are the ones who must endure the reforms' effects.

As Przeworski makes clear, the argument against neoliberalism rests on the assumption that neoliberal economic reforms are bad for public welfare and worse for public welfare than some non-neoliberal set of policies. If neoliberalism were not worse for public welfare than gradualism, publics would not have an interest in resisting it. If publics did not have an interest in resisting it, policymakers implementing neoliberal economic reforms would face no need to undermine representative institutions. If the relationship between economic liberalization and social welfare were not negative, the argument that economic liberalization is bad for democracy would be weakened. It would lack a causal mechanism specifying why economic liberalization would require governments to coerce, hoodwink, exclude, or ignore the people. If rapid reforms are indeed worse for welfare than gradual reforms, then the hypothetical causal chain linking neoliberal economics and antidemocratic politics is potentially sound.

What, then, is the relationship between economic policy and human welfare? Is Przeworski's assumption, which is accepted as an axiom by many scholars, sound?

Given the paucity of data on economic liberalization over the 1990s that cover the whole world, here I will stick with the postcommunist region alone, for which we may use the cumulative economic liberalization index for 1989–97. Welfare is assessed using the Human Development Index (HDI), the measure of well-being constructed by the UNDP and used widely in development studies (UNDP, 2003). Countries are scored on a 0–1 scale. In 2001, the most recent year for which data are available, the range in the postcommunist region extended from 0.881 (for Slovenia) to 0.661 (for Mongolia). Assessing change requires comparing the recent numbers with those available at the time of the demise of Communist Party regimes. For the year 2001, data are available for all postcommunist countries; for 1990, for 20 of them. The analysis is therefore limited to 20 countries. In order to assess change, I subtract each country's score for 1990 from its score for 2001. Higher scores represent greater positive change. Scores higher than 0 represent improvement in welfare between 1990 and 2001; scores below 0 show deterioration.

Figure 6.6 illustrates the relationship between economic liberalization and change in social welfare in the postcommunist region. The picture defies Przeworski's contention. The relationship between economic liberalization and change in the HDI is positive.

The simple bivariate relationship illustrated in Figure 6.6 might be deceptive, since countries that started with higher welfare might have had an easier time both undertaking economic liberalization and containing the human cost of it. In order to assess whether the starting point made all the difference, I regress HDI_{2001} minus HDI_{1990} on the Cumulative Economic Liberalization Index and the HDI in 1990. The results, shown in Table 6.4, suggest that the positive link between economic liberalization and welfare improvement holds when controlling for starting points in welfare.

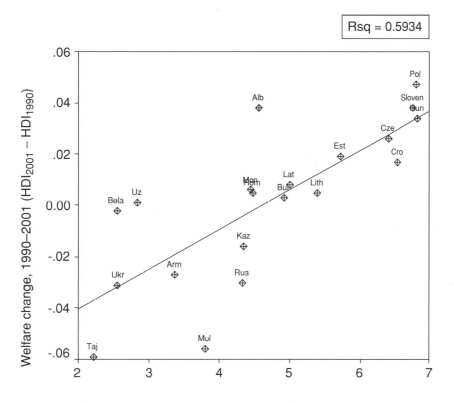

Figure 6.6. Change in Social Welfare and Economic Liberalization, Postcommunist Region

More economic reform spelled less, not more, socioeconomic trauma, even when accounting for countries' level of development at the beginning of the transformations of the 1990s.

It is possible that the faster reformers did worse at first and that their advantage in welfare change was delayed until the positive socioeconomic consequences of economic liberalization kicked in later. Figure 6.7 and Table 6.5 present the evidence relevant to this question. They test the relationship between welfare changes from 1990 to mid-decade, measured as HDI_{1995} minus HDI_{1990}, and the sum of the annual scores on the Economic Liberalization Index for 1991–3. The regression presented in Table 6.5 is similar to the one shown in Table 6.4, except that the dependent variable in Table 6.5 is HDI_{1995} minus HDI_{1990} rather than HDI_{2001} minus HDI_{1990},

Table 6.4. *Multiple Regression of Change in Welfare*
(HDI$_{2001}$ minus HDI$_{1990}$) on Hypothesized
Determinants, Postcommunist Region

Variable	
Constant	0.01
	(0.01)
Human Development	−0.11
Index, 1990	(0.11)
Cumulative Economic	0.02***
Liberalization Index, 1989–97	(0.003)
Adj. R^2	.57

$N = 20$ countries.
*p < 0.05; **p < 0.01; ***p < 0.001

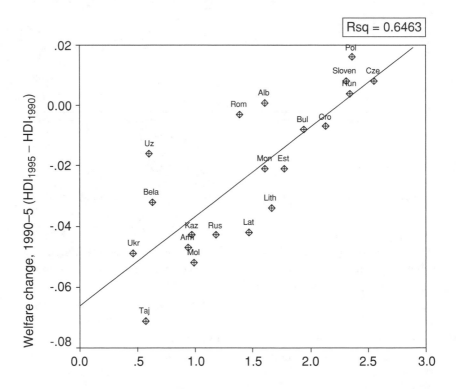

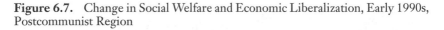

Economic Liberalization Index, Summary of Scores for 1991–3

Figure 6.7. Change in Social Welfare and Economic Liberalization, Early 1990s,
Postcommunist Region

Table 6.5. *Multiple Regression of Change in Welfare During the First Half of the 1990s (HDI$_{1995}$ Minus HDI$_{1990}$) on Hypothesized Determinants, Postcommunist Region*

Variable	
Constant	−0.01
	(0.06)
Human Development Index, 1990	−0.07
	(0.08)
Economic Liberalization Index, sum	0.03***
for 1991–3	(0.01)
Adj. R^2	.62

$N = 20$ countries.
*p < 0.05; **p < 0.01; ***p < 0.001

and the independent variable is the earlier, three-year sum of the Economic Liberalization Index rather than the Cumulative Economic Liberalization Index. Again a control is included for HDI$_{1990}$. The results show precisely the same dynamic as in the analysis of change over the longer period. More economic liberalization was better for socioeconomic welfare than was less liberalization, even in the short run.

The analysis speaks to why any leaders ever pursue economic liberalization. Why any politician who has to face the voters would ever implement economic liberalization has vexed many scholars. Neoliberal reforms are assumed to straiten the majority; why, then, would any politician who cared about his or her political career ever carry them out? Some writers believe that they have solved the puzzle by showing that politicians may expect – rightly or not – neoliberal economic policies to bear fruit before the politicians must again face the electorate (Stokes, 2001[a]; Stokes, ed., 2001[b]). But perhaps there is no conundrum at all. If more economic liberalization improves welfare more quickly than less economic liberalization, there is no riddle to solve. If one simply *assumes* that neoliberal economics must be more exclusionary, painful, and traumatic to the people than non-neoliberal alternatives, as most writers do, then of course the riddle remains.

The small number of cases included in the analysis suggests the wisdom of caution in interpreting the findings, but the information that analysis offers is unequivocal. At least in the postcommunist region, the notion that faster liberalization produced greater welfare losses is untenable. The empirical evidence further suggests that economic liberalism – and liberalization – are decisive and rapid allies of open politics.

For the moment, enough empirical evidence; let us return instead to logical connections. As economists like to say (albeit not publicly), perhaps it works in fact, but does it work in theory? What are the theoretical bases for the strong empirical link between economic freedom and democratic politics?

The Logic of the Case for Shock Therapy

William Riker has argued: "Although it has become fashionable in this century to deride economic freedom, capitalism remains essential for faction. No government that has eliminated economic freedom has been able to attain or keep democracy, probably because, when all economic life is absorbed into government, there is no conceivable financial base for opposition" (1982, p. 7). This passage, which refers to *absolute* state control of the economy, provides a compact theoretical summary of why countries where markets are shut down completely invariably become dictatorships. The statement applies to the Soviet Union, sovietized East Europe, Maoist China, and several Southeast Asian and African countries from the 1950s to the 1980s when their economies were thoroughly statized.

But Riker's statement applies in a strict sense to these countries alone; only in them was "economic freedom" actually "eliminated" and "all economic life . . . absorbed into government." The logic of Riker's proposition may be rendered more useful by reducing its absolutism and reformulating it as a matter of degree. A hypothesis offered by Robert Dahl does just that: "The likelihood that a government will tolerate an opposition increases as the resources available to the government for suppression decline relative to the resources of an opposition" (1971, p. 48). If Dahl is right, greater latitude for private actors to pursue their interests independent of the state might promote a higher degree of political openness.

Riker's and Dahl's maxims point out why economic liberalization may be an especially vital prerequisite to genuine political contestation in post-communist countries. In many countries where political regime change has taken place over the past three decades, large and powerful private sectors were already functioning at the time of transformation. The communist world was different. Private sectors were minuscule and poorly developed, and commerce was controlled almost entirely by the state. There was, to use Riker's phrase, "no conceivable financial base for opposition." Without economic liberalization, none would have emerged.

156

In fact, little if any financial base for opposition emerged where there was minimal change in the extent of economic statization after the end of the Soviet period. Belarus, Uzbekistan, and Turkmenistan are the clearest examples. In these countries, to borrow Dahl's formulation, governments need not tolerate serious oppositions since the resources available to opponents of the government are so minimal. In countries with long heritages of economic statism, rapid liberalization opened the gates to pluralism. The absence of rapid liberalization kept the doors shut. Political oppositions are of course essential to democracy, as many contemporary theorists have argued (Shapiro, 1996).

Economic reform may be crucial to the emergence of other politically relevant societal organizations as well. Thoroughgoing economic liberalization may spur the emergence of class and occupational identities and, therefore, associations representing those identities, including labor unions and professional associations (Titma, Tuma, and Silver, 1998; Zaslavsky, 2001).

Many writers have argued that the formation of a large class of small property holders – that is, a middle class – facilitates democratization. Karl Marx regarded the bourgeoisie as the agent of democratization (which, in Marx's scheme, would be superseded by proletarian dictatorship) due to the bourgeoisie's lack of immediate dependence on overlords – be they rulers, bosses, or landowners – and its ability to demand and pursue its rights as a result of its autonomy. Barrington Moore, who explicitly agrees with Marx and who sums up part of his magisterial analysis of the origins of political regimes with the maxim "No bourgeoisie, no democracy," similarly views the middle classes' independence from the state as crucial to their pro-democratic influence (1966, p. 418; Marx and Engels, 1998).

Some theorists have argued that those who hold economic power not only are more able to stand up to the state and other potential agents of control; they also are more psychologically disposed to do so. Writing in the early nineteenth century, Benjamin Constant argued that economic independence transforms the psychology of individuals in a manner that promotes open politics. In Constant's phrase: "Commerce inspires in men a vivid love of individual independence" (2000, p. 315). He claimed that autocrats and would-be autocrats encountered resistance to their pretensions among those engaged in commerce, and he concluded that free commercial life undermined autocracy and promoted political self-rule.

Rapid economic opening may also lessen the state's ability to control political behavior by distributing patronage and bribery. In almost every polity, including fully open ones, politicians build support by using their access to state funds and their ability to time the distribution and target the recipients of those funds. But the state's patronage resources are less likely to be decisive in shaping voters' and social groups' political behavior where a great deal of autonomous economic power exists in society and where the state has limited resources and fewer levers of economic control at its disposal. A lower level of reliance of economic actors – be they private citizens, associations, or enterprises – upon the state for the money, goods, access to credit, licenses, and permits spells less societal dependence on the state, which in turn means less influence for politicians' patronage and lower concentration of power in state agencies.

In sum, rapid economic policy change may encourage open politics by creating a financial basis for the formation of autonomous societal organizations, including groups that oppose those in power. It may also loosen the dependence of individuals and whole classes on the state and reduce the state's ability to orchestrate politics by means of its control of patronage. The logic of the link between more rapid economic reform and greater political openness, then, is about pluralism, or pluralization. It is about multiplying and diversifying the holders of economic resources and empowering a wider range of actors.

What, then, does all this have to do with Russia?

Economic Policy Doctrine in Russia

Many scholars have claimed that Russia carried out "shock therapy" and that this policy undermined, or at least created social and economic conditions that hindered, democratization (Arbatov, 2001; Cohen, 2000; Pomer, 2001; Reddaway and Glinski, 2001). These authors are right to claim that economic reform has affected political reform. So too are they right to hold that democratization has faltered. But there are two problems with their arguments. First, Russia did not carry out shock therapy. Its economic reforms have been a hodgepodge of half measures and schemes that have little to do with shock therapy. Second, rapid economic liberalization is not bad for democracy.

The Cross-National Picture: Where Russia Fits In

The cross-national data leave ample room for questioning whether Russia undertook shock therapy. Tables 6.6, 6.7, and 6.8 show how Russia compares to other postcommunist countries on measures of economic freedom.

Table 6.6. *Economic Freedom Indices, 1995–2001 (Seven-Year Average), Postcommunist Countries*

Czech Republic	3.78	**Russia**	**2.47**
Estonia	3.67	Croatia	2.43
Latvia	3.18	Albania	2.37
Hungary	3.14	Kyrgyzstan	2.34
Poland	3.04	Georgia	2.28
Slovakia	3.01	Ukraine	2.27
Lithuania	3.00	Kazakhstan	2.15
Slovenia	2.90	Belarus	2.09
Mongolia	2.75	Tajikistan	1.95
Armenia	2.62	Turkmenistan	1.70
Moldova	2.54	Azerbaijan	1.66
Romania	2.54	Uzbekistan	1.56
Bulgaria	2.51		

Table 6.7. *Fraser Economic Freedom Scores, 2000, Postcommunist Countries*

Estonia	7.09	Poland	5.72
Czech Republic	6.99	Croatia	5.64
Latvia	6.82	Bulgaria	5.51
Hungary	6.66	Albania	5.49
Lithuania	6.48	Romania	4.85
Slovenia	6.10	**Russia**	**4.73**
Slovakia	5.84	Ukraine	4.47

Table 6.6 ranks countries according to the EFI, Table 6.7 according to Fraser scores, and Table 6.8 by the CELI.

In terms of the EFI, Russia ranks 14th of 25 postcommunist countries (Macedonia and Yugoslavia/Serbia and Montenegro are not ranked). In global perspective, Russia ranks 102d of 143 countries. In the Fraser scores, Russia ranks 13th of the 14 postcommunist countries included in the survey and 108th of 115 countries in the world. In the CELI, which scores only postcommunist countries, Russia places 16th of 26. Thus, by the standards of the EFI and the CELI, Russia scores in roughly the 40th percentile of countries in the postcommunist region. In terms of Fraser scores, which evaluate only 14 postcommunist countries, Russia comes out one spot from the bottom. In global perspective, Russia scores in the bottom third in the EFI and in the bottom tenth in the Fraser scores. There is little evidence that economic policy was defined by radical, rapid reform. In comparative

159

Table 6.8. *Cumulative Economic Liberalization Indices, 1989–97,*
Postcommunist Countries

Hungary	6.84	Mongolia	4.44
Poland	6.81	Kazakhstan	4.35
Slovenia	6.77	**Russia**	**4.32**
Croatia	6.53	Moldova	3.80
Czech Republic	6.40	Kyrgyzstan	3.39
Macedonia	6.34	Armenia	3.37
Slovakia	6.05	Georgia	3.26
Estonia	5.72	Uzbekistan	2.83
Lithuania	5.39	Azerbaijan	2.64
Latvia	5.00	Ukraine	2.55
Bulgaria	4.92	Belarus	2.54
Albania	4.56	Tajikistan	2.21
Romania	4.47	Turkmenistan	1.53

perspective, gradualism, rather than shock therapy, best characterizes economic policy in post-Soviet Russia.

Economic Policy Reform: The Macroenvironment

There is a large literature on post-Soviet economic policymaking in Russia
(Appel, 2004; Freeland, 2000; Frye, 2000; Goldman, 1994 and 2003;
Johnson, 2000; Kokh, 1998; Rutland, ed., 2000; Shleifer and Treisman,
2000; Woodruff, 2000). Instead of offering a detailed account of economic
policy in Russia, I intend only to characterize in general terms the process
of economic policy reform, drawing on the works just cited to illuminate
some facts relevant to the current discussion.

The Gorbachev era was a time of dramatic political reform but also of half
measures and timidity in economic policy change. Gorbachev's economic
reforms included three prominent initiatives, each of which was encoded
in law in 1987–8 and took effect in 1988 or 1989. The first was a relaxation
of the ban on private enterprise. The effect of the measure was the emergence of so-called cooperatives, which were small-scale private enterprises.
Some cooperatives were underground cottage industries that were now allowed to operate in the open. Others were new enterprises that emerged in
small-scale retail, trading, or production. Most cooperative production,
however, occurred within state enterprises, whose managers set aside some
portion of the material inputs and labor they controlled and devoted them to
production for private profit. The second policy initiative was a new law on

joint ventures that ended the traditional Soviet ban on foreign investment. The third took the form of the "law on state enterprises," which provided for what at the time were dubbed "self-management" and "self-financing" for enterprises.

The government pursued each of the reforms in a tepid, desultory manner. It stopped short of implementing measures that would have put teeth in the policy changes. The laws on private enterprise opened the door a crack to private production, retail, and service provision, but included no effective measures to promote or protect new private businesses. The new rules brought some underground black market activity to the surface and stimulated some new small-scale business activity, but heavy and inconsistent regulation, predation by officials, and the absence of protection for property rights meant that the cooperatives never had a chance to create a sizable private sector. The law on joint ventures, which the government expected would release a torrent of foreign investment, had no such effect. Only a tiny trickle of investment entered the country, due to the requirement of entering the Soviet Union with a Soviet partner, severe restrictions on repatriating profits, and the near impossibility of sourcing inputs in the Soviet Union or of freely selling output in the country. The law on state enterprises was expressly designed to get state enterprises to operate the way businesses do in a market economy – meaning that the enterprises would keep and balance their own books, wean themselves from state subsidies, and operate in the black. The problem here was that enterprise managers, while being told to act like capitalists, were not given the incentive (a profit motive), or the information (market prices), or the ability (the right to hire and dismiss employees and to ignore planning directives) to act like capitalists. The law did not have its intended effect.

At the same time that he pursued economic reform partially and inconsistently, Gorbachev also adopted policies that accelerated the Soviet economic decline. The government undertook a binge of foreign borrowing and pursued monetary policies that were alternately confiscatory and inflationary (though inflation remained partially repressed due to fixed prices). By the end of the Soviet period, the Soviet government's monetary policy had become reckless by any standard, be it market/capitalist or Soviet/planned.

Largely as a result of Gorbachev's inconsistent reforms and the collapse of the Soviet state in 1991, Yeltsin and his associates inherited an economy in ruins. At the time of the dissolution of the Soviet regime, major cities, including Moscow, were suffering from shortages of basic goods that were acute even by Soviet standards. Anything resembling normal production and distribution of goods had evaporated. In 1991, inflation topped 160 percent and industrial output fell by 15 percent. In this environment, Yeltsin entrusted economic reform to a group of young, inexperienced, liberal economists led by Egor Gaidar, who served as acting prime minister between January and December of 1991, and Anatolii Chubais, who headed the State Property Committee and presided over the privatization program.

Gaidar-Chubais had five major aims. The goals required a new liberal policy doctrine that indeed merited the label "shock therapy." First, Gaidar-Chubais sought to get the state out of the business of setting prices. To this end, they drew up a plan for rapid price liberalization. They intended to render redundant and irrelevant the mighty lords of the state planning agencies, Gosplan and Gostsen, that ruled the Soviet economy. Second, Gaidar-Chubais sought to reduce the size of the government budget deficit, which had multiplied many times over during the Gorbachev years. Any move toward greater fiscal discipline required drastic, permanent reductions in state subsidies to enterprises, which Gaidar-Chubais intended to carry out. Third, they wanted to create a modern banking sector. Fourth, they desired to clear the obstacles to small-scale private business activity. To this end, they wanted to undertake massive deregulation and allow private producers and sellers the opportunity to operate freely. Fifth, Gaidar-Chubais intended to carry out rapid, large-scale privatization of state-owned enterprises. The goals were a form of privatization that would create (or at least create the appearance of) widespread ownership, as well as the emergence of a middle class, which they thought would make the return of communism and central planning impossible. Equally importantly, they favored privatization that would include a leading role for outside owners. They feared that buyouts of enterprises by their managers and employees would not create the needed stimulus to restructure enterprises and enhance efficiency (Berger, 1992; Filippov, 1994; "Parlament ostanovil protsess," 1993; Vulf, 1992).

The proponents of gradualism favored a different course. They were represented prominently among politicians by the speaker of the Supreme Soviet, Ruslan Khasbulatov, and the vice-president, Aleksandr Rutskoi, who broke with Yeltsin in 1992. The gradualist position was also championed by Arkadii Volskii, the head of the Russian Union of Industrialists and Entrepreneurs (RUIE; RSPP in Russian), who had worked as a top industrial manager in government from the time of Andropov until the end of the Gorbachev period. Volskii spoke for many enterprise directors.

162

Khasbulatov-Rutskoi-Volskii favored gradual, piecemeal price liberalization, rather than lifting controls across the board. They strenuously opposed slashing government subsidies for enterprises and favored continued large-scale deficit spending. They had little interest in reforming the banking sector. Stimulating new small-business entry was a low priority. They did not favor dramatic deregulation of economic activity and did not assign great value to sparking new business start-ups. They supported privatization of large-scale enterprises, but they sought insider privatization, rather than sales to outsiders. In practice, they favored granting ownership rights to sitting enterprise managers. Khasbulatov touted what he called a "third way" between socialism and capitalism and held that insider privatization, which he said created "collective ownership," was the way to the third way. Many enterprise managers found this program appealing (Appel, 2004; Khasbulatov, 1992; Parkhomenko, 1992).

The third camp was represented most clearly by Gennadii Ziuganov and the forces that he pulled together to form the Communist Party of the Russian Federation (CPRF). While his economic program was in general poorly articulated, Ziuganov clearly was not enamored with the market. Despite professions that he realized that the state could not own everything, he wanted to restore central planning and preserve state ownership of the means of production. He had little use for either the first or the third way; he preferred the second. He opposed liberalizing prices and doing away with Gosplan. The idea of cutting the government's budget deficit did not appeal to him in the conditions of 1991 and 1992, though returning to pre-Gorbachev Soviet-style fiscal discipline once the command economy was back on its feet made good sense to him. Reducing state regulation of the economy and spurring small-business starts, in contrast, made no sense, since he did not like small private enterprises or economic destatization. Privatizing large enterprises was not on his agenda. Unlike Khasbulatov-Rutskoi-Volskii, Ziuganov was no gradualist; he was a restorationist. He regarded a Soviet-style command economy, infused with an Andropovite spirit of administrative discipline and shorn of the half-hearted compromises with the market that Gorbachev initiated, as superior to the alternatives.

How did the struggle over policy turn out? Ziuganov and his restorationists got virtually nothing. After Yeltsin won the violent showdown with the motley coalition of his opponents in the fall of 1993, the restorationists had to adjust their plans. The restorationists took another hit when Yeltsin beat Ziuganov in the 1996 presidential contest, leaving Ziuganov and the

CPRF to pursue what Boris Kapustin (2000) has called "left-conservatism," meaning a defensive effort to preserve or restore some Soviet-era amenities (also Flikke, 1999). For many restorationists the dream never died, but lack of progress toward reviving the old system reshaped the policy orientations of many in this camp.

The real battle was between the shock therapists and the gradualists. At the onset of the post-Soviet period, the shock therapists seemed to have the upper hand. Yeltsin enjoyed overwhelming authority as well as decree powers, and he placed his trust in Gaidar. In January 1992, the government freed prices on most items, including almost all consumer goods, and presented a budget that slashed subsidies for enterprises, including and especially military industry. Yeltsin signed a decree that essentially legalized trucking and bartering. Chubais presided over a voucher privatization program whose stated goal was to create a broad stratum of small property owners.

Yet, while the shock therapists won on early price liberalization, immediately after that their command began to erode. Gaidar's plans for restructuring state spending and especially for slashing cheap state credits to enterprises encountered the powerful opposition of enterprise directors, many of whom were represented by Volskii. The directors were well represented in parliament and enjoyed Khasbulatov's and Rutskoi's sympathy. In April 1992, Yeltsin gave a speech in which he promised to consult more closely with parliament, and he followed through by appointing Georgii Khizha and Viktor Chernomyrdin as deputy prime ministers. Khizha, the former director of a large military enterprise, managed to overturn parts of Gaidar's plan to slash spending on military industry. The government also reversed itself on aspects of price liberalization, freezing gas and oil prices. By midsummer, Gaidar's control over policy was waning. Yeltsin perceived the need to compromise with opponents in parliament and in the factories, and he justifiably feared the consequences of a sharp rise in unemployment at a time when many Russians were already reeling from years of economic chaos. In December, Yeltsin gave in to pressure from Khasbulatov-Rutskoi-Volskii and replaced Gaidar with Chernomyrdin, a veteran manager of Gazprom, the behemoth state gas company. Chernomyrdin, who had good relations with the captains of Soviet industry and with many of Yeltsin's opponents in parliament, announced that the period of "market romanticism" was past (McFaul, 2001; Shokhin, 1995).

It had been a short romance. Gaidar had guided economic policy for less than a year, and only for about the first third of that year had Yeltsin wholeheartedly supported his policies. After that, the program of forcing

164

enterprises to sink or swim was abandoned, and the government ran prodigious deficits and borrowed from abroad even more prodigiously. Chernomyrdin did not prove friendly to the restorationists' policy preferences, but nor did he embrace Gaidar's shock therapy. During the Chernomyrdin years, Yeltsin was concerned above all with stabilizing the macroeconomic situation without following Gaidar's unabashedly liberal policies. The resulting policy doctrine was a strange cocktail that required extravagant fiscal chicanery, which included covering government deficits by issuing short-term bonds with astronomical interest rates, spending tens of billions of (borrowed) dollars to sustain an overvalued ruble, forcing Gazprom to provide free energy to enterprises, and adopting tax policies that were at once confiscatory and ineffective. The tax policies allowed enterprises to keep virtually none of their profits, but the government had little ability to enforce its own tax laws. The policies created a class of well-bribed tax inspectors, a bankrupt national treasury, and enterprise managers who often had to spend as much energy cooking their books as they did producing (Freeland, 2000).

Policy on banking also amounted to a peculiar and largely inauspicious mix. During the first several years of the post-Soviet period and again between 1998 and 2002, the Central Bank was directed by Viktor Gerashchenko, who had headed Gosbank, the Soviet-era state bank, during the 1980s. Gerashchenko was a favorite of the gradualists. His policy preferences ran in the direction of generosity to enterprises, regardless of the effect on price stability. After taking over as head of the Central Bank in July 1992, he launched a policy of printing money and boosting credits to enterprises, which quickly undermined Gaidar's plans for bridling inflation. By the end of 1992, Central Bank credits amounted to 31 percent of GDP, and monthly inflation was running in double digits. In terms of administrative style, Gerashchenko was the epitome of the holdover Soviet bureaucrat: cunning in guarding his fiefdom, unimaginative, and opposed to modernization or transparency in his agency. He vigorously resisted reforms in the banking sector, including liberalization that would have allowed some foreign banks to operate in Russia (Granville, 1995; Mereu, 2002).

The massive deregulation that proponents of shock therapy wanted in order to spark large-scale start-ups of small businesses simply never occurred. Russian businesses throughout the 1990s and early 2000s were among the most highly – and arbitrarily – regulated in the world. The unwieldy and irrational tax system ensured that harassment by tax inspectors would be an institutionalized part of doing business. Constant inspections by bribe-seeking police and by officials from agencies of public health and sanitation, energy consumption, fire inspection, licensing and certification, and sundry other agencies, in addition to harassment by private criminal groups, severely depressed new business start-ups. It was only after Yeltsin that the Putin government, in an attempt to lighten the regulatory burden, would be able to push through reforms that included banning multiple inspections of a single business by a given agency over a period of less than two years, fixing the fees required for the acquisition of licenses and permits, and setting a five-year minimum on the life span of licenses. While the reforms might eventually help reduce the regulatory burden, surveys conducted in 2002 and 2003 showed that most small businesses in Russia continued to endure frequent, multiple inspections by single agencies, pay more than the legally established price for licenses, receive licenses that are valid for less than the legally prescribed time period, and experience police harassment. Hiring "consultants" with close ties to local administrations in order to obtain licenses and certifications and reduce the frequency of visits by grasping inspectors remains common practice for private businesses (Bianova and Selivanova, 2003; Centre for Economic and Financial Research, 2003; Frye, 2002[b]; Frye and Shleifer, 1997).

Finally, large-scale privatization took place, but it was not the type that the liberals in Russia sought or that liberals in power in any other post-communist country implemented. The first major stage of privatization, launched in the fall of 1992, involved the distribution of vouchers to the population as a whole. The vouchers could be invested as their holders wished. While appearing to spread property broadly, the program had no such effect. In conformity with the preferences of Khasbulatov-Rutskoi-Volskii, recipients of vouchers received special incentives to invest their vouchers in their own workplaces. In practice, management bought up employees' vouchers and assumed formal ownership rights over their enterprises. Such "nomenklatura privatization" dominated the process: Fully two-thirds of privatized enterprises were acquired by their sitting managers. This was the structure of ownership that Chubais had opposed. He thought that such an outcome, which excluded a large role for outside ownership and which involved minimal change in patterns of authority in the workplace, would not stimulate enterprise restructuring and would simply reproduce Soviet-era patterns of proprietorship. But Chubais compromised mightily in order to speed up privatization. According to Hilary Appel (2004, p. 85), he accepted management-employee buyouts even though he "recognized that this form was preferred by Khasbulatov and others in the legislature." Chubais's desire to get destatization moving, according to Appel, overrode his plans to do it right (also Kokh, 1998; Kryshtanovskaya and White, 1996; Rutland, 1994).

Chubais continued to compromise in the loans-for-shares privatization program of 1995 and 1996. In this scheme, the government handed out huge blocs of shares in the largest and most valuable firms to a clique of banks as security against loans that these banks made to the state. Soon after granting the shares in exchange for the loans, the government sold the enterprises to the same banks for a fraction of their real worth. The banks had been established during the late Soviet and early post-Soviet periods as currency speculation machines and magnets for attracting cheap state credits. Their owners now found themselves in an extraordinarily favorable situation. The enterprises were sold at what amounted to closed auctions, some of which were actually organized by the buyers themselves.

The combination of management-employee buyouts and rigged auctions created an economy dominated by Financial-Industrial Groups (FIGs), most of which encompassed a large bank or productive enterprise at the top and an affiliated network of smaller enterprises. By 1996, the FIGs in some ways resembled the prewar Japanese *zaibatsu* or the postwar Korean *chaebol* in their enormity, their complexity, and their intimate ties with the state. Indeed, many high officials who favored a statist approach, preeminently the first deputy prime minister, Oleg Soskovets, characterized the FIGs in precisely such terms. They cast the FIGs as the fruits of a policy that staked out a middle way between free market capitalism and the Soviet-style command economy. According to Soskovets and others, the policies that led to the formation of the FIGs were especially appropriate for Russia, where the state had traditionally played a leading role in the economy and where the necessity of playing catch-up with the advanced industrialized West dictated the necessity of *dirigisme*, the concentration of capital, and hierarchical organization ("Glava gosudarstva podderzhal FPG," 1996; Johnson, 1997; Soskovets, 1996).

The privatization program transferred ownership rights from the state to private entities. In strictly formal terms, by 1996 private enterprise produced more than half of output. But the private sector that the policies of 1992–6 spawned was a profoundly peculiar creature. It was made from above and enmeshed with state agencies on all levels. Its ownership structure was opaque and its system of corporate governance arbitrary. What was truly private, half private and half public, or mostly public – or controlled in one way or another by the state regardless of formal ownership – was unclear.

None of the government's economic polices (with the exception of early price liberalization) had much to do with the liberals' initial intentions or with economic liberalism. In fiscal policy, banking reform, deregulation of small-business activity, and privatization, neither the shock therapists nor their diametric opposites, the restorationists, got much of what they wanted. Rather, the gradualists, with their preference for high government spending, aversion or indifference to deregulation, and advocacy of privatization that would ensconce Soviet-era management and reproduce Soviet-era paternalism and hierarchy, won most of the battles. Russia's economic policy differed starkly from that pursued by governments that wholeheartedly embraced the market, such as those in the Czech Republic, Estonia, and Poland. Economic liberalization also fared worse in Russia than in some countries that embraced the market only belatedly or haphazardly, such as Bulgaria, Mongolia, Romania, and Slovakia. At the same time, however, Russia made more of a move to the market than the most conservative postcommunist countries. Prices were freed early, some space – however cramped – for small-scale private enterprise emerged, and privatization of state assets occurred. Russia was no Uzbekistan, which moved from an autarkic economy with a planning system run by the Communist Party and administered from Moscow to an autarkic economy with a planning system run by a dictator and administered from Tashkent. Russia's low-to-middling rating on economic reform shown in Tables 6.6, 6.7, and 6.8 is justified by the evidence.

Those who won most of the battles in Russia were not, of course, the authors of a finely crafted, phased-in program of institution-building-followed-by-careful-liberalization advocated by Western critics of neoliberalism. Even if one assumes that such an approach to economic reform is optimal, it was scarcely possible in the post-Soviet Russian environment. It was more romantic in its view of "institution building" than was the liberal plans' view of "marketization." As Stephen Kotkin (2001, p. 116) has asked rhetorically, speaking of Western critics of rapid economic reform: "Who was supposed to have implemented their suggested state-led 'gradualist' policies – the millions of officials who had betrayed the Soviet state and enriched themselves in the bargain?"

Kotkin is right to suggest that there was no cadre of competent, incorruptible officials waiting in the wings, ready to fashion the proper institutions and then launch a controlled program of destatization – all without touching the public purse. In fact, such a cadre existed nowhere in the postcommunist world. "Gradualism" of the type touted by so many

Western academic critics of shock therapy happened nowhere. Something approaching genuine "shock therapy," in the sense of rapid, thoroughgoing liberalization, took place only in the Czech Republic, Estonia, and Poland. The Czech Republic's government did maintain more state involvement in social welfare provision than its radical rhetoric admitted, and Poland's leaders did delay the privatization of large enterprises. But on the whole, leaders in both countries, like their counterparts in Estonia, undertook rapid destatization of their economies, including wholesale deregulation that sparked a surge of new business starts (Winiecki, 2002). Less shocking but still extensive liberalization took place in Hungary, Lithuania, Mongolia, Romania, Slovakia, and Slovenia. Still less shocking liberalization – in practice, reform of the Khasbulatov-Rutskoi-Volskii type – was implemented in Russia. Full nonreform characterized economic policy in Uzbekistan, Belarus, and Turkmenistan. But in no country did agents of the state straighten out institutions – organize a civil service, get the property-rights laws right, rebuild the agencies of law enforcement – and then proceed with prudent, incremental economic reform. Governments had the ability to liberalize more or less rapidly and thoroughly. But no governments even remotely had the capacity to execute the nimble, state-led adjustment programs and institution-building campaigns that so many opponents of rapid liberalization in the West have advocated.

The View from Below: The Microenvironment

State penetration of economic life in Russia cannot be understood fully by examining policy doctrine alone. It must be lived to be wholly appreciated, though a few examples will suffice to illustrate the phenomenon. The way that many people experience the state's presence in their everyday lives has not changed markedly since Soviet times, and most state agencies operate the way they did for most of the twentieth century. Vladimir Pastukhov, a lawyer and professor at the Moscow School of Economics, rightly notes: "The everyday life of Russians largely depends on the nature of their relations to various administrative agencies" (2002, p. 72). What is more, "The main principle of postcommunist law is the presumption of guilt on the part of economic actors. Whatever freedoms are proclaimed for the latter, however much control of economic activities is liberalized, contemporary Russian law is constructed in such a way that economic actors must prove their innocence with regard to the law at any stage in the realization of their rights." Such a condition leads logically to "the overdevelopment of control mechanisms at the expense of mechanisms for the law's realization" (p. 69; also Barkhatova, 2000).

Pastukhov cites numerous examples of how the system works in practice. His account of how one goes about receiving medicines shipped from abroad is instructive (pp. 69–70):

By definition, humanitarian aid should not be subject to customs duties when crossing the state border. Registration of documents to transport humanitarian aid is done by the State Customs Committee. But the State Customs Committee can accept documents for consideration only if it receives special permission from the Interdepartmental Commission for Humanitarian Aid under the Government of the Russian Federation, which meets once in two months and considers each case of importation of humanitarian aid as submitted by the commission secretariat. The secretariat prepares these cases requesting the same documents as the customs. But the Commission for Humanitarian Aid will not even consider the matter if permission is not received from the pertinent ministry. In the most common cases, involving medicine deliveries, the relevant ministry would be that of health. In order to apply to the Interdepartmental Commission for Humanitarian Aid, it is therefore necessary to obtain approval in the Humanitarian Aid Department of the Health Ministry of the Russian Federation. This approval, in its turn, can be given provided there is permission to import humanitarian aid from the regional health committee for the region for which the humanitarian aid is intended, and also if an expert opinion is furnished on the quality of the medicine. This must come from a research institute in the Ministry of Health system (this service usually requires payment) as well as the Pharmaceutical Committee and several other less-important organizations. Only after collecting all of these documents is it possible to return to the Customs Committee, where the freight has been in a temporary warehouse and where each day of storage is paid at a commercial rate. If all the paperwork is in order, the shipment is moved from the temporary customs warehouse to the recipient's own storage facility. But this does not mean that it can be used right away. In order to obtain permission to use the humanitarian aid released by customs, it is necessary to register the entire procedure, up to this point, with the State Tax Inspectorate and the Main Department to Combat Economic Crimes in the Internal Affairs Ministry. And only when the last two agencies grant permission, is it possible to begin using the aid. But subsequent supervision is carried out by all six agencies every month, each in its field. In order to provide an idea of the extent of supervisory control, it suffices to point out that in the case of deliveries of vaccines or other injected substances, the Committee for Humanitarian Aid requires the recipient of the humanitarian aid to give account of the aid in the shape of used syringes, which must be collected from each doctor making the injections together with a filled-out form.

Pastukhov notes that "a normal person" would never be willing or able to work this system. Thus, "it is natural that with the existence of such obstacles only an out-and-out criminal pursuing personal gain and with

170

hidden motives would agree voluntarily to go through such administrative ordeals." Furthermore, "since this person is a criminal he will pay for the officials' work at every step in the process of approval" (p. 70).

Even changing one's residence requires Herculean effort, as many Russian citizens know from personal experience. Here is how one gets permission (Pastukhov, p. 73):

In order to register at a new address, as the result, say, of the purchase of a new apartment, a Muscovite must take the following steps. First of all, it is necessary to obtain from the passport official at the housing office of one's former residence a special form to cancel the old registration; one must wait several days for this form, since it is issued at the local Internal Affairs section, to which he or she cannot apply directly, while the passport offices receive documents through the housing office. Second, it is necessary to go to the passport official in the housing office of the new residence for preliminary confirmation of the new registration. It is necessary to wait for a few days at this point, as well, since confirmation is also done through the passport office of the Internal Affairs section. The citizen must now return with the same form to the passport lady at the previous residence and submit documents to cancel registration. Once you receive, several days later, the passport with a stamp canceling the old registration from the same Internal Affairs section, you must once again apply with a request to be registered at the new place of residence with the whole package of accumulated documents. It is possible, after a few more days of waiting, to get the passport with the registration stamp indicating the new place of residence. This procedure can take much longer if it turns out, at one of the stages, that some paper is missing from the package of documents. For example, it is necessary to submit at every point in the journey, in addition to papers confirming the right to live at the new place of residence, a certain document based on the tenants register at the previous residence, a copy of the financial account, and a certificate confirming the absence of any arrears. If a minor is involved in the process, special permission from the guardianship and wardship agencies may be required. If, God forbid, the applicant is divorced, notarized approval from the former spouse (whose place of residence, after all, might be unknown) may be required. In view of the need to have at hand the complete package of these and other documents, and taking into account the fact that passport officials in housing offices work three days a week, and, as a rule, the queues waiting outside their offices are so long that, realistically, it is not possible to be received within one day, one must expect that the registration procedure at a new place of residence could last for months. Meanwhile, the citizen who does not have the final registration cannot send his children to school, receive a medical-insurance policy, or solve any of the big or little problems of everyday life.

Operating a business, which sometimes may require something as radical as hiring someone from out of town, is an entirely different game in Russia than it is elsewhere. So too is running a household. Even in most other postcommunist countries, citizens need not endure such statization of daily life.

The costs of the persistence of the Soviet-era regulatory bureaucracy in Russia are immense. Evgenii Iasin, a former minister of the economy, has assembled a team to investigate conditions and calculate the price. According to Iasin's analysts, small businesses each year spend $850 million on coping with the myriad inspections and requirements for approvals, $400 million in "voluntary contributions" to bureaucrats' pet projects, and $3.3 billion on bribes to individual officials to gain the opportunity to lease property from government agencies. The total cost of official harassment of small business therefore amounts to $4.55 billion, or 1.6 percent of GDP. This sum does not include taxes or any other legally legitimate expenses. Given such conditions, it is unsurprising that as of the beginning of 2003, only 800,000 small businesses were registered in Russia. This works out to about six small businesses per 1,000 people in Russia; the analogous figure in the EU is 30. The number of small businesses per 1,000 inhabitants in the fastest-liberalizing East European economies, including the Czech Republic and Poland, approaches the EU norm. The difference between such countries and Russia is due to the pace of new business start-ups in the postcommunist period. While conclusive cross-regional data from Russia are not yet available, there is evidence that the (relatively few) provinces whose governors have made a strong and sustained effort to ease the regulatory burden have witnessed greater-than-average growth of small-scale private entrepreneurship ("Data on Small Moscow Businesses Posted," 2003; Khakamada, 2003; Kihlgren, 2002; Nechaeva, 2002; Petro, 1999).

In sum, Russia did move away from full-blown, Soviet-style state control over the economy. The plan-and-command system began to wither during the late 1980s and underwent an unceremonious demise in the 1990s. But it was not replaced by a market economy. Instead, the reforms that Russia's post-Soviet leaders pursued spurred the rise of what may be dubbed a racket economy (Breslauer, 1992; Fish, 1998[c]). This creature is defined by the intimate proximity of public and private economic power, even despite the movement of a great deal of property into private hands, and the presence of a regulatory hand that is at once grasping, fumbling, and arbitrary.

Why the Myth of Shock Therapy?

Considering the availability of evidence to the contrary, why have so many Western scholars claimed that the Russian government undertook radical

172

liberalization and destatization of the economy, and why have so many blamed the failures of democratization on such policies? Even more importantly, why have so many Russians identified their postcommunist economic crisis with shock therapy, rather than with the aftereffects of six decades of Stalinist planning? Several interrelated facts may explain the phenomenon.

Yeltsin's rhetoric during the second half of the Gorbachev period, when Yeltsin was emerging as the most popular politician in Russia, indeed differed radically from Gorbachev's argot of commitment to "market socialism" and half-hearted economic reforms. By 1990, Yeltsin was embracing capitalism without qualification. In 1990, when Gorbachev instructed his pro-market advisers and his conservative prime minister to work out a middle way on economic reform, Yeltsin accused Gorbachev of trying to mate a hedgehog and a snake. If socialism was the hedgehog, Yeltsin liked the snake. Unlike many pro-reform intellectuals who surrounded him, moreover, Yeltsin did not bother with the niceties of whether a Swedish, Korean, or some other market "model" would be most appropriate for Russia. He knew, and he said he knew, that all command economies were disasters and that capitalism seemed to work. That was what mattered.

Yeltsin took charge of the economy at the end of the Soviet period without changing his tune. He appeared fiercely intent on transforming his rhetoric into reality. With considerable fanfare he appointed Gaidar, Chubais, and several other young, pro-Western, pro-market economists to oversee economic policy. Gaidar's and Chubais's own rhetoric was even more fundamentally and consistently pro-capitalist than Yeltsin's. Gaidar and Chubais believed in the market like Nikita Khrushchev believed in the plan – they really believed. They fully embraced the slogan of Václav Klaus, the architect of the Czech Republic's economic reform: "The Third Way is the way to the Third World." They lived in the homeland of the Second Way and knew where that path led. The First Way – capitalism – seemed vastly preferable to the alternatives.

The team that took over economic policy at the outset of the post-Soviet period was, therefore, vocally and vociferously liberal. It was also articulate and youthful. This combination of traits – in Russian policymakers no less – guaranteed that the team got a great deal of media attention, in Russia and abroad. What is more, reform did start with a bang. Gaidar's price liberalization produced a near-trebling of prices. By the end of 1992, the streets of Russian cities, gray and commercially moribund for nearly three-quarters of a century, teemed with small-scale traders parked behind makeshift tables and kiosks. The reformers sounded radical and the reforms, at first, looked dramatic. Furthermore, since coverage in the media of most events the world over tends to focus on the initial stages of any given process, the images that stuck in the minds of many were Yeltsin's and Gaidar's dramatic statements, the angry pensioners who lost savings in the inflation that followed price liberalization, and the long-bare shelves in shops quickly filling up with goods that Russians had not seen for years – or had never seen at all.

The problem was that the reforms were not sustained – or, more precisely, that the highly liberal character of the doctrine was diluted and then undone as Yeltsin encountered resistance and sought to placate his opponents. He quickly abandoned most of his lieutenants who were set on radically reducing state subsidies to enterprises and dismantling the agencies that maintain the sovietesque relations between the people and the bureaucracy depicted in the long passages quoted in the previous section.

And yet he left one major liberal (Chubais) in charge of a very important policy (privatization). Even as most of Yeltsin's original team of liberals filed out and were replaced with more cautious figures, Chubais remained in place and presided over the destatization of property. As mentioned, however, Chubais had to give at every step – and he proved to be a willing compromiser. Chubais's motives for shifting strategies are hard to know. He might have felt that rapid destatization of any type was better than nonprivatization, particularly given the risk of a comeback by restorationists. George Soros (2000) shares this view. In an article published in 2000 (p. 15), he stated: "In my opinion [Chubais] is a genuine reformer who sold his soul to the devil in order to fight what he called the red-brown menace, a combination of nationalism and socialism, which he believed would come to dominate Russia unless he did something to prevent it." Perhaps Chubais was motivated by naked self-interest; he did, after all, end up profiting handsomely from the privatization process. Whatever his motives, Chubais abandoned his earlier commitment to transparency of process and outside ownership of firms and his resistance to management-employee buy-outs.

Yet Chubais had established an unshakable reputation as a liberal crusader before privatization was carried out. Thus, many observers naturally associated the privatization program with Chubais's (and Gaidar's) earlier liberal idealism – though privatization, as carried out, was driven at least as much by political as by economic concerns and was extremely corrupt.

What is more, Yeltsin – the face of the new, noncommunist Russia – fended off opponents and remained in power until the end of the 1990s.

174

He vanquished some of the highest-profile gradualists – most notably, Khasbulatov and Rutskoi – in the October 1993 battle that ended with his shelling of the parliament building. He defeated his strongest foe among the restorationists, Ziuganov, in the 1996 presidential election, and Yeltsin's hand-picked successor beat Ziuganov again in 2000. Furthermore, the restorationists realized none of their major goals in the first post-Soviet decade. Despite the impressive showing of Zhirinovskii's LDPR in the 1993 parliamentary elections and of Ziuganov's CPRF in the parliamentary elections of 1995 and 1999, the extreme nationalists and the communists had little serious influence on policy. The real battle was between the forces I am calling the shock therapists and the gradualists. Yeltsin's retention of power and Chubais's leading role in privatization could, and often did, create the impression that the shock therapists won and controlled policy. Yet as both the cross-national comparative analysis and the actual trajectory of policy change recounted here show, the policy that Russia adopted during the first post-Soviet decade was decidedly not shock therapy.

The behavior of international lending institutions may have also clouded the picture. The IMF usually insists upon liberalization in exchange for loans, and Russia received a great deal of money from the IMF during the Yeltsin years. While the IMF sometimes withheld this or that portion of a multibillion dollar loan to protest the Russian government's unresponsiveness to its advice, in the end the Fund always coughed up. Bad behavior – indeed, even the market-ignoring and market-distorting behavior that brought on the crash of 1998 – prompted the Fund to rush in on the eve of the debacle with a promise of a fresh infusion of $23 billion. Russia is not Haiti or Bolivia. International lending institutions have never been in a position, or at least never considered themselves to be in a position, to tell the Russian government to take or leave a package of loans and conditions. With Russia, they made the loans and looked the other way (Hedlund, 2000). Part of the problem might have stemmed from simple incompetence, ignorance, or lack of will on the part of IMF officials. As noted in Chapter 3, the Fund's remarkably lenient policy was probably also rooted in a feeling among the international community's leading governments that the Russian economy simply could not be "allowed" to fail. Whatever the reasons for its policy, the IMF bolstered the impression that Russia was right on the liberal track – even long after it had run off it completely.

Thus, there are good explanations for why so many people, Russians and outside observers alike, have incorrectly believed that Russia pursued shock therapy. Still, the belief is mistaken. Russia did not, compared to other postcommunist countries or in view of its own liberal policymakers' designs, implement radical liberalization.

The Consequences of Economic Statism for Open Politics in Russia

The economic statism described in this chapter has hindered democratization in Russia. The consequence is consistent with the theoretical propositions outlined in the discussion of the case for shock therapy.

The Weakness of Organized Opposition and Civil Society

The first inauspicious effect is the feebleness of organizations that engage in competition for public office and particularly opposition organizations. As Marc Howard (2003) has shown in a major empirical study, the strength of political and civil associations in postcommunist countries is substantially lower than in postauthoritarian polities outside the postcommunist world. Even by postcommunist standards, however, the size and strength of associations in Russia is modest. The disadvantages that such organizations face vis-à-vis the state may help account for their weakness.

The main organizations that contest elective office in most polities, including in Russia, are political parties. According to many scholars, parties are the linchpin in state–society relations. They enjoy a degree of legitimacy that, due to their aims for advancing the causes of particular groups, interest associations cannot pretend to attain (Key, 1961; Kitschelt, 1992; Lipset, 1960; Rose, Munro, and White, 2001; Sartori, 1976). In Russia, political parties are diminutive and relatively marginal. The CPRF, which benefits from the prior loyalties of holdover members of the Communist Party of the Soviet Union, is the largest party, with a membership of one-half million. United Russia, the conglomeration of the Unity party, which was created by the presidential apparatus in late 1999, and the Fatherland and All Russia parties, which several provincial chiefs formed on the eve of the same elections, claimed 400,000 members as of August 2003, though this figure may be inflated. No other party exceeds 100,000 in formal membership.

Table 6.9 shows figures for the percentage of the population made up of people who called themselves active members of political parties in postcommunist countries as of 1995. The picture has not changed dramatically since that time. As the table shows, Russia ranks low. Less than 1 percent of the population is active in parties. It merits mention that Albania's

Table 6.9. *Percentage of the Population Active in Political Parties, 1995, Postcommunist Region*

Albania	13.17	Azerbaijan	1.80
Macedonia	5.73	Slovenia	1.30
Romania	5.08	Armenia	1.15
Croatia	2.77	Lithuania	1.09
Hungary	2.62	Moldova	0.91
Georgia	2.59	**Russia**	**0.78**
Czech Republic	2.54	Ukraine	0.64
Bulgaria	2.24	Estonia	0.59
Slovakia	2.20	Belarus	0.43

Source: World Values Survey 1995, as reported in Raiser et al., 2002.

Table 6.10. *Multiple Regression of Percentage of the Population Active in Political Parties on Hypothesized Determinants, Postcommunist Region*

Variable	
Constant	25.27***
	(6.48)
Economic	−8.32**
development	(2.15)
Cumulative Economic	1.18*
Liberalization Index, 1989–97	(0.42)
Adj. R^2	.44

$N = 18$ countries.
*p < 0.05; **p < 0.01; ***p < 0.001

conspicuously high rate of activism in parties has been recorded consistently across successive waves of the World Values Surveys. Public participation in groups of other types also tends to be high in Albania; Albanians are, in regional perspective, "joiners" (Inglehart et al., 2004).

Does economic liberalization affect participation in parties? It might. Table 6.10 presents the results of a regression of party activism on the CELI and a control for economic development. Economic liberalization, measured as the CELI, is statistically significant. The effect is not overwhelming; the entire range of the CELI, which is measured as 0–1, is associated with a 1.18 percent difference in the size of the population that participates actively in parties. Still, since in no country in the region does the proportion of the population active in parties reach even 6 percent (with the exception of Albania), a 1 percent difference in the dependent variable is substantial.

The next step is to assess whether participation in parties affects political openness. There is some evidence that it does. In a partial correlation controlling for economic development, the relationship between the proportion of the population active in parties and VA scores is noteworthy (r = .47, p < .05). The available evidence suggests that economic liberalization might aid the growth of parties and that the growth of parties might, in turn, facilitate political openness.

It is impossible precisely to assess the role that enduring economic statization has on party development. But several facts suggest that the weakness of economic liberalization retards the growth and maturation of parties. There is a substantial literature on parties in post-Soviet Russia, and many writings note parties' underdevelopment. Many studies also note parties' shortage of resources (S. Hanson, 2003; Ishiyama, 1999; Kolosov, 1995; McFaul, 1997; Pshizova, 1998; Stoner-Weiss, 2001; White, Rose, and McAllister, 1997; Wyman, White, and Oates, eds., 1998). I arrived at a similar conclusion following my field research during the late 1990s and early 2000s. While parties are better developed in some provinces than others, well-endowed organizations are rare.

The exception, however, is the party supported by the presidential administration. Whichever party that is, it is invariably flush and has much more money to spend in electoral campaigns than does its competitors (Colton and McFaul, 2000; Fish, 1997; Petrov, 2003[c]; Urban, 1994). Such was the case with Democratic Choice of Russia (DCR) in 1993, Our Home Is Russia (OHR) in 1995, the Unity party in 1999, and United Russia (an amalgam of Unity and the Fatherland-All Russia party) in 2003. Here, the lopsided balance between the resources of the state and those of society comes into bold relief. In each election, the president's favorite party has access to unlimited resources while the other parties do the best they can. In presidential elections, the incumbent has never relied on a party, since he has been able to use the state apparatus, in effect, as his campaign staff.

Part of the problem here is that laws limiting campaign spending are not enforced and the president manages to tap state funds. But societal organizations that oppose the president (or that oppose governors, on the provincial level) also often do not have the wherewithal to fight back. Even the major opposition parties, such as the liberal Iabloko and the leftist CPRF, have relied on meager funding. Such parties have their financial backers, but they do not enjoy a broad base of contributors who can help

Table 6.11. *Percentage of the Population Active in Professional Associations, 1995, Postcommunist Region*

Croatia	6.13	Moldova	1.73
Hungary	6.00	Georgia	1.54
Albania	4.94	Estonia	1.27
Slovenia	4.88	Lithuania	1.19
Macedonia	4.32	**Russia**	**0.88**
Romania	3.71	Azerbaijan	0.85
Czech Republic	3.60	Ukraine	0.85
Slovakia	3.21	Bulgaria	0.56
Armenia	2.35	Belarus	0.14

Source: World Values Survey 1995, as reported in Raiser et al., 2002.

guarantee the parties a voice. As will be discussed in the next chapter, part of the problem is that the distribution of power among state agencies depresses incentives for well-endowed private actors to invest in parties. But part of the problem is also that the socioeconomic backbones of liberal or leftist parties – say, the middle class and industrial workers – are not well developed as groups and do not have a lot to spend on political parties.

Parties are not the only site of organizational weakness. Russia ranks near the bottom on activism in societal organizations of many types. Some of the founders of social science, most prominently Émile Durkheim (1997 and 1992), as well as contemporary theorists of democracy and democratization, including Philippe Schmitter (1992 and 1981) and Paul Hirst (1994), have regarded professional and occupational associations as the social-organizational bedrocks of open politics. Such groups are small in Russia even by postcommunist standards, as is evident in Table 6.11.

Economic liberalization may influence popular participation in professional associations. Table 6.12 shows a regression of membership in professional associations on the CELI, along with the usual control for economic development. The results are broadly similar to those that tested the effects of economic liberalization on party membership.

Furthermore, popular involvement in professional associations might affect political openness. In a partial correlation controlling for economic development, the relationship between the proportion of the population active in professional associations and VA scores is substantial ($r = .47$, $p < .05$). This correlation is precisely the same as that between the proportion of the population active in political parties and VA scores, which was discussed earlier.

Table 6.12. *Multiple Regression of Percentage of the Population Active in Professional Associations on Hypothesized Determinants, Postcommunist Region*

Variable	
Constant	2.39
	(4.10)
Economic	−1.43
development	(1.35)
Cumulative Economic	1.07***
Liberalization Index, 1989–97	(0.27)
Adj. R^2	.49

$N = 18$ countries.
*p < 0.05; **p < 0.01; ***p < 0.001

These analyses provide just one piece of evidence. Data are missing for many countries, and the number of observations is too small for the regression analysis to provide firmly reliable estimates. What is more, measuring the strength of civil society is difficult. The figures on participation in organizations used here are not the only possible measure, though they may be the best source of quantitative data.

The Tenuousness of the Socioeconomic Basis for Civil Society

The management-employee buyouts that predominated in privatization reproduced some Soviet-era patterns of subordination and dependence in the workplace. The free availability of consumer goods in the stores in the post-Soviet setting has reduced managers' control. During the Soviet period, employees often had to rely for the means of subsistence on goods distributed in the workplace. But during the Soviet era, fear of being dismissed weighed only on workers who were politically active; now, the danger of unemployment for all workers is higher. In general, the paternalist nature of authority relations is largely the same as during the Soviet period. Mikhail Kasimov, a longtime pro-democratic activist and a deputy in Perm's oblast Duma, notes:

The urban latifundia that dominated production during the Soviet era are still in place, though some of course are dying. The directors still control their employees and play the big papa. If they play the good papa and seem to fight for their subordinates, they can use their power in the workplace to win a seat here in the Duma. About half of our deputies are enterprise directors and got elected using their employees and their employees' families as their base of support. They enter politics in order to get closer to the governor's office, where everyone knows the power lies, and they can promote their business interests by having better relations with local executive power. Now, obviously this whole system is not very favorable for the organization of opposition to power. I'd like to be able to rely on some independent societal organizations to support me as a deputy here in my efforts to push some reforms, but I'm not an enterprise director, and there really aren't any strong societal organizations on which I can rely. (Kasimov, personal interview, March 2, 2001, Perm)

Such conditions do not empower labor, and help explain the endurance of the dependence and passivity of much of the workforce (Ashwin, 1999; Crowley, 1994; Zaslavsky, 2001).

According to Kasimov, the structure of authority relations in the workplace is not the only check on independent societal organizations. Asked if small-scale entrepreneurs served as a potential base for autonomous organization in society, he replied:

Oh no! Our small and medium businessmen do not stick together at all. They are all in competition with each other, and the fastest way to weaken a competitor is to sic the tax police on him. Just report something, whatever you want, to the tax police. That's how they relate to each other: They sic the police on each other. If the police were not so eager and responsive to accusations, the businesspeople might relate to each other in other ways, but not under these conditions.

Kasimov's reasoning suggests that the threat to small-scale entrepreneurs from officialdom would not be so salient, and something like a "business community" might even have the chance to form, if the regulatory system were not so encompassing and penetrative and if the police were not so omnipresent. Here, the link between the ubiquity of petty officialdom, on the one hand, and the political atomization of a socio-occupational group, on the other, is evident (Barkhatova, 2000).

In broader terms, the predatory regulatory environment has retarded the growth of a new middle class. A middle class has emerged in post-Soviet Russia, but it may be smaller, less self-confident, and less capable of organization than it would be in a situation that afforded entrepreneurs more scope for independent action. Measuring the size and strength of the middle class precisely is impossible, particularly in highly fluid environments. Most analysts who have addressed the matter, however, regard the growth of Russia's middle class as relatively sluggish (Balzer, 1998; Rutkevich, 1997; Zaslavskaia, 1995).

181

   This problem is not lost on policymakers who would like to see faster growth of private enterprise and the middle class. In late 2001, Putin stated: "We, the federal, regional and municipal governments, are to blame for Russia's middle class never developing. Administrative organizations that feed off of small businesses at every stage of its development, including licensing and registration bodies, the fire department and health department, have created a whole market of legalized corruption" (Ostrovsky, 2001). Putin may be unconcerned about the consequences of the middle class's underdevelopment for democracy. But he does care about economic development, and he has stated that the fact that small and medium-sized private businesses in Russia employ just 14 percent of the workforce and account for only 10 percent of GDP – one-fifth the figure in Poland – is an imposing barrier to his economic goals. Putin has repeatedly decried Russia's overdependence on oil – again, apparently not out of concern for oil's debilitating effects on open government, but due to what he regards as the pernicious economic consequences. According to Putin, "Russia will depend on energy exports until it develops a strong layer of small businesses" (Ostrovsky, 2001). Putin's awareness of the problem has led to some reforms, including recent efforts by the federal government to rein in the tax police. As of this writing, however, conditions for businesspeople do not appear to have changed substantially (Easter, 2002; Khakamada, 2003; Nicholson, 2003). The possible effects of recent policy changes on the climate for business and the development of autonomous economic power will be taken up again in the final chapter of the book.

   From the standpoint of the development of an independent entrepreneurial class, one noteworthy and possibly inauspicious trend that bureaucratic regulation and predation has produced is the movement of talent out of ownership of small private firms and into management of large enterprises. Working as a manager in a large firm may be less interesting to many businesspeople, but so too is it less onerous. Vladimir Orlov, a leading businessman in Tomsk, explains the problem in the following terms:

Local administration officials clearly understood that success in elections depends on the availability of funds. Where could the funds come from? Obviously from the businessmen. And not only in the form of taxes, but also as forced sponsorship. Racket on the part of regional administration has become ubiquitous. "Whose are you, boy?" If you're not with anyone you have to choose. In case of resistance there are always means to apply pressure in the form of the tax police. . . . This phenomenon undermines many entrepreneurs. Therefore, an unfortunate tendency has appeared: Entrepreneurs accept positions as hired managers [in large firms]. That way they feel psychologically comfortable or at least there is no forced affiliation: once you're hired [by a large firm] the rules of the game are different. (Orlov, personal communication, September 24, 2003)

Does the size and autonomy of the business class necessarily affect democracy's prospects? Perhaps official predation on businesses is rampant and depresses new start-ups and the growth of existing businesses. But does the development of an entrepreneurial class necessarily advance open politics?

As many writers have shown, middle classes may abandon democracy as quickly as any other groups when their interests are threatened (Rueschemeyer, Stephens, and Stephens, 1992). Still, Marx's and Barrington Moore's assertion that the bourgeoisie is important for democracy's emergence, and Benjamin Constant's claim that those accustomed to commerce are particularly resistant to autocratic interference, may be relevant to Russia. In a study based on an extensive survey, Timothy Frye (2003) found that support for open politics in Russia was especially pronounced among the managers of private firms that were created after 1989. Many factors often considered determinants of political orientation, such as age and level of education, had little effect, while leadership of a new private business was strongly and positively correlated with support for democratic practices. Such evidence is consistent with surveys conducted on the eve of the 1996 presidential election, which showed that among Russians employed in small private businesses, 96 percent supported Yeltsin in the runoff against Ziuganov ("NG – Stsenarii," 1996). Yeltsin's own "democratic" credentials, of course, are open to debate; voting for Yeltsin certainly did not necessarily qualify one as a dyed-in-the-wool democrat. Still, the lack of Ziuganov's commitment to democracy is not open to debate; Ziuganov never pretended to be a democrat. His political sympathies include large dollops of red and brown, but no other hues (Vujacic, 1996). Opposition to Ziuganov may be regarded in some respects as opposition to communism and extreme nationalism, and those who worked in small private businesses were nearly unanimous in their opposition to Ziuganov.

Excursus: Does Civil Society Matter for Open Politics?

Is the strength of society important for open politics? Perhaps economic liberalization does promote the growth of autonomous societal organizations, as suggested. But if civil society is not conducive to democratization, then economic liberalization's positive effect on democratization may not work through its tendency to strengthen civil society.

During the past decade, two major arguments have emerged in the debate over the role of civil society. One judges its impact on democratization as positive. The other regards civil society as at best a neutral force. The latter argument emphasizes the bad apples – in particular, anti-democratic and extremist groups of all types – as well as the possibility of democratization in the absence of strong societal organizations.

The benign image has been advanced mostly by scholars who stand in one or several of the liberal traditions of John Locke, Benjamin Constant, Alexis de Tocqueville, and J. S. Mill. The darker image has also been shared by some contemporary liberals, but is championed mostly by socialists and social democrats, postmodernists, and skeptics who stand in one or several of the nonliberal traditions of G. W. F. Hegel, Karl Marx, Friedrich Nietzsche, and Carl Schmitt. In general, writers who embrace the first image regard society as capable of taking care of itself. They also see maintenance of the primacy of the individual over the group and society over the state as essential to democracy. Scholars who adhere to the latter image are usually less enamored of individualism, more keen on the importance of institutions of control and administration, and less trusting of markets.

The empirical touchstone of the case against civil society is Weimar Germany, where a plethora of nonstate organizations existed at the time that the Nazis seized power. In a celebrated work that figures prominently in the writings of civil-society skeptics, Sheri Berman (1997, p. 402) claims: "During the inter-war period, Germans threw themselves into their clubs, voluntary associations, and professional organizations out of frustration with the national government and political parties, thereby helping undermine the Weimar Republic and facilitate Hitler's rise." Had civil society been weaker, "the Nazis would never have been able to capture so many citizens for their cause or eviscerate their opponents so swiftly." In another piece of civil-society skepticism, Omar Encarnación argues that Chile and Brazil, which lead South America in the density of individual membership in societal organizations, have not been leaders in democratization in Latin America. He goes as far as claiming that civil society, without proper direction from above, may be one of democracy's greatest foes: "Those fronting the revival of civil society have not only failed to recognize that a flourishing of civil society is a poor indicator for forecasting the sustainability of democracy but also that civil society's very existence is premised on the viability of political institutions. In their absence, the construction of a vibrant and robust civil society is likely to remain a fleeting dream but also a threat to democracy itself." Relying upon Samuel Huntington's much-cited conceptual framework, Encarnación asserts that "instability, disorder, and even violence are the likely outcomes of the pairing of highly organized and mobilized publics with low political institutionalization" (Encarnación, 2002, pp. 128–29). Skepticism is also evident in the writings of Peter Evans, who ridicules what he terms the "charisma of civil society" that, he says, has captured all too many hearts and minds (1997, p. 78; see also Armony, 2004; Carothers, 1999–2000; Chambers and Kopstein, 2001).

Such thinking has been applied to Russia and the postcommunist region as well. Stephen Hanson and Jeffrey Kopstein (1997) have conjectured that Russia's weak society may have helped thwart a repetition of the Weimar scenario in the early post-Soviet period. They hold that a stronger society, particularly under conditions of economic stress and national humiliation, would have included a plethora of extremist parties and movements that might have undermined Russia's democratic gains.

The main problem with these arguments is a shortage of empirical support. The evidence even on Nazi Germany is debatable. A temporal correlation between Germans throwing themselves into professional organizations and Hitler's rapid evisceration of his opponents may exist, but Berman's anecdotes do not establish a causal link. Encarnación's analysis of Latin America is also questionable. First, his claim that Chile's post-Pinochet democratization has been especially problematic is open to contrary interpretation. There may be no such thing as a smooth and fully successful regime change, but whatever one's comparative referent, Chilean democratization since the late 1980s has hardly been a failure. Second, Encarnación's claim that civil society has not advanced democracy in Latin America during the 1980s and 1990s is peculiar. In Chile, the lingering shadow of military autonomy undoubtedly deferred the advent of full-blown democracy. But was an overly vigorous civil society to blame? Who sparked and carried through Chile's democratic transition – the Pinochet government's ministers, military officers, and bureaucrats or the social movements and revived political organizations of Chilean civil society? The Brazilian experience also raises questions. Why did the Brazilian military withdraw to the barracks in the 1980s? Did the generals turn out to be democrats, weary of power and eager to usher in a free society? Or did pressure from labor unions, the independent press, and the Catholic Church have something to do with democratization? Would Brazilian politics be more open if Brazil's labor movement were less powerful and its media less assertive?

In practice, in few places affected by political regime change in recent decades has democratization been stymied or democratic regimes destroyed by powerful, politicized societal groups. The Weimar model – assuming Berman's causal story is sound – is exceptional, and analyses that draw on the "lessons" of Weimar for contemporary politics have an anachronistic ring. In every case in the postcommunist region where democratization did not happen or was initiated and then reversed, a top-down dynamic has been at work. Despite a decade and a half of anxious waiting for the rise of mass movements for fascism or the revival of Sovietism, anti-democratic restoration has been effected in no case by such movements. Officeholders attired in cravats have been the agents of political closure. Society's poverty of organization and inability to resist the imposition of autocracy from above has undermined open government or prevented its emergence in the first place.

Aleksandr Lukashenko, the terminator of Belarus's short-lived experience with open politics, was not swept to the presidency in the mid-1990s with a roar of social approval. Instead, he came to office amidst the din of a thin whine of discontent with corruption. No mass societal organization supported him, or for that matter any of his opponents; he was elected strictly on the basis of his ability to convince a demobilized electorate that he would take a few simple measures against corruption. Democratization in Belarus, accordingly, died not with a bang but with a whimper. No grassroots campaign prevailed upon Lukashenko to shut down parliament, emasculate the courts, and assemble hit squads to deal with people he did not like. He did these things on his own initiative and on behalf of his own interests in a context that lacked organized societal forces capable of challenging him. The conversion of Turkmenistan into a shrine to its president, Saparmurat Niyazov (known universally in the Turkmen press as "Turkmenbashi the Great"), did not result from the triumph of a mass movement of Niyazov enthusiasts. Like most other rulers in Central Asia, he converted his Communist Party first secretaryship into the presidency of the newly independent republic in 1990–1. He subsequently thwarted the emergence of challengers and established a dictatorship insulated from popular pressure by the secret police. In Belarus and Turkmenistan, chief executives ran roughshod over inarticulate societies that were poor in autonomous organizations.

In Russia, a similar dynamic has been at work. The agents of de-democratization have been sitting executives, not mass political movements. It was not popular pressure that prompted Yeltsin to order the invasion of Chechnya in December 1994, setting off a conflict that has already endured for a decade and harmed Russian democracy. Public opinion at the time was overwhelmingly opposed to the operation (Lapidus, 1998; Lieven, 1998). Putin did not seize control of the independent electronic media in the wake of an upsurge of popular demands that he do so. Instead, he got away with constricting press freedoms because no one was able to stand up to him. Neither Putin nor Yeltsin, or any governor or republican president, has presided over electoral fraud in response to popular demands or even relied upon societal organizations to carry out his dirty work. The beneficiaries of falsification can and do rely on state agents alone. Stephen Holmes (2003, p. 130) is right to argue, in a discussion of Russia, that "the granular makeup of society disempowers the electoral majority, making it politically impotent." Societal "granularity," or lack of cohesiveness, rather than coherence, has been democratization's foe.

Strong, autonomous societal organizations and networks may not always be democracy's allies, but their absence is almost always democracy's enemy. Societal demobilization, atomization, and passivity – not assertiveness, politicization, and hyperactivity – spell trouble for open politics in the contemporary world, including in the postcommunist region (Bermeo, 2003; Bunce, 2004; Gill, 2000; Green, 2002; Isaac, 2000). Democratization in the postcommunist region, including in Russia, has been derailed behind closed doors, not in the streets.

The State's Leverage over Societal Organizations

This section returns to and completes the discussion of the consequences of economic statism for open politics in Russia. It focuses specifically on how the endurance of economic statism enables politicians to manipulate – and, when they desire, emasculate – societal organization.

A handful of examples help make the point. The first is the well-known case of the state's assault on NTV, formerly the main private television company in Russia. Many well-wishers of press freedom placed great hope in NTV's ability to broadcast information that power holders did not necessarily like, especially after Putin began to tighten the reins on the media. The hope in NTV seemed justified, not only by the pugnacity of its then-owner, Vladimir Gusinskii, but also by NTV's independent status. Many believed that even if Putin insisted on docility in state-owned TV, NTV would still be there to shine light in places the government preferred to keep out of public view. To be sure, NTV was not "objective." Its manager worked for Yeltsin's presidential campaign in 1996. But it was independent.

No one compelled anyone at NTV to work for Yeltsin. What is more, although NTV supported Yeltsin in his campaign against Ziuganov, the network supplied the public with a stream of information that embarrassed high officials, including Yeltsin. It also broadcast grimly incisive reporting from Chechnya during the first war of 1994–6.

But there was a catch: The state owned a stake in NTV. During the Yeltsin period, no one paid any attention to this fact; it seemed irrelevant. But when Putin decided to bring the media to heel, he used state share-holders to take over the company and drive out its independent-minded – and top-caliber – journalists. Putin's agents used Gusinskii's insolvency and alleged financial improprieties as pretexts, claiming that NTV's reporting and independence had nothing to do with their actions. The absurdity of the claim was obvious, but the government still got its way – without firing a shot or even throwing people in jail. Its cut of the company provided the toehold needed to avoid such unpleasantness.

The second example involves producers of goods rather than information. The producers are workers in general, and the organization they make up is the Federation of Independent Trade Unions of Russia (FITUR; FNPR in Russian), the successor to the Soviet-era All-Union Central Committee of Trade Unions (AUCCTU; VTsSPS in Russian). The role of the FITUR's predecessor was largely to support management, which in turn answered to Communist Party authorities. Only secondarily, if at all, did it defend workers. After the Soviet collapse, the union, renamed the FITUR, claimed that it would begin to represent its members in earnest. The FITUR inherited sufficient resources to take on a major role. Its sanatoria, health clinics, children's camps, offices, apartments, and recreational facilities are valued at some $6 billion, and the union generates $300 million per year in income. Membership in the union is high, standing at roughly 40 million. Ninety-five percent of unionized workers in Russia are members.

Nevertheless, the union has joined ranks with management on virtually every issue. In the early 1990s, it supported the privatization scheme promoted by Khasbulatov-Rutskoi-Volskii, which ended up giving managers ownership rights and workers virtually nothing. Despite enormous problems of wage arrears in the 1990s, caused in part by embezzlement and other machinations by managers and politicians, the FITUR did not mobilize members. Instead, it joined with managers in lobbying the state for higher subsidies. Members sometimes enjoy access to services provided by the union, but they certainly do not feel represented by it. In a large survey of Russian workers conducted in 1997, when asked who defended their interests, 54 percent said no one, 35 percent said either their immediate bosses or the directors of the enterprise, and 9 percent said the union (Kovaleva, 1997; also Ashwin, 2004; Clarke and Ashwin, 2003; Crowley and Ost, eds., 2001).

Why does the union not stand up for its members? The question raises another question: Who "owns" the FITUR? A union is normally "owned," of course, by its members. But the FITUR is a bit different. It maintains colossal resources, in part, by virtue of its right to take 1 percent of its members' paychecks. The Soviet government gave the AUCCTU this right, and the Yeltsin government continued the practice. The Putin government has done still more for the union. In the labor code that it drew up and that was passed in 2001, it included a rule obligating employers to bargain only with those unions representing a majority of the firm's workers – meaning the FITUR. The new law powerfully inhibits the formation of smaller, more assertive unions (Gordon, 1995; Kubicek, 2002; Vodolazov, 2001).

To say that the state "owns" the FITUR would be too strong. But to say that it controls it would not be an exaggeration. An organization that was once a state agency dedicated to averting strikes and to administering paternalist programs for employees continues to enjoy a virtual monopoly on representing workers by virtue of rights and privileges that the state bestows. In return for those rights and privileges, the union continues to avert strikes and administer paternalist programs for employees. It would be hard to imagine an organizational arrangement better tailored to ensuring that laborers do not become a nuisance to their employers or the government.

Russian workers' passivity in the post-Soviet environment has been attributed to a number of causes. Rising unemployment and economic contraction undoubtedly checked the growth of labor power. Debra Javeline (2003) has argued that poor economic circumstances alone, however, do not explain labor quiescence. She holds that Russian workers endured the nonpayment of wages in the 1990s with minimal protest due to their inability even to assign blame for their predicament. In a sophisticated empirical study, she shows that workers at once blamed central governmental authorities, local governmental authorities, enterprise managers, and the general economic situation, without managing collectively to fix the responsibility for their plight. Employees lacked the information they needed to assign blame, which was a prerequisite to mass action.

Such information shortage was undoubtedly due in part to truly compli-cated circumstances and the blame-avoiding strategies that blameworthy individuals and groups devised, and Javeline discusses these problems in depth. So too, however, may the de facto statization of labor organization and weakness of autonomous labor unions account for worker passivity. One of unions' most important tasks in any environment is supplying members with information and interpreting that information in a way that makes sense of the challenges and foes that members face. With the FITUR blan-keting the terrain of labor organization, it is little wonder that workers lacked relevant information about the sources of their misery. Their repre-sentatives were in bed with their overlords.

The third example focuses on an organization whose sole mission is producing information, though not as part of the news media. It is the All-Russia Center for the Study of Public Opinion (ARCSPO; VTsIOM in Russian), which until September 2003 was Russia's leading organization engaged in the study of public opinion. ARCSPO's surveys commanded attention in Russia and abroad. ARCSPO was headed by Iurii Levada, an intrepid sociologist whose record of independent thinking stretched back to the Khrushchev period. He directed a staff of about 100, which included some of Russia's best survey researchers.

That was all before September 2003, when Levada and company found themselves ejected from their offices. Orders came from the Property Min-istry, which, in classic Putin form, claimed that it wished only to make ARCSPO more financially accountable. Levada's replacement was an un-known 29-year-old man from the pro-Putin Unity Party, Valerii Federov, who bore more than a faint resemblance to the deadly serious but intellec-tually and sartorially challenged stereotype of the Brezhnev-era Komsomol youth leader. Upon taking over, Federov announced that the agency would shift the focus of its surveys from political to social questions. Aleksandr Parshukov, the Property Ministry spokesman, of course denied that upcoming parliamentary and presidential elections, ARCSPO's surveys showing rising disaffection for the war in Chechnya, or any other polit-ical matter had the slightest bearing on the government's move.

Despite his cynicism and mendacity, Parshukov did utter an important truth in his discussion of the case. Responding to a question about whether the government was encroaching upon the independence of ARCSPO, Parshukov replied: "This independence . . . is pure fiction. Levada is a civil servant who responds directly to the labor minister. It's just so happened that

[Labor Minister Aleksandr] Pochinok hasn't been interfering in his affairs" (Yablokova, 2003[a]). Levada himself, though vocal in his condemnation of the government's move, understood who owned what. In an interview he gave shortly before losing his job, he rightly stated: "We have nothing but our reputation. We have bought everything you see here, but if we are forced to leave, we will have to leave with nothing. We would have no chairs to sit on, no offices and no computers. They all belong to the state" (Yablokova, 2003[a]).

Indeed they do. Though ARCSPO under Levada financed its own operations entirely with contributions from companies and political parties that used its polling services, it is a so-called GUP, or a state-owned entity with the right to engage in commercial activity. Levada was thus a civil servant, and his organization answered to the Labor Ministry, though few people paid any attention to this fact until the Putin administration decided to seize control. The government executed the move against ARCSPO's de facto independence by invoking its formal ownership rights, announcing that it was turning ARCSPO into a joint-stock company, and appointing a new board of directors that excluded Levada and anyone else then working at ARCSPO. The government also announced that shares of stock in the company would be offered soon. To no one's surprise, however, Parshukov confirmed that no sales of shares would take place before the March 2004 presidential election. As he candidly explained: "There aren't any insane people in the government who would transfer [ARCSPO] into private hands ahead of the elections" (Yablokova, 2003[a]; also Yablokova, 2003[b]; Shlapentokh, 2003[b]).

In sum, state custody of assets enables officials to move against perceived opponents without breaking the law, through the use of commercial levers alone. The state's stakeholdership gives officials an easy and relatively elegant way to control or eliminate groups and activities they do not like. The government's disposal of NTV and ARCSPO illustrates the problem. So too can state control over assets, even if indirect, greatly reduce the potential for the emergence of autonomous organizations, as is evident in the case of labor unions and the FITUR.

Not all organs of state are equally inclined or able to engage in such democracy-degrading behavior, however. One particular set of state agencies tends to be more dangerous than others. Institutional arrangements that invest great power in that set of agencies create special hazards for open government. This matter is the subject of the next chapter.

Summary

Despite the prominence of claims that radical economic liberalization undermines democratization, cross-national analysis and evidence drawn from Russia suggest that it actually helps it. The evidence also shows that Russia did not undertake "shock therapy" in economic policy. Russia's post-Soviet economic policies have been marked by tepid gradualism, rather than by radical liberalism. The piecemeal nature of economic reforms produced a persistence of economic statism. Enduring economic statism retarded the development of independent societal organizations and the socioeconomic bases for the development of such groups, and it circumscribed the autonomy of the organizations that did emerge. The sluggish growth of societal organizations and their vulnerability to state pressure and control, in turn, inhibited democratization.

7

The Institutional Problem

SUPERPRESIDENTIALISM

In themselves, technical changes in the form of government do not make a nation vigorous or happy or valuable. They can only remove technical obstacles and thus are merely means for a given end. Perhaps it is regrettable that such bourgeois and prosaic matters, which we shall discuss here with deliberate self-limitation and exclusion of all of the great *substantive* cultural issues facing us, can be important at all. But that is the way things are.

— Max Weber, *Parliament and Government in a Reconstructed Germany* (1917; 1978)

It is not because we have made a certain law or because it has been willed by so many votes, that we submit to it; it is because it is a good one – that is, appropriate to the nature of the facts, because it is all it ought to be and because we have confidence in it. And this confidence depends equally on that inspired by the organs that have the task of preparing it. What matters, then, is the way in which the law is made, the competence of those whose function it is to make it and the nature of the particular agency that has to make this particular function work. Respect for the law depends on the quality of the legislators and the quality of the political system.

— Emile Durkheim, *Professional Ethics and Civic Morals* (1890; 1982)

One of the potentially most consequential institutions in any polity is the constitution. In monocracies and some highly closed oligarchies, the constitution is a dead letter. It may prescribe a bouquet of rights and protections, as well as the dispersion of power among state agencies, but the rules may have nothing to do with the way the polity works. In Russia, however, as in many other countries, the constitution's provisions, while sometimes ignored by power holders, do shape the overall distribution of power among state agencies and the relationships between the citizens and the state.

A prominent feature of the Russian constitution is the preeminence of the presidency. How this institution affects Russia's failure to democratize is the subject of this chapter.

The first part of the chapter discusses the debate over the effects of constitutional forms on democracy. It classifies postcommunist countries and takes a preliminary look at the correlation between constitutional arrangements and political openness. The second part offers a differentiated set of criteria for assessing the powers of the legislature. It holds Russia up to the light of these criteria. The third section investigates where constitutions come from and, in particular, that which shapes the choices of constitutional types. Russia's experience with constitutional choice is discussed. The fourth part examines how a constitution that tilts power away from the parliament and toward the president hinders democratization. The chapter closes with further rumination about constitutional choice.

The Debate over Constitutional Types and Democracy

Overview of Constitutional Types and Their Merits

The relative merits of constitutional types for democratization are the source of a lively debate. Some scholars advocate parliamentarism. Under such a constitution, the government is formed by elements of the legislature, the prime minister exercises the bulk of executive power and answers to parliament, and the president either does not exist, is elected by the legislature, or is elected by direct suffrage but holds only modest power. Advocates of parliamentarism see it as highly representative, meaning that the main governing body looks like the people, whether in ideological, ethnic, or other terms. In general, parliamentarism's defenders are suspicious of unconstrained executive power and laud the permanent dependence of the most powerful executive (the prime minister) and his/her government on the legislature. They note that no matter how powerful the prime minister might be, in a parliamentary system s/he serves at the pleasure of the assembly and can be dismissed by that assembly if s/he loses his/her majority. They contrast the rigidity of the fixed terms that presidents serve – which may force electorates to live with an incompetent executive for years – with the flexibility of parliamentarism, where legislatures may depose prime ministers and their governments in short order (Linz and Valenzuela, eds., 1994; Stepan and Skach, 1993).

Presidentialism also has its advocates. It is a system in which the president is directly elected, the government is appointed by and answerable to the president, and the president enjoys considerable prerogatives. Presidentialism's advocates sometimes tout the advantages of the separation of power. The presence of two entities (the presidency and the legislature), each with its own source of electoral legitimacy and an ability to check the other, may reduce the hazard of radical missteps. A president elected by the whole people may better embody the national will and rise above social cleavages than a legislature. In times of crisis, a president, as a unitary actor, may be more capable of rapid, decisive action than a legislature (Gunther and Mughan, 1993; Horowitz, 1996; Mainwaring and Shugart, eds., 1997; Shugart and Carey, 1992).

Semipresidentialism, sometimes called a "dual" or "mixed" system, combines features of presidentialism and parliamentarism. Maurice Duverger (1980) formulated the classical definition (see also Elgie, ed., 1999; Protsyk, 2003; Roper, 2002; Wu, 2000). According to Duverger, and in his own words, a system is semipresidential if the constitution that established it combines three elements: 1) The president of the republic is elected by universal suffrage; 2) he possesses quite considerable powers; and 3) he has opposite him, however, a prime minister and ministers who possess executive and governmental power and can stay in office only if the parliament does not show its opposition to them.

The first two points require some minimum of presidential authority; the third sets some minimum of parliamentary influence over the government and, thus, policymaking. The third point specifies what is often considered the distinctive feature of semipresidentialism: the mutual, and often contested, control of the prime minister and the government as a whole by both the president and the legislature.

Semipresidentialism may be defended on the same grounds that parliamentarism and presidentialism are. Since it provides for some separation of powers, it may, like presidentialism, moderate the blunders of either the parliament or the president. Since it involves direct election of the president, the people as a whole have a decisive voice in the selection of the chief executive. Yet since it affords the legislature some say over the government, it may reduce the risks of overweening presidential power.

Classification of Postcommunist Political Systems

Specialists sometimes differ on how to classify this or that country, including some in the postcommunist region (Baylis, 1996; Derbyshire and Derbyshire, 1996; Easter, 1997; Elgie, 1998). Adhering to the basic criteria discussed here can help solve the problem. If the president is not directly elected or the presidency does not exist, the system is parliamentary. Such conditions obtain in Albania, Estonia, Latvia, the Czech Republic, Hungary, and until 1999, Slovakia. The system is also parliamentary if the president is directly elected but has little power. If the president does not have substantial voice in the choice of the prime minister and/or the composition of the cabinet and lacks the power to dissolve parliament under nonemergency conditions, the system is parliamentary, even if the president is directly elected. Bulgaria, Macedonia, Slovenia, and Slovakia after 1999 fit that description. In Bulgaria, the president has the formal right to appoint the prime minister, but this right is largely devoid of content, since the president is obligated to appoint the candidate nominated by the party holding the largest number of seats in parliament. The president may dissolve the legislature, but only if the three largest parliamentary factions fail in three successive votes to form a government. In practice, then, the president's dissolution powers do not come into force without full parliamentary cooperation. In Macedonia, Slovakia, and Slovenia, presidents also lack substantial sway over the government (Krouwel, 2000).

Presidential systems – those in which the president is directly elected, the government is appointed by and answerable to the president alone, and the president enjoys considerable prerogatives – are also common in the region. Some are essentially presidential dictatorships with decorative parliaments. Belarus, Turkmenistan, and Uzbekistan fit that profile. Parliaments in Azerbaijan and Tajikistan have more power but are, for the most part, subordinate to the president. In Azerbaijan, Belarus, and Tajikistan, legislatures at some point during the Gorbachev years or the immediate post-Soviet period did play a noteworthy role, but presidents subsequently brought the legislatures under their tutelage. In Turkmenistan and Uzbekistan, legislatures never gained the opportunity to play a meaningful role. Conditions in Kyrgyzstan are more ambiguous. There, the constitution provides for a presidential system, but whether it is a presidential dictatorship or a "normal" presidential system with a president who habitually oversteps his authority is open to debate. The constitution was changed several times during the 1990s to enhance the president's powers, although in 2003, a major crisis and public demonstrations forced the president to accede to constitutional changes that would enhance the legislature's powers. Georgia and Armenia have more "normal" presidential systems, meaning that they are not dictatorships and have the usual features of presidentialism. Both countries have suffered tumult since independence, but both have, as of this writing, maintained presidential systems.

The remaining nine countries – Croatia, Kazakhstan, Lithuania, Moldova, Mongolia, Poland, Romania, Russia, and Ukraine – have semipresidential systems. Moldova adopted changes in 2001 that provided for parliamentary election of the president, but for the first decade of its postindependence existence, it had a semipresidential constitution with a directly elected president. Each of these countries fulfills (in Moldova's case, fulfilled) Duverger's criteria for semipresidentialism. In each, the president is directly elected and possesses considerable powers, but so too is the government in some way dependent on parliamentary approval.

Yugoslavia/Serbia and Montenegro is excluded here. It was formally parliamentary but was run by a junta and was at war during the 1990s. It formally switched to presidentialism when the dictator, Slobodan Milosevic, gave up the prime ministership to take over the presidency.

A Preliminary Empirical Probe

Which form of constitution is most compatible with open politics in the postcommunist region? Table 7.1 provides some preliminary evidence. The answer seems clear. Parliamentary systems do well, semipresidential systems less well, and presidential systems worst. The difference between categories relative to the difference within categories is large enough for the analysis

Table 7.1. *Analysis of Variance (ANOVA): Political Openness and Constitutional Type, Postcommunist Region*

	Mean VA Score	Minimum VA Score	Maximum VA Score
Presidential (8 countries)	−1.07	−1.85	−0.30
Semipresidential (9 countries)	0.09	−1.05	1.11
Parliamentary (9 countries)	0.70	−0.29	1.17

$F = 18.00$ (p < 0.001)

197

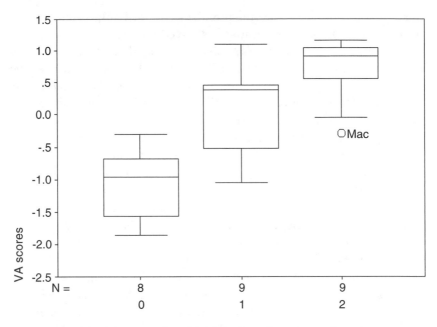

presidential = 0; semipresidential = 1; parliamentary = 2

Figure 7.1. Political Openness and Constitutional Type

of variance (ANOVA) test to be statistically significant at a demanding level. The boxplot shown in Figure 7.1 provides illustration.

The semipresidential category is of special interest. The four largest countries in the region, including Russia, have semipresidential systems. As Table 7.1 and Figure 7.1 show, moreover, the range in political openness among countries with semipresidential regimes is particularly great. Eight of the nine countries with parliamentary constitutions (all but Macedonia) are reasonably high achievers. None of the countries with presidential systems is a high achiever. But semipresidential systems cover a broad spectrum. What accounts for the vast variation in political openness among countries with semipresidential constitutions?

The Centrality of Parliamentary Power

The rudimentary analysis presented here suggests that countries where parliaments stand at the center of national politics have more open

198

political systems, while presidential systems have less-open politics. Since parliamentary systems generally have more powerful parliaments than presidential systems do, the finding suggests that stronger parliaments may be better for democracy than weaker parliaments. To this point, the direction of causation has not been shown. Later I will take up this matter and show that strong parliaments indeed are conducive to political openness; they are not merely the effect of greater political openness. For now, discussion will proceed from the elementary finding just presented. This finding raises the possibility that differences in parliamentary powers across countries with semipresidential constitutions might be correlated with variation in political openness. One would predict that countries with semipresidential regimes that have stronger parliaments will be more politically open.

Some Criteria of Parliamentary Power in Light of Duverger's Conception

According to Duverger's third criterion for semipresidentialism, the president has "a prime minister and ministers who possess executive and governmental power and can stay in office only if the parliament does not show its opposition to them." This criterion specifies the requirement for parliamentary control over the government. It may be operationalized using several concrete measures of the legislature's control. The first is whether the legislature itself appoints individual ministers or at least has the right to confirm or reject the ministers individually. Right of individual appointment or confirmation confers more power than the mere opportunity to vote up or down on the prime minister alone or the government as a whole. Even in some presidential systems, such as in the United States, the legislature (in this case, the Senate) must confirm each minister (secretary) individually. This rule gives the legislature real influence over the composition of the cabinet, even if the president makes the appointments. The second measure regards parliament's power to dismiss the government. Crucial is whether legislators may terminate a government without automatically risking their own seats. If opposition to the government triggers new parliamentary elections, legislators may be permanently reluctant to withhold confidence, which reduces parliament's leverage over the executive. The third measure is parliament's control over government operations. Such control is achieved by oversight, which may take the form of the power to summon ministers to testify before parliamentary committees or the parliament as a whole, the right to investigate the president and the government, and the right to monitor government agencies.

Thus, parliament's powers of confirmation of ministers, dismissal of government, and control of government activities operationalize Duverger's third criterion for semipresidentialism. These powers determine in practical, concrete terms the legislature's influence over the government.

The following generalizations may be made. In Croatia, Mongolia, and Poland, the parliament either appoints or must confirm individual ministers; in Lithuania, Kazakhstan, Moldova, Romania, Russia, and Ukraine, the parliament neither appoints the ministers nor has the right to confirm/reject them individually. In this respect, parliament's powers are more substantial in Croatia, Mongolia, and Poland. In Croatia, Moldova, Mongolia, Poland, Romania, and Ukraine, parliament may vote to dismiss a government without triggering its own dissolution; in Lithuania, Kazakhstan, and Russia, parliament faces likely or certain dissolution if it brings down a government. On this score, the Croatian, Moldovan, Mongolian, Polish, Romanian, and Ukrainian parliaments have an advantage. The Croatian, Lithuanian, Moldovan, Mongolian, Polish, and Romanian parliaments enjoy substantial powers of oversight over the executive branch, while the Kazakh, Russian, and Ukrainian parliaments do not. Here, Croatia's, Lithuania's, Moldova's, Mongolia's, Poland's, and Romania's parliaments are the stronger.

To this short list of parliamentary prerogatives one may add another fundamental right: a monopoly on legislative power. Where presidents do not have decree power or enjoy it only in highly exceptional circumstances (such as national emergencies), the legislature enjoys a monopoly on legislative power. Where presidential decree powers are not limited to emergencies and inconsequential functions, the legislature shares legislative power with the president. Such a condition obviously affects the balance between president and parliament. Duverger's third point specifies that the legislature has an independent hand in executive power; the question I now pose extends Duverger's criteria and asks whether the executive has an independent hand in legislation. If s/he does, the power of the legislature is diminished.

In Lithuania, the president has decree powers, but they are limited to diplomatic exchanges and titles, conferral of military rank, declaration of states of emergency, and granting of citizenship. These rights do not give the president much real lawmaking power. Practically speaking, the legislature monopolizes legislative power. In Croatia, Moldova, Mongolia,

Poland, and Romania, the president also lacks substantial decree power. In these countries, legislatures do the legislating. In Kazakhstan, Russia, and Ukraine, presidents enjoy broad powers of decree; legislatures must share lawmaking powers with the president.

This brief examination of parliamentary powers in light of Duverger's criteria reveals ample variation in varieties of postcommunist semipresidentialism. The powers of legislatures differ considerably across countries with semipresidential constitutions. The following section delves more deeply into measuring parliamentary powers.

Assessing the Status of Legislatures: The Parliamentary Powers Index

In an effort to measure the powers of national legislatures around the world, a colleague and I have created a Parliamentary Powers Index (or PPI; Fish and Kroenig, 2004). Several efforts to quantify the powers of parliaments are available in the literature (Krouwel, 2000; Shugart and Carey, 1992). Yet they are dated, cover a small number of polities, or are based on only a handful of criteria. The PPI overcomes these limitations. It encompasses a broader array of dimensions of power and many more criteria than do other assessments. It is based on 32 questions. The first 9 address the influence of the legislature on executive power; 10–18 deal with the institutional autonomy of the legislature; 19–26 address the powers and prerogatives of parliament; and 27–32 measure parliament's institutional capacity. The index therefore covers the parliament's ability to monitor the president and the bureaucracy, its freedom from presidential control, the authority of the legislature on specific tasks, and the resources that the legislature brings to its work. The answers to some questions are available in constitutions; the answers to others are not. In order to enhance the accuracy of assessments, we administered the questionnaire as a survey to experts. We obtained a minimum of five expert responses per country. We conducted the survey for 130 countries and gathered responses over a three-year period between 2002 and 2004. Here we focus only on postcommunist countries. The items in the survey are posed such that affirmation of the statement indicates greater rather than lesser power for the legislature (one could also think in terms of a "check mark" next to each statement). A greater number of affirmative answers indicates a more powerful legislature. The Legislative Powers Survey (LPS) is presented in Table 7.2.

The Parliamentary Powers Index is calculated for each country by dividing the number of affirmative answers by the total number of questions.

201

Table 7.2. *The Fish-Kroenig Legislative Powers Survey*

1. The legislature alone, without the involvement of any other agencies, can impeach the president or replace the prime minister.
2. Ministers may serve simultaneously as members of the legislature.
3. The legislature has powers of summons over executive branch officials and hearings with executive branch officials testifying before the legislature or its committees are regularly held.
4. The legislature can conduct independent investigation of the chief executive and the agencies of the executive.
5. The legislature has effective powers of oversight over the agencies of coercion (the military, organs of law enforcement, intelligence services, and the secret police).
6. The legislature appoints the prime minister.
7. The legislature's approval is required to confirm the appointment of individual ministers; or the legislature itself appoints ministers.
8. The country lacks a presidency entirely or there is a presidency, but the president is elected by the legislature.
9. The legislature can vote no confidence in the government without jeopardizing its own term (that is, without, the threat of dissolution).
10. The legislature is immune from dissolution by the executive.
11. Any executive initiative on legislation requires ratification or approval by the legislature before it takes effect; that is, the executive lacks decree power.
12. Laws passed by the legislature are veto-proof or essentially veto-proof; that is, the executive lacks veto power, or has veto power but the veto can be overridden by a simple majority in the legislature.
13. The legislature's laws are supreme and not subject to judicial review.
14. The legislature has the right to initiate bills in all policy jurisdictions; the executive lacks gatekeeping authority.
15. Expenditure of funds appropriated by the legislature is mandatory; the executive lacks the power to impound funds appropriated by the legislature.
16. The legislature controls the resources that finance its own internal operation and provide for the perquisites of its own members.
17. Members of the legislature are immune from arrest and/or criminal prosecution.
18. All members of the legislature are elected; the executive lacks the power to appoint any members of the legislature.
19. The legislature alone, without the involvement of any other agencies, can change the Constitution.
20. The legislature's approval is necessary for the declaration of war.
21. The legislature's approval is necessary to ratify treaties with foreign countries.
22. The legislature has the power to grant amnesty.
23. The legislature has the power of pardon.
24. The legislature reviews and has the right to reject appointments to the judiciary; or the legislature itself appoints members of the judiciary.
25. The chairman of the central bank is appointed by the legislature.
26. The legislature has a substantial voice in the operation of the state-owned media.
27. The legislature is regularly in session.
28. Each legislator has a personal secretary.
29. Each legislator has at least one non-secretarial staff member with policy expertise.
30. Legislators are eligible for re-election without any restriction.
31. A seat in the legislature is an attractive enough position that legislators are generally interested in and seek re-election.
32. The re-election of incumbent legislators is common enough that at any given time, the legislature contains a significant number of highly experienced members.

This technique, which assigns equal weight to each item, obviously involves difficult and arbitrary distinctions. So too would weighting the questions involve difficult and arbitrary distinctions. Despite the obvious limitations inherent in this or any other index, the PPI may provide a tool for comparative assessment of the power of national legislatures.

Table 7.3 shows the answers for each postcommunist country that has a semipresidential constitution. The final row presents the PPI for each country.

The survey reveals disparities in the powers of parliaments. In Croatia, Lithuania, Moldova, Mongolia, Poland, and Romania the legislature is potent; in Russia and Ukraine it is much less powerful; in Kazakhstan it is weak. For comparative purposes, one may consider the following scores: Germany's PPI is .78; India's, .66; Brazil's, .53; Nigeria's, .50; and Uzbekistan's, .28. Unlike in Uzbekistan, the legislature in Russia is not a decoration that merely lends an aura of legitimacy to presidential or monarchical hegemony. But nor is it a commanding political actor.

The Legislature's Powers in Russia

What makes the Russian constitution semipresidential? According to Duverger's definition and in the judgment of leading specialists on Russia's political institutions, Russia does have a semipresidential system (Huskey, 1999; Remington, 2001). Crucially, however, it is semipresidential by virtue of a single provision: the right of the Duma, the lower house of parliament, to reject the president's choice for prime minister.

In practice, this is a flimsy reed. In order to block the president's nominee for prime minister, the legislature must reject him or her not once or twice but three times – at which point the president, without having to place him/herself up for reelection, automatically dissolves the legislature and calls new elections. This provision explains why the Duma has never rejected a prime minister, even though it was at loggerheads with the president during the entire Yeltsin period. On some occasions – most notably in 1998, when he backed away from bringing Viktor Chernomyrdin back as prime minister – Yeltsin bowed to parliamentary opposition. Yet Yeltsin was still able to dismiss and appoint prime ministers at will and even with abandon, as he did during the last two years of his presidency.

Yeltsin's choice of Sergei Kirienko to head the government in 1998 provides a stark illustration of the limitations on parliament's control. A young, bookish, liberal neophyte, Kirienko embodied everything that the Duma's

Table 7.3. *Legislative Powers Survey and Parliamentary Powers Indices for Postcommunist Countries with Semipresidential Systems*

	Country								
Question #	Croatia	Kazakhstan	Lithuania	Moldova	Mongolia	Poland	Romania	Russia	Ukraine
1	x		x		x	x	x		
2			x		x	x	x		
3	x		x	x	x	x	x		x
4	x		x	x	x	x	x	x	
5	x		x	x	x	x	x		
6									
7	x				x	x			
8									
9				x	x	x	x		x
10					x		x		x
11	x		x	x	x	x	x		
12	x		x	x			x		
13									
14	x	x	x	x	x	x	x	x	x
15	x		x	x	x	x	x		x
16	x	x	x	x	x	x	x	x	x
17	x	x	x	x	x	x	x	x	x
18	x		x	x	x	x	x		x
19	x		x	x	x				
20	x	x	x	x	x	x	x	x	x
21	x	x	x	x	x		x	x	x
22	x	x	x	x	x			x	x
23									
24	x		x	x	x			x	
25	x		x	x	x		x		
26	x		x	x		x	x		
27	x	x	x	x	x	x	x	x	x
28		x	x		x	x		x	x
29						x		x	
30	x	x	x	x	x	x	x	x	x
31	x	x	x	x	x	x	x	x	x
32	x			x		x	x	x	x
PPI	.72	.31	.72	.72	.81	.66	.72	.44	.50

204

communists and nationalists despised. To goad his fellow oppositionists to place principles above job security, Gennadii Ziuganov, the leader of the CPRF, ostentatiously swore on Lenin's grave that he would oppose Kirienko's nomination. Yet when Yeltsin stuck with Kirienko, the opposition folded. Only about 10 percent of deputies in a legislature whose majority avowedly opposed the nominee voted to put their seats at risk. If the legislature's rejection of a prime minister or government spells its own dissolution, its prerogative may amount to a paper power that no president need fear.

The Russian parliament's control over the executive is tenuous in other respects as well. It does not have the right to reject individual ministers. It has scant oversight powers. Although it can investigate the president and the government, as noted in question 4 in the LPS, it lacks the resources to do so and almost never does so in fact. Ministers do not answer to the parliament and are not summoned to testify before it. Parliament has no ability to monitor the military, the police, or the organs of state security (see Knight, 2000). The president enjoys wide decree authority, and so parliament must share legislative functions with the executive. The parliament does not even control the resources that finance its own internal operation and provide for its members' perquisites (question 16 in the LPS). An agency in the presidential apparatus dispenses the benefits, such as the luxurious (or not so luxurious, depending on the member's orientation toward the president) apartments in Moscow that house the parliamentarians.

Examination of Russia in light of the LPS shows that a regime may be both semipresidential and superpresidential. Some students of Russian politics have used the "superpresidential" label to depict the Russian constitution (Colton, 1995; Fish, 2001[b]; Walker, 1993/4). The constitution is semipresidential by reason of a single provision that lacks bite. In practice, the president enjoys virtually full control over the government's composition and operations.

Parliamentary Powers, Semipresidentialism, and Democracy

The preliminary empirical probe presented here showed that parliamentary systems scored higher on political openness than semipresidential systems, which in turn scored higher than presidential systems. But the analysis also showed that countries with semipresidential constitutions covered a broad spectrum in political openness. Subsequent discussion revealed that among semipresidential constitutions, the powers of parliaments varied greatly.

The PPI provides a measure that makes possible a more rigorous test of the relationship between parliament's powers and political openness. Using the measure, however, costs a case, since one of the region's countries, Turkmenistan, lacks a legislature and is not assessed. An entity known as the "People's Council" occasionally gathers to lavish awards upon President Saparmurat Niyazov, known in the (entirely state-run) Turkmen press as "Turkmenbashi the Great." It has proclaimed him president-for-life, voted to name months of the year after him, and declared a book of his poems a classic of world literature. It has unanimously approved turning Ashgabat into a shrine to the Great Father. The shrine includes innumerable statues of Niyazov, including an immense gold figure placed on a vaulted pedestal that rotates so that the Leader's visage is always facing the sun. The legislature has never held any legislative powers; to call the body a rubber stamp would be an understatement (Albion, 2003).

Table 7.4 shows the PPI for postcommunist countries. Albania, Belarus, Kazakhstan, Kyrgyzstan, Moldova, Poland, and Slovakia made constitutional changes between the time of the adoption of their first post-Soviet constitutions and the present day that may be of relevance to the powers of their legislatures. Albania adopted its first postcommunist constitution in May 1991 but revised it in October 1998. The basic powers of the legislature, which are of concern here, are essentially the same in the two constitutions, though they are spelled out with greater clarity in

Table 7.4. *The Parliamentary Powers Index, Postcommunist Countries*

Country	PPI		
Albania	.75	Lithuania	.72
Armenia	.53	Macedonia	.78
Azerbaijan	.44	Moldova	.72
Belarus	.28	Mongolia	.81
Bulgaria	.78	Poland	.66
Croatia	.72	Romania	.72
Czech Republic	.78	**Russia**	**.44**
Estonia	.75	Slovakia	.72
Georgia	.59	Slovenia	.78
Hungary	.69	Tajikistan	.41
Kazakhstan	.31	Ukraine	.50
Kyrgyzstan	.41	Uzbekistan	.28
Latvia	.84		

the later document. Since 1998, officials have observed the constitution more faithfully than during 1991–8, when the then-president, Sali Berisha, made a habit of trying to break out of the constitution's constraints. Belarus adopted changes in November 1996 that strengthened the president's powers. Kazakhstan and Kyrgyzstan enacted changes that strengthened presidencies in August 1995 and February 1996, respectively. Moldova changed its constitution to put the parliament in charge of electing the president in 2001. Poland did not have a constitution until May 1997, but between 1992 and 1997 operated under a "Little Constitution" that was the blueprint for the constitution that it finally enacted formally in 1997. Slovakia switched from election of the president by parliament to direct election of the president in 1999. The scores shown in Table 7.4 and used in this chapter reflect the powers of legislatures in the countries' original constitutions, before the amendments just mentioned were made.

Figure 7.2 shows a scatterplot of the relationship between the PPI and VA scores. The correlation is high and positive. Table 7.5 shows a regression of VA scores on the PPI and a control for economic development. The power of the legislature may strongly affect political openness.

The analysis suggests that semipresidentialism per se is not democracy's antagonist, and that Russia's democratic deficit cannot be ascribed to semipresidentialism. Semipresidentialism may sometimes have what appear to be pathological effects, including policy paralysis and awkward "cohabitation," in which rival political forces must share control of the government. Semipresidentialism yielded gridlock in Mongolia in 1999, when a liberal parliament and a socialist president clashed over who would head the government, leaving the country without a prime minister for months. So too is the Polish experience rife with interbranch brawls over control of the government.

Yet Mongolia and Poland have done remarkably well in democratization. At the end of the 1980s, remote, impoverished Mongolia was nobody's pick to become a vigorously open polity – but it became one. Poland's democratization has been successful by any standard. The same may be said of Lithuania, which also has a semipresidential system. Democratization in Romania, which labored under homegrown Stalinism until 1989, has exceeded the expectations of many. The experiences of Croatia and Moldova have been more ambiguous, though after the death of Franjo Tudjman, the Croatian polity opened quickly and Moldova averted the reversal of political opening that occurred in Russia. Russia and Ukraine, with their president-heavy forms of semipresidentialism, have done much worse.

Table 7.5. *Multiple Regression of Voice and Accountability Scores on Hypothesized Determinants, Including the Parliamentary Powers Index, Postcommunist Region*

Variable	
Constant	-5.78^{***} (0.72)
Economic development	1.02^{***} (0.22)
Parliamentary Powers Index	3.86^{***} (0.38)
Adj. R^2	.86

$N = 25$ countries.
$^*p < 0.05; ^{**}p < 0.01; ^{***}p < 0.001$

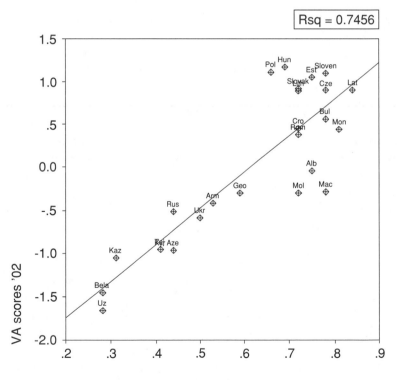

Figure 7.2. Political Openness and Parliamentary Powers

Semipresidentialism need not impede democratization; but neither does it ensure it.

What, though, of the argument that Russia already tried a form of semipresidentialism that afforded the legislature more power and that this system only came to grief? One might argue that Russia experimented with balanced semipresidentialism between the time of the Soviet Union's demise and late 1993, when the new constitution was adopted by referendum. During this period, some observers hold, the legislature (then the holdover Supreme Soviet) had substantial powers – but the result was irreconcilable interbranch conflict, culminating in the violent showdown of October 1993 between Yeltsin and the parliament (Mikheyev, 1996).

This argument is faulty, since it mischaracterizes the political system that was in place during the first years of the post-Soviet period. That system was not semipresidential or, for that matter, parliamentary or presidential. It was a Soviet-era holdover, a hodgepodge of legal fictions and ad hoc amendments attached during the liberalization of the Gorbachev era. According to the Soviet constitution, the sitting parliament, the Supreme Soviet, held supreme authority, though during the Soviet period, the Communist Party monopolized power and the legislature was a rubber stamp. In the post-Soviet setting, some leaders of parliament seized on the old Soviet provision and aimed to make it reality. In practice, however, Yeltsin enjoyed decree powers that the Supreme Soviet granted him at the onset of the post-Soviet period, when his popularity was at its zenith and before relations between the Supreme Soviet and Yeltsin soured. The parliament had little say in the composition of the government, which the president appointed and which answered to him alone. The holdover constitution's contestedness and opacity were higher barriers to normal interbranch relations than was the fact that power was supposedly shared by the president and the legislature (Brudny, 1995). The constitution in force in Russia during 1991–3 did not represent bona fide semipresidentialism.

The constitution in force since the end of 1993 *is* semipresidential – but only formally and only barely. A single, lifeless provision enables it to fulfill Duverger's criterion for minimal parliamentary control over the government (his point number 3).

The analysis suggests that what matters for democracy is the strength of the legislature, rather than whether the constitutional system is formally parliamentary, semipresidential, or presidential. Countries with more potent parliaments have done better than those with weaker parliaments.

The Origins of Parliamentary Powers

The Roots of Constitutional Choice

Before concluding that stronger parliaments foster more open politics, we must consider whether stronger parliaments are a mere effect of more open politics. Some writers have claimed that the strength of the legislature (or the presidency), as prescribed in the constitution, is an effect of political openness at the time of constitutional choice (Kitschelt, 2003; Roeder, 2001; Way, 2004). Others have treated constitutional type as an independent variable that may affect political openness (Linz and Valenzuela, eds., 1994; Mainwaring and Shugart, eds., 1997; Stepan and Skach, 1993).

Establishing the direction of causation is difficult. The data do not lend themselves to a Granger causality test or other statistical techniques that may tease out the direction of causation, such as multiple-stage least squares regression. One might hope to be able to establish unequivocally that one factor is cause and the other is effect. But reality probably is not so tidy. The causal arrow probably goes both ways. The extent of political openness at the time of the constitution's inauguration may well influence the powers granted to parliament. Certainly one would expect that constitutions drawn up in thoroughly closed polities would provide for weak legislatures while lodging the bulk of power in the president (or the general secretary of the hegemonic party or the head of the military).

There is a correlation between the openness of the polity at the time that the constitution was adopted and the strength of the legislature. To measure political openness, it is necessary here to leave behind VA scores and return to the Freedom House (FH) freedom scores, since the latter are issued yearly. Here I use the last scores issued before the adoption of the constitution. They capture the state of political openness at the constitutional moment. Table 7.6 shows the time that each country adopted its constitution and the FH freedom score that reflects conditions at that time.

Some countries must be excluded. Those of the former Yugoslavia enacted constitutions before FH freedom scores were published for them. Latvia is excluded for the same reason. In May 1990, before the demise of the Soviet Union and before FH freedom scores were available for Latvia, the republican legislature reverted to the 1922 constitution of the Republic of Latvia. The document has subsequently been amended but has remained in force to the present day. Alone in the region, Latvia did not adopt a new

Table 7.6. *Freedom House Freedom Scores at the Time of Constitutional Choice*

Country	FH freedom score (year)
Albania	1.5 (May 1991)
Armenia	4.5 (July 1995)
Azerbaijan	2.0 (November 1995)
Belarus	3.5 (March 1994)
Bulgaria	4.5 (July 1991)
Czech Republic	6.0 (December 1992)
Estonia	5.5 (June 1992)
Georgia	3.0 (October 1995)
Hungary	3.5 (October 1989)
Kazakhstan	3.0 (January 1993)
Kyrgyzstan	5.0 (May 1993)
Lithuania	5.5 (October 1992)
Moldova	3.0 (July 1994)
Mongolia	5.5 (February 1992)
Poland	6.0 (November 1992)
Romania	2.5 (December 1991)
Russia	**4.5 (December 1993)**
Slovakia	6.0 (January 1993)
Tajikistan	1.0 (December 1994)
Ukraine	4.5 (June 1996)
Uzbekistan	2.5 (December 1992)

postcommunist constitution. As mentioned earlier, Turkmenistan lacks a legislature and for that reason is not included.

As always in this book, the FH freedom scores are reversed such that higher numbers represent more political openness. Figure 7.3 shows the relationship between them and the PPI. In general, countries that had more open politics at the time that they chose their constitutions created stronger national legislatures.

Yet the correlation is not overwhelming. In many countries, the powers of parliament are not what one would expect them to be if more political openness translated into a more expansive role for parliament. Hungary was just beginning democratization at the time that it adopted its fundamental law, and its FH freedom score was still quite low, yet it embraced a constitution that provided for a powerful legislature. Romania's FH freedom score was even lower at the time it adopted its constitution. Nicolae Ceauşescu, the Stalinist psychopath who ruled Romania for two decades, had been deposed, but the presidency was occupied by Ion Iliescu, a thuggish former

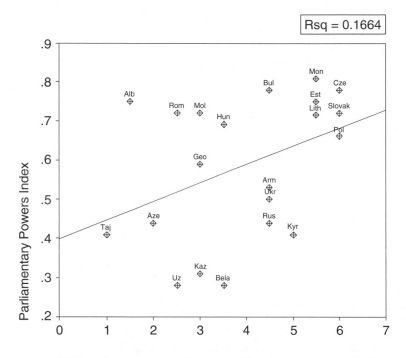

Figure 7.3. Parliamentary Powers and Political Openness at the Constitutional Moment

associate of Ceaușescu who was in no hurry to democratize. Yet Romania adopted a semipresidential system that included a strong legislature. In contrast, Kyrgyzstan was a relatively open polity when it adopted a constitution that vested modest powers in the legislature. Russia was more open in 1993, when it adopted its constitution, than was Hungary in 1989 or Romania in 1991; yet Russia's constitution created a comparatively weak legislature. The evidence does not provide strong backing for the assertion that the powers of legislatures were merely functions of the openness of the polity at the time that the legislature's powers were defined.

Another argument that does not withstand scrutiny attributes the balance of powers between the president and the parliament to the strength of the state. Timothy Frye (2002[a]) suggests that expansive presidential power resulted from state weakness. He argues that weak states gave rise to powerful coalitions that supported strong presidents as protectors of their property rights. Gerald Easter (1997) has also characterized strongly presidential systems as a response to state weakness. Measuring the strength of the state is tricky and will not be attempted here, and so testing the hypothesis rigorously is difficult. Brief consideration of the postcommunist experience, however, casts doubt on this argument. The state was no stronger during the period of regime change in, say, Albania, Romania, Moldova, or Mongolia than it was in Russia. The state apparatus virtually dissolved under the stress of social chaos in Albania, was buffeted by internal divisions and violence in Romania and Moldova, and labored under near collapse induced by the evaporation of financial resources in Mongolia (Biberaj, 1999; Pomfret, 2000; Tismaneanu, 2003; Way, 2003). The Russian state still had formidable organizational, bureaucratic, coercive, financial, and personnel assets inherited from the Soviet period. Its capital had been the capital of the Soviet Union and the hub of political life in the communist region. Yet among these countries, Russia alone ended up with a president-dominated system; the others opted for strong parliaments.

In fact, neither the extent of political openness nor state strength at the time of the constitution's adoption determined the powers of parliament. Myriad factors that can be understood only in the context of each country's political experience and struggles shaped the decisions that established the role of legislatures. Many constitutions were adopted hastily in the heat of regime change. Some analysts treat constitution making as a bargaining game among elite actors pursuing their own interests (Elster, ed., 1996; Geddes, 1996; Przeworski, 1991; Roeder, 2001). That game undoubtedly underlay constitutional choices. Yet it is important to remember that under the conditions that obtained in most postcommunist countries, many elite actors could not gauge which institutional arrangements would best serve them. The fog of struggle shrouded the arenas in which calculations were made, and the density and hue of the fog varied from place to place. What is more, mass opinion molded constitutional choice in some countries, including in Russia.

In Hungary, as in Czechoslovakia and several other East European countries, leaders reached for the form of noncommunist constitution they knew best, which was what they had lived under during the precommunist period and/or what most West European countries had. In Estonia, Latvia, and Lithuania, creating a strong legislature was completely uncontroversial. Powerful parliaments are the norm in Western Europe, and the Balts longed above all to join the West. Romania adopted a semipresidential constitution in large part because France had such a constitution. As the Western country that paid Romania the closest attention and whose culture the Romanians knew the best, France seemed the country to emulate. For Romanians, moreover, who suffered homegrown fascism between the wars and home-grown Stalinism in the 1970s and 1980s, embracing a time-worn foreign model was appealing.

Mongolia also selected a semipresidential system with a strong legislature, but not out of a desire to emulate Europe. Nor did the Mongolian constitution empower the legislature merely because the country's political life had already opened up by the time the constitution was adopted. As I found during interviews in Mongolia in the late 1990s, concern for protecting the country against foreign pressure weighed heavily on the Mongolians (Fish, 1998[b]). Elites, bolstered by a public consensus, were concerned above all with thwarting the specter of a Chinese or Russian threat to national independence. Mongolians regarded dispersion of power as a prophylactic against foreign manipulation. The reasons for such a view may be found in Mongolia's communist-era past. Mongolians tend to remember their communist-era regime less as a partyocracy than as a one-man dictatorship headed by a puppet in Moscow's employ. This view is the product of the way Mongolia was ruled. The country had just two Communist Party general secretaries from the time of Lenin to that of Chernenko. In contrast with Khrushchev and Brezhnev and their contemporaries in East Europe, neither of Mongolia's top leaders pretended to govern collegially (or to live modestly). To Mongolians, for whom maintaining national independence during a vulnerable time was paramount, dispersing power was seen as the way to minimize the danger of manipulation by a foreign hegemon, since multiple sources of power would be harder for Russia or China to buy off and control than would a single source of power. This concern produced elite and public support for a parliament-heavy form of semipresidentialism that reflected exquisite preoccupation with deconcentration of power.

Poland also ended up with a semipresidential system that provided for a powerful legislature, though for reasons that were entirely specific to Polish circumstances and that differed greatly from those that led Romania and Mongolia to their parliament-heavy forms of semipresidentialism. In the early constitution-making process launched in 1989, the powers of the presidency were tailored to allow the communist leader, General Wojciech Jaruzelski, to guarantee some continuity in Poland's foreign and military policies and to allow him to serve as an arbiter among forces in the rapid political transformation that was engulfing Poland at the time. Direct elections were held for the presidency at the end of 1990, and the first elected president, Lech Wałęsa, took full advantage of the prerogatives that his predecessor, who had earlier been his jail keeper, built into the constitution. In response to Wałęsa's imperiousness in office, the legislature adopted what came to be known as the "Little Constitution" in the fall of 1992, which attempted to bridle presidential powers, though it left the president considerable room for influencing the government. After winning parliamentary elections in 1993, the leftist coalition led by the communist-successor party promoted the bolstering of parliament at the expense of the president. Yet after its leader, Aleksandr Kwaśniewski, defeated Wałęsa in presidential elections in late 1995, the leading coalition in parliament backed off of its efforts to augment parliamentary powers. As Krzysztof Jasiewicz (2003, p. 112) notes, the whole process "was driven not by the pursuit to a well-balanced, cohesive system of formal rules, but by the substantive political ends of the parties involved."

The constitution that finally emerged in 1997 was the product of myriad struggles and deals among political forces whose strength waxed and faded along the way. What is more, in the end, the constitution still bore the marks of the conditions and compromises of 1989, which led critics such as Zbigniew Stawrowski to hold that the 1997 constitution was "based on recognizing the former rulers of the Polish People's Republic as the founders of the Republic of Poland." According to Stawrowski, such recognition "is unacceptable for all those who, despite everything, have not yet forgotten about the past," and explains why 45 percent of voters rejected the new constitution in the referendum that confirmed it (2003, p. 86). The thinking underlying this view and the details of the constitution itself need not detain us. The point is that the constitution, including its provisions for the distribution of power and relations between the parliament and the president, was the outcome of conditions that were entirely specific to Poland.

Who held which office at a particular moment also shaped the outcome of constitutional debates in Ukraine in 2004. Parliamentary opponents of President Leonid Kuchma blocked a constitutional amendment backed by Kuchma that would have strengthened parliament at the expense of the presidency (Mydans, 2004). Kuchma engineered the proposed amendment for the sole purpose of clinging to some leverage in case he was tossed out of office in upcoming presidential elections, since he had some influence over a substantial portion of parliament. Given the multitude of crimes for which he was suspected, including murder, electoral fraud, and all manner of corruption, he was keen to maintain some influence after leaving office. The preferences of both Kuchma and his antagonists were fully comprehensible.

215

Still, the struggle was paradoxical, since most of the parliamentarians who opposed the proposed amendment in principle favored empowering parliament and would have supported the measure had it not been introduced by the president as a naked gambit for shielding himself from prosecution in the event of his loss of the presidency.

Constitutional Choice in Russia

Constitutional choice in Russia was also both paradoxical and deeply influenced by struggles that were particular to the country. In contrast with conditions in, say, Mongolia, circumstances in Russia led advocates of national independence and democracy to favor concentration of powers in the presidency. The Russian constitution's passage by referendum occurred only in late 1993, but the origins of what became an ironic choice lie in the struggle that dominated politics in the waning years of the Soviet Union.

The democratic movement's strategy at the end of the 1980s and the beginning of the 1990s was to undermine the communist regime by asserting the sovereignty of Russia (that is, the Russian Soviet Federated Socialist Republic) and thereby withdrawing Russia from the Soviet Union. The surest way to do so was to create new governmental agencies and institutions that were independent of all-Union (that is, USSR) authorities. The best bet at the time was a directly elected president of the RSFSR. The RSFSR Supreme Soviet, which became the Supreme Soviet of the Russian Federation upon the dissolution of the Soviet Union, served as a springboard for Yeltsin and other proponents of regime change, but it was elected in early 1990 under a system devised by the Gorbachev government, and not more than about one-third of its members were committed to radical change. The formation of an entirely new center of power – necessarily, under prevailing conditions, a presidency – was the route to revolution. In response to a question in a referendum held in the spring of 1991, citizens of the RSFSR endorsed creating such an office. The result was a vote for Russian sovereignty and the anticommunist movement (Walker, 2003). So too was it a vote for Yeltsin, who was the paramount leader of the democratic movement and the most popular politician in Russia at the time. Voters knew that Yeltsin would capture the new office in the event of its creation; indeed, they made it for him (Fish, 1995; Urban, 1997). In the ensuing election for the new office in June 1991, on the eve of the dissolution of the Soviet Union, Yeltsin captured three-fifths of the vote – more than three times that of the second-place finisher, Nikolai Ryzhkov, who was the most attractive candidate the Communist Party could find.

During 1992 and 1993, the presidency continued to be associated with the democratic movement and the parliament with the old order. Yeltsin refrained from calling fresh elections for a new legislature in late 1991 or early 1992, thus bypassing a momentous opportunity to capitalize on his formidable public stature at the time. Had he called new elections, he could have discarded the holdover Russian Supreme Soviet, elected in March 1990, in favor of a legislature that almost certainly would have been friendlier. Yeltsin may have regarded the prospect of a legislature with a fresh mandate, even if closer to him in political spirit, as potentially more constraining than a holdover legislature with declining public support. A feeble foe can be less bothersome than a potent and independent ally. In the event, nationalists and communists did become the dominant forces in the Supreme Soviet during 1992 and 1993; the liberal minority stopped attending sessions. The speaker of the legislature, Ruslan Khasbulatov, an ethnic Chechen known for personal coarseness and a comically transparent lust for power, did not enjoy lofty public stature. When Yeltsin called a referendum to clarify his own popularity vis-à-vis that of the parliament in April 1993, he won convincingly. Voters answered four questions: whether they supported Yeltsin, whether they endorsed his policies, whether they wanted new elections for president, and whether they wanted new elections for parliament. Yeltsin's preferred outcome – " *da, da, net, da*" – was precisely what voters handed him. Falsification such as would become common later in the 1990s was still probably not rampant at the time; the vote showed that Yeltsin continued to enjoy considerable public support. Pro-democratic forces were elated, and many expected fast action to break the impasse between the president and the Supreme Soviet (Alekseev, 1993).

In a remarkable case of inaction, however, Yeltsin sat still. His constitutional right to call new elections for parliament was murky, but everything was murky at the time, and the moment immediately following the April 1993 referendum offered a precious opportunity. But Yeltsin failed to act decisively. He convoked a constitutional assembly to hash out a revised version of a draft constitution, but he did little to push the matter to closure. Finally, six months later, after the Supreme Soviet had grown even more intransigent and the glow of legitimacy lent by the referendum had dissipated, Yeltsin abruptly announced the legislature's dissolution. The ill-timed test of wills produced a showdown in the streets of Moscow between groups loyal to the (mostly but not entirely) communist and nationalist parliamentarians and Yeltsin's government. Firepower decided the outcome. Yeltsin deployed the army to destroy parts of the parliament building where holdout legislators where holed up in defiance of his order to disband. Khasbulatov was jailed and parliament was shut down.

Under these conditions, Yeltsin called elections for a new parliament, to be held concurrently with a referendum on a new constitution. The vote was held in December 1993. Voters approved the new fundamental law. Unsurprisingly, given Yeltsin's dominance at the time (at least relative to the disbanded parliament), the constitution that voters were asked to endorse or reject was largely the president's creation. It provided for presidential control over the levers of public expenditure, presidential decree powers, rules that make impeachment of the president virtually impossible, a legislature with little oversight authority, and a judiciary that is controlled largely by the president. While it did not prescribe a large presidential apparatus, it created a permissive environment for the creation of such an apparatus, which subsequently proceeded apace (Huskey, 1999; McFaul, 2001).

The constitution, by imposing few constraints on the president and investing the legislature with modest powers, had a pernicious effect on democratization. But as this story suggests, voters who endorsed the draft constitution in December 1993 were not opposing democracy; the contrary was true. At the time, supporting the constitution meant backing Yeltsin, and voting against it meant siding with Khasbulatov. Given political circumstances, Russians could not possibly separate the actors from the institutions. Yeltsin and his government, for all their liabilities, still represented a relatively pro-democratic position. As Gleb Iakunin, then a leader of Democratic Choice of Russia (DCR) and an Orthodox priest who was defrocked for his liberal political activism, stated on the eve of the showdown between Yeltsin and his opponents: "Yes, we must criticize Yeltsin and his mistakes, and he is a transitional figure, but we must also recognize that he remains much closer to democracy than his enemies, and he is still key to avoiding a takeover by the Front for National Salvation" (author's minutes, August 28, 1993, Moscow). The group to which Iakunin referred, the Front for National Salvation (FNS), was the union of communist and nationalist forces that was congealing at the time. It was not a responsible opposition. Its leadership, which prominently featured General Albert Makashov, Colonel Viktor Alksnis, Colonel Stanislav Terekhov, Nikolai

Lysenko, Sergei Baburin, and Nikolai Pavlov, was a collection of misanthropes, militarists, and fascists. Having managed to elude the credential checkers and attend the Second National Congress of the Front for National Salvation in July 1993 in Moscow, I saw the ferocious anti-Semitism and seething resentment that pervaded the organization. This was the group that represented the mainstay of support for the parliament and the spearhead of the effort to oust Yeltsin in October 1993 (also author's minutes of press conferences on July 25, 1993 [Ilia Konstantinov] and July 27, 1993 [Nikolai Pavlov and Nikolai Lysenko], Moscow; Timofeev, 1993; Vujacic, 1996).

Given these circumstances, the overwhelming majority of Russia's democrats supported the constitution. Indisputably pro-democratic figures helped write it and defended it after its enactment (Gerber, personal interview, July 30, 1994, Moscow; Sheinis, personal interview, December 8, 1995, Moscow). In interviews carried out in a dozen cities in Russia since 1994, I have queried nearly a hundred politicians on how they voted in the referendum, and nearly all of those many who associate themselves with a pro-democratic position say that they voted for the constitution. Many saw the constitution's hazards. Staneslav Radkevich (personal interview, July 11, 1994, Moscow), a leading political scientist and consultant to liberal deputies in the Duma in the mid-1990s, remarked that the constitution provided for "a president who is too strong," but he added that "of course it is still better than we had before, and it does reduce the scope for open conflict." The mayor of St. Petersburg during much of the 1990s, Anatolii Sobchak (1993), expressed concern in 1993 that the constitution concentrated too much power in the executive, but he supported it all the same.

With some embarrassment at both my lack of political foresight and my less-than-impeccable respect for the law, I must admit that I too voted for it. I resided in Russia at the time and accompanied to the polls a friend who knew of my avid interest in politics. After she signed in at the polling place, we walked to the voting area, where she turned her ballot over to me. With tongue in check, she remarked that Americans were not allowed to vote in Russian elections, but that she knew that I was more interested in politics than she was (which was true), that I would vote the same way that she would (which was also true), and that I would really enjoy participating in the event (which was very true). Many voters were milling about the area. Groups of stout and voluble babushki stood in circles, arguing over whom to vote for. No one was on hand to prevent foreigners from filling out ballots for their Russian friends. Along with endorsing the liberal Iabloko party, I also voted the same way that most other Iabloko voters did – for the constitution. This choice amounted to – or felt like – resisting the forces of nostalgia.

Factors other than the political battle that engulfed Russia in the early 1990s may have shaped constitutional choice in Russia as well. While residing in Russia and discussing the matter with politicians and social scientists in the early 1990s, I was struck by the absence of discussion of a parliamentary alternative. Even before the battle lines between Yeltsin and Khasbulatov were clearly drawn, nearly everyone assumed that the new constitution would include a powerful president. Some would-be framers, including Oleg Rumiantsev, the liberal parliamentarian and constitutional specialist, favored a balanced system, but even his plan provided for a strong executive presidency. Only the communists advocated pure parliamentarism, and their preference had nothing to do with adopting a European-style system and everything to do with getting back to the good old days. Anatolii Luk'ianov (personal interview, December 19, 1995, Moscow), a member of the Duma and CPRF stalwart, held that an all-powerful parliament could "facilitate a return to Soviet power." In Luk'ianov's plan, a certain "party that speaks for all the working people" would "come to power in the parliament and again be in a position to establish the working people's control over the state." Besides the communists, however, virtually no one favored parliamentarism. From interviews and discussions at the time, I gleaned that a reason that presidentialism of some type seemed the logical choice even to most liberals, in addition to Yeltsin's control of the presidency and communists' and nationalists' predominance in parliament, was the perception that Russia needed a strong president as a guardian of its great-power status. People often mentioned the United States as a model and remarked that a country with serious international responsibilities needed a powerful president who could act quickly and decisively. Many were unaware of the heavy constraints that Congress and the courts place on the president of the United States. Other observers of the constitutional debate in Russia have also noted this phenomenon (Walker, 1992).

Constitutional Choice as a Determinant of Political Regime

The Russian story, as well as the experiences of other countries, illuminates several important facts. First, country-specific circumstances shaped constitutional choices. Second, popular preferences often influenced those choices. Constitutions were not merely the products of an elites' game. In Russia, from the advent of the idea of a Russian presidency in late 1990 and early 1991 to the vote that ratified the new constitution in late 1993, popular opinion, expressed repeatedly at the polls, shaped outcomes. Third, the openness of the political system did not necessarily determine the powers that the constitution granted the legislature. Russia was more politically open than either Hungary or Romania at the respective times that each country chose its constitution. Yet, for reasons rooted in historical or proximate political circumstances, Russia's constitution provided for a much weaker legislature than did the Hungarian and Romanian constitutions.

Although the *roots* of constitutional choice varied across cases, the *consequences* of that choice are tractable to generalization. The choice of a stronger legislature facilitated subsequent democratization. Figure 7.2 illustrated the intimacy of the tie between the powers of legislatures and VA scores as of 2002. Use of FH freedom scores rather than VA scores produces the same result. Figure 7.4 plots the relationship between the PPI and FH freedom scores for 2002.

As mentioned earlier, determining the direction of the causal arrow in the relationship between political openness and the power of legislatures is difficult, and in practice, the relationship almost certainly runs both ways. But the correlations shown in Figures 7.2 and 7.4 are much stronger than that shown in Figure 7.3. This evidence suggests that the strength of parliamentary powers, as established in constitutions adopted between the late 1980s and mid-1990s, predicts political openness in the early 2000s more accurately than political openness at the time of the adoption of constitutions predicts the strength of legislatures.

Calculating changes in FH freedom scores between the time of the constitution's adoption and 2002, and examining the correlation between these numbers and the PPI, provides further evidence that constitutional choice subsequently influenced political openness. Figure 7.5 shows the relationship. The correlation is strong. All seven of the countries whose FH score deteriorated over the years between the constitution's adoption and 2002 had a PPI score of less than .6. Eleven of the 14 countries whose FH score improved (all but Azerbaijan, Georgia, and Tajikistan) had a PPI score higher than .6. As Table 7.7 shows, the effect of the PPI score on change in FH scores is robust to controls for economic development and FH scores at the time of the constitution's adoption.

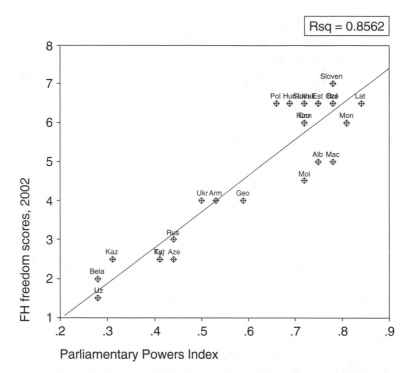

Figure 7.4. Political Openness (as FH Freedom Scores) and Parliamentary Powers

Thus, constitutional choices may have weighty consequences for democratization further down the line. The data also show unequivocally that investing parliaments with greater powers was better for democratization than investing them with lesser powers. The findings challenge conclusions that leading scholars have issued on the relationship between constitutional type and political regime. In the early 2000s, for example, Timothy Frye (2002[a], p. 102) stated: "Despite strong arguments made by some of the most prominent scholars in the field, the debate over the merits of presidential and parliamentary institutions for countries in transition remains unresolved." The present analysis shows that stronger conclusions than Frye's are warranted by the evidence.

Yet simply having a reasonably powerful legislature is the key; whether the legislature is extremely powerful, as in Latvia, or merely quite powerful, as in Poland, is not of great consequence. Neither is whether the constitution is formally parliamentary or semipresidential decisive. As Figure 7.4

Table 7.7. *Multiple Regression of Change in FH Freedom Scores on Hypothesized Determinants, Postcommunist Region*

Variable	
Constant	−5.12** (1.52)
Economic development	1.22* (0.49)
FH score at time of constitution's adoption	−0.87*** (0.10)
Parliamentary Powers Index	8.78*** (0.70)
Adj. R^2	.90

$N = 21$ countries.
*$p < 0.05$; **$p < 0.01$; ***$p < 0.001$

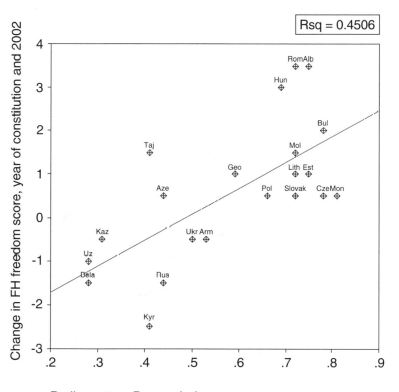

Figure 7.5. Change in Political Openness and Parliamentary Powers

shows, the bulk of countries whose PPI score is above .6 do well in democratization, and among those countries, differences in the PPI are not necessarily of great consequence for democratization. As Figure 7.5 illustrates, moreover, every country with a PPI score above .6 improved its FH freedom score between the time of the constitution's adoption and 2002. Again, differences in democratization among countries that surpass the threshold of .6 in the PPI are relatively inconsequential. What is more, whether a system is classified as parliamentary, semipresidential, or presidential is of less moment for democracy than is the strength of the legislature, though all countries that have parliamentary systems have a PPI score over .6 and no countries with a PPI score under .6 have parliamentary systems. Semipresidential systems range widely in the extent of parliamentary powers, from Mongolia (.81) to Kazakhstan (.31). So too do they range just as widely in the extent of democratization, which is closely related to the power of parliament. There is nothing essentially good or bad about semipresidentialism per se for democratization; what matters is how much power the legislature has. The more, the better.

How, specifically, does a weak legislature inhibit democratization?

What's Wrong with Superpresidentialism?

Tenuous Regime Legitimacy

Superpresidentialism has compromised the legitimacy of the post-Soviet regime in Russia by identifying democracy itself with a single person. On the eve of the passage of the constitution in late 1993, Edward Walker (1993/4, p. 119) predicted: "Unfortunately, the power concentrated in the presidency will also mean that the declining popularity of the president will probably be accompanied by declining support for democracy. Russia appears destined to acquire a new institutional order that makes the already precarious process of democratic consolidation even more problematic." Events proved Walker's prescience. Public skepticism about democracy climbed as Yeltsin's effectiveness waned. Since so much power is vested in a single person, it is unsurprising – especially in a fledgling democracy with little history of open politics – that many citizens would associate the regime with the person. Had Yeltsin been the perfect politician and had social and economic circumstances been sunny, the close association of president and regime might not have damaged the legitimacy of democracy. In fact, Yeltsin was often debilitated and conditions for many people were arduous. In the post-Yeltsin era, the legitimacy of the regime has been tied to Putin. While Putin is more competent and popular than his predecessor, the problem remains: The legitimacy of the political system is tethered to one individual's performance (White and McAllister, 2003).

Semipresidential constitutions that provide for truly joint control over the government and multiple centers of real power are different. The president and the parliament habitually blame one another for their country's travails – but they may do so without impugning the political system itself. Citizens can fix blame for their woes on a particular political target without necessarily condemning the whole regime (Walker, 1993/4). As parliament and the president in Poland lashed one another for rising unemployment in the early to mid-1990s, so too could Poles feel that their pain was inflicted by either the simpleminded liberal-nationalist president, Lech Wałęsa, or the treacherous, atheistic former communists who predominated in parliament. Both branches, in fact, had real influence over policy, and so blaming either one made perfectly good sense and did not necessarily require blaming "democracy."

The legitimacy-preserving effects of a reasonably strong legislature are also evident in Lithuania. In December 2002, Rolandas Paksas, a politician with a weakness for shady arms deals and 1930s-style torchlit rallies, swamped the incumbent, Valdas Adamkus, an émigré politician known for his probity, in presidential elections (Donskis, 2003). The victory of Paksas, a Zhirinovskii with administrative experience, was all the more disturbing given that Lithuania's economy had performed well during Adamkus's term. But Paksas's election did not have the same meaning in Lithuania as a Zhirinovskii victory would have in Russia. With Algirdas Brazauskas, a seasoned social democrat, ensconced in the prime minister's office and in command of a parliamentary coalition capable of counterbalancing the president, there was little reason for Lithuanians who disliked Paksas to reexamine their own commitment to open politics. The electorate indeed elevated to the presidency a figure whose own commitment to democracy was in doubt. But no one politician in Lithuania is capable of jeopardizing the legitimacy of the political system. What is more, the legislature itself could impeach the president and force his removal from office – which it did in April 2004.

The same cannot be said for Russia. There, a politician who launched his bid for power as the voice of the people but who declined dramatically in office turned the term "democrat" into a curse word for many of his countrymen, and the legislature did not have the capacity to dislodge him.

Legitimacy means more than "popularity" and cannot be captured fully by public opinion polls. It refers to a generally positive orientation toward the political regime. According to the conventional measures, including trust (or lack thereof) in public institutions, respect (or lack thereof) for the law, and the size of the vote for parties that are (or are not) committed to open politics, the legitimacy of the post-Soviet regime in Russia is low even by postcommunist standards (Holmes, 2003; Robinson, 2001; Rose, 1996; Rose and Shin, 1998; Rose and Munro, 2002; Vujacic, 2001).

Listless Political Parties

Superpresidentialism also has a chilling effect on party development. The impetus to build parties depends on the power of the national legislature. Parties typically attract public attention, form identities and reputations, and find their voices in parliaments and parliamentary elections (Linz and Valenzuela, eds., 1994). Since half of all deputies are elected on party lists and committee chairmanships are distributed on the basis of party affiliation, parties do play a role in the Duma (Fish, 2003; Golosov, 2003; Smith and Remington, 2001; Wyman, White, and Oates, eds., 1998). But the countervailing effects of the legislature's diminutive role wipe away the auspicious effects of these rules. The weakness of the legislature deadens interest in party building. For the political operative, the attractive positions are in the executive branch, and party work is not a prerequisite for a position there. For the businessperson, targeting the executive-branch official responsible for policy in one's area of concern is more promising than contributing to political parties. The system of strong-president-weak-legislature animates the growth not of political parties but rather of closed, compact organizations that are skilled at pressuring and bribing officials in executive-branch agencies. Consequently, well-heeled cliques representing narrow business interests, rather than political parties, have constituted the growth sector in sociopolitical organization in post-Soviet Russia (Golosov, 1997; McFaul, 1997; Shevtsova, 1995; Zudin, 1999).

Figure 7.6 plots the relationship between the percentage of people active in political parties and the PPI. The data on party activism are the same as those used in Chapter 6. As the figure shows, countries with stronger legislatures generally have more activism in political parties. Dropping Albania improves the goodness of fit, with the R^2 rising to .21. Table 7.8, which includes Albania, shows that the relationship holds when controlling for economic development.

Table 7.8. *Multiple Regression of Percentage of the Population Active in Political Parties on Hypothesized Determinants, Including the Parliamentary Powers Index, Postcommunist Region*

Variable	
Constant	16.33* (6.68)
Economic development	−5.76** (1.93)
Parliamentary Powers Index	9.12* (3.87)
Adj. R^2	.39

$N = 18$ countries.
*$p < 0.05$; **$p < 0.01$; ***$p < 0.001$

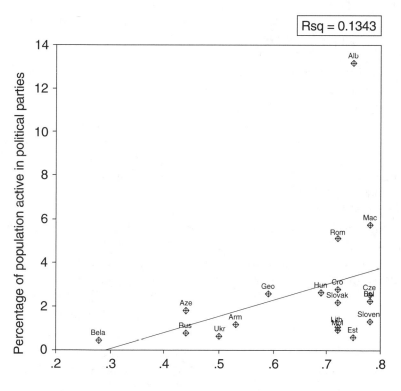

Figure 7.6. Party Activism and Parliamentary Powers

The debilitating effects of parliamentary weakness on party development have long been abundantly clear in Russia. Parliamentary elections are held several months before presidential elections. Voters view – and politicians treat – the parliamentary elections as a first heat for the contest that really counts. After the Unity Party, which Putin endorsed, performed well in the parliamentary elections of December 1999, Putin was widely assumed to be the front-runner for the presidency. Similarly, the poor showing of the Fatherland-All Russia Party knocked its leaders, Iurii Luzhkov and Evgenii Primakov, out of the presidential race.

The relative weightlessness of the parliament makes a career there unattractive, while the presidency and posts in the executive branch are attractive. The system creates perverse incentives for leading politicians, at least in regards to party building. As little more than a first heat for the presidential race, the legislative election encourages intracamp, rather than intercamp, competition. Party leaders who have presidential aspirations lack an incentive to maximize their parties' vote share vis-à-vis parties whose ideological orientation is starkly different from their own. They have little reason to cooperate with like-minded parties or even to maximize their own party's share of the total vote. Instead, the supremacy of the presidency, especially given the timing of elections, encourages party leaders to maximize their own party's vote share *within* a particular camp, even to the extent of undermining potential allies.

The behavior of Iabloko's leader, Grigorii Iavlinskii, illustrates the dynamic. Throughout the 1990s, Iavlinskii's overriding aim was becoming president (Fish, 1997; Rutland, 1999). In the 1995 and 1999 parliamentary campaigns, Iavlinskii spewed invective against fellow liberals. In 1995, he denounced DCR and Forward, Russia (FR, *Vpered Rossiia* in Russian), two parties that shared Iabloko's liberalism and that were logical allies of Iabloko in the Duma. Iavlinskii hardly criticized anti-democratic parties. He even spoke respectfully of the communists. His aim was transparent: to emerge from the parliamentary elections as the only viable liberal candidate for president. DCR and FR were also headed by figures with national stature and ambitions, Egor Gaidar and Boris Federov, respectively. Thus, maximizing Iabloko's share of the vote, after the point at which the party received the 5 percent minimum needed for representation in the Duma, was far less important to Iavlinskii than ensuring that neither DCR nor FR cross the 5 percent barrier and thereby establish a foothold in parliament. Despite Iabloko's mediocre performance (its share fell from the 8 percent it received in 1993 to 7 percent in 1995), the result suited Iavlinskii well,

228

since neither DCR nor FR cleared the 5 percent threshold. The day after the parliamentary vote, Iavlinskii announced that the field for the 1996 presidential election was set. It consisted, he proclaimed, of the leaders of the four parties that had cleared the 5 percent barrier, meaning himself, the LDPR's Zhirinovskii, OHR's Chernomyrdin, and the CPRF's Ziuganov, as well as Yeltsin (Fish, 1997). Iavlinskii was indeed the lone liberal candidate to stand for the presidency in 1996 (unless one also counts Yeltsin as a liberal). In the event, he was disappointed, finishing with roughly the same percentage of the vote as his party won in the parliamentary elections. Iavlinskii pursued the same strategy in the 1999 parliamentary campaign, again training his fire on other liberals, though this time Iabloko was bested by another liberal party, the URF.

The shadow of the impending presidential elections also meant that Iavlinskii dared not let other leaders of his own party upstage him. In the 1995 parliamentary campaign, no one else represented the party in the media, though Iabloko had a half dozen other leaders who might have enhanced the party's appeal, including Vladimir Lukin and Aleksei Arbatov. In 1999, the party added other high-profile figures to its ranks, including Sergei Stepashin and Nikolai Travkin. Yet Iavlinskii never ceded the limelight; as in 1995, he alone spoke for the party.

Iavlinkskii's behavior did not endear him to fellow leaders in the party, many of whom parted ways with the party after 1999. In December 2003, Iavlinskii repeated his well-worn patterns of behavior, but this time Iabloko failed even to cross the 5 percent threshold (Belin, 2003[b]). As discussed in Chapter 3, there is reason to believe that electoral fraud, rather than the will of the people, shut Iabloko out of the Duma. In a fair count, Iabloko might have crossed – if only barely – the 5 percent minimum. At any rate, it is safe to say that Iavlinskii's behavior between 1993 and 2003 did not enhance the coherence of liberal forces in Russia. Nor did it promote the growth and development of Iabloko. Yet it is fully comprehensible, given the centrality of the presidency and the marginality of parliament.

Innumerable observers have claimed that Russian voters care little for parties, programs, and principles, but rather focus on personalities. Donald Jensen (2003) holds that "the preeminence of candidates' personalities over their views on the issues" is a central feature of post-Soviet Russian politics. In its report on Russia's 2003 parliamentary elections, *The Economist* quipped that parties and ideologies meant little to Russians; instead "it is faces that voters latch on to" ("Putin's Way," 2003). Many others agree (Bukharin, 1995; Chekalkin, 1995; see also Brader and Tucker, 2002; Miller and Klobucar, 2000; Wishnevsky, 1995). Yet no one has demonstrated the veracity of this claim in comparative perspective. None has ever shown that Russians care more about faces and less about principles than do American or French or Indonesian voters. None has offered a theory of why Russians would be so extraordinarily attached to personalities. Perhaps Russians are not, in comparative terms, inordinately enamored with personalities. Instead, it is possible that institutionally defined incentives, rather than popular demand, encourage candidates to base their appeals on themselves. The apparent hyperpersonalization of elections may result more from political institutions that encourage candidates to engage in personalization than out of a predisposition of Russian voters to shun interests in favor of faces.

Amateurish Politicians

The superpresidential system not only encourages party leaders to advance their interests as loners rather than team players but also reduces the quality of the political class. The president, by occupying so much of the field, stifles the entrance into national politics of other people of ability and ambition.

Max Weber's polemic on behalf of resurrecting parliament in early post–World War I Germany illuminates with singular acuity the role that the legislature plays in the formation of the political class. In his *Parliament and Government in a Reconstructed Germany* (Weber, 1978), Weber assailed the emasculation of parliament and exposed its devastating consequences. According to Weber, Otto von Bismarck's domination of politics during his time as chancellor from 1871 to 1890, achieved by Bismarck's political brilliance and specific measures that he took to sideline parliament, left Germany with an otiose legislature.

A patriot as well as a democrat, Weber yearned for a postwar regime in Germany that was both open and effective, and he regarded a muscular legislature as a precondition for both democracy and effectiveness. He held that parliament, at a minimum, must be "the agency for enforcing the *public control of administration,* for determining the *budget* and finally for deliberating and passing *laws*" (1978, p. 1454, italics here and following in the original). He favored a system in which the ministers of government were members of parliament or at least were required to "account for their actions exhaustively to parliament" and to "run the administration according to the guidelines approved by parliament" (p. 1408).

Weber regarded a strong parliament as the key to recruiting individuals with the capacity for leadership into the affairs of state. According to

Weber, only genuine politicians made good leaders, and only the type of men who crave glory and thrive on struggle were cut out to be politicians. A powerful legislature drew such men into public life, and since a legislature was composed of hundreds of seats, it could attract a substantial number of potential leaders into the political arena.

Weber drew a distinction between politicians and bureaucrats. The politician loved asserting mastery. He was skilled at swaying opinion (to get elected) and battling other politicians (to represent those who elected him and ensure his reelection and advancement). He had an independent base of power (his constituents) and got ahead by besting his peers (other politicians). The bureaucrat was by nature a security seeker. He was expert at executing tasks assigned by others. He succeeded by ingratiating himself with superiors. For the bureaucrat, "the quality which best guarantees promotion is a measure of pliancy toward the apparatus, the degree of the subordinate's 'convenience' for his superior. The selection is, on the average, certainly not one of born leaders" (p. 1449). Since the bureaucracy was not congenial to "born leaders," it could not attract them to the affairs of state.

Legislatures were different: "Every conflict in parliament involves not only a struggle over substantive issues but also a struggle for personal power" (p. 1409). That was the kind of environment that attracted real leaders. But real leaders would compete for a place in parliament only if the latter was the arena of high-stakes conflict. Otherwise, "a man with a strong power drive and the qualities that go with it" would stick with applying his energies "in fields such as the giant industrial enterprises, cartels, banks, and wholesale firms" (p. 1413). Some men, to be sure, will be happy to participate in a weak parliament. But they will usually be the type who desire office as entrée to a comfortable position in the state's bureaucratic-administrative apparatus. Alternatively, they may be demagogues who revel in publicity but have scant desire to wield power. True leaders seek office, according to Weber, "not for the sake of salary and rank, but of *power* and the attending *responsibility*." The difference between a strong parliament and a weak one spelled the "difference between making parliament a recruiting ground for leaders or for bureaucratic careerists [and] demagogic talents" (pp. 1411, 1416).

An authoritative parliament was not only essential for drawing real leaders into public life; it was also crucial for training them. Since "the essence of politics – as we will have to emphasize time and again – is *struggle*, the recruitment of *allies* and of a *voluntary* following," then it followed that

231

"for the modern politician the proper palaestra is the parliament and the party contests before the general public; neither competition for bureaucratic advancement nor anything else will provide an adequate substitute" (p. 1414). In the heated debate over the powers of parliament that percolated in Germany at the time that Weber wrote, nothing less than the quality of the nation's political leadership was at stake: "Only a *working*, not merely speech-making parliament can provide the ground for the growth and selective ascent of genuine leaders" (p. 1416).

Let us move east and push the clock forward by about 90 years. The Russian parliament lacks what Weber regarded as the minimal functions of a working legislature. It exerts virtually no control over public administration. It must contend with the president's ability to impound funds and otherwise manipulate the budget. It shares lawmaking authority with the president, who can legislate by decree.

So too is Russia short on genuine *politicians*. The problem is especially acute among democrats. The superpresidential system, according to Weber's logic, may be partially to blame. Since Yeltsin was widely regarded as the leader of the democrats, one might expect to find especially little room left for real politicians in the pro-democratic portion of the political spectrum. If parliament were a site of real power, liberal-minded individuals who had what Weber called "a strong power drive and the qualities that go with it" would find it an attractive place to make a career. But the parliament did not and does not offer the "*power* and the attending *responsibility*" that Weber said it must in order to attract people suited to leadership.

Russia does not lack liberal leaders. Some are extraordinary individuals. Many are extremely intelligent. No one would ever accuse Egor Gaidar or Anatolii Chubais, leaders of DCR and then the URF; Irina Khakamada, a leader of the URF; or Sergei Kirienko, a former leader of the URF, of mental sluggishness. Grigorii Iavlinskii, the leader of Iabloko, is also intellectually gifted. Some Russian liberals are moral paragons. Sergei Kovalev, a human rights activist and former parliamentarian, spent much of the Brezhnev period in prison for political activity. He tenaciously opposes the war in Chechnya and has risked his life traveling to war zones there.

And yet, none of these people is capable of what Weber regarded as the politician's central affair – that is, "struggle" by means of "the recruitment of *allies* and of a *voluntary* following." Based on close observation over more than a decade, I would add that few are capable of carrying on a conversation with a nonintellectual without quickly turning condescending or simply losing interest. These people are not politicians in Weber's sense. Several have served stints in the executive branch and are able administrators. But none has, or ever will, recruit a substantial popular following. To say that each lacks the common touch would be to understate the point.

A brief look of how they ran their campaigns in a parliamentary election provides illustration. In 1995, the two major liberal parties were DCR and Iabloko. I resided in Russia at the time and saw the campaigns up close. Iabloko's campaign on the airwaves relied on two stock ads. Both gave prominence to the fruit used by the party as its name. (An assembly of the party's founders' names created an acronym that roughly spells *Iabloko*, which means "apple" in Russian.) In one ad, a man dressed as Isaac Newton sits under a tree. Predictably, an apple falls on his head. The jolt gives him the bright idea of voting for Iabloko. In the second ad, a young couple sit on a park bench. The young man, turning away from his girlfriend, munches an apple. His girlfriend whines: "Do you love the apple more than me?" Her boyfriend, now smiling, turns to her and answers: "No, dear, I love *you* – but I am *voting* for Iabloko." A voice-over then assures viewers that "one does not contradict the other" – meaning that one could love one's sweetheart and vote for Iabloko, too. When queried about their party's television strategy after the election, several of Iabloko's leaders stated that they regarded the ads as hopelessly fatuous, but that Iavlinskii esteemed the agency that produced the ads and could not be dissuaded from using them (Vladimir Averchev and Viacheslav Igrunov, personal interviews, January 6, 1996, Moscow).

The centerpiece of Iabloko's print-media campaign was a *350-page hardcover book* that was exceedingly hard to find outside the offices of party leaders. The volume, which the party called its program, was entitled *Reforms for the Majority* (*Reformy dlia bol'shinstva*). Here was no loose chatter. The 200 pages that were devoted to economic policy included a magnificent statistical apparatus and graphs depicting "the dynamic of real monetary supply M0 and M2" over a three-year period. Crime and corruption, which were matters of overriding public concern at the time, were dealt with in a half-dozen pages. Solutions to crime were to be found in "a change in the economic course," "a system of strengthening the family," and "a system of rehabilitating criminals." Corruption was simply condemned as a very bad thing (*Reformy dlia bol'shinstva*, 1995).

DCR's political acumen matched that of Iabloko. A central part of DCR's television pitch was a monologue that stretched on for several minutes. A long-faced Gaidar, sitting behind a desk, offers a somber disputation on Russia's economic woes. Adducing comparative data on the economic performance of neighboring countries, Gaidar intones that had he had three years rather than eleven months in the prime minister's office, the country's economy would be in much better shape. The centerpiece of DCR's print-media effort was the party's campaign brochure, grippingly entitled *Notes from the Hall* (*Zapiski iz zala*). The document was an 80-page-long interview with Gaidar (1995). In the first half of the booklet, Gaidar held forth on budgetary, tax, bankruptcy, and exchange-rate policies. In the second half, he answered questions about himself, his opinions of Yeltsin, and other issues that were presumably of burning urgency to the voters.

So went the 1995 campaign. Did the liberals' political acumen subsequently improve? In the 1999 parliamentary elections, the URF, led by Gaidar, Kirienko, Khakamada, Chubais, and Boris Nemtsov, captured 11 percent of the vote. Yet the party's main asset was an eleventh-hour pat on the back from Putin. The gesture, which became the party's main television ad, took the form of a meeting between Putin and Kirienko in which Putin gestured toward the URF's program and stated: "There are some good ideas here." Putin was already allied with the Unity Party, but he saw fit to give the young liberals of the URF a boost as well. By the 2003 parliamentary campaign, Putin was regarding the URF as a nuisance. Left to their own devices, the liberals again proved shy on shrewdness. The URF's main ad featured Chubais, Khakamada, and Nemtsov flying in a private jet. The ad was meant to appeal to ambitious, fortunate young people (Belin, 2003[a]). The only problem was that Chubais, who presided over Russia's privatization program, made his fortune – which by most accounts could finance a fleet of private jets – during his time in government service. Due in part to this unsavory fact, he is one of the most despised public figures in Russia (Freeland, 2000).

There is nothing quite as ineffective in modern mass politics as ingenuous hubris. The ad with the URF's leaders in the private jet showcases this peculiar quality. So too does much of the discourse that Russia's liberal leaders have generated since the downfall of the Soviet regime. Enlightening and edifying, rather than convincing and mobilizing, has been the standard approach to voters (Shlapentokh, 2003[a]). Iavlinskii has never tired of reminding his audiences that he is a professional economist. His answers to questions in interviews are habitually prefaced with remarks such as "your question [or comment] shows that you know nothing about economics." In the 1995 parliamentary campaign, in response to what appeared to be an offer by Gaidar to pool their efforts, Iavlinskii stated that a union was improbable, but added: "Gaidar is a professional economist and it is always possible to find common ground with a professional economist" (Orttung, 1995).

Economists indeed; Gaidar and Iavlinskii, as well as Chubais and Khakamada, are economists by profession. But politicians they are not. Their paucity of political prowess may have something to do with the atrophy of the pro-democratic vote.

There have been exceptions. Sergei Stankevich, who was deputy major of Moscow and a leader of the democratic movement in the late Gorbachev period, may have been one, though Stankevich fled abroad under the cloud of corruption allegations in the early 1990s. Anatolii Sobchak, who first achieved fame as a member of the USSR Congress of People's Deputies for his electrifying denunciations of Soviet rule, and who went on to serve two terms as mayor of Leningrad/St. Petersburg, also had a politician's instincts, though he was narrowly defeated for a third term in 1996 and died in 2000.

The most obvious surviving exception is Nemtsov, but his experience illustrates how the system stymies talent. Nemtsov started his political career at the end of the Soviet period as a young governor of Nizhnii Novgorod oblast. He first worked in Moscow when Yeltsin called him to serve as deputy prime minister in 1997. Nemtsov agonized over the decision. He seemed to realize intuitively what Weber spelled out explicitly: Politicians often do not make good bureaucrats. The position Yeltsin offered seemed to carry real power, however, and Nemtsov took it. But he was chewed up by work in the governmental apparatus and left in frustration after little more than a year in office. He then turned to parliamentary politics. Yet the Duma did not hold much appeal for him. He lent his name to the URF in 1999 and 2003 but never invested much in his role as a parliamentarian. His public stock shrank along with his job satisfaction. By the end of the 1990s, Nemtsov, whom Yeltsin once touted as a potential future president, was no longer a highly regarded national figure. In December 2003, the URF did not reach the 5 percent threshold required for parliamentary representation ("Boris Nemtsov," 2003; Chinayeva, 1996).

In countries with strong parliaments, figures like Nemtsov have a great deal to do in national politics without having to go to work for a chief executive who may or may not be personally stable or managerially competent. In the Czech Republic, Nemtsov could have followed the path of Milos Zeman or Václav Klaus; in Bulgaria, that of Ivan Kostov or Ahmed Dogan; and in Mongolia, that of Radnaasumbereliin Gonchigdorj or Janlav Narantsatsralt. Each of these individuals, like Nemtsov, is a reformer and also what Weber called a "born leader." Unlike Nemtsov, each also has the benefit of working in a system in which the central arena of national politics is what Weber called "the proper palaestra" for the modern politician.

One might argue that an office of supreme importance that did not exist in the Germany of Weber's time is present in today's Russia: a presidency filled by popular election. Weber made his plea for a powerful parliament at a time when the monarch still reigned (though he was on the verge of exit). The alternative to parliamentary struggle was bureaucratic rivalry.

The presidency may also serve as a magnet and a proving ground for real political talent. Yet the presidency creates but a single political job; all who work for the president, like all who worked for the German chancellor, are bureaucrats. What is more, in the event that a "born leader" occupies the presidency in a political system that invests great power in the presidency, he or she may actually stifle the development of an able political class – precisely what Weber accused Bismarck of doing in Germany.

Indeed, Yeltsin's and Putin's domination of national politics has had all of the pathological effects that Weber attributed to Bismarck's rule. While Yeltsin held the presidency, his presence tended especially to crowd out pro-democratic talent, as he was regarded as a – or the – representative of the pro-democratic tendency. There was little room left for other "democrats." What is more, even though Yeltsin did sometimes promote relatively liberal figures, his patronage was always short-lived. Yeltsin tended to distrust talent and regard it as a threat to his own dominance, something Gaidar, Kirienko, Nemtsov, and other liberals learned from personal experience (Breslauer, 2002). This state of affairs helps explain why liberal political figures, while by no means holding a monopoly on political incompetence, did display an especially conspicuous degree of it during the 1990s. They could not really form a spirited opposition when one of their own was president. Yet "their" president gave them little to do; indeed, he did more to crush their ambitions than to nurture them.

When a strong president who is not identified with a particular political orientation holds office, as in the case of Putin, his presence may virtually sweep the field clean, leaving little or no talent left to spar with him. Such a situation was on lurid display in the 2004 presidential elections, in which some of Putin's "rivals" endorsed Putin (Myers, 2004[a]).

In the meantime, then, where are the individuals "with a strong power drive and the qualities that go with it" who, Weber said, were crucial for effective national leadership, but who would stick with "fields such as the giant industrial enterprises, cartels, banks, and wholesale firms" unless a powerful parliament attracted them to political life? (p. 1413). They are just where Weber would expect them to be.

Frail State Agencies

Among the arguments in favor of superpresidentialism, perhaps the one that seems most intuitively sensible is that the concentration of power in the president strengthens the state. Legislatures are often messy, quarrelsome places. In polities under stress, where decisive action is often urgent, an executive who can sidestep or overrule the legislature might seem like a vital asset.

In practice, however, superpresidentialism undermines state capacity. Measuring state capacity is difficult, and I will not try to do so here. Yet, however one assesses state strength, the Russian state, even in the context of the postcommunist region, is not known for its effectiveness in carrying out steering, administrative, service-providing, and other functions (Holmes, 1997[b]; Sperling, 2000). George Breslauer (2002) has demonstrated that administrative organization during the 1990s was the antithesis of rationalization. Zoltan Barany (2001) has shown that Yeltsin's management of the armed forces amounted to little more than a jumble of fleeting personalistic arrangements in which the president abolished agencies of control as suddenly as he created them.

Superpresidentialism enervates state agencies mainly by means of the personalistic, anti-institutional impulse that it builds into political life. If a single actor enjoys or potentially enjoys mastery, he or she has an incentive to block the formation of foci of organization and influence that can challenge him or her. The ruler may say – and even sincerely believe – that he or she desires stable agencies that operate according to well-established rules. And yet, such entities are in reality a threat to the ruler's supremacy and freedom of action.

The conundrum is rooted in a perennial problem of politics and rule, which is the relationship between rulers and their agents. This issue lay at the center of much of Weber's thinking about rulership and administration. He held that "[h]istorical reality involves a continuous, though for the most part latent, conflict between chiefs and their administrative staffs for appropriation and expropriation in relation to one another" (1978, p. 264). According to Weber, the problem posed a perpetual challenge to effective administration. Yet one of his great insights was to perceive that a workable system of administration, in which the tension between the ruler and his agents did not continuously undermine government, could emerge even in a system based on patrimonialism, in which rulers considered their realm as personal chattel. Several conditions had to obtain. One was obvious: that "technical training should be available." Another was less obvious and much more interesting. It was the presence of "sharp competition between a plurality of patrimonial powers within the same cultural area" (p. 240). In such a condition, "the patrimonial ruler, in the interest of his own power and financial provision, develops a rational system of administration with technically specialized officials." Weber implies that the challenges of "sharp competition" among a "plurality" of rulers leads the latter to embrace an efficient apparatus and rule-bound relationships with subordinates, since such arrangements may be crucial to successful struggle and survival. In a word, the danger posed by competition from equals forces rulers to trust subordinates enough to facilitate, rather than undermine, their effective organization, and to enlist their subordinates in their struggle against other rulers.

Joel Migdal's (1988) comparative study of state building in developing countries provides some evidence from contemporary politics. Migdal establishes the logic for why rulers sometimes destroy institutions as quickly as they create them. He characterizes rulers who say that they aim to build a strong state and to deploy it for laudable ends as sincere; he does not cast them as egoistic predators. And yet, he shows, rulers often emasculate even institutions that they created themselves. Since institutions may beget rival power centers, rulers concerned with staying in power and maximizing control – meaning most rulers – find themselves pursuing deinstitutionalization as soon as they have accomplished institutionalization. According to Migdal (p. 207): "Bizarre as it may seem, state leaders with limited capacity to mobilize their public have themselves crippled the arms of the state, especially those organs that ultimately could have given the leaders not only mobilizational ability but also . . . enhanced security."

Migdal sees the paradox as arising out of the nature of society. With special reference to Egypt under Gamal Abdul Nasser, Migdal holds that the ruler's efforts at transformation collide with "the vast, but fragmented social control embedded in the nonstate organizations of society," which in turn "has dictated a particular, pathological set of relationships with the state organization itself, between the top state leadership and its agencies" (p. 207). Migdal focuses on how society, with its multifarious structures of authority and control, affects the state. In his view, prior-existing bases of societal power co-opt the ruler's agencies, forcing the ruler constantly to intervene to undercut his own agents and institutions in order to thwart challenges and ensure his survival.

Migdal furnishes valuable insight into the deinstitutionalizing impulse. But he only illuminates the paradox and provides a glimpse at its possible sources; he does not reveal the logic of the deinstitutionalizing urge or show precisely under what conditions the opposite impulse might guide the ruler's behavior. There is no logical reason why "the vast, but fragmented social control embedded in the nonstate organizations of society" must be the main source of the ruler's suspicions that his agents will escape his domination. Migdal writes about countries where societies rich in long-standing clan or tribal ties, chiefdoms, well-off peasants, and other sources of nonstate authority meshed with and co-opted state agents, thereby challenging rulers' transformational goals and supremacy. Even without the societal challenges that he emphasizes, rulers may fear loss of control over their agents – especially if the latter can break out of exclusively vertical, dependent relations and work within agencies that might escape the ruler's monitoring and command. In fact, Russia did not enter the post-Soviet period with, nor did it subsequently spawn, a dense, weblike society of the type that Migdal found in his postcolonial cases. Stalinism leveled classes and destroyed the nascent civil society of the late imperial period, and strong clan and tribal ties were virtually nonexistent. Post-Soviet Russian society bears little resemblance to the societies that Migdal investigated; yet its presidents' anti-institutional habits of rule are as pronounced as Nasser's. Like Nasser, Russia's presidents have feared institutions' potential for spawning sources of power that may elude personal control.

How do rulers' orientations toward institutions differ when power is not concentrated in a single actor? Rulers may still spurn institutionalization. But when power at the national level is dispersed between two or more branches or camps, power holders are often guided by an urge to build institutions, rather than undermine them. If power holders do not and cannot hope to achieve complete mastery, the best strategy may be to outdo competitors in building institutions that can serve as sources of support – even given the risk that they may elude total control.

In fact, the origins of institutions and institutional development are usually found in competition for the right to rule, rather than in ruling. Samuel Huntington (1968, p. 11) argues: "Historically, political institutions have emerged out of the interaction among and disagreement among social forces, and the gradual development of procedures and organizational devices for resolving those disagreements." Charles Tilly (1990) shows that the impetus to construct robust agencies and rules at the dawn of state formation grows out of rivalry between proto-states, not from the practice of despotism within a single, unchallenged polity. Axel Hadenius (2001, p. 199) holds that particularly robust states arose in England, Sweden, the Netherlands, and the United States largely because in these countries, "no decisions of any import could be made without negotiating with society's leading groups." Competition among powerful, autonomous social groups and between these groups and the state promoted the emergence of both strong states and relatively open politics. In contrast, in Russia, Spain, and France, autocratic regimes bolstered by highly centralized or militarized states neither provided channels for representation of societal interests nor were able to avoid disintegration when the rulers' capacity for extracting taxes waned or when the countries were defeated in war. Dankwart Rustow's (1970) theory of regime change outlines how competition between evenly matched forces spurs the genesis of democratic institutions. The rules that emerge to regulate the conflict become the institutional infrastructure of the new democratic regime. Democratic institutions arise willy-nilly out of heated competition, not by design and bestowal from above. Some works that adopt a formal choice-theoretic approach have also shown that the dominance of a single actor is inimical to institutional building and institutional reform (Andrews and Montinola, 2004; Geddes, 1994).

Even Migdal illustrates the importance of competition and the dispersion of power for institution building, though he does not fully explicate the implications of his own narrative. His sole case of successful postcolonial state building, Israel, is chock full of conflict and balancing. Strife among the state builders, the absence of a single dominant personage or organization in the anticolonial movement, and the consequent necessity of resolving conflict by creating durable rules stand out as the most obvious differences between Israel and the cases of failed state building. Migdal does not emphasize these differences in his conclusions, but instead stresses the skill of Israeli politicians and the structural characteristics of society.

In short, the concentration of power, particularly in a single individual or office, counters institution building. In this case, institutions tend never to be born, to be subverted by their creator if they are born, or to rot from lack of reform even if they are not subverted. Institutions reduce arbitrariness, and their weakness dims the prospects for nonarbitrary rule. Democracy requires that rules rule rulers; it cannot emerge without institutional development and stability.

Such a dynamic is at work in present-day Russia. As John Squier (2004, p. 172) notes in an incisive review article: "Rather than reaching out to the public and trying to build lasting institutions – a strategy that would serve both to support his goals and to impose accountability on the unruly system he faces – Putin seems to have decided to impose order by eliminating as many independent sources of influence as possible." One may add that the office he holds enables and encourages Putin to pursue such an approach.

Unbridled Corruption

The extraordinary extent of corruption in Russia was discussed in previous chapters. The corruption-stoking effects of natural resource abundance were shown in Chapter 5. The superpresidential system exacerbates corruption. The relationship is evident in cross-national perspective. Figure 7.7

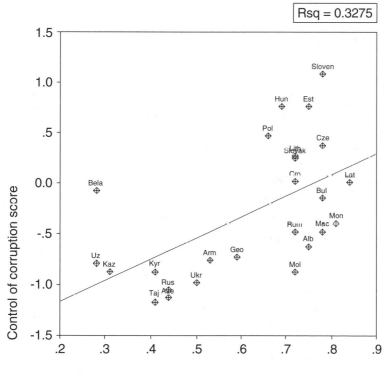

Figure 7.7. Control of Corruption and Parliamentary Powers

Table 7.9. *Multiple Regression of Control of Corruption Score on Hypothesized Determinants, Including the Parliamentary Powers Index, Postcommunist Region*

Variable	
Constant	-5.59^{***} (0.83)
Economic development	1.29^{***} (0.25)
Parliamentary Powers Index	1.60^{***} (0.44)
Adj. R^2	.67

$N = 25$ countries.
$^*p < 0.05$; $^{**}p < 0.01$; $^{***}p < 0.001$
Source: Data for control of corruption score, which are for 2000, from Kaufmann et al., 2003.

illustrates the correlation between the PPI and Kaufmann's control of corruption scores. Table 7.9 shows a regression of the corruption scores on the PPI plus the control for economic development. Stronger legislatures are conducive to higher control of corruption.

The link between corruption and superpresidentialism is found in the executive's control over public expenditure and the weakness of checks on executive-branch officials. The president controls the disposal of most of the central government's resources. As the results of the Legislative Powers Survey shown in Table 7.3 reveal, the president enjoys impoundment powers (question 15), meaning that parliament can legislate expenditure but the president can block the dispersal of the funds. The president's powers of decree (question 11) further enhance his control over spending. The parliament does not even control the budget that finances its members' perks (question 16); instead, an office in the presidential administration doles out the goodies (Huskey, 1999). Whenever the legislature's cooperation is desirable, the president can buy it. Yeltsin obtained support for his budgets even from a Duma whose majority was hostile to him. Shortly after coming to office, Putin made full use of his control over perks to ensure smooth sailing for his agenda, dispatching his agents to discuss with the recently elected parliamentarians such matters as the size and quality of the apartments that they would receive in Moscow (Skorobogatko, 2000). Such circumstances help explain why the parliament does little to check corruption in executive-branch agencies. Even if they are inclined to refuse the president's inducements, parliamentarians have little capacity to monitor the executive. They lack powers of summons over executive branch officials (question 3 in the LPS). They lack control over the agencies of coercion (question 5). Not only are the military, the FSB, and the interior ministries entirely under presidential direction, but the legislature also lacks even rudimentary powers of oversight. The legislature formally has the right to conduct independent investigation of some executive agencies (question 4), but it lacks the wherewithal to do so and does not do so in practice. The legislature formally has responsibility for confirmation of some judicial appointments (question 24), but the executive makes the key appointments and exercises effective control, including over the prosecutor general, who by law is supposed to be independent of the government (Feifer, 2000).

Thus, corruption in the sprawling executive-branch bureaucracy rages unchecked by legislative or judicial oversight. Those who control the state's resources at the national level are accountable only to the president. Were he deeply committed to controlling his subordinates, perhaps the president could prevent abuse of office for private gain. But Yeltsin's obvious incompetence in this area allowed officials to route public funds into personal bank accounts, portfolios, and real estate empires abroad. Putin cultivates a reputation for intolerance of corruption, but there is little evidence that official rectitude has risen markedly on his watch. He may be more engaged in administration than his predecessor, but the KGB men who dominate his administration know very well the KGB way: Do not stoop to the level of the ordinary police, who extract a steady stream of revenue from petty bribes. Instead, take bribes rarely – but then very large ones. The sternness of Putin's rhetoric notwithstanding, official corruption will not diminish substantially in the absence of potent checks.

Closing Ruminations

What About Culture and Tradition?

Russia's superpresidential system has its defenders. Some hold that it suits Russian political culture. The argument goes roughly as follows: Russia has almost always been ruled by a strongman (or strongwoman), be he or she a monarch or Communist Party first secretary. Russians are accustomed to a strong hand. Superpresidentialism, which allows the masses to have their father figure and vote for him, too, is a good fit for post-Soviet Russia (Brovkin, 1996; Mikheyev, 1996; Nichols, 2001; Pipes, 2004).

Let us assume for a moment that such an image of Russian political culture is on target, though the point is debatable. If Russians are used to laboring under a strong hand, are arrangements that reproduce familiar conditions and reinforce old habits appropriate? Or might institutions that countervail tradition be desirable? Japan had a culture of autocracy and rigid social hierarchy at the end of World War II. Would restoring the monarchy to its prewar status, or perhaps creating a political system that was open but dominated by a president, therefore have provided a better basis for postwar political development than the parliamentary system that Japan actually adopted? Would postwar Germany, given its political heritage and culture, also have been better served by a superpresidential constitution than by the parliamentarism that it embraced?

Analogous questions may be asked of the postcommunist region. Few countries there enjoy traditions of open politics. Political culture in most places – local mythmaking notwithstanding – has been shaped no more strongly by democratic thought and pluralist practice than it has in Russia. In some sense, a dominant presidency would have been consonant with tradition and culture in every postcommunist country. Lech Wałęsa held that cultural and historical circumstances favored a strong presidency in Poland. Zhelyu Zhelev, the first president of Bulgaria, said after leaving office that he coveted the power that Yeltsin had in Russia and that Bulgaria would have been much better off had he had it (Zhelev, personal interview, January 14, 1998, Sofia). Unsurprisingly, the refrain was heard around the region from presidents and would-be presidents. Yeltsin said that a strong presidency suited Russia's traditions; Nursultan Nazarbaev made the same claim about Kazakhstan. In a sense, all of these leaders were right. But not all got what they wanted. Wałęsa and Zhelev did not, and democratization in Poland and Bulgaria has been remarkably robust. Yeltsin and Nazarbaev got what they wanted, and democratization has been durable in neither Russia nor Kazakhstan. Perhaps constitutions that were less consonant with preexisting conditions furnished a firmer basis for democratization. Institutions that countervailed culture may have spurred the growth of new traditions and provided a superior basis for political progress.

What About the Legislature's Foibles?

Another case for Russia's constitution is based on counterfactual thinking about what *would have* happened had the legislature been vested with more power. Given the prominence in Russia's post-Soviet legislatures of nondemocrats and even anti-democrats, one can plausibly argue that a strong legislature would have harmed democratization even more than the superpresidential order has. Despite his liabilities, Yeltsin was a better anti-authoritarian than his communist and nationalist foes in parliament. Wasn't Russia blessed to have a presidency that outweighed the legislature?

Perhaps it was; but the argument that a more balanced system would have yielded more anti-democratic outcomes holds only if one assumes that the behavior of both the legislature and the electorate would have been the same under a different constitution as it was in fact. This assumption cannot be tested, but one may question whether everything would have been the same except that communists and nationalists would have held more sway. Voters might have acted differently if the Duma's decisions really mattered. If they were voting for a body that held real power, would the same electorate that chose Yeltsin over his communist and nationalist opponents in 1991 and 1996 have elected a parliament with a communist-nationalist majority in 1995? If voters believed that the parliamentary elections offered a chance to shape policy, rather than merely to register disgruntlement, might they have voted differently?

Even had voters behaved similarly under a different system, may one safely assume that legislators would have acted no differently? It is possible that a more powerful parliament still would have become what the Duma became – a forum for demagogic grandstanding, rampant absenteeism, and the near-unanimous passage of ludicrous motions. But a legislature endowed with greater authority might have been taken more seriously by its own members. So too might it have exerted a stronger pull on serious talent. Weber's appeal for parliamentary resurrection in Germany (p. 1392) furnishes a fitting last word:

This powerlessness of parliament also meant that its intellectual level was greatly depressed. The naïve moralizing legend of our unpolitical literati reverses the causal relationship and maintains that parliament remained deservedly powerless *because* of the low level of parliamentary life. But simple facts and considerations reveal the actual state of affairs, which in any case is obvious to every soberly reflecting person. The level of parliament depends on whether it does not merely discuss great issues but decisively influences them; in other words, its quality depends on whether what happens there matters.

8

Can Democracy Get Back on Track?

> In essence, we are witnessing a unique experiment – whether one person with
> absolute power can run a country as enormous as Russia all by himself.
> – Mikhail Rostovskii and Aleksandr Budberg (in *Moskovskii Komsomolets*,
> March 2, 2004)

In his celebrated article penned in the late 1960s, Dankwart Rustow (1970) left a stamp on thinking about regime change in the late twentieth century. Rustow claimed that socioeconomic and cultural "prerequisites" for democratization might not be prerequisites at all. He held that the factors that made for the incremental emergence of democracy in the First World in the nineteenth and early twentieth centuries may be very different from those that facilitate democratization elsewhere. In light of the empirical evidence of the past several decades, many scholars have embraced Rustow's claim. It is easy to forget, however, that Rustow considered one generation the normal time frame for democratization. Many of us have come to think of democratization as something that happens on short order. This view is not necessarily naive; democratization can happen overnight. In Lithuania and Chile, the overthrow of dictatorship and the inauguration of a robust open regime occurred in a few short years. But these cases are atypical. The failure of democratization to take place rapidly does not necessarily spell the failure of democracy in general. Revisiting Rustow reminds us that twenty years, rather than just one or two, may be the proper interval for framing our expectations.

Yet three-quarters of that interval has already passed in Russia; it is not too early for a preliminary assessment. The bulk of the evidence shows that the dominant trend since the breakdown of the Soviet Union has been negative. The early post-Soviet period was a time of relative political openness.

Rather than building on the gains of the late Gorbachev and early Yeltsin periods, however, Russia slid backward. It has not passed through the stages that Rustow or any other theorist characterizes as the path to open rule. Russia has authored a tale of the closure of a nascent open polity, rather than a story of democratization.

Recap and Discussion of the Causal Argument

Synopsis of the Explanation

In this book's story, three variables explain Russia's failure to democratize. They are too much oil, too little economic liberalization, and too weak a national legislature.

Russia's raw materials abundance, which is reflected in the dominance of hydrocarbons and precious metals in its export profile, has undermined democratization in two ways. First, it has fueled corruption. The dominance in the economy of a few items that are extracted and exported by a small number of companies, entirely out of public view, and the vast enticements for predation that producers and regulators face due to the products' superabundance and high value on world markets, encourage corrupt behavior. High corruption, in turn, reduces popular enthusiasm for open politics, particularly in a fledgling neodemocracy such as Russia at the end of the Soviet era. Citizens who are victimized by a colossal diversion of resources to the consumption wants of officials and private actors allied with them are receptive to the appeals of politicians who promise to attack corruption even at the expense of liberty. Popular tolerance of Putin's high-handedness is comprehensible in terms of his promises to discipline grasping public officials and quasi-private "oligarchs" who made fabulous fortunes in oil, gas, and precious metals. Rampant corruption has not only boosted popular demand for a furrowed brow and a heavy hand; it has also enhanced elites' interest in political closure. People who have prospered from treachery dislike public scrutiny. Unfortunately for Russian democracy, these included people who might have helped forge an open polity. Filching public assets and giving or taking bribes – particularly if the lucre runs into the billions of dollars, as it does in resource-rich Russia – dulls one's taste for public accountability. In sum, resource superabundance has encouraged corruption, and corruption has undermined open politics. Resource abundance has also encouraged economic statism. The concentration of economic power in a handful of actors, which often occurs in economies based on a few

247

extractive industries, does not rule out deregulation and privatization. But it does present state officials with opportunities and incentives to maintain a controlling, or at least meddling, hand in production, distribution, and finance. It may encourage pseudoprivatization and the maintenance of an extraordinary regulatory burden.

Economic statism has had its own depressing effects on democratization. The predatory regulatory environment has slowed the growth of an entrepreneurial class and the middle class more generally, which in turn has circumscribed the social basis for liberal political parties and professional associations. The management buyouts and corrupt loans-for-shares deals that dominated the privatization of productive property have reproduced Soviet-era dependencies in the workplace and attenuated the social bases for parties and occupational groups that represent workers' interests. Officials' regulatory powers and control over resources have enabled them to manipulate politics through control of patronage, which has further reduced incentives to participate in political parties and interest associations and exacerbated their sluggish growth. State custody of assets even in companies or organizations that are (or were) largely privately owned or operated has enabled officials to control interest representation and to eliminate perceived opponents using commercial levers alone. In short, the endurance of economic statism has curbed the development and restricted the autonomy of societal associations. It has left society underorganized, inarticulate, and incapable of holding rulers accountable.

The third major impediment to democratization is the "superpresidential" system, meaning a constitutional arrangement that invests great power in the presidency and much less power in the legislature. This asymmetry has inhibited democratization in five ways. First, it has damaged the legitimacy of the post-Soviet regime. The concentration of power in a single pair of hands has identified the regime itself with one fallible individual. During the first post-Soviet decade, that individual was widely regarded as a "democrat" and at least as widely regarded as incompetent. Many Russians came to identify democracy with incompetence and a strong hand with the promise of salvation.

Second, the superpresidential system has inhibited the development of political parties. The constitutional system only reinforces the negative effect of economic statism on parties. The drive to build parties depends largely on the stature of the national legislature. In Russia, where the constitution relegates parliament to a subordinate role, parties have had a difficult time winning the loyalty and securing the participation of ordinary voters and well-endowed elites, whose resources are better spent pressuring agencies and officials in the executive branch. The underdevelopment of parties has left the political arena unstructured and voters incapable of controlling rulers.

Third, the overpowering presidency has degraded the quality of the political class. The president, by occupying so much of the political field, has retarded the entrance into politics of other people of ability and ambition. This problem has been particularly acute in the liberal portion of the political spectrum, since Yeltsin was considered a democrat. This state of affairs left little room for other democrats to build reputations, wield power, and gain real experience as politicians (as opposed to bureaucrats in the president's employ). The Duma's relative powerlessness restricted its potential as a magnet and a training ground for political talent. The consequent amateurishness of the political class, and especially the liberal portion of it, left the polity short on effective democratizers.

Fourth, the president-heavy constitutional order undermines state capacity, specifically by infecting the political system with an anti-institutional virus. When a single leader can hope to dominate everyone, he or she has an incentive, perverse as it might be, to undermine institutions, since institutions may aid challengers. When the rules do not allow anyone to aspire to domination, leaders have an incentive to engage in competitive institution building. Most rulers, of course, want to be dictators. But if one cannot possibly indulge this desire, one must adopt a strategy aimed at more modest goals. Establishing robust rules and agencies that favor oneself and that one can use to compete against other leaders is then often one's best strategy. If they cannot hope to control everything, competitors for power are often more willing to incur the risks of building institutions, which include the danger that those institutions might beget sources of power that escape direct control. The Russian experience illustrates how the theory works in practice. The Russian president, given his constitutional powers, can reasonably aspire to dominance, rather than mere eminence. Yeltsin was notoriously suspicious of institutions. He almost always favored personal arrangements between himself and a subordinate to regular, rule-bound agencies and procedures that could elude his personal control. Putin, despite his incessant insistence upon rationalizing government, has attached highest priority to scotching rules that he did not make himself and undermining organizations and agencies that he does not control. Since open political regimes require that rules rule rulers, democracy cannot function without some institutional development and stability. The

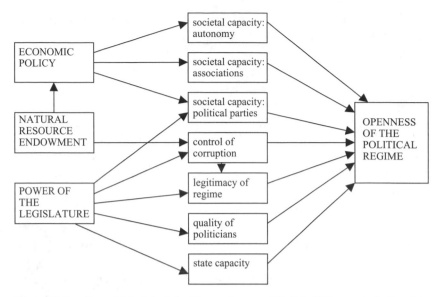

Figure 8.1. Causal Model of the Determinants of Political Openness in Russia

superpresidential system is bad for state institutions and therefore for state capacity.

Lastly, the superpresidential system is bad for controlling corruption. Unconstrained power is corruption's closest companion. Russia's super-presidential system, with its legislature that cannot monitor and discipline the executive branch, provides rich soil for the luxuriant growth of corruption. Fossil fuels and precious metals add their own pungent fertilizer; as discussed, Russia's superabundance of raw materials also corrupts. Corruption, in turn, undermines democratization by heightening demand for a firm (even if anti-democratic) hand among corruption's victims (the people) and by erasing interest in official transparency among corruption's beneficiaries (grasping officials and their comrades-in-crime).

Figure 8.1 summarizes the causal explanation. Figure 8.2 is identical to Figure 8.1, except that it includes partial correlation coefficients for the postcommunist region, controlling for economic development. Each of the partial correlations is statistically significant at the 5 percent level. The three main explanatory variables are listed on the left, and the dependent variable is located on the right. The means by which the explanatory variables affect the dependent variable are the intervening variables; they

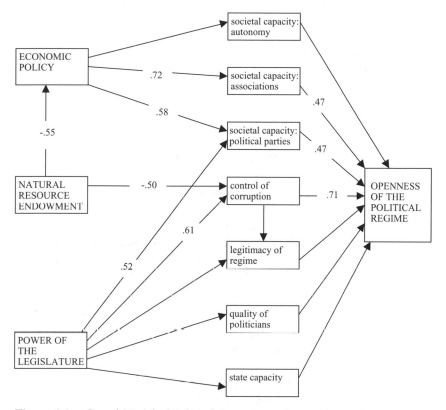

Figure 8.2. Causal Model of Political Openness with Partial Correlation Coefficients, Postcommunist Region

are posted between the independent variables and the dependent variable. The indicators for the variables are those used in the previous chapters. "Economic policy" is measured by the cumulative economic liberalization index (CELI). It indicates the extent of economic liberalization; higher scores mean greater liberalization. "Natural resource endowment" is the percentage of exports accounted for by raw materials, and so higher numbers mean greater economic dependence on fossil fuels and precious metals. "Power of the legislature" is measured by the Parliamentary Powers Index (PPI); higher scores spell a stronger legislature. "Societal capacity: associations" is measured by the percentage of the population active in professional associations, while "societal capacity: parties" is the percentage of the population active in political parties. "Control of corruption" is the Kaufmann score; higher scores indicate less corruption. "Openness of the political regime" is measured by the Kaufmann Voice and Accountability (VA) score. The autonomy of society from the state, the legitimacy of the political regime, the quality of politicians, and state capacity were also found to be important intervening variables, but I could not measure them with quantitative indictors.

What Kind of Explanation Is This?

According to Durkheim (1982, p. 159), social science "has no need to take sides between the grand hypotheses which divide the metaphysicians. Nor has it to affirm free will rather than determinism. All that it asks to be granted it, is that the principle of causality should be applicable to social phenomena." I acknowledge and embrace this limitation. At best, the present study makes a modest, plausible contribution to understanding the causality behind political regime change. It certainly cannot pretend to present findings that adjudicate between the primacy of free will and determinism.

That said, the "agency versus structure" debate is the subject of much attention in contemporary social science, just as it has been, in various guises, as long as people have analyzed people. Agency refers to human beings and the things they make. Since institutions are artifacts (meaning human creations), explanations that highlight institutions as explanations for outcomes are often said to show the centrality of agency. Explanations that focus on the role of leaders are also agent-centric. A so-called "great man" theory of history, which attributes change to a small number of event-making individuals, represents an extreme form of the agency-centric explanation. It is rare in contemporary social science. A more moderate agency-centric framework takes close account of the influence of people and the things they create but situates them within the context of constraints. Sidney Hook's classic work on great leaders (1955) is an example. In contemporary social science, George Breslauer's (2002) and Richard Samuels's (2003) writings exemplify judicious agency-centric analysis.

Structural explanations stress the importance of things that people do *not* make. Structures by definition are not artifacts. They include level of economic development and class configurations. These are things that people cannot change (or cannot change easily). They normally vary across cases but not within them. When they do vary within cases, they do so only over long periods of time. The work of Gregory Luebbert serves as an example of pure structuralism. According to Luebbert (1991, p. 306), "leadership and meaningful choice" in no way affected the phenomenon he sought to explain, variation in the type of political regime that emerged in several European countries between the wars. Mass material interests and class structures alone determined outcomes. Theda Skocpol's early writings (1979) provide another example of structuralism, though Skocpol leaves a bit of room for nonstructural variables.

The causal explanation presented in the present book does not fit squarely into either an agency-centric or a structuralist mold, though it is closer to the former than the latter. One structural variable, natural resource endowment, plays an important role. Yet the other two explanatory variables, economic policy and the power of the legislature, are partly products of human design. Natural resource endowment, a structural variable, truncated economic liberalization, which in turn compromised open politics. Yet variables other than natural resource endowment surely shaped the economic policies that leaders chose. As discussed in Chapter 6, choice played some role in economic policy.

For the purposes of the present study, the constitutional system is not a structural variable. Russia's superpresidential system was codified in the 1993 constitution, which Yeltsin's advisers wrote and which the electorate endorsed in a referendum. It is an institution par excellence, a creation of human design. And yet, as Chapter 7 showed, the constitution was not the product of unconstrained choice. People did not make their institutions as they chose. Conditions that emerged from the whirlwind of the late 1980s set the stage for an ironic constitutional choice in late 1993. Prominent among those conditions were the fortuitous but unfortunate facts that creating an elected republican president provided a better way to beat the Soviet system than relying on the sitting republican legislature, and that in the early post-Soviet period, the president was more liberal and more popular than the legislature.

Agency therefore plays a prominent role in the explanatory tale. Two of the three causal variables are nonstructural. What is more, Russia is no prisoner of its own historically determined conditions, be they economic or cultural. Cross-national analysis showed that economic development affects political openness, but that Russia is a stark underachiever in democratization for its level of economic development. Russia's prospects for democracy would be higher if the country were richer, but its level of economic development is plenty high to allow for open politics. The analysis does not show that Orthodox Christian tradition is a foe of democracy, and so Russia's religious tradition probably does not foreclose democratization. Nor does Russia's ethnic diversity counter political openness. The data show that ethnic diversity is no foe of democracy in global comparative perspective, and Russia is not, at any rate, especially heterogeneous.

Although nonstructural factors shaped regime change, it is important to note that nonstructural does not mean unconstrained. Economic policy was influenced by natural resource endowment, a structural factor, and the document that encoded the balance of power between the president and the legislature was shaped by conditions that emerged willy-nilly from the heat of political struggle that no one directed or controlled.

The Explanation's Limitations

The discussion raises the problem of what stands behind the independent variables. What caused the causes? Like all explanations in social science, mine is subject to that discomfiting question. Even structural and cultural variables, whose origins may lie in the mists of the distant past, are vulnerable to the query. Level of economic development and class structure, for example, may have deep roots, and they may change slowly, but even they were caused by something other than themselves. This fact poses the conundrum of infinite causal regress, meaning that one may question the cause of any cause, and so a "complete" explanation moves back through a limitless chain of causation. Obviously this problem is intractable and one must draw a line somewhere. Still, all explanations are limited by where they draw the line.

Raw materials endowment, the first causal variable, is relatively unproblematic. To be sure, the indicator used in this study, the percentage of exports accounted for by fuels and ores, is imperfect. It does not fully capture raw material *endowment* per se, but rather an economy's reliance on its raw material endowment, which may change over time. Still, the indicator provides a reasonably good reflection of endowment, which cannot be readily traced to some other cause. Like geographical location, resource endowment is a physical factor.

The other two independent variables are more susceptible to the "what caused the cause" query. Neither is structural, and both were the products of decisions. Something must stand behind them.

In the case of economic policy, a structural factor, natural resource endowment, was influential. Yet other factors that I did not investigate undoubtedly affected economic policy as well.

What else shaped it? In an article published in 1998, I presented evidence that a crucial political juncture, the outcome of the first postcommunist

254

election, accounted for a great deal of cross-national variation in economic reform (Fish, 1998[a]). Where initial elections displaced communist-era elites, economic reform was relatively quick and complete. In these cases, communist successor parties rapidly underwent either reformation, which involved embracing the market, or marginalization. Thus, where communist successor parties returned to power after having been thrashed in the first elections, they sustained policies of economic liberalization initiated by their noncommunist predecessors. Where initial elections produced partial turnover, economic liberalization was more tentative and less thoroughgoing. Where the communists held onto power through the first elections, economic liberalization was more modest yet. The article explicated the multistaged process by which the outcome of the initial elections influenced subsequent economic reform.

For several reasons I did not pursue this argument in this book. First, data on the initial postcommunist elections that I coded and used in the 1998 article were limited to the postcommunist region. Analogous data cannot be generated for countries elsewhere. Postcommunist countries had their initial elections at virtually the same time (that is, within a few years of each other), and the extent of the old elite's defeat or persistence could be gauged fairly easily. Countries outside the postcommunist area could not be analyzed in the same way. Furthermore, I am not satisfied with my earlier explanation for economic reform within the postcommunist region. I am convinced that cross-national variation in the initial election decisively influenced subsequent differences in economic policy. But I still cannot explain what I then treated as the independent variable, the outcome of the initial elections. Nor has anyone else explained it. Using rudimentary measures, I found that no cultural, economic-structural, or institutional factor determined the outcome of the first elections. In subsequent tests I have used more differentiated measures but have still not hit upon a convincing answer. I have also found that plausible explanations that I did not test earlier – most notably economic starting points, such as the size of the nonstate sector and the depth of national indebtedness at the time of the demise of Soviet-type regimes – did not determine subsequent patterns of economic reform. I suspect, as I did in the late 1990s, that variables that are not tractable to quantitative measurement may have shaped cross-national differences in the outcome of the initial elections. Such factors may include the way that the rapid-fire succession of events in the late 1980s forged (or did not forge) space for new leaders who were not closely tied to the old regimes.

In research for the current book, I found that economic liberalization powerfully advanced democratization and that Russia's anemic economic liberalization helps explain its failure to sustain democratization. But when it came to explaining the explanation, I did not find my previous work especially usable or compelling. Further investigation reinforced my opinion that I would not be able fully to explain cross-national variation in economic reform or why economic reform took the form that it did in Russia. Investigating many countries' late-Soviet experiences, as well as the histories of myriad countries outside the postcommunist region – a task beyond my capacity – would be necessary. I did encounter evidence that natural resource abundance may inhibit economic liberalization. Statistical tests presented in Chapter 5 confirmed this possibility.

Yet that is where my explanation for economic policy ends. It is obviously incomplete. The many scholars who are better qualified than I to explain cross-national variation in economic policies, as well as precisely why Russia adopted the economic policies that it did, will undoubtedly address the puzzle in the future. Here, I treated economic policy as an independent variable and did not explain it, other than to note that it appears to have been influenced by natural resource endowment.

The third major causal variable in my explanation, the power of the national legislature, is also nonstructural for the purposes of this investigation. Treating it as an independent variable also raises the question of where it came from. I addressed this matter in Chapter 7. In Russia, the powers of the legislature were the paradoxical product of a political battle that began before the dissolution of the Soviet Union. In the postcommunist region more generally, no single factor, including the extent of political openness at the time that constitutions were adopted, explains the distribution of power between the president and the legislature. Interests, hopes, fears, and emulation played roles. During the 1990s and early 2000s, I carried out extensive field work in 12 of the region's 28 countries, from Croatia to Mongolia (including Russia, of course). After interviewing many constitution framers, I was disappointed to find that I could not locate a common factor that determined the distribution of power between branches of government.

My explanation for Russia's constitutional choice relies on the tracing of decision making back through a series of events that do not necessarily have analogues elsewhere. I am confident that the legislature's powers, working through five intervening variables, affected democratization, but I cannot say with certainty what determined the constitutionally defined strength of the legislatures. Scholars may eventually explain systematically what I am here treating as an independent variable. In short, my explanation is limited by my inability to trace the chain of causation back further than I have done.

Data also impose limitations. The three independent variables and the dependent variable can be measured quantitatively, but only three of the seven intervening variables in the causal map are amenable to quantitative measure. There is nothing inherently inferior about qualitative evidence. Given the tractability of the independent variables and the dependent variable to quantification, however, one might hope that the intervening variables would readily lend themselves to quantitative measure as well. Yet not all do. I therefore employed an approach to explanation that relied on what I considered to be the most appropriate evidence, quantitative or qualitative, for the problem at hand.

How Will We Know If This Explanation Is Faulty?

All theoretical explanations should be falsifiable, meaning that one should be able to specify the conditions under which the explanation would be proven wrong or at least seriously weakened. It is not difficult to imagine the conditions that would falsify my explanation for the derailment of democratization in Russia.

The most obvious sign that my explanation is off target will be if none of the three independent variables change appreciably but democratization moves forward anyway. It is possible that something other than the factors in my causal framework will spur political opening. Perhaps rapid economic growth, a shift in public attitudes, the outlook of the president or something else will push democratization back on the rails, even without change in the variables I treat as decisive. Such a development would cast doubt on the soundness of this book's explanation or at least show the explanation to have been time-bound and no longer relevant. So too will the book's explanation be weakened if the independent variables change for the better but the political regime does not. If dependence on natural resources falls, economic destatization takes place, and the power of the legislature is enhanced, and yet Russia does not undergo democratization, one will have to look beyond this book for explanation. The argument would also be weakened by the presence elsewhere in the world of countries that undergo successful democratization even in the presence of economic reliance on raw materials, a high degree of economic statism, and relatively weak legislatures.

If this book's argument is at least partially sound, the future of democracy depends on changes in raw materials dependence, economic liberalization, and the power of the national legislature. Given conditions and trends, what are the prospects for change?

The Paradoxes of Putinism and the Prospects for Democracy

Natural Resources: The Curse Endures

Russia's dependence on natural resources presents a paradox in the making. On the one hand, Putin is acutely aware of the problem. He frets about it publicly and claims that he will not rest until the economy breaks its addiction. He and his advisers call loudly for economic diversification. Putin may have little concern for how resource dependence affects democracy, but he does care about how it endangers economic stability, foreign investment, and the sustainability of economic growth. In 2004, he raised export duties on oil, gas, and minerals in what he portrayed as an effort to reduce dependence on natural resources ("Kudrin," 2002; Prince, 2003).

Yet the place of natural resources in Russia's export profile has only increased on Putin's watch. Sales of oil, gas, and metals rose from 60 percent to 75 percent of export earnings between 2002 and 2003. Some of the change came from an increase in oil prices, which moved from $24 to $28 per barrel. Some of the increase is also attributable to Putin's decision to encourage oil companies to raise production levels as quickly as possible, which most did, leading to an increase in output of about 8 percent per year during Putin's first term. The rise in prices and production has had some auspicious economic effects. The central government balanced its books while increasing pensions and smoothly overcoming a spike in debt servicing (Aris, 2002[b]; Prince, 2003; Sokolowski, 2002).

Yet the oil boom has not been accompanied by diversification of production. The Putin government can hardly be faulted for not weaning Russia off oil in a few years. Oil dependence and its attendant pathologies are deeply rooted and probably could not be reversed quickly by any government in Russia, regardless of its intentions (P. Hanson, 2003). But trends do not even hint at a decrease in natural resource dependence. In late 2003, Callum Henderson of Bank of America Securities pointed out: "Oil price strength masks a multitude of sins within the Russian economy which will eventually come back to haunt it. Productivity gains are entirely focused on energy, while the rest of the Russian industrial capacity remains extremely unproductive" (Prince, 2003). A rise in investment in sectors other than fuels and ores might signal diversification. Yet, as Laza Kekic (2004), the director for Central and East Europe of *The Economist* Intelligence Unit noted in early 2004, "a disproportionate amount of investment is still directly attributable to the energy sector." There was no evidence, she held, "that [economic] recovery is becoming more broadly based and less dependent – directly and indirectly – on the energy sector." The main focus of growth in investment outside of hydrocarbons has been in the mining of nickel, gold, and other metals (Prince, 2003; also Ickes, 2004; Wallace, 2003).

The lack of diversification in production dims the prospects for open politics. The first way that enduring natural resource dependency affects politics is by exacerbating corruption. The Putin government has been unrelenting in its rhetorical assault on corruption ("Government Challenged to Root out Corruption," 2004; "Putin Declares War on Corruption," 2003). It has waged high-profile assaults on the oligarchs of the 1990s, most of whom are (or were) associated with oil or other raw materials production. Boris Berezovskii, the one-time chief of Sibneft, was driven into exile soon after Putin's ascent to power. Mikhail Khodorkovskii, the head of Yukos, was arrested in 2003 on a barrage of charges of financial impropriety. In early 2004, Berezovskii's successor at Sibneft, Roman Abramovich, was informed by the Tax Ministry that his company owed the government $1 billion in back taxes.

The Putin government has characterized every such action purely as an attack on corruption. There is no doubt that the heads of targeted companies originally acquired capital by dubious means. Most benefited from the loans-for-shares privatization schemes of the mid-1990s. Yet by the early 2000s, most were operating relatively openly and paying their taxes. Investors regarded Yukos as one of the few Russian companies that reached Western levels of professionalism and transparency. The government's declarations that it was motivated exclusively by zeal to quash malfeasance had a hollow ring; the evidence in support of the claim is not obvious.

The aggressive reassertion of state control over the energy industry *is* obvious. Despite initial claims that its move against Khodorkovskii was not motivated in the least by a desire to gain control over Yukos, the government followed his arrest with a sustained series of blows to Yukos that left the company sinking. The government proved more than willing to pick up the pieces – and take control of assets. The government's claims against Sibneft are similarly the opening shot in an effort to establish state control (Belton, 2004; Walsh, 2003; "Yukos Stake Sale," 2002).

The relevant question for present discussion is whether state control over extractive industries will reduce corruption. There can be no doubt that state control is growing. Putinism in raw materials industries means the same thing that it does in every other realm: boosting state control and tightening the president's grip. Still, even if the government is motivated by expanding control rather than reducing corruption, its actions could still reduce corruption. Blessed results do not require pure motives. Sometimes good things happen by accident or as side effects. But have they?

The government has certainly reigned in some of the buccaneer entrepreneurs of the Yeltsin period, and humbling the oligarchs may look like fighting corruption. But there is room for skepticism. Writing in the wake of the government raid on Yukos, Alexander Lukin shrewdly noted: "A regime run by billionaires who came by their wealth illegally during the Yeltsin years is obviously a bad thing. But in terms of democratization, the power of hundreds of faceless and equally corrupt functionaries is far worse" (2004; also Iavlinskii, 2001).

It is too early to know the effect of Putin's policies, but not too early for a preliminary probe. Transparency International's (TI) Corruption Perceptions Index assigns scores to countries on an annual basis. They range from 10 (squeaky clean) to 1 (filthy). For assessing change over time, this index provides a better measure than Kaufmann and colleagues' control-of-corruption scores, since the latter are not issued annually. In 1999, the last year of the Yeltsin administration, TI assessed 99 countries. The actual empirical range ran from Denmark (a perfect 10) to Cameroon (1.5). Russia was tied for 82d place with Ecuador with a score of 2.4. In 2003, the most recent year available, TI assessed 133 countries, and the actual empirical range stretched from Finland (9.7) to Bangladesh (1.3). Russia was tied for 86th place with Mozambique; both countries received a 2.7. Russia moved from the 17th to the 35th percentile, but this change was due mainly to the expansion of the sample to include many impoverished countries. Russia's score in 1999 placed it below Egypt, Morocco, Senegal, India, and Malawi – and its score for 2003 did as well. In terms of absolute scores, which are roughly comparable across years, Russia scored 0.3 points higher in 2003 than in 1999 (Transparency International, 2004[a]). This is a modest difference. What is more, as Transparency International (2004[b]) noted in its report for 2004, high-profile attacks on corruption, such as the televised arrests of corrupt police officers on programs narrated by Boris Gryzlov, the minister of the interior and head of United Russia, amounted to election-year public relations stunts, rather than manifestations of major policy changes.

This section may be summarized as follows. First, despite the government's stated intention to diversify the economy, reliance on oil, gas, and metals is intensifying rather than abating. Second, despite the government's claims that its offensive against energy companies is designed to penalize corruption, all evidence points to statization, rather than rectitude, as the driver of policy. Third, while it is too early fully to assess the effects of the government's actions, Putin's stern gaze has not yet dented corruption.

Economic Policy: Liberal Principles Versus Statist Interests

According to the analysis offered in Chapter 5, raw materials superabundance not only exacerbates corruption; but also may cramp economic liberalization. As Chapter 6 showed, economic liberalization aids democratization. The enduring dependence of Russia on raw materials would seem to bode ill for economic liberalization, which in turn would hinder political opening.

Such relationships do and will hold, but economic policy, as discussed earlier, is not determined exclusively by raw materials dependence. Policymakers have some room for maneuver. Here it would seem that Putinism might promote democratization. Putin characterizes himself as pro-market. He pursued several initiatives early in his presidency that bolstered his claim. He pushed through a 13 percent flat tax on personal incomes. So too did he successfully advocate a new Land Code. Despite much talk about land reform during the 1990s, at the close of the decade the laws were still essentially Soviet. Putin changed that, expanding the categories of land that could be privately owned.

Putin certainly has not allowed concerns for socioeconomic equality to interfere with economic policy. Neither he nor his party, Unity (and then United Russia) even use the language of egalitarianism. As Sergei Satiukov, the leader of Unity in Arkhangel'sk noted: "We are against social leveling [*uravnenie*]. We even shun the term 'social justice' in our documents, and you won't hear Vladimir Vladimirovich [Putin] use the term much either. Our principles are traditionalism, patriotism, and great power status, not social justice [*Nashie printsipy – traditsionalizm, patriotizm, i derzhavnost', ne sotsial'naia spravedlivost'*]" (personal interview, May 30, 2001, Arkhangel'sk). Putin used some of the proceeds from the oil windfall to benefit pensioners, among whom turnout rates in elections are high. So too has he pulled down some of the highest-flying oligarchs of the 1990s. But for the most part, he has neither pursued nor pretended to pursue economic policies that place equality above efficiency.

Despite his rhetoric and the liberal cast of some of his early economic policies, however, Putin's commitment to economic liberalization has never been tightly held or consistently followed. He has swung between the red-blooded liberalization advocated by former economic adviser Andrei Illarionov and the gradualism touted by his finance minister, Aleksei Kudrin. Sometimes German Gref, a moderate liberalizer and Putin's minister of economic development and trade, has appeared to hold sway. Many officials surrounding Putin – prominently the so-called *siloviki* from law enforcement and the KGB/FSB – do not like economic liberalization at all. As Alexander Bim and Kim Iskyan (2003) noted, economic policy under Putin is buffeted by "lack of an ideological rudder and the president's apparent difficulties with grasping a broad conceptual framework." What Putin *is*, however, is unwaveringly committed to increasing the state's control over society and his own control over the state. Here, the president lacks neither ideological rudder nor the ability to grasp a broad conceptual framework.

Indeed, precisely because it threatens to strengthen nonstate actors and loosen state control, economic liberalization does not fit comfortably in Putin's overarching program. It is the piece of Putinism that does not go with the others. As such, it will often have to give. At best, it will be pursued intermittently and incoherently. In Putin's Russia, when the requirements of economic liberalization clash with the imperatives of political control, the latter will win every time.

Evidence is found in the economic reforms that have not happened, even as Putin has amassed formidable power. Tax reform ran out of steam by 2003 (Liashenko, 2003; Visloguzov, 2004). Meaningful banking reform, without which all other economic reforms are bound to founder, has been deferred year after year. Deregulation of private business activity, while touted by Putin as crucial to Russia's economic future, has collided with the interests of the officials who profit from the richly textured layers of restrictions that remain in place. An economist specializing in business in Russia, Edward Parker, stated in 2003: "Behind the froth, the underlying improvements are not so spectacular. In the area of business deregulation, the evidence suggests that the burden on business is getting worse rather than better" (Hurst, 2003). As a result, the burst of new business entry that many observers anticipated during Putin's early years did not materialize (Kekic, 2004). Reforming Gazprom, the behemoth that accounts for nearly a quarter of all output, has been deferred again and again. The president's political interests trump economic considerations. As Bim and Iskyan (2003) state: "The restructuring of Gazprom is critical to ending the Soviet legacies of super-monopolization and non-transparency, but it would also make it much harder for the company to be used as a slush fund for financing Kremlin-backed political parties and other projects." After repeated efforts by advocates of restructuring have quietly come to naught, Bim and Iskyan note, "it is pretty clear that the message not to touch Gazprom is coming from Putin himself." Similarly, restructuring the electricity industry has been stymied by state officials who stand to lose from change.

In fact, while Putin has been eager to cut down select private actors and provincial officials who do not answer to him, he has shown scant inclination to reduce the rent-seeking opportunities of officials in the "executive vertical" atop which he sits. Quite the opposite: Every move against a company such as Yukos or an elected provincial official translates into greater access to resources for functionaries in Putin's employ. It is difficult to avoid the impression that Putin's strategy for controlling his own agents – the ruler's conundrum outlined by Weber and Migdal and discussed in Chapter 7 – relies not only on blocking the formation of rival power centers but also on increasing rent-seeking opportunities for those who are beholden to him.

In this respect, Putin seems to be smarter than his predecessor. Yeltsin, like Putin, was suspicious of his own agents. He thwarted the growth of impersonal rules and the agencies required to follow and enforce them. But Yeltsin, while enriching a small circle of businessmen and their allies at the top level of government, failed to feed his functionaries. Putin, like Yeltsin, blocks depersonalization of power and therefore institutional development. But he is far better at generating rewards for loyalty through the length and breadth of the governmental apparatus. So too is he adept at redefining corruption as corruption that takes place *outside* the agencies of the national government's executive branch. The house that Putin is building bears a striking resemblance to the edifice that ran the Soviet system prior to Gorbachev's rise to power. Its custodians might be even better fed. As Andrei Repnevskii, a leader of the CPRF in Arkhangel'sk, noted sardonically: "The bureaucrats have it better under Putin than they did in Soviet times" (personal interview, May 29, 2001, Arkhangel'sk). A communist, Repnevskii does not fret over the effects of Putin's methods of political control on economic liberalization. But if his statement is on target, the future of economic liberalization may not rest in nurturing hands.

Cross-national evidence supports skepticism. The Economic Freedom Index, used as one indicator of economic liberalization in Chapters 5 and 6, assigns ratings and rankings to most of the world's countries on an annual basis. Between 1999, the last year of the Yeltsin period, and 2004, the most recent year for which data are available, Russia's score improved (that is, economic policy was rated more "free") by 0.14 points on a 5-point scale, which is a negligible change. In comparative perspective, Russia's rating actually deteriorated. In 1999, the survey included 161 countries, and Russia ranked 110th. In 2004, it included 155 countries and Russia ranked 114th. Thus, in 1999, Russia placed in the 32d percentile; in 2004, in the 26th percentile. Table 8.1 shows the global percentile rankings for the 24 postcommunist countries for which data are available for both 1999 and 2004. The rankings of 15 countries improved between the 1999 and 2004 assessments; they declined in 9, including in Russia. In 1999, Russia placed

Table 8.1. *Economic Freedom Indices, 1999 and 2004, Global Percentile Ranks, Postcommunist Countries*

Country	Global Percentile Ranking, 1999	Global Percentile Ranking, 2004
Albania	27th	48th
Armenia	34th	72nd
Azerbaijan	9th	32nd
Belarus	14th	6th
Bulgaria	32nd	50th
Croatia	27th	47th
Czech Republic	86th	79th
Estonia	81st	96th
Georgia	28th	41st
Hungary	57th	73rd
Kazakhstan	16th	15th
Latvia	70th	81st
Lithuania	58th	86th
Moldova	41st	49th
Mongolia	43rd	59th
Poland	68th	64th
Romania	41st	17th
Russia	**32nd**	**26th**
Slovakia	50th	77th
Slovenia	61st	66th
Tajikistan	16th	6th
Turkmenistan	7th	3rd
Ukraine	22nd	25th
Uzbekistan	6th	4th

higher on economic freedom than 10 other postcommunist countries. In 2004, it was higher than only 7 (Miles, Feulner, and O'Grady, 2004).

While Putin has pursued economic liberalization halfheartedly, he has labored zealously to thwart the potentially auspicious effects for democracy of the economic liberalization that he has carried out. As discussed in Chapter 6, economic liberalization promotes democratization mainly by enhancing pluralism, and specifically by promoting the development and autonomy of nonstate organizations. But Putin has striven to curb the autonomy and strength of societal groups. As discussed in Chapter 3, the 2001 law on political parties requires a party to have 10,000 members and a substantial presence in at least half of Russia's 89 provinces in order to receive legal recognition and participate in elections. So too did it mandate state financing for parties and virtually ban private contributions. In some established democracies, state financing may help level the political playing field. But in Russia, the law has in no way promoted freer competition. Georgii Satarov, the head of the INDEM Center for Applied Political Studies in Moscow and a former Yeltsin adviser, rightly stated that Putin's intention "was not to improve the party system, but to make presidential and governmental influence on parties more efficient." Boris Nadezhdin, a parliamentary deputy from the liberal URF, was more categorical, stating that the law on parties spelled "the end of liberal politics in Russia" (Uzelac, 2001).

The December 2003 parliamentary election provides evidence. Despite the presence of a law on the media that requires equal coverage for all candidates and parties, the airwaves were saturated during the campaign with favorable reporting on Putin's party, United Russia. The party's coffers were cavernous; the campaign evidenced no limits to its resources. Mikhail Khodorkovskii, a backer of Iabloko and the URF, was arrested and his assets frozen during the campaign. In short, the laws are enforced selectively. All parties are forced to rely on state support. But only one party really gets it – and its cup overflows. The media are required to provide balanced coverage, but this law is simply ignored.

Labor organizations have also felt the astringent embrace of the state. The right to organize has been undermined by governmental action that, like the law on parties, was cloaked in the garb of overcoming disorder and furnishing paternal assistance. According to the labor code of 2001, only unions that represent a majority of a firm's workers may represent workers in collective bargaining agreements. The Federation of Independent Trade Unions of Russia (FITUR), the holdover monopolist from the Soviet period that remains beholden to the state, happened to be the only union that enjoyed this status in the vast majority of Russian enterprises. The heads of the FITUR, unsurprisingly, applauded the new law. The Russian Union of Industrialists and Entrepreneurs (RUIE), the association of enterprise directors that successfully pushed for management-friendly privatization in the early and mid-1990s, endorsed it as well. Thus, the Putin administration, the holdover Soviet-era trade union, and the managers of large enterprises were all satisfied. And no wonder: The law granted a de facto monopoly on labor representation to the domesticated FITUR, thereby extinguishing the specter of independent unions (Nikol'skii, Bekker, and Kochetov, 2001; Visloguzov, 2001; Vodolazov, 2001).

The Power of the Legislature: The Institutionalization of Incapacity

The powers of the legislature have not changed markedly since the constitution established them in 1993. Members of the Federation Council, the upper house of parliament, are no longer elected as they were in the 1990s. Since the early 2000s, they have been appointed by provincial authorities under the influence of the president. In this respect, the legislature might be even weaker than it was in 1993, though the upper house was never the site of much influence or public attention. The Duma, the lower house, has been more important, and its powers have not changed.

During the late 1990s, the idea of altering the constitution to reduce presidential powers surfaced in Russia (Sharlet, 1997 and 2001). The baleful effects of Yeltsin's infirmity began to elicit something like an elite consensus on the desirability of change. The liberals of Iabloko and the communists of the CPRF alike favored empowering the legislature vis-à-vis the president. Changing the constitution, however, is difficult – at least unless the president cooperates. Unsurprisingly, Yeltsin did not.

By the time the consensus began to gel, the prospect of fresh elections drew the momentum out of what may have otherwise become a serious movement to reduce presidential prerogatives. The two-term limit on incumbency ensured that Yeltsin's days were numbered, and interest in reducing presidential powers gave way to a scramble among politicians to position themselves for the presidential election of 2000. Yeltsin's sudden resignation at the end of 1999 and the election three months later of a young, vigorous figure delivered the coup de grâce to the idea of redistributing power.

Thus, the powers of the legislature have remained more or less constant since 1993. The parliamentary election of December 2003 gave Putin a friendly majority. With the help of some manipulation and fraud, he converted an ineffectual assembly that sometimes posed a nuisance into an ineffectual assembly that never disturbed him at all. The legislature's marginal status has become a fixture of political life.

I argued in Chapter 7 that the concentration of power in the presidency and the weakness of the legislature tether the legitimacy of the political regime to a single person, rendering regime legitimacy tenuous. Putin's skill might seem to shore up regime legitimacy. Indeed, as of this writing, Putin enjoys – or at least appears to enjoy – astronomical popularity, which would seem to bolster the legitimacy of the system. Yet two problems remain. First, the legitimacy of the regime still rests on the popularity of a single individual, which is a sandy foundation. Second, the regime that Putin's popularity is (at least temporarily) boosting is not a democracy.

For all of Yeltsin's shortcomings as a democrat, the regime that he aimed to legitimate even to the end of his tenure was at least partially open. Electoral fraud and the erosion of rights in the 1990s compromised the democratic ideals that Yeltsin championed during the late Gorbachev period. But he never broke entirely with his commitment to open politics. He placed himself at risk of losing reelection, and he never lost his ability to suffer public criticism. What is more, he consistently touted an inclusive, supraethnic definition of the polity. As George Breslauer (2002, p. 147) states of Yeltsin: "He eschewed nostalgic, invidious, imperial, and ethnic designations of the character of the state and promoted instead a non-ethnic definition of citizenship within Russia." Furthermore, as Breslauer notes, Yeltsin attempted to build his authority in part on civic values and an ideology of individualism. Thus, Yeltsin never completely lost his reputation as a democrat – which is, ironically, why democracy's reputation declined along with him.

Putin shares with Yeltsin an inclusive, nonethnic notion of national belonging. The first chairman of the Unity Party was Sergei Shoigu, a Tuvanese whose handsome and distinctly Asian countenance adorned Unity Party offices. Putin includes numerous nonethnic Russians in high positions. He always refers to his countrymen as *rossiiane* (inhabitants of Russia), as Yeltsin did, rather than *russkie* (ethnic Russians), the term preferred by many nationalists. In other respects, however, Putinism differs from Yeltsinism. Putin's understanding of citizenship lacks a civic dimension. Membership in the national community, social solidarity, and unwavering loyalty to the state should, in Putin's view, form the core of citizens' public consciousness and identity. The social cement that Putin is intent upon manufacturing is largely a neo-Soviet elixir. In place of the Communist Party and allegiance to it, however, Putin substitutes the state – with himself as its embodiment – and devotion to it. This formula requires a personality cult. By the time of the 2004 election, such a cult – even if a miniature one, by comparison with others that Russians have known – was very much in evidence (Lipman, 2004). A regime based on exultation of the leader is not a democracy. To the extent that Putin succeeds in legitimating the political order over which he presides, he undermines, rather than shores up, the legitimacy of democracy.

Putin's own decline in popularity, if and when it comes, may be a pre-requisite for reviving the legitimacy of the idea of democracy. This circumstance, along with the way that the debility of a "democratic" president diminished democracy's reputation in the 1990s, highlights how super-presidentialism may damage the legitimacy of open politics.

The subordination of the legislature also ensures that political parties will not undergo rapid development. It sustains disinterest in parties, except in the party the president controls. The 2003 Duma election neither evinced nor promoted party development. In the party-lists portion of the vote, United Russia, whose sole raison d'être is supporting Putin, won a large plurality, taking 37 percent. Vladimir Zhirinovskii's LDPR, which does little but collect payment from the presidential administration in exchange for unstinting support, picked up 12 percent. A nondescript, mainly pro-Putin organization that emerged only months before the election, the Motherland Party, received 9 percent. The CPRF, which won pluralities in both 1995 and 1999, received 13 percent. The two main liberal parties, Iabloko and the URF, failed to cross the 5 percent threshold. The results weakened the only party with a genuine mass base, the CPRF, and eclipsed Iabloko and the URF, both of which had a genuine, if diminutive, public following. The ultimate consequence of the superpresidential system for the party system is the reduction of the parties to supplicants for presidential favor. In early 2004, the LDPR earned the right to claim victory in the obsequiousness contest when Zhirinovskii called for anointing Putin president-for-life.

As the legislature's power remains modest, so too, as Max Weber would predict, does the quality of politicians. The cast of characters who "opposed" Putin in the 2004 election illustrated the denouement of the superpresidency's crippling effect on the political class. Putin's main "rivals" refused to express a hope or an intention to win. Sergei Mironov endorsed Putin in the same speech in which he threw his hat in the ring. Sergei Glazev characterized his candidacy as an exercise in publicizing particular concerns but not as a sincere attempt to become president. The SPS's

Irina Khakamada, the lone liberal, did apparently hope to do well, but she ran a quixotic campaign and expressed skepticism about her own candidacy (Myers, 2004[a]).

Not all candidates were tepid in their pursuit of the prize. Ivan Rybkin, a former speaker of the Duma, was backed by Boris Berezovskii, the exiled prince of Russia's robber baron oligarchs. Rybkin did not shrink from criticizing Putin. Yet his credibility suffered a bit when he vanished for five days during the waning weeks of the campaign. He failed to tell his wife, his campaign staff, or anyone else that he had decided to take a short vacation, and he cut off all communication during the time. His disappearance attracted international attention and prompted a manhunt and speculation that he had been murdered. Upon returning to Moscow from Kiev, his chosen vacation spot, Rybkin remarked to his bewildered campaign manager: "Can't a person take some rest?" But his time away from the hustings did nothing to soften his oppositional spunk. To the swarm of journalists who met him at the airport upon his return from Kiev, he announced: "Such tyranny as now, I have not seen or experienced in my 15 years in politics. Tyranny is tyranny. Tyranny in Africa is tyranny, only there they eat people" (Myers, 2004[b]; also "Rybkin uzhe v Moskve," 2004). Such was the clarion voice of intransigent opposition in 2004.

Even if politicians are amateurish and growing more so, can one deny that the strength of the state is growing? Putin has landed some blows in his fight to draw power back to Moscow. He convinced the gangster governor of Primorskii krai, Evgenii Nazdratenko, to resign. St. Petersburg came under virtually direct rule by Putin shortly after he came to office. The city's governor at the time, Vladimir Iakovlev, whom Putin despises, wisely decided that serving Putin was preferable to resisting him. In 2003, Putin managed to have Iakovlev depart a few months early and got a hand-picked candidate, Valentina Matvienko, elected as Iakovlev's successor. Iurii Luzhkov, the overweening mayor of Moscow, shows Putin deference. Putin has launched an effort to bring the imperious president of Bashkortostan, Murtaza Rakhimov, into line. In 2003 and 2004, the communist governors of Briansk, Krasnodar, Kursk, Vladimir, and Volgograd deserted the CPRF to swear loyalty to Putin (Koreneva, 2003; Mereu, 2004; Petrov, 2003[a] and [c]).

Observers differ over the success of Putin's efforts to recentralize power. Some believe that his victories have been more apparent than real. Donald Jensen, director of communications for Radio Free Europe/Radio Liberty, argued in 2003: "One could more properly speak of the Virtual President, or Virtual Putin, since the power centers are popularly seen to be carrying out Putin's wishes even when they act against each other, against him, or are otherwise obstacles to the achievement of what Putin says he wants" (quoted in Filipov, 2003). Many analysts point out that Putin had to offer Nazdratenko and Iakovlev high posts in Moscow in order to coax them into leaving their baronies (Borisova, 2001; Filipov, 2003; Jack, 2003).

Still, the ambitiousness of Putin's effort is undeniable, and he has clearly exceeded Yeltsin in his ability to influence provincial politics. His establishment of seven "superregions," superimposed on the country's 89 territorial units, represents a serious push to bring regional officials to heel. Each superregion is headed by a "supergovernor" who reports directly to the president. Putin has also sent a "federal inspector" to each of the country's 89 territories to keep an eye on the governors and republican presidents.

Putin may well have achieved some recentralization, and recentralization per se is not necessarily inconsistent with democratization. But has recentralization strengthened state institutions in general? Perhaps in some ways it has, but given the hyperpersonalization of power at the center, it is difficult to conclude that Putinism really strengthens overall state capacity. Building personal power and building institutions are not the same thing. The jury is still out on whether the superpresidential system under Putin's direction will enhance state capacity. It is not yet obvious that it will.

Nor may one conclude that Putin's management of the superpresidency has reduced corruption. The persistence of high corruption in Putin's Russia was noted earlier. The weakness of the legislature leaves the executive branch unchecked, keeping the doors to subornment wide open to executive-branch officials.

A Final Word

Can democracy get back on track in Russia? If the thrust of this book is sound, it can, but will not for the foreseeable future.

It can get back on track because the conditions that derailed democratization are changeable. Russia's superabundance of resources will not change, but economic diversification can reduce the importance of raw materials in the economy, which would improve democracy's prospects. Economic policy, while influenced by raw materials dependence, is not fully its hostage. Policymakers have leeway, and acceleration of economic liberalization would promote democratization. The constitutional framework that prescribes the superpresidential system is also subject to change.

Altering the constitution to empower the legislature would not be easy, but it is possible.

Yet democratization will not resume in the foreseeable future for the reasons outlined in this chapter. Trends point toward entrenchment of oligarchy – or even movement toward monocracy – rather than resumption of political opening. Signs of democratization's unceremonious reversal are everywhere, from the constriction of choice in elections to the saturation of the airwaves with obsequious plaudits for the president.

The answer to the question posed in the epigram to this chapter – "whether one person with absolute power can run a country as enormous as Russia all by himself" – is, of course, no. But the man who has the pretensions to being that person does not seem to know it. Perhaps the clearest evidence of Putin's urge to control is found in the gratuitousness of so many of his power grabs. A single independent television station (NTV), an independent polling agency (ARCSPO), several diminutive liberal political parties (the URF and Iabloko), and a handful of independent trade unions hardly threatened his grip on power. Yet Putin drove them out of business. In its every suppressive action, the Putin government claims to be guided exclusively by a desire to impose order. Conditions in post-Soviet Russia, however, scarcely necessitate such suppression. From Putin's actions, one might think that Russia resembles Germany on the verge of Nazi takeover or Chile on the eve of the military coup of 1973. But post-Soviet Russia has never bristled with politicized, combative organizations that are deeply rooted in society and capable of mass mobilization. Putin moves against independent groups as if they were dangerous enemies. Yet they posed little more than irritations – and irritations of the type that Boris Yeltsin and Mikhail Gorbachev were willing to countenance.

In his reflexive gluttony for power, Putin is not unusual. With tragic frequency, presidents vested with great power lose their capacity to grasp their personal limitations with each passing year in office. Open politics will not come to Russia on Putin's watch. It remains to be seen whether Putin's drive toward dictatorship will trigger counteraction on behalf of the right to self-government.

References

Abakumova, Mariia. "Vybory nachalis' so skandala." *Vremia-Moskovskie novosti*, October 19, 2001.

Abbott, Andrew. *Time Matters: On Theory and Method*. Chicago: University of Chicago Press, 2001.

Afrobarometer Network. "Afrobarometer Round 2: Compendium of Comparative Results from a 15-Country Survey." *Afrobarometer Working Paper No. 34*, March 2004. Online at afrobarometer.org. Site consulted June 2004.

Albats, Evgenia. "Kremlin Has Killed Russian Democracy." *St. Petersburg Times*, May 8, 2001.

Albion, Adam. "Reinventing Turkmen Government." *Central Asia Report of Radio Free Europe/Radio Liberty* 3, 28, August 22, 2003. Online at rfefr.org/reports/centralasia. Site consulted February 2004.

Alekseev, Sergei. "Drama vlasti v Rossii." *Izvestiia*, April 29, 1993.

Alesina, Alberto, Arnaud Devleeschauwer, William Easterly, Sergio Kurlat, and Romain Wacziarg. "Fractionalization." December 2002. Online at stanford.edu/~wacziarg/~downloads/fractionalization. Site consulted December 2002.

Alexander, James, and Jörn Grävingholt. "Evaluating Democratic Progress Inside Russia: The Komi Republic and the Republic of Bashkortostan." *Democratization* 9, 4 (Winter 2002): 77–105.

Alexander, James, Andrei A. Degtyarev, and Vladimir Gelman. "Democratization Challenged: The Role of Regional Elites." In Blair A. Ruble, Jodi Koehn, and Nancy Popson, eds., *Fragmented Space in the Russian Federation*. Washington, DC: Woodrow Wilson Center, 2002: 157–218.

Ames, Barry. *The Deadlock of Democracy in Brazil: Interests, Identities, and Institutions in Comparative Perspective*. Ann Arbor: University of Michigan Press, 2001.

Amsden, Alice H., Jacek Kochanowicz, and Lance Taylor. *The Market Meets Its Match: Restructuring Economies in Eastern Europe*. Cambridge, MA: Harvard University Press, 1998.

"'And They Call This Elections?'" Editorial in the *Moscow Times*, December 16, 1999.

Anderson, Richard D., M. Steven Fish, Stephen E. Hanson, and Philip G. Roeder. *Postcommunism and the Theory of Democracy*. Princeton, NJ: Princeton University Press, 2002.

Andrews, Josephine T., and Gabriella R. Montinola. "Veto Players and the Rule of Law in Emerging Democracies." *Comparative Political Studies* 37, 1 (February 2004): 55–87.

Andrusenko, Lidiia, and Aleksandr Shapovalov. "TsIK reshil pomoch' kommunistam." *Nezavisimaia gazeta*, September 8, 2001.

Appel, Hilary. *A New Capitalist Order: Privatization and Ideology in Russia and Eastern Europe*. Pittsburgh, PA: University of Pittsburgh Press, 2004.

Arbatov, Georgi. "Origins and Consequences of 'Shock Therapy.'" In Lawrence R. Klein and Marshall Pomer, eds. *The New Russia: Transition Gone Awry*. Stanford, CA: Stanford University Press, 2001: 171–8.

Aris, Ben. "Weaning off the Barrel." *Moscow Times*, June 3, 2002.

Armony, Ariel C. *The Dubious Link: Civic Engagement and Democratization*. Stanford, CA: Stanford University Press, 2004.

Arnett, Anthony. "Social Fractionalization, Political Instability, and the Size of Government." IMF Staff Papers 48, 3 (2001). Online at ideas.repec.org. Site consulted March 2003.

Ashwin, Sarah. *Russian Workers: The Anatomy of Patience*. Manchester, UK: Manchester University Press, 1999.

Ashwin, Sarah. "Social Partnership or a 'Complete Sellout'? Russian Trade Unions' Responses to Conflict." *British Journal of Industrial Relations* 42, 1 (March 2004): 23–46.

Åslund, Anders. *Building Capitalism*. Cambridge: Cambridge University Press, 2000.

Auty, Richard. *Resource-Based Industrialization: Sowing the Oil in Eight Developing Countries*. Oxford: Clarendon Press, 1990.

Badkhen, Anna. "Greens' Signatures Dumped by CEC." *Moscow Times*, November 30, 2000.

Bahry, Donna, Cynthia Boaz, and Stacy Burnett Gordon. "Tolerance, Transition and Support for Civil Liberties in Russia." *Comparative Political Studies* 30, 5 (August 1997): 484–510.

Balian, Hrair. "OSCE: Election-Fraud Report Was Unfair." *Moscow Times*, October 28, 2000.

Balzer, Harley. "Managed Pluralism: Vladimir Putin's Emerging Regime." *Post-Soviet Affairs* 19, 3 (July–September 2003): 189–227.

Balzer, Harley. "Russia's Middle Classes." *Post-Soviet Affairs* 14, 2 (April–June 1998): 165–86.

Barany, Zoltan D. "Politics and the Russian Armed Forces." In Zoltan D. Barany and Robert G. Moser, eds., *Russian Politics: Challenges of Democratization*. Cambridge: Cambridge University Press, 2001: 175–214.

Barkhatova, Nonna. "Russian Small Business, Authorities, and the State." *Europe-Asia Studies* 52, 4 (June 2000): 657–76.

References

Barro, Robert J. "Determinants of Democracy." *Journal of Political Economy* 6, 107 (December 1999): 158–83.

Bashkirova, Elena, and Andrei Melville. "Russian Public Opinion Between Elections." *International Social Science Journal* 47, 4 (December 1995): 553–65.

Baylis, Thomas A. "Presidents Versus Prime Ministers: Shaping Executive Authority in Eastern Europe." *World Politics* 48, 3 (April 1996): 297–323.

Beinin, Joel, and Joe Stork, eds. *Political Islam*. Berkeley: University of California Press, 1997.

Belin, Laura. "The SPS's Television Ads: A Case Study of Poor Image Construction." *RFE/RL Russian Election Special*, December 9, 2003[a].

Belin, Laura. "The Yabloko Campaign on Television." *RFE/RL Russian Election Special*, December 10, 2003[b].

Bellin, Eva. "The Robustness of Authoritarianism in the Middle East: Exceptionalism in Comparative Perspective." *Comparative Politics* 36, 2 (January 2004): 139–57.

Belton, Catherine. "Sibneft Hit with $1 Billion Tax Claim." *Moscow Times*, March 3, 2004.

Berger, Mikhail. "Privatizatsiia ugrozhaet dikatura proletariata." *Izvestiia*, June 3, 1992.

Berman, Sheri. "Civil Society and the Collapse of the Weimar Republic." *World Politics* 49, 3 (April 1997): 401–29.

Bermeo, Nancy. *Ordinary People in Extraordinary Times: The Citizenry in the Breakdown of Democracy*. Princeton, NJ: Princeton University Press, 2003.

Biberaj, Elez. *Albania in Transition: The Rocky Road to Democracy*. Boulder, CO: Westview, 1999.

Biianova, Nataliia, and Mariia Selivanova. "'O kakom razvitii malogo biznesa mozhno govorit': Otkaza odnogo vedmstva ot odnoi iz funktsii dlia etogo iavno nedostatochno." *Gazeta GZT.ru*, August 21, 2003. Online at gzt.ru. Site consulted September 2003.

Bim, Alexander, and Kim Iskyan. "The End of the Putin Reform Era." *Moscow Times*, October 21, 2003.

Bobbio, Norberto. *The Future of Democracy*. Minneapolis: University of Minnesota Press, 1987.

Bobbio, Norberto. *Liberalism and Democracy*. London: Verso, 1990.

Boix, Carles, and Susan Stokes. "Endogenous Democratization." *World Politics* 55, 4 (July 2003): 517–49.

"Boris Nemtsov" and "The Russian Federation Votes, 2003–2004." *RFE/RL Election Special*, December 2003. Online at rferl.org/specials/russianelection/bio/nemtsov.asp. Site consulted January 2004.

Borisov, Sergei. "Russia: A President Without Rivals." *Transitions Online*, January 6–12, 2004. Online at tol.cz. Site consulted March 2004.

Borisova, Yevgenia. "Fury as Fisheries Job Goes to Nazdratenko." *St. Petersburg Times*, February 27, 2001.

275

Borisova, Yevgenia, and Timur Aliev. "Activists See Fraud at Chechen Poll." *Moscow Times*, October 8, 2003.

Borisova, Yevgenia, Gary Peach, Nonna Chernyakova, and Mayerbeck Nunayev. "Baby Boom or Dead Souls?" *Moscow Times*, September 9, 2000[a]. Online at themoscowtimes.com. Site consulted January 2003.

Borisova, Yevgenia, Gary Peach, Nonna Chernyakova, and Mayerbeck Nunayev. "How Many Forgeries?" *Moscow Times*, September 9, 2000[b]. Online at themoscowtimes.com. Site consulted January 2003.

Borisova, Yevgenia, Gary Peach, Nonna Chernyakova, and Mayerbeck Nunayev. "Special Report on the Presidential Election: And the Winner Is?" *Moscow Times*, September 9, 2000. Part 1 is 2000[c]; Part 2 is 2000[d]; Part 3 is 2000[e]. Online at themoscowtimes.com. Site consulted January 2003.

Borón, Atilio A. "Faulty Democracies? A Reflection on the Capitalist 'Fault Lines' in Latin America." In Felipe Agüero and Jeffrey Stark, eds., *Fault Lines of Democracy in Post-Transition Latin America*. Coral Gables, FL: North-South Center Press at the University of Miami, 1998: 41–65.

Brader, Ted, and Joshua A. Tucker. "It's Nothing Personal? The Appeal of Party Leaders and the Development of Partisanship in Russia." Paper delivered at the annual meeting of the Midwest Political Science Association, Chicago, April 2002.

Bransten, Jeremy. "Russia: Corruption Continues to Thrive, Say Researchers." *Radio Free Europe/Radio Liberty Report*, June 4, 2002. Online at www.rferl.org. Site consulted July 2003.

Bratton, Michael. "State-Building and Democratization in Sub-Saharan Africa: Forwards, Backwards, or Together?" Paper delivered at the conference on Democratic Advancements and Setbacks: What Have We Learned? Uppsala University, Uppsala, Sweden, June 2004.

Bratton, Michael, Robert Mattes, and E. Gyimah-Boadi. *Public Opinion, Democracy, and Market Reform in Africa*. New York: Cambridge University Press, 2004.

Breslauer, George W. *Gorbachev and Yeltsin as Leaders*. New York: Cambridge University Press, 2002.

Breslauer, George W. "Reflections on the Anniversary of the August 1991 Coup." *Post-Soviet Affairs* 8, 2 (April–June 1992): 164–73.

Brovkin, Vladimir. "The Emperor's New Clothes: Continuity of Soviet Political Culture in Contemporary Russia." *Problems of Post-Communism* 43, 2 (March–April 1996): 21–8.

Brown, Frank. "Spreading the Word in a Gray Area." *Moscow Times*, March 21, 1998.

Brudny, Yitzhak M. "Ruslan Khasbulatov, Aleksandr Rutskoi, and Intraelite Conflict in Postcommunist Russia, 1991–1994." In Timothy J. Colton and Robert C. Tucker, eds., *Patterns in Post-Soviet Leadership*. Boulder, CO: Westview, 1995: 75–101.

Brzezinski, Matthew. *Casino Moscow: A Tale of Greed and Adventure on Capitalism's Wildest Frontier*. New York: Free Press, 2001.

Bukharin, Nikolai. "Novyi sub"ekt politicheskoi zhizni." *Vlast'* 7, 1995: 19–21.

References

Bunce, Valerie. "Comparative Democratization: Big and Bounded Generalizations." *Comparative Political Studies* 33, 6/7 (August–September 2000): 703–34.

Bunce, Valerie. "The Political Economy of Postsocialism." *Slavic Review* 58, 4 (Winter 1999): 756–93.

Bunce, Valerie. "Recent Democratization in Postcommunist Eurasia: Regional Trends and Cross-Regional Comparisons." Paper delivered at the conference on Democratic Advancements and Setbacks: What Have We Learned? Uppsala University, Uppsala, Sweden, June 2004.

Bunce, Valerie. "Rethinking Recent Democratization: Lessons from the Postcommunist Experience." *World Politics* 55, 2 (January 2003): 167–92.

Burawoy, Michael. "Industrial Involution: The Russian Road to Capitalism." In Burgit Müller, ed., *A La Recherche des Certitudes Perdues*. Berlin: Centre Marc Bloch, 1996[a]: 11–57.

Burawoy, Michael. "The State and Economic Involution: Russia Through a China Lens." *World Development* 24, 6 (1996[b]): 1105–17.

Burkhart, Ross E., and Indra de Soysa. "Open Borders, Open Regimes? Testing Causal Direction Between Globalization and Democracy, 1970–2000." *ZEF Discussion Papers on Development Policy* No. 67, Center for Development Research, Bonn, April 2003.

Callaghy, Thomas M. "Africa: Back to the Future?" *Journal of Democracy*, 5, 4 (October 1994): 133–45.

Callaghy, Thomas M. "Political Passions and Economic Interests: Economic Reform and Political Structure in Africa." In Thomas M. Callaghy and John Ravenhill, eds., *Hemmed In: Responses to Africa's Economic Decline*. New York: Columbia University Press, 1993: 463–519.

Carothers, Thomas. "Civil Society: Think Again." *Foreign Policy* 117 (Winter 1999/2000): 18–29.

Central Intelligence Agency. *The World Factbook 2000*. Washington, DC: Brassey's, 2000.

Central Intelligence Agency. *The World Factbook 2003*. Washington, DC: Brassey's, 2003.

Centre for Economic and Financial Research. "Monitoring Administrative Barriers to Small Business Developments in Russia: Second Round." Report of the Centre for Economic and Financial Research and the World Bank, February 5, 2003, Moscow. Online at cfir.ru. Site consulted September 2003.

Chambers, Simone, and Jeffrey Kopstein. "Bad Civil Society." *Political Theory* 29, 6 (December 2001): 838–66.

Chaudhry, Kiren Aziz. *The Price of Wealth: Economies and Institutions in the Middle East*. Ithaca, NY: Cornell University Press, 1997.

Chekalkin, Vladimir. "Osobennosti otechestvennoi izbiratel'noi kampannii." *Vlast'* 7, 1995: 13–18.

Chinayeva, Elena. "Profile: Boris Nemtsov, a Rising Star in the Russian Provinces." *Transition* 2, 4 (February 23, 1996): 36–38.

Chua, Amy. *World on Fire: How Exporting Free Market Democracy Breeds Ethnic Hatred and Global Instability*. New York: Doubleday, 2003.

Clark, John F. "Petro-Politics in Congo." *Journal of Democracy* 8, 3 (July 1997): 62–76.

Clark, Victoria. *Why Angels Fall: A Journey Through Orthodox Europe from Byzantium to Kosovo*. New York: Palgrave Macmillan, 2000.

Clarke, Simon, and Sarah Ashwin. *Russian Trade Unions and Industrial Relations in Transition*. New York: Palgrave Macmillan, 2003.

Cohen, Stephen F. *Failed Crusade: America and the Tragedy of Post-Communist Russia*. New York: Norton, 2000.

Collier, David, and Steven Levitsky. "Democracy with Adjectives: Conceptual Innovation in Comparative Research." *World Politics* 49, 3 (April 1997): 430–51.

Colton, Timothy J. "Superpresidentialism and Russia's Backward State." *Post-Soviet Affairs* 11, 2 (April–June 1995): 144–8.

Colton, Timothy J. *Transitional Citizens: Voters and What Influences Them in the New Russia*. Cambridge, MA: Harvard University Press, 2000.

Colton, Timothy J., and Michael McFaul. "Are Russians Undemocratic?" *Post-Soviet Affairs* 18, 2 (April–June 2002): 91–121.

Colton, Timothy J., and Michael McFaul. *Popular Choice and Managed Democracy: The Russian Elections of 1999 and 2000*. Washington, DC: Brookings, 2003.

Colton, Timothy J., and Michael McFaul. "Reinventing Russia's Party of Power: 'Unity' and the 1999 Duma Election." *Post-Soviet Affairs* 16, 3 (July–September 2000): 201–24.

Committee to Protect Journalists. *Attacks on the Press, 2001: Russia*. Online at www.cpj.org. Site consulted December 2002.

Constant, Benjamin. *Political Writings*. Cambridge: Cambridge University Press, 2000.

Coppedge, Michael. "The Conditional Impact of the Economy on Democracy in Latin America." Paper delivered at the conference on Democratic Advancements and Setbacks: What Have We Learned? Uppsala University, Uppsala, Sweden, June 2004.

"Court Cancels Far East Race." *Moscow Times*, December 18, 1999.

Crowley, Stephen. "Barriers to Collective Action: Steelworkers and Mutual Dependence in the Former Soviet Union." *World Politics* 46, 4 (July 1994): 589–615.

Crowley, Stephen, and David Ost, eds. *Workers After Workers' States: Labor and Politics in Postcommunist Eastern Europe*. Oxford: Rowman and Littlefield, 2001.

Dahl, Robert A. *Dilemmas of Pluralist Democracy*. New Haven, CT: Yale University Press, 1982.

Dahl, Robert A. *Polyarchy*. New Haven, CT: Yale University Press, 1971.

Dahl, Robert A. "Why Free Markets Are Not Enough." *Journal of Democracy* 3, 3 (July 1992): 82–9.

"Data on Small Moscow Businesses Posted." *Pravda. RU*, February 25, 2003. Online at Pravda.ru. Site consulted September 2003.

Davis, Charles L., Roderic Ai Camp, and Kenneth M. Coleman. "The Influence of Party Systems on Citizens' Perceptions of Corruption and Electoral Response in Latin America." *Comparative Political Studies* 37, 6 (August 2004): 677–703.

References

De Melo, Martha, Cebdet Denizer, and Alan Gelb. "Patterns of Transition from Plan to Market." *World Bank Economic Review* 10, 3 (1996): 397–424; and subsequent updates.

Derbyshire, J. Denis, and Ian Derbyshire. *Political Systems of the World.* New York: St. Martin's, 1996.

Dewhirst, Martin. "Censorship in Russia, 1991 and 2001." *Journal of Communist Studies and Transition Politics* 18, 1 (March 2002): 21–34.

Diamond, Larry. *Deepening Democracy: Toward Consolidation.* Baltimore: Johns Hopkins University Press, 1999.

Diamond, Larry. "Democracy and Economic Reform." In Edward P. Lazear, ed., *Economic Transition in Eastern Europe and Russia.* Stanford, CA: Hoover Institution Press, 1995: 107–58.

Dine, Thomas A. "Free Press in Russia and Ukraine: A Key to Integration in Europe." In Karin Deutsch Karlekar, ed., *Freedom of the Press 2003: A Global Survey of Media Independence.* New York: Freedom House, 2003: 41–6.

Di Palma, Giuseppe. "Legitimation from the Top to Civil Society: Politico-Cultural Change in Eastern Europe." *World Politics* 44, 1 (October 1991[a]): 49–80.

Di Palma, Giuseppe. *To Craft Democracies: An Essay on Democratic Transitions.* Berkeley: University of California Press, 1990.

Di Palma, Giuseppe. "Why Democracy Can Work in Eastern Europe." *Journal of Democracy* 2, 1 (Winter 1991[b]): 21–31.

Dolgov, Anna. "New Fears Arise over Danger to Journalists." *St. Petersburg Times,* March 9, 2001.

Donskis, Leonidas. "The Autumn of Lithuania's Discontent." *Transitions Online,* December 5, 2003. Online at tol.cz. Site consulted January 2004.

Drobizheva, Leokadiya. "Comparison of Elite Groups in Tatarstan, Sakha, Magadan, and Orenburg." *Post-Soviet Affairs* 15, 4 (October–December 1999): 387–406.

Dryzek, John S., and Leslie Holmes. "The Real World of Civic Republicanism: Making Democracy Work in Poland and the Czech Republic." *Europe-Asia Studies* 52, 6 (September 2000): 1043–68.

Duncan, Peter J. S. *Russian Messianism: Third Rome, Holy Revolution, Communism and After.* London: Routledge, 2000.

Durkheim, Emile. *The Division of Labor in Society.* New York: Free Press, 1997.

Durkheim, Emile. *The Elementary Forms of Religious Life.* New York: Free Press, 1995.

Durkheim, Emile. *Professional Ethics and Civic Morals.* London: Routledge, 1992.

Durkheim, Emile. *The Rules of the Sociological Method,* ed. Steven Lukes. New York: Free Press, 1982.

Duverger, Maurice. "A New Political System Model: Semi-Presidential Government." *European Journal of Political Research* 8, 1 (June 1980): 165–87.

Easter, Gerald M. "Preference for Presidentialism: Postcommunist Regime Change in Russia and the NIS." *World Politics* 49, 2 (January 1997): 184–211.

Easter, Gerald M. "The Russian Tax Police." *Post-Soviet Affairs* 18, 4 (October–December 2002): 332–62.

EastWest Institute. *Russian Regional Report* 5, 42 (November 15, 2000). Online at www.isn.ethz.ch. Site consulted July 2003.

Ebel, Robert, and Rajan Menon, eds. *Energy and Conflict in Central Asia and the Caucasus*. Lanham, MD: Rowman and Littlefield, 2000.

"Editor Attacked." *Moscow Times*, July 1, 1998.

Elgie, Robert. "The Classification of Democratic Regime Types: Conceptual Ambiguity and Contestable Assumptions." *European Journal of Political Research* 33, 2 (March 1998): 219–38.

Elgie, Robert, ed. *Semi-Presidentialism in Europe*. Oxford: Oxford University Press, 1999.

Elklit, Jørgen, and Andrew Reynolds. "The Impact of Election Administration on the Legitimacy of Emerging Democracies: A New Comparative Politics Research Agenda." *Commonwealth and Comparative Politics* 40, 2 (July 2002): 86–119.

Elster, Jon, ed. *The Roundtable Talks and the Breakdown of Communism*. Chicago: University of Chicago Press, 1996.

Encarnación, Omar G. "On Bowling Leagues and NGOs: A Critique of Civil Society's Revival." *Studies in Comparative International Development* 36, 4 (Winter 2002): 116–31.

Esposito, John L., and John O. Voll. *Islam and Democracy*. New York: Oxford University Press, 1996.

Evans, Peter. "The Eclipse of the State? Reflections on Stateness in an Era of Globalization." *World Politics* 50, 1 (October 1997): 62–87.

Fairbanks, Charles H. "The Feudalization of the State." *Journal of Democracy* 10, 2 (April 1999): 47–53.

Fearon, James D., and David D. Laitin. "Ethnicity, Insurgency, and Civil War," *American Political Science Review* 97, 1 (February 2003): 75–90.

Fearon, James D., and David D. Laitin. "Explaining Interethnic Cooperation." *American Political Science Review* 90, 4 (December 1996): 715–35.

Feifer, Gregory. "Who Pulls Prosecutor's Strings?" *St. Petersburg Times*, July 18, 2000.

Filipov, David. "Putin's Paradox: In Public, He's Boss; Behind the Scenes, He Takes Cues." *Boston Globe*, June 21, 2003.

Filippov, Petr. "Kuda poshel protsess?" *Delovoi mir*, February 6–13, 1994.

Fish, M. Steven. "Democracy and Russian Politics." In Zoltan D. Barany and Robert G. Moser, eds., *Russian Politics: Challenges of Democratization*. Cambridge: Cambridge University Press, 2001[a]: 215–54.

Fish, M. Steven. *Democracy from Scratch: Opposition and Regime in the New Russian Revolution*. Princeton, NJ: Princeton University Press, 1995.

Fish, M. Steven. "The Determinants of Economic Reform in the Post-Communist World." *East European Politics and Societies* 12, 1 (Winter 1998[a]): 31–78.

Fish, M. Steven. "The Impact of the 1999–2000 Parliamentary and Presidential Elections on Political Party Development." In Vicki L. Hesli and William M. Reisinger, eds., *The 1999–2000 Elections in Russia: Their Impact and Legacy*. Cambridge: Cambridge University Press, 2003: 186–212.

References

Fish, M. Steven. "Islam and Authoritarianism." *World Politics* 55, 1 (October 2002): 4–37.

Fish, M. Steven. "Mongolia: Democracy Without Prerequisites." *Journal of Democracy* 9, 3 (July 1998[b]): 127–41.

Fish, M. Steven. "The Predicament of Russian Liberalism: Evidence from the December 1995 Parliamentary Elections." *Europe-Asia Studies* 49, 2 (March 1997): 191–220.

Fish, M. Steven. "Putin's Path." *Journal of Democracy* 12, 4 (October 2001[b]): 71–8.

Fish, M. Steven. "The Roots of and Remedies for Russia's Racket Economy." In Stephen S. Cohen, Andrew Schwartz, and John Zysman, eds., *The Tunnel at the End of the Light: Privatization, Business Networks, and Economic Transformation in Russia.* Berkeley: University of California International and Area Studies, 1998[c]: 86–137.

Fish, M. Steven, and Robin S. Brooks. "Does Diversity Hurt Democracy?" *Journal of Democracy* 15, 1 (January 2004): 155–66.

Fish, M. Steven, and Matthew Kroenig. *The Legislative Powers Survey* and *The Parliamentary Powers Index.* 2004.

Flikke, Geir. "Patriotic Left-Centrism: The Zigzags of the Communist Party of the Russian Federation." *Europe-Asia Studies* 51, 2 (March 1999): 275–98.

Freeland, Chrystia. *Sale of the Century: Russia's Wild Ride from Communism to Capitalism.* New York: Crown, 2000.

Friedman, Milton. *Capitalism and Freedom.* Chicago: University of Chicago Press, 1962.

Frye, Timothy. *Brokers and Bureaucrats: Market Institutions in Russia.* Ann Arbor: University of Michigan Press, 2000.

Frye, Timothy. "Markets, Democracy, and New Private Business in Russia." *Post-Soviet Affairs* 19, 1 (January–March 2003): 24–45.

Frye, Timothy. "Presidents, Parliaments, and Democracy: Insights from the Post-Communist World." In Andrew Reynolds, ed., *The Architecture of Democracy: Constitutional Design, Conflict Management, and Democracy.* New York: Oxford University Press, 2002[a]: 81–103.

Frye, Timothy. "Private Protection in Russia and Poland." *American Journal of Political Science* 46, 3 (July 2002[b]): 572–84.

Frye, Timothy and Andrei Shleifer. "The Invisible Hand and the Grabbing Hand." *American Economic Review* 87, 2 (May 1997): 354–8.

Fuller, Liz. "Ballot Fails to Elect New President After Strongest Candidate Excluded from Ballot." *RFE/RL Russian Report* 4, 13 (April 10, 2002[a]).

Fuller, Liz. "No Holds Barred in North Ossetian Election Campaign." *Caucasus Report of Radio Free Europe/Radio Liberty* 5, 4 (January 2002[b]).

Gaidar, Egor. *Zapiski iz zala.* Moscow: Evraziia, 1995.

Geddes, Barbara. "Initiation of New Democratic Institutions in Eastern Europe and Latin America." In Arend Lijphart and Carlos H. Waisman, eds., *Institutional Design in New Democracies: Eastern Europe and Latin America.* Boulder, CO: Westview, 1996: 15–41.

Geddes, Barbara. *Politician's Dilemma: Building State Capacity in Latin America.* Berkeley: University of California Press, 1994.

Gelman, Vladimir. "Regime Transition, Uncertainty and Prospects for Democratisation: The Politics of Russia's Regions in Comparative Perspective." *Europe-Asia Studies* 51, 6 (September 1999): 939–65.

Gelman, Vladimir, Sergei Ryzhenkov, and Igor Semenov. "Saratovskaia oblast': Pobeditel' poluchaet vse." In Vladimir Gelman et al., eds., *Rossiia regionov: Transformatsiia politicheskikh rezhimov.* Moscow: Ves' mir, 2000: 109–45.

Geremek, Bronislaw. "The Transformation of Central Europe." In Larry Diamond and Marc F. Plattner, eds., *Democracy After Communism.* Baltimore: Johns Hopkins University Press, 2002: 120–4.

Gerring, John. *Social Science Methodology: A Critical Framework.* Cambridge: Cambridge University Press, 2001.

Gerschenkron, Alexander. *Economic Backwardness in Historical Perspective.* Cambridge, MA: Harvard University Press, 1962.

Gibson, James L. "Becoming Tolerant? Short-Term Changes in Russian Political Culture." *British Journal of Political Science* 32, 2 (April 2002): 309–34.

Gibson, James L. "The Russian Dance with Democracy." *Post-Soviet Affairs* 17, 2 (April–June 2001): 101–28.

Gibson, James L. "The Struggle Between Order and Liberty in Contemporary Russian Political Culture." *Australian Journal of Political Science* 32, 2 (July 1997): 271–90.

Gill, Graeme J. *The Dynamics of Democratization: Elites, Civil Society and the Transition Process.* New York: Palgrave Macmillan, 2000.

"Glava gosudarstva podderzhal FPG." *Segodnia,* April 2, 1996.

Globachev, Mikhail. "A Shot of Fright." *New Times,* June 2003. Online at www.newtimes.ru. Site consulted June 2003.

Goldman, Marshall I. *Lost Opportunity: Why Economic Reforms in Russia Have Not Worked.* New York: Free Press, 1994.

Goldman, Marshall I. *The Piratization of Russia: Russian Reform Goes Awry.* New York: Routledge, 2003.

Goldman, Marshall I. "Russian Energy: A Blessing and a Curse." *Journal of International Affairs* 53, 1 (Fall 1999): 73–84.

Goldthorpe, John H. "Current Issues in Comparative Macrosociology: A Debate on Methodological Issues." *Comparative Social Research* 16 (1997): 1–26.

Golosov, Grigorii V. "Russian Political Parties and the 'Bosses': Evidence from the 1994 Provincial Elections in Western Siberia." *Party Politics* 3, 1 (January 1997): 5–21.

Golosov, Grigorii V. "The Vicious Circle of Party Underdevelopment in Russia: The Regional Connection." *International Political Science Review* 24, 4 (October 2003): 427–43.

Goodwin, Jan. *Price of Honor: Muslim Women Lift the Veil of Silence in the Islamic World.* New York: Penguin, 1995.

Gordon, Leonid. *Nadezhda ili ugroza.* Moscow: IMEMO, 1995.

References

Gott, Richard. *In the Shadow of the Liberator: The Impact of Hugo Chavez on Venezuela and Latin America*. London: Verso, 2001.

"Government Challenged to Root out Corruption." *Russia Journal*, February 19, 2004. Online at russiajournal.com. Site consulted March 2004.

Granville, Brigitte. *The Success of Russian Economic Reforms*. Washington, DC: Brookings, 1995.

Green, Andrew T. "Comparative Development of Post-communist Civil Societies." *Europe-Asia Studies* 54, 3 (May 2002): 455–71.

Grimes, Barbara F., ed. *Ethnologue Languages of the World*, 14th ed. Dallas: SIL International, 2000.

Gudkov, Lev. "O legitimosti sotsial'nogo poriadka v Rossii." *Vestnik obshchestvennogo mneniia* 70, 2 (March–April 2004): 8–17.

Gunnemark, Erik V. *Countries, Peoples, and Their Languages: The Geolinguistic Handbook*. Dallas: SIL International, 1991.

Gunther, Richard, and Anthony Mughan. "Political Institutions and Cleavage Management." In R. Kent Weaver and Bert A. Rockman, eds., *Do Institutions Matter? Government Capabilities in the United States and Abroad*. Washington, DC: Brookings, 1993: 272–301.

Gurr, Ted Robert, Monty G. Marshall, and Keith Jaggers. *Polity IV Project: Political Regime Characteristics and Transitions, 1800–2002*. Online at cidcm.umd.edu/inscr/polity/index.htm#data. Site consulted April 2004.

Gvosdev, Nikolas K. *Emperors and Elections: Reconciling the Orthodox Tradition with Modern Politics*. Hauppauge, NY: Nova, 2000[a].

Gvosdev, Nikolas K. "The New Party Card? Orthodoxy and the Search for Post-Soviet Russian Identity." *Problems of Post-Communism* 47, 6 (November–December 2000[b]): 29–38.

Gwartney, James, and Robert Lawson with Neil Emerick. *Economic Freedom of the World: 2003 Annual Report*. Vancouver, BC: The Fraser Institute, 2003. Online at fraserinstitute.ca. Site consulted August 2003.

Hadenius, Axel. *Institutions and Democratic Citizenship*. Oxford: Oxford University Press, 2001.

Hadenius, Axel, and Jan Teorell. "Evaluating Alternative Indices of Democracy." Paper delivered at the annual meeting of the American Political Science Association, Chicago, August 2004.

Hahn, Jeffrey W. "St. Petersburg and the Decline of Local Self-Government in Post-Soviet Russia." *Post-Soviet Affairs* 20, 2 (April–June 2004): 107–31.

Hale, Henry E. "Explaining Machine Politics in Russia's Regions: Economy, Ethnicity, and Legacy." *Post-Soviet Affairs* 19, 3 (July–September 2003): 228–63.

Hale, Henry E. "The Regionalization of Autocracy in Russia." PONARS Policy Memo 42, Harvard University, November 1998.

Hall, Peter A. "Aligning Ontology and Methodology in Comparative Politics." In James Mahoney and Dietrich Rueschemeyer, eds., *Comparative Historical Analysis in the Social Sciences*. Cambridge: Cambridge University Press, 2003: 373–404.

Hanson, Philip. "The Russian Economic Recovery: Do Four Years of Growth Tell Us That the Fundamentals Have Changed?" *Europe-Asia Studies* 55, 3 (May 2003): 365–82.

Hanson, Stephen E. "Instrumental Democracy: The End of Ideology and the Decline of Russian Political Parties." In Vicki L. Hesli and William M. Reisinger, eds., *The 1999–2000 Elections in Russia: Their Impact and Legacy*. Cambridge: Cambridge University Press, 2003: 163–85.

Hanson, Stephen E., and Jeffrey S. Kopstein. "The Weimar/Russia Comparison." *Post-Soviet Affairs* 13, 3 (July–September 1997): 252–84.

Hedlund, Stefan. *Russia's Market Economy: A Bad Case of Predatory Capitalism*. London: UCL Press, 2000.

Hefner, Robert W. *Civil Islam*. Princeton, NJ: Princeton University Press, 2000.

Hellman, Joel S. "Winners Take All: The Politics of Partial Reform in Postcommunist Transitions." *World Politics* 50, 2 (January 1998): 203–34.

Herbst, Jeffrey. *States and Power in Africa*. Princeton, NJ: Princeton University Press, 2000.

Herrera, Yoshiko M. "Russian Economic Reform, 1991–1999." In Zoltan Barany and Robert G. Moser, eds., *Russian Politics: Challenges of Democratization*. New York: Cambridge University Press, 2001: 135–74.

Hirschman, Albert O. *The Passions and the Interests*. Princeton, NJ: Princeton University Press, 1977.

Hirst, Paul. *Associative Democracy: New Forms of Economic and Social Governance*. Amherst: University of Massachusetts Press, 1994.

Holmes, Stephen. "Crime and Corruption After Communism." *East European Constitutional Review* 6, 4 (Fall 1997[a]): 69–70.

Holmes, Stephen. "Potemkin Democracy." In Theodore K. Rabb and Ezra N. Suleiman, eds., *The Making and Unmaking of Democracy: Lessons from History and World Politics*. New York: Routledge, 2003: 109–33.

Holmes, Stephen. "What Russia Teaches Us Now: How Weak States Threaten Freedom." *The American Prospect* 8, 33 (July 1–August 1, 1997[b]): 30–9.

Hook, Sidney. *Hero in History: A Study in Limitation and Possibility*. Boston: Beacon Press, 1955.

Horowitz, Donald L. "Comparing Democratic Systems." In Larry Diamond and Marc F. Plattner, eds., *The Global Resurgence of Democracy*, 2d ed. Baltimore: Johns Hopkins University Press, 1996: 143–9.

Horowitz, Donald L. "Democracy in Divided Societies." *Journal of Democracy* 4, 4 (October 1993): 18–38.

Horowitz, Donald L. *Ethnic Groups in Conflict*. Berkeley: University of California Press, 1985.

Hout, Michael, and Theodore P. Gerber. "More Shock than Therapy: Market Transition, Employment, and Income in Russia, 1991–95." *American Journal of Sociology* 104, 1 (July 1998): 1–50.

Howard, Marc Morjé. *The Weakness of Civil Society in Post-Communist Europe*. Cambridge: Cambridge University Press, 2003.

References

Huber, Evelyne, Dietrich Rueschemeyer, and John D. Stephens. "The Paradoxes of Democracy: Formal, Participatory, and Social Dimensions." In Lisa Anderson, ed., *Transitions to Democracy*. New York: Columbia University Press, 1999: 168–92.

Huntington, Samuel P. *The Clash of Civilizations and the Remaking of the Modern World*. New York: Simon and Schuster, 1996.

Huntington, Samuel P. *Political Order in Changing Societies*. New Haven, CT: Yale University Press, 1968.

Huntington, Samuel P. *The Third Wave: Democratization in the Late Twentieth Century*. Norman: University of Oklahoma Press, 1991.

Huntington, Samuel P. "Will More Countries Become Democratic?" *Political Science Quarterly* 99, 2 (Summer 1984): 193–218.

Hurst, Andrew. "Investment Grade Still a Ways Off, Analysts Say." *Moscow Times*, February 10, 2003.

Huskey, Eugene. *Presidential Power in Russia*. Armonk, NY: M. E. Sharpe, 1999.

Iavlinskii, Grigorii. "Russia Risks Becoming a Corporate Police State." *Novye izvestiia*, February 24, 2001. Online at eng.yabloko.ru. Site consulted 2004.

Ickes, Barry W. "The Russian Economy in 2003." In Peter Reddaway, Gail W. Lapidus, Barry W. Ickes, Carol Saivetz, and George W. Breslauer, "Russia in the Year 2003." *Post-Soviet Affairs* 20, 1 (January–March 2004): 19–31.

INDEM. "Diagnostika rossiiskoi korruptsii: Sotsiologicheskii analiz" (2002). Online at www.anti-corr.ru/awbreport. Site consulted June 2003.

Inglehart, Ronald. "Trust, Well-Being and Democracy." In Mark E. Warren, ed., *Democracy and Trust*. Cambridge: Cambridge University Press, 1999: 88–120.

Inglehart, Ronald. *World Values Surveys*, 2002. Online at worldvaluessurvey.org. Site consulted March 2003.

Inglehart, Ronald, Miguel Basáñez, Jaime Díez-Medrano, Loek Halman, and Ruud Luijkx, eds. *Human Beliefs and Values: A Cross-Cultural Sourcebook Based on the 1999–2002 Values Surveys*. Mexico City: Siglo Veintiuno, 2004.

Inglehart, Ronald, and Christian Welzel. "Political Culture and Democracy: Analyzing Cross-Level Linkages." *Comparative Politics* 36, 1 (October 2003): 61–79.

International League for Human Rights. "Belarusian Orthodox Church Supports Lukashenko Regime." *Belarus Update* 3, 15 (April 2000). Online at ilhr.org. Site consulted February 2003.

International Monetary Fund. Statistical Appendices from reports for 2000, 2001, and 2002. Online at imf.org/external/country/index.htm. Site consulted May 2003.

Isaac, Jeffrey C. "1989 and the Future of Democracy." In Sorin Antohi and Vladimir Tismaneanu, eds., *Between Past and Future: The Revolutions of 1989 and Their Aftermath*. Budapest: CEU Press, 2000: 39–60.

Ishiyama, John T. "Political Parties and Candidate Recruitment in Post-Soviet Russian Politics." *The Journal of Communist Studies and Transition Politics* 15, 4 (December 1999): 41–69.

Ivanov, Mikhail. "Golosovaniie vtemnuiu." *Rossiiskaia gazeta*, May 21, 2002.

Jack, Andrew. "Putin Eases the Way for Pro-Kremlin Candidate." *Financial Times*, June 17, 2003.

Jackman, Robert. "Cross-National Statistical Research and the Study of Comparative Politics." *American Journal of Political Science* 29, 1 (February 1985): 161–82.

Janos, Andrew C. *East Central Europe in the Modern World*. Stanford, CA: Stanford University Press, 2000.

Jasiewicz, Krzysztof. "Dead Ends and New Beginnings." In Marek Jan Chodakiewicz, John Radzilowski, and Dariusz Tolczyk, eds., *Poland's Transformation: A Work in Progress*. Charlottesville, VA: Leopolis Press, 2003: 89–123.

Javeline, Debra. *Protest and the Politics of Blame: The Russian Response to Unpaid Wages*. Ann Arbor: University of Michigan Press, 2003.

Jensen, Donald N. "Russia's 'Vertical of Power' Goes to the Polls." *RFE/RL Newsline* 7, 182, September 24, 2003. Online at rferl.org/newsline. Site consulted January 2004.

Johnson, Juliet. *A Fistful of Rubles: The Rise and Fall of the Russian Banking System*. Ithaca, NY: Cornell University Press, 2000.

Johnson, Juliet. "Russia's Emerging Financial-Industrial Groups." *Post-Soviet Affairs* 13, 4 (October–December 1997): 333–65.

Jowitt, Ken. "The Leninist Legacy." In Ivo Banac, ed., *Eastern Europe in Revolution*. Ithaca, NY: Cornell University Press, 1992: 207–24.

Jung, Courtney, and Ian Shapiro. "South Africa's Negotiated Transition." *Politics and Society* 23, 3 (September 1995): 269–308.

Kahn, Jeffrey. *Federalism, Democratization, and the Rule of Law in Russia*. Oxford: Oxford University Press, 2002.

Kapustin, Boris. *Ideologiia i politika v postkommunisticheskoi Rossii*. Moscow: Editorial URSS, 2000.

Karatnycky, Adrian. "The 2001 Freedom House Survey." *Journal of Democracy* 13, 1 (January 2002): 99–112.

Karatnycky, Adrian, Aili Piano, and Arch Puddington, eds. *Freedom in the World: The Annual Survey of Political Rights and Civil Liberties 2003*. Boulder, CO: Rowman and Littlefield, 2003.

Karl, Terry Lynn. "Dilemmas of Democratization in Latin America." *Comparative Politics* 23, 1 (October 1990): 1–22.

Karl, Terry Lynn. *The Paradox of Plenty: Oil Booms and Petro-States*. Berkeley: University of California Press, 1997.

Karlekar, Karin Deutsch, ed. *Freedom of the Press 2003: A Global Survey of Media Independence*. New York: Freedom House, 2003.

Karush, Sarah. "Priest Brings Schoolchildren into the Fold." *St. Petersburg Times*, March 28, 2001.

Kaufmann, Daniel, Aart Kraay, and Massimo Mastruzzi. "Governance Matters III: Governance Indicators for 1996–2002." June 30, 2003. Online at worldbank.org/wbi/governance. Site consulted May 2004.

Keane, John, ed. *Civil Society and the State*. London: Verso, 1988.

Kekic, Laza. "How Dependent Is Growth on the Oil Price?" *Moscow Times*, January 23, 2004.

References

Key, V. O. *Public Opinion and American Democracy*. New York: Knopf, 1961.

Khakamada, Irina. "Small Enterprises Not Smiling Yet." *Moscow Times*, February 13, 2003.

Khasbulatov, Ruslan. "Ne tam by diktatorov ishchete." *Komsomolskaia pravda*, October 9, 1992.

Khripunov, Igor. "Red Army Blues." *Bulletin of the Atomic Scientists* 52, 3 (May/June 1996): 13.

Kihlgren, Alessandro. "Small Business in Russia: A Case Study of St. Petersburg." William Davidson Institute Working Paper No. 439, January 2002. Online at eres.bus.umich.edu/docs. Site consulted September 2003.

King, Gary, Robert O. Keohane, and Sidney Verba. *Designing Social Inquiry*. Princeton, NJ: Princeton University Press, 1994.

Kirkow, Peter. "Regional Warlordism in Russia: The Case of Primorskii Krai." *Europe-Asia Studies* 47, 6 (September 1995): 923–48.

Kirkow, Peter. *Russia's Provinces: Authoritarian Transformation Versus Local Autonomy?* New York: Palgrave Macmillan, 1998.

Kishkovsky, Sophia. "A Bright Future: Russian Higher Education." *Carnegie Reporter* 1, 1 (Summer 2000). Online at carnegie.org/reporter/01/russia. Site consulted May 2004.

Kitschelt, Herbert. "Accounting for Postcommunist Regime Diversity: What Counts as a Good Cause?" In Grzegorz Ekiert and Stephen E. Hanson, eds., *Capitalism and Democracy in Central and Eastern Europe: Assessing the Legacy of Communist Rule*. New York: Cambridge University Press, 2003: 49–86.

Kitschelt, Herbert. "The Formation of Party Systems in East Central Europe." *Politics and Society* 20, 1 (March 1992): 7–50.

Klein, Lawrence R., and Marshall Pomer, eds. *The New Russia: Transition Gone Awry*. Stanford, CA: Stanford University Press, 2001.

Knight, Amy. "The Enduring Legacy of the KGB in Russian Politics." *Problems of Post-Communism* 47, 4 (July–August 2000): 3–15.

Knox, Zoe. "The Symphonic Ideal: The Moscow Patriarchate's Post-Soviet Leadership." *Europe-Asia Studies* 55, 4 (June 2003): 575–96.

Kokh, Alfred R. *The Selling of the Soviet Empire: Politics and Economics of Russia's Privatization, Revelations of the Principal Insider*. New York: SPI Books, 1998.

Kollontai, Vladimir. "Social Transformations in Russia." *International Social Science Journal* 51, 1 (March 1999): 103–21.

Kolosov, Vladimir. "Partii v regionakh: vliianie i perspektivy." *Vlast'* 7, 1995: 22–38.

Koreneva, Marina. "Kremlin Candidate Wins St. Petersburg Vote, but Turnout Is Low." *Agence France-Presse*, October 6, 2003, posted online by ISI Emerging Markets. Online at securities.com. Site consulted January 2004.

Kotkin, Stephen. *Armageddon Averted: The Soviet Collapse 1970–2000*. New York: Oxford University Press, 2001.

Kovaleva, Natalia. "Konflikty, profsoiuzy, sotsial'naia zashchita: otsenki rabotnikov i rukovoditelei predpriiatii." In *Monitoring obshchestvennogo mneniia* 5, 31 (September–October 1997): 26–32.

Kovalyev, Vladimir. "Putin Named 'Enemy' of Journalists." *St. Petersburg Times,* May 8, 2001.

Krain, Matthew. "Ethnic Fractionalization Data." Online at wooster.edu/polisci/mkrain/Ethfrac. Site consulted September 2001.

Krasikov, Anatoly. "From the Annals of Spiritual Freedom: Church-State Relations in Russia." *East European Constitutional Review* 7, 2 (Spring 1998): 75–84.

Krouwel, André. "The Presidentialisation of East-Central European Countries." Paper prepared for presentation at the ECPR Joint Sessions Workshop on the Presidentialisation of Parliamentary Democracies, Copenhagen, April 2000.

Kryshtanovskaya, Olga, and Stephen White. "From Soviet Nomenklatura to Russian Elite." *Europe-Asia Studies* 48, 5 (July 1996): 711–33.

Kubicek, Paul. "Civil Society, Trade Unions and Post-Soviet Democratisation: Evidence from Russia and Ukraine." *Europe-Asia Studies* 54, 4 (June 2002): 603–24.

"Kudrin: State Hopes to Break Free from Oil." *Moscow Times,* April 19, 2002.

——. "Liberal Elites, Socialist Masses, and Problems of Russian Democracy." *World Politics* 51, 3 (April 1999): 323–58.

——. "The Political Foundations of Post-Communist Regimes: Marketization, Agrarian Legacies, or International Influences." *Comparative Political Studies* 35, 5 (June 2002): 524–53.

——. "The Implications of Constructivism for Constructing Ethnic Fractionalization Indices." *Newsletter of the Comparative Politics Section of the American Political Science Association* 12, 1 (Winter 2001): 13–17.

Lallemand, Jean-Charles. "Politics for the Few: Elites in Bryansk and Smolensk." *Post-Soviet Affairs* 15, 4 (October–December 1999): 312–35.

Lapidus, Gail W. "Contested Sovereignty: The Tragedy of Chechnya." *International Security* 23, 1 (Summer 1998): 5–49.

Lardeyret, Guy. "The Problem with PR." In Larry Diamond and Marc F. Plattner, eds., *The Global Resurgence of Democracy,* 2d ed. Baltimore: Johns Hopkins University Press, 1996: 175–80.

Lehoucq, Fabrice. "Electoral Fraud: Causes, Types, and Consequences." *Annual Review of Political Science* 6, 2003: 233–56.

Le Huérou, Anne. "Elites in Omsk." *Post-Soviet Affairs* 15, 4 (October–December 1999): 362–86.

Leite, Carlos, and Jens Weidmann. "Does Mother Nature Corrupt? Natural Resources, Corruption, and Economic Growth." IMF Working Paper, WP/99/85 (July 1999).

Levitsky, Steven, and Lucan A. Way. "The Rise of Competitive Authoritarianism." *Journal of Democracy* 13, 2 (April 2002): 51–65.

Lewis, Peter. "From Prebendalism to Predation: The Political Economy of Decline in Nigeria." *Journal of Modern African Studies* 34, 1 (March 1996): 79–103.

Liashenko, Galina. "Nalogovoi reformy v 2004 godu ne budet." *Kommersant,* March 25, 2003.

Lieven, Anatol. *Chechnya: Tombstone of Russian Power.* New Haven, CT: Yale University Press, 1998.

References

Lijphart, Arend. *Democracy in Plural Societies*. New Haven, CT: Yale University Press, 1977.

Lindblom, Charles E. *Politics and Markets*. New York: Basic Books, 1977.

Linz, Juan J. *The Breakdown of Democratic Regimes: Crisis, Breakdown, and Reequilibration*. Baltimore: Johns Hopkins University Press, 1978.

Linz, Juan J., and Alfred Stepan. *Problems of Democratic Transition and Consolidation: Southern Europe, South America, and Post-Communist Europe*. Baltimore: Johns Hopkins University Press, 1996.

Linz, Juan J., and Arturo Valenzuela, eds. *The Failure of Presidential Democracy*. Baltimore: Johns Hopkins University Press, 1994.

Lipman, Masha. "The Putin Toothpick." *New Yorker*, March 8, 2004.

Lipset, Seymour Martin. "The Centrality of Political Culture." In Larry Diamond and Marc F. Plattner, eds., *The Global Resurgence of Democracy*, 2d ed. Baltimore: Johns Hopkins University Press, 1996: 150–3.

Lipset, Seymour Martin. *Political Man*. Garden City, NY: Doubleday, 1960.

Lipset, Seymour Martin, and Gary Marks. *It Didn't Happen Here: Why Socialism Failed in the United States*. New York: Norton, 2001.

Litvinovich, Dmitri. "Russia: Recounting, Swindling, Regrouping." *Transitions Online*, December 9–15, 2003. Online at tol.cz. Site consulted January 2004.

Luebbert, Gregory M. *Liberalism, Fascism, and Social Democracy: Social Classes and the Political Origins of Regimes in Interwar Europe*. Oxford: Oxford University Press, 1991.

Lukin, Alexander. "Authoritarianism Deposing 'Clan Democracy.'" *Moscow Times*, January 21, 2004.

Luong, Pauline Jones, and Erika Weinthal. "Contra Coercion: Russian Tax Reform, Exogenous Shocks, and Negotiated Institutional Change." *American Political Science Review* 98, 1 (February 2004): 139–52.

Luong, Pauline Jones, and Erika Weinthal. "Prelude to the Resource Curse: Explaining Oil and Gas Development Strategies in the Soviet Successor States and Beyond." *Comparative Political Studies* 34, 4 (May 2001): 367–99.

Macpherson, C. B. *Democratic Theory: Essays in Retrieval*. Oxford: Clarendon, 1973.

Mahoney, James, and Dietrich Rueschemeyer, eds. *Comparative Historical Analysis in the Social Sciences*. Cambridge: Cambridge University Press, 2003.

Mainwaring, Scott, Daniel Brinks, and Aníbal Pérez-Liñán. "Classifying Political Regimes in Latin America, 1945–1999." *Studies in Comparative International Development* 36, 1 (Spring 2001): 37–65.

Mainwaring, Scott, and Matthew Soberg Shugart, eds. *Presidential Democracy in Latin America*. New York: Cambridge University Press, 1997.

Maravall, José Maria. *Regimes, Politics and Markets: Democratization and Economic Change in Southern and Eastern Europe*. New York: Oxford University Press, 1997.

Marshall, T. H. *Class, Citizenship, and Social Development*. Garden City, NY: Anchor, 1965.

Marx, Karl, and Friedrich Engels. *The German Ideology*. Amherst, NY: Prometheus Books, 1998.

McCauley, Martin. *Bandits, Gangsters and the Mafia: Russia, the Baltic States and the CIS Since 1991*. London: Longman, 2001.

McDaniel, Tim. *The Agony of the Russian Idea*. Princeton, NJ: Princeton University Press, 1998.

McFaul, Michael. *Russia's 1996 Presidential Election: The End of Polarized Politics*. Stanford, CA: Hoover Institution Press, 1997.

McFaul, Michael. *Russia's Unfinished Revolution: Political Change from Gorbachev to Putin*. Ithaca, NY: Cornell University Press, 2001.

McFaul, Michael, and Nikolai Petrov, eds. *Politicheskii al'manakh Rossii 1997, tom 2, kniga 1: Sotsial'no-politicheskie portrety regionov*. Moscow: Carnegie Center, 1998.

Medetsky, Anatoly. "Voters in Far East Region Left with Little Choice." *Moscow Times*, December 17, 1999.

Medetsky, Anatoly, and Francesca Mereu. "Communists Say Vote Count 'a Scam.'" *St. Petersburg Times*, December 11, 2003.

Medvedev, Roy. *Post-Soviet Russia: A Journey Through the Yeltsin Era*. New York: Columbia University Press, 2000.

Mehlum, Halvor, Karl Moene, and Ragnar Torvik. "Institutions and the Resource Curse." August 28, 2002. Online at folk.uio.no/karlom/natres. Site consulted March 2003.

Mendelson, Sarah E. "The Putin Path: Civil Liberties and Human Rights in Retreat." *Problems of Post-Communism* 47, 5 (September–October 2000): 3–12.

Mendras, Marie. "How Regional Elites Preserve Their Power." *Post-Soviet Affairs* 15, 4 (October–December 1999): 295–311.

Menon, Rajan, and Graham E. Fuller. "Russia's Ruinous Chechen War." *Foreign Affairs* 79, 2 (March/April 2000): 32–44.

Mereu, Francesca. "Red Governors Swear Loyalty to Putin." *Moscow Times*, March 25, 2004.

Mereu, Francesca. "Russia: Central Bank Head Tenders Resignation." *RFE/RL Report*, March 19, 2002.

Meyer, Henry. "Polling Stations Deserted in War-Torn Chechnya." *Agence France-Presse*, March 14, 2004, posted online by ISI Emerging Markets. Online at securities.com. Site consulted March 2004.

Migdal, Joel S. *Strong Societies and Weak States: State-Society Relations and State Capabilities in the Third World*. Princeton, NJ: Princeton University Press, 1988.

Mikheyev, Dmitry. *Russia Transformed*. Indianapolis: Hudson Institute, 1996.

Miles, Marc, Edwin J. Feulner, and Mary Anastasia O'Grady. *2004 Index of Economic Freedom*. Washington, DC: The Heritage Foundation and Dow Jones & Co., 2004.

Miliband, Ralph. "The Socialist Alternative." *Journal of Democracy*, 3, 3 (July 1992): 118–24.

Millar, James R. "From Utopian Socialism to Utopian Capitalism: The Failure of Revolution and Reform in Post-Soviet Russia." *Problems of Post-Communism* 42, 3 (May–June 1995): 7–14.

Miller, Arthur H., and Thomas F. Klobucar. "The Development of Party Identification in Post-Soviet Societies." *American Journal of Political Science* 44, 4 (October 2000): 667–86.

References

Moore, Barrington. *Social Origins of Dictatorship and Democracy: Lord and Peasant in the Making of the Modern World.* Boston: Beacon, 1966.

Moses, Joel C. "Voting, Regional Legislatures and Electoral Reform in Russia." *Europe-Asia Studies* 55, 7 (November 2003): 1049–75.

Munck, Gerardo L., and Jay Verkuilen. "Conceptualizing and Measuring Democracy: Evaluating Alternative Indices." *Comparative Political Studies* 35, 1 (February 2002): 5–34.

Mungiu-Pippidi, Alina. "The Ruler and the Patriarch: The Romanian Eastern Orthodox Church in Transition." *East European Constitutional Review* 7, 2 (Spring 1998): 85–91.

Murphy, Kevin M., Andrei Shleifer, and Robert Vishney. "The Transition to a Market Economy: Pitfalls of Partial Reform." *Quarterly Journal of Economics* 107, 3 (August 1992): 889–906.

Murrell, Peter. "The Transition According to Cambridge, Mass." *Journal of Economic Literature* 33, 1 (March 1995): 164–78.

Muslim Population Worldwide. Online at www.islamicpopulation.com. Site consulted June 2003.

Mydans, Seth. "Ukraine: Move Seen as Leader's Ploy Fails." *New York Times,* April 9, 2004.

Myers, Steven Lee. "Nine Candidates Run to Praise Putin, Not to Beat Him." *New York Times,* January 9, 2004[a].

Myers, Steven Lee. "Now You Don't See Him, Now You Do: Putin Foe Resurfaces." *New York Times,* February 11, 2004[b].

Myers, Steven Lee. "Observer Team in Russia Lists Election Flaws." *New York Times,* March 16, 2004[c].

Myers, Steven Lee. "Russia's Voting for Parliament Bolsters Putin." *New York Times,* December 8, 2003.

"Napadeniia na zhurnalistov i redaktsii, 2003." *Arkhiv fonda zashchity glasnosti izbitye zhurnalisty, 2003.* Online at www.gdf.ru/arh/crym/crym2003.shtml. Site consulted January 2004.

Nations in Transit 2003: Russia. New York: Freedom House, 2003.

Nechaeva, Marina. "Development of Small and Medium Enterprises in the Samara Region." Report of the Business Information Service for the Newly Independent States (BISNIS), July 2002. Online at www.bisnis.doc.gov. Site consulted September 2003.

Nelson, Daniel N. "Civil Society Endangered." *Social Research* 63, 2 (Summer 1996): 345–68.

Newburg, Paula L. "Corrupt Elections: What's an NGO to Do About It?" *St. Petersburg Times,* December 8, 2000.

"News Editor Beaten in Russian Enclave." *Moscow Tribune,* July 3, 1998.

Nezhdanova, Vera. "Enticed or Forced, Russians Flock to Vote." *Agence France-Presse,* March 14, 2004, posted online by ISI Emerging Markets. Online at securities.com. Site consulted March 2004.

"NG – Stsenarii." *Nezavisimaia gazeta,* June 29, 1996.

Nichols, Thomas M. *The Russian Presidency: Society and Politics in the Second Russian Republic.* Basingstoke: Macmillan, 2001.

Nicholson, Alex. "No Tearful Goodbyes for the Tax Police." *Moscow Times*, March 13, 2003.

Nikol'skii, Aleksei, Aleksandr Bekker, and Sergei Kochetov. "Vse dovol'ny." *Vedomosti-Business News Media*, July 16, 2001, posted online by ISI Emerging Markets. Online at securities.com. Site consulted March 2004.

Oates, Sarah. "The 1999 Russian Duma Elections." *Problems of Post-Communism* 47, 3 (May–June 2000): 3–14.

O'Donnell, Guillermo A. "Democracy, Law, and Comparative Politics." *Studies in Comparative International Development* 36, 1 (Spring 2001): 7–36.

O'Driscoll, Gerald P., Kim R. Holmes, and Mary Anastasia O'Grady. *2002 Index of Economic Freedom*. New York: The Heritage Foundation and Dow Jones & Co., 2002.

Okonta, Ike, and Oronto Douglas. *Where Vultures Feast: Shell, Human Rights, and Oil*. New York: Verso, 2003.

Orenstein, Mitchell. "Lawlessness from Above and Below: Economic Radicalism and Political Institutions." *SAIS Review* 18, 1 (Winter-Spring 1998): 35–50.

Organization for Security and Cooperation in Europe (OSCE). *Russian Federation, Presidential Election, 26 March 2000, Final Report*. Warsaw: OSCE Office for Democratic Institutions and Human Rights, May 19, 2000.

Orttung, Robert. "Gaidar Calls for Unified Democratic Bloc." *OMRI Daily Digest*, February 13, 1995.

Ost, David. "Illusory Corporatism in Eastern Europe." *Politics and Society* 28, 4 (December 2000): 508–30.

Ostrovsky, Simon. "Putin: Graft Killing Small Business." *Moscow Times*, December 20, 2001.

Oxhorn, Philip D., and Graciela Ducatenzeiler, eds. *What Kind of Democracy? What Kind of Market? Latin America in the Age of Neoliberalism*. University Park: Pennsylvania State University Press, 1998.

Pacific Media Watch. "Russian Anti-Terrorism Law Tightens Grip on the Media." *Scoop*, October 31, 2002. Online at www.scoop.co.nz. Site consulted May 2003.

"Parlament ostanovil protsess, kotoryi uzhe poshel." *Megapolis Express*, July 28, 1993.

Pastukhov, Vladimir. "Law Under Administrative Pressure in Post-Soviet Russia." *East European Constitutional Review* 11, 3 (Summer 2002): 66–74.

Payne, Anthony. "Westminster Adapted: The Political Order of the Commonwealth Caribbean." In Jorge I. Dominguez, Robert A. Pastor, and R. DeLisle Worrell, eds., *Democracy in the Caribbean*. Baltimore: Johns Hopkins University Press, 1993: 57–73.

Peach, Gary. "Kaliningrad's Open Season on Journalists." *Moscow Times*, December 16, 1999.

Petro, Nicolai. "The Novgorod Region: A Russian Success Story." *Post-Soviet Affairs* 15, 3 (July–September 1999): 235–61.

Petro, Nicolai. *The Rebirth of Russian Democracy: An Interpretation of Political Culture*. Cambridge, MA: Harvard University Press, 1995.

Petrov, Nikolai. "Bashkir Bargaining." *Moscow Times*, December 4, 2003[a].

Petrov, Nikolai. "Electoral Centralization." *Moscow Times*, June 17, 2003[b].

References

Petrov, Nikolai. "Russia's 'Party of Power' Takes Shape." *Jamestown Foundation Russia and Eurasia Review* 2, 16 (August 5, 2003). Online at russia.jamestown.org. Site consulted September 2003[c].

Pierson, Paul. *Politics in Time: History, Institutions, and Social Analysis.* Princeton, NJ: Princeton University Press, 2004.

Pipes, Richard. "Flight from Freedom: What Russians Think and Want." *Foreign Affairs* 83, 3 (May/June 2004): 9–15.

Pomer, Marshall. "Demise of the Command Economy." In Lawrence R. Klein and Marshall Pomer, eds., *The New Russia: Transition Gone Awry.* Stanford, CA: Stanford University Press, 2001: 139–69.

Pomfret, Richard. "Transition and Democracy in Mongolia." *Europe-Asia Studies* 52, 1 (January 2000): 149–60.

"Postanovlenie Tsentral'noi izbiratel'noi komissii Rossiiskoi Federatsii ot 22 ianvaria 2004 g. N 80/679–4 g. Moskva ob otkaze v registratsii kandidata na dolzhnost' Prezidenta Rossiiskoi Federatsii V. V. Gerashchenko, vydvinutogo politicheskoi partiei 'Partiia rossiiskikh regionov.'" *Rossiiskaia gazeta*, January 27, 2004.

Poznanski, Kazimierz P. "The Crisis of Transition as a State Crisis." In Frank Bonker, Klaus Muller, and Andreas Pickel, eds., *Postcommunist Transformation and the Social Sciences.* Lanham, MD: Rowman and Littlefield, 2002: 55–76.

Prince, Todd. "S&P Says Russia Still Too Hooked on Oil." *Moscow Times*, December 17, 2003.

Prodromou, Elizabeth. "The Ambivalent Orthodox." *Journal of Democracy* 15, 2 (April 2004): 62–75.

Protsyk, Oleh. "Troubled Semi-presidentialism: Stability of the Constitutional System and Cabinet in Ukraine." *Europe-Asia Studies* 55, 7 (November 2003): 1077–95.

Przeworski, Adam. *Democracy and the Market: Political and Economic Reforms in Eastern Europe and Latin America.* Cambridge: Cambridge University Press, 1991.

Przeworski, Adam. "Economic Reforms, Public Opinion, and Political Institutions: Poland and Eastern Europe in Comparative Perspective." In Luis Carlos Bresser Pereira, José Maria Maravall, and Adam Przeworski, *Economic Reforms in New Democracies: A Social-Democratic Approach.* Cambridge: Cambridge University Press, 1993.

Przeworski, Adam. "The Neoliberal Fallacy." *Journal of Democracy* 3, 3 (July 1992): 45–59.

Przeworski, Adam, Michael Alvarez, José Antonio Cheibub, and Fernando Limongi. "Classifying Political Regimes." *Studies in Comparative International Development* 31, 2 (Summer 1996[a]): 3–36.

Przeworski, Adam, Michael Alvarez, José Antonio Cheibub, and Fernando Limongi. *Democracy and Development: Political Institutions and Well-Being in the Modern World, 1950–1990.* New York: Cambridge University Press, 2000.

Przeworski, Adam, Michael Alvarez, José Antonio Cheibub, and Fernando Limongi. "What Makes Democracies Endure?" *Journal of Democracy* 7, 1 (January 1996[b]): 39–56.

Pshizova, Susaina. "Kakuiu partiinuiu model' vosprimet nashe obshchesto." *Polis* 4, 1998: 101–13.

"Putin Declares War on Corruption." *Russia Journal*, November 25, 2003. Online at russiajournal.com. Site consulted March 2004.

"Putin's Way: Special Report on the Russian Elections." *The Economist*, December 13, 2003. Online at economist.com/world/europe/displayStory.cfm? story_id=2282403. Site consulted June 2004.

Putnam, Robert D. *Making Democracy Work: Civic Traditions in Modern Italy*. Princeton, NJ: Princeton University Press, 1993.

Rabushka, Alvin, and Kenneth A. Shepsle. *Politics in Plural Societies*. Columbus, OH: Merrill, 1972.

Radio Free Europe/Radio Liberty. *Media Matters* 2, 27 (July 8, 2002). Online at www.rferl.org. Site consulted May 2003.

Raiser, Martin, Christian Haerpfer, Thomas Nowotny, and Claire Wallace. "Social Capital in Transition: One Cheer for Civic Association." Paper delivered at the conference on Political Economy of Transition: Institutions, Politics, and Policies, University of Bonn and the Centre for Economic Policy Research, Bonn, Germany, May 2002.

Reddaway, Peter, and Dmitri Glinski. *The Tragedy of Russia's Reforms: Market Bolshevism Against Democracy*. Washington, DC: U.S. Institute of Peace, 2001.

Reformy dlia bol'shinstva. Moscow: Pervaia obraztsovaia tipografiia, 1995.

. "Political Values in Russia, Ukraine, and Lithuania: Sources and Implications for Democracy." *British Journal of Political Science* 24, 2 (April 1994): 183–223.

Remington, Thomas F. *The Russian Parliament: Institutional Evolution in a Transitional Regime, 1989–1999*. New Haven, CT: Yale University Press, 2001.

Riker, William H. *Liberalism Against Populism*. Prospect Heights, IL: Waveland, 1982.

Robinson, Neil. *Russia: A State of Uncertainty*. London: Routledge, 2001.

Roeder, Philip G. "The Rejection of Authoritarianism." In Richard D. Anderson, Jr., M. Steven Fish, Stephen E. Hanson, and Philip G. Roeder, *Postcommunism and the Theory of Democracy*. Princeton, NJ: Princeton University Press, 2001: 11–53.

Roper, Steven D. "Are All Semipresidential Regimes the Same? A Comparison of Premier-Presidential Regimes." *Comparative Politics* 34, 3 (April 2002): 253–72.

Rose, Richard. "Economics in Transition: A Multidimensional Approach to a Cross-Cultural Problem." *East European Constitutional Review* 11/12, 4/1 (Fall 2002/Winter 2003): 62–70.

Rose, Richard. "Postcommunism and the Problem of Trust." In Larry Diamond and Marc F. Plattner, eds., *The Global Resurgence of Democracy*, 2d ed. Baltimore: Johns Hopkins University Press, 1996: 251–63.

Rose, Richard, and Neil Munro. *Elections Without Order: Russia's Challenge to Vladimir Putin*. Cambridge: Cambridge University Press, 2002.

Rose, Richard, Neil Munro, and Stephen White. "Voting in a Floating Party System: The 1999 Duma Election." *Europe-Asia Studies* 53, 3 (May 2001): 419–43.

References

Rose, Richard, and Doh Chull Shin. "Qualities of Incomplete Democracies: Russia, the Czech Republic and Korea." Studies in Public Policy No. 302, Centre for the Study of Public Policy, University of Strathclyde, 1998.

Rose-Ackerman, Susan. "Trust, Honesty, and Corruption: Reflection on the State-Building Process." *Archives of European Sociology* XLII, 3 (2001): 27–71.

Rosefielde, Steven. "Premature Deaths: Russia's Radical Economic Transition in Soviet Perspective." *Europe-Asia Studies* 53, 8 (December 2001): 1159–76.

Rosenberg, Tina. "In Colombia, Muckrakers Have Become Scarce." Editorial. *New York Times*, July 3, 2003.

Ross, Cameron, ed. *Regional Politics in Russia*. Manchester: Manchester University Press, 2002.

Ross, Michael. "Does Oil Hinder Democracy?" *World Politics* 53, 3 (April 2001): 325–61.

Rostovskii, Mikhail, and Aleksandr Budberg. "Fradkov podkralsia nezametno." *Moskovskii Komsomolets*, March 2, 2004.

Rueschemeyer, Dietrich, Evelyne Huber Stephens, and John D. Stephens. *Capitalist Development and Democracy*. Chicago: University of Chicago Press, 1992.

Rustow, Dankwart. "Transitions to Democracy: Toward a Dynamic Model." *Comparative Politics* 2, 3 (April 1970): 337–63.

Rutkevich, Mikhail. "Transformatsiia sotsial'noi struktury rossiiskogo obshchestva." *Sotsiologicheskie issledovaniia* 7, 1997: 3–19.

Rutland, Peter. "Mission Impossible? The IMF and the Failure of the Market Transition in Russia." *Review of International Studies* 25, Special Issue (December 1999): 183–200.

Rutland, Peter. "Privatization in Russia: One Step Forward, Two Steps Back?" *Europe-Asia Studies* 46, 7 (1994): 1109–31.

Rutland, Peter, ed. *Business and the State in Contemporary Russia*. Boulder, CO: Westview, 2000.

"Rybkin uzhe v Moskve." *Grani.ru*, March 3, 2004. Online at grani.ru. Site consulted March 2004.

Sachs, Jeffrey. "Why Russia Has Failed to Stabilize." In Anders Aslund, ed., *Russian Economic Reform at Risk*. London: Pinter, 1995: 53–62.

——. "The Curse of Natural Resources." *European Economic Review* 45 (2001): 827–38.

Sakwa, Richard. "Elections and National Integration in Russia." In Vicki L. Hesli and William M. Reisinger, eds., *The 1999–2000 Elections in Russia: Their Impact and Legacy*. Cambridge: Cambridge University Press, 2003: 121–41.

——. "Vserossiiskii dispanser." *Gazeta.ru*, March 15, 2004. Online at gazeta.ru. Site consulted March 2004.

Samuels, Richard J. *Machiavelli's Children: Leaders and Their Legacies in Italy and Japan*. Ithaca, NY: Cornell University Press, 2003.

Sapir, Jacques. "The Washington Consensus and Transition in Russia: History of a Failure." *International Social Science Journal* 52, 4 (December 2000): 479–91.

Saradzhyan, Simon. "Moscow Takes over Probe of Slain Editor." *Moscow Times*, June 11, 1998.

Sartori, Giovanni. *Parties and Party Systems: A Framework for Analysis*. Cambridge: Cambridge University Press, 1976.

Sartori, Giovanni. *The Theory of Democracy Revisited*. Chatham, NJ: Chatham House, 1987.

Satter, David. *Darkness at Dawn: The Rise of the Russian Criminal State*. New Haven, CT: Yale University Press, 2003.

Satter, David. "Symposium on Democracy in Russia." *Insight on the News* 18, 26 (July 22, 2002).

Schedler, Andreas. "Measuring Democratic Consolidation." *Studies in Comparative International Development* 36, 1 (Spring 2001): 66–92.

Schmitter, Philippe C. "Interest Intermediation and Regime Governability in Contemporary Western Europe and North America." In Suzanne Berger, ed., *Organizing Interests in Western Europe: Pluralism, Corporatism, and the Transformation of Politics*. Cambridge: Cambridge University Press, 1981: 285–327.

Schmitter, Philippe C. "Interest Systems and the Consolidation of Democracies." In Gary Marks and Larry Diamond, eds., *Reexamining Democracy: Essays in Honor of Seymour Martin Lipset*. Newbury Park, CA: Sage, 1992: 156–81.

Schmitter, Philippe C., and Terry Lynn Karl. "What Democracy Is . . . and Is Not." In Larry Diamond and Marc F. Plattner, eds., *The Global Resurgence of Democracy*. Baltimore: Johns Hopkins University Press, 1996: 49–62.

Schumpeter, Joseph A. *Capitalism, Socialism, and Democracy*. New York: Harper, 1950.

Shapiro, Ian. *Democracy's Place*. Ithaca, NY: Cornell University Press, 1996.

Sharlet, Robert. "The Politics of Constitutional Amendment in Russia." *Post-Soviet Affairs* 13, 3 (July–September 1997): 197–227.

Sharlet, Robert. "Russian Constitutional Change: Proposed Power-Sharing Models." In Roger Clark, Ferdinand Feldbrugge, and Stanislaw Pomorski, eds., *International and National Law in Russia and Eastern Europe*. Amsterdam: Kluwer Law International, 2001: 361–72.

Shelley, Louise. "Is the Russian State Coping with Organized Crime and Corruption?" In Valerie Sperling, ed., *Building the Russian State: Institutional Crisis and the Quest for Democratic Governance*. Boulder, CO: Westview, 2000: 91–112.

Shevtsova, Liliia. *Postkommunisticheskaia Rossiia: Logika razvitiia i perspektivy*. Moscow: Moscow Carnegie Center, 1995.

Shishkunova, Elena. "Viktor Gerashchenko poluchil otkaz." *Gazeta.ru*, March 10, 2004. Online as gazeta.ru. Site consulted March 2004.

Shkolnikov, Vladimir, Martin McKee, and D. A. Leon. "Changes in Life Expectancy in Russia in the Mid-1990s." *The Lancet* 357 (9260), (March 24, 2001): 917–21.

Shlapentokh, Vladimir. "Hobbes and Locke at Odds in Putin's Russia." *Europe-Asia Studies* 55, 7 (November 2003[a]): 981–1007.

Shlapentokh, Vladimir. "What the Russians Are Thinking." *New York Times*, August 18, 2003[b].

Shleifer, Andrei, and Daniel Treisman. "A Normal Country." *Foreign Affairs* 83, 2 (March/April 2004): 20–38.

Shleifer, Andrei, and Daniel Treisman. *Without a Map: Political Tactics and Economic Reform in Russia*. Cambridge, MA: MIT Press, 2000.

References

Shokhin, Aleksandr. *Moi golos budet vse-taki uslyshan: Stenogramma epokhi peremen.* Moscow: Nash dom – L'Age d'Homme, 1995.

Shugart, Matthew Soberg, and John M. Carey. *Presidents and Assemblies: Constitutional Design and Electoral Dynamics.* Cambridge: Cambridge University Press, 1992.

Skocpol, Theda. *States and Social Revolutions: A Comparative Analysis of France, Russia, and China.* Cambridge: Cambridge University Press, 1979.

Skorobogatko, Tatiana. "Housewarming of First Reading: Will the Government Manage to Trade in Budget Approval for Elite Apartments for Duma Deputies?" *Moscow News*, September 20, 2000.

"Sluchai gibeli zhurnalistov." *Arkhiv fonda zashchity glasnosti – pogibshie zhurnalisty, 2003.* Online at www.gdf.ru/arh/mort/2003.shtml. Site consulted January 2004.

Smith, Peter H., and Scott R. Bailey. "Latin American Democracy – Electoral, Liberal, Illiberal." Paper delivered at the conference on Democratic Advancements and Setbacks: What Have We Learned? Uppsala University, Uppsala, Sweden, June 2004.

Smith, Steven S., and Thomas F. Remington. *The Politics of Institutional Choice: The Formation of the Russian State Duma.* Princeton, NJ: Princeton University Press, 2001.

Sobchak, Anatolii, et al. "Konstitutsiia ne 'sh'etsia' po vechnoi merke." *Kuranty*, May 14, 1993.

Sokolowski, Alexander. "Grounds for Optimism." *Moscow Times*, October 21, 2002.

Soros, George. "Who Lost Russia?" *New York Review of Books*, April 13, 2000: 10–16.

Soskovets, Oleg. "My ne otkazhemsia ot reform." *Nezavisimaia gazeta*, March 12, 1996.

Sperling, Valerie. "Introduction: The Domestic and International Obstacles to State-Building in Russia." In Valerie Sperling, ed., *Building the Russian State: Institutional Crisis and the Quest for Democratic Governance.* Boulder, CO: Westview, 2000: 1–23.

Squire, John. "Putin's Deep Freeze." *Journal of Democracy* 15, 1 (January 2004): 167–74.

Stan, Lavinia, and Lucian Turcescu. "The Romanian Orthodox Church and Postcommunist Transition." *RFE/RL East European Perspectives* 3, 5 (March 7, 2001).

Stark, David, and Laszlo Bruszt. *Postsocialist Pathways.* Cambridge: Cambridge University Press, 1998.

Stavrakis, Peter J. "The East Goes South: International Aid and the Production of Convergence in Africa and Eurasia." In Mark R. Beissinger and Crawford Young, eds., *Beyond State Crisis? Postcolonial Africa and Post-Soviet Eurasia in Comparative Perspective.* Washington, DC: Woodrow Wilson Center Press, 2002: 263–90.

Stavrakis, Peter J. "State-Building in Post-Soviet Russia: The Chicago Boys and the Decline of Administrative Capacity." Kennan Institute for Advanced Russian Studies, Occasional Paper No. 254, 1993.

Stawrowski, Zbigniew. "The Constitutional Debate in Poland after 1989." In Marek Jan Chodakiewicz, John Radzilowski, and Dariusz Tolczyk, eds., *Poland's Transformation: A Work in Progress.* Charlottesville, VA: Leopolis Press, 2003: 77–88.

Stepan, Alfred. *Arguing Comparative Politics*. New York: Oxford University Press, 2001.

Stepan, Alfred, and Cindy Skach. "Constitutional Frameworks and Democratic Consolidation: Parliamentarianism Versus Presidentialism." *World Politics* 46, 1 (October 1993): 1–22.

Stokes, Susan C. *Mandates and Democracy: Neoliberalism by Surprise in Latin America*. Cambridge: Cambridge University Press, 2001[a].

Stokes, Susan C., ed. *Public Support for Market Reforms in New Democracies*. Cambridge: Cambridge University Press, 2001[b].

Stoner-Weiss, Kathryn. "The Limited Reach of Russia's Party System: Underinstitutionalization in Dual Transitions." *Politics and Society* 29, 3 (September 2001): 385–414.

Stoner-Weiss, Kathryn. *Local Heroes: The Political Economy of Russian Regional Governance*. Princeton, NJ: Princeton University Press, 1997.

Taylor, Charles L., and Michael C. Hudson. *World Handbook of Political and Social Indicators*, 2d ed. New Haven, CT: Yale University Press, 1972.

Thompson, Ginger. "Former Mexican President Reveals '88 Presidential Election Was Rigged." *New York Times*, March 9, 2004.

Tilly, Charles. *Capital, Coercion, and European States, A.D. 990–1990*. Oxford: Oxford University Press, 1990.

Timofeev, Lev. "Natsional-kommunisty vozrazhdaiut ideologiiu nenavisti." *Izvestiia*, April 20, 1993.

Tismaneanu, Vladimir. *Stalinism for All Seasons: A Political History of Romanian Communism*. Berkeley: University of California Press, 2003.

Titma, Mikk, Nancy Brandon Tuma, and Brian Silver. "Winners and Losers in the Postcommunist Transition: New Evidence from Estonia." *Post-Soviet Affairs* 14, 2 (April–June 1998): 113–46.

Transparency International. "The Corruption Perceptions Index." Online at http://wwwuser.gwdg.de/~uwvw/icr.htm. Site consulted March 2004[a].

Transparency International. *Global Corruption Report 2004*. Sterling, VA: Pluto Press, 2004[b].

Treisman, Daniel. *After the Deluge: Regional Crises and Political Consolidation in Russia*. Ann Arbor: University of Michigan Press, 2001.

Treisman, Daniel. "Blaming Russia First." *Foreign Affairs* 79, 6 (November–December 2000): 146–55.

Treisman, Daniel. "Russia's 'Ethnic Revival': The Separatist Activism of Regional Leaders in a Postcommunist Order." *World Politics* 49, 2 (January 1997): 212–49.

Tsukanova, Liubov. "Few Guarantees on Elections." *Novoe vremia* 23, June 2002. Online at http://www.eng.yabloko.ru/Publ/2002/papers/nv-230602.html. Site consulted June 2003.

Tsygankov, Valerii. "Veshniakovu podrezhut kryl'ia." *Obshaia gazeta*, March 7, 2002.

United Civil Party. "Some Are More Equal Than Others in Belarus." *Belarus Today*, October 16, 2002. Online at ucpb.org. Site consulted February 2003.

United Nations Development Programme (UNDP). *Human Development Report 1999: Russian Federation*. Moscow: Human Rights Publishers, 1999.

References

United Nations Development Programme (UNDP). *Human Development Report 2000.* New York: Oxford University Press, 2000.

United Nations Development Programme (UNDP). *Human Development Report 2000: Russian Federation.* Moscow: Human Rights Publishers, 2001.

United Nations Development Programme (UNDP). *Human Development Report 2003.* New York: Oxford University Press, 2003.

United Nations Statistics Division. "Indicators on Income and Economic Activity." Online at unstats.un.org. Site consulted April 2002.

United States Census Bureau. International Data Base. Online at www.census.gov. Site consulted March 2003.

United States Department of State. *Annual Reports on International Religious Freedom, 2001.* Various countries. Online at www.state.gov/g/drl/irf/rpt. Site consulted February 2003.

United States Information Agency (USIA). "The People Have Spoken: Global Views of Democracy." January 1998. Online at dosfan.lib.uic.edu/usia/usiahome/pdforum/demopeop. Site consulted June 2003.

Urban, Michael. "December 1993 as a Replication of Late-Soviet Electoral Practices." *Post-Soviet Affairs* 10, 2 (April–June 1994): 127–58.

Urban, Michael. *The Rebirth of Politics in Russia.* Cambridge: Cambridge University Press, 1997.

"U.S. Shares Russian Poll Concerns." *BBC News,* December 8, 2003. Online at newsvote.bbc.co.uk. Site consulted December 2003.

Uzelac, Ana. "Putin Wins Vote to Limit Parties." *Moscow Times,* May 25, 2001.

Uzzell, Lawrence. "Church Has to Reconsider Old Borders with the State." *St. Petersburg Times,* December 15, 2000.

Uzzell, Lawrence. "Keston Letter, April 2001." Online at prcenter.newmail.ru/oldnews/keston_letter.htm. Site consulted July 2003.

Uzzell, Lawrence. "Legislating Intolerance." *Moscow Times,* September 4, 1997.

Vandewalle, Dirk. *Libya Since Independence: Oil and State Building.* Ithaca, NY: Cornell University Press, 1998.

Varese, Federico. *The Russian Mafia: Private Protection in a New Market Economy.* Oxford: Oxford University Press, 2001.

Varshney, Ashutosh. *Ethnic Conflict and Civic Life: Hindus and Muslims in India.* New Haven, CT: Yale University Press, 2003[a].

Varshney, Ashutosh. "Nationalism, Ethnic Conflict, and Rationality." *Perspectives on Politics* 1, 1 (March 2003[b]): 85–99.

Vassilev, Rossen. "The 'Third-Worldization' of a 'Second-World' Nation: De-development in Post-Communist Bulgaria." *New Political Science* 25, 1 (March 2003): 99–112.

Veniamin, Igumen. "Termin, kotoromu ne povezlo." *Nezavisimaia gazeta,* June 20, 2001.

Verdery, Katherine. "Privatization as Transforming Persons." In Sorin Antohi and Vladimir Tismaneanu, eds., *Between Past and Future: The Revolutions of 1989 and Their Aftermath.* Budapest: CEU Press, 2000: 175–97.

Visloguzov, Vadim. "Belyi dom gotovitsia k zaversheniiu nalogovoi reformy." *Kommersant,* February 16, 2004.

Visloguzov, Vadim. "Reforma na marshe." *Infomaker-Russia Focus,* July 23, 2001, posted online by ISI Emerging Markets. Online at securities.com. Site consulted March 2004.

Vodolazov, Aleksandr. "RAO 'FNPR'." *Vremia Moskovskie Novosti,* February 24, 2001.

Volkov, Vadim. *Violent Entrepreneurs: The Use of Force in the Making of Russian Capitalism.* Ithaca, NY: Cornell University Press, 2002.

Vujacic, Veljko. "Gennadiy Zyuganov and the 'Third Road.'" *Post-Soviet Affairs* 12, 2 (April–June 1996): 118–54.

Vujacic, Veljko. "Serving Mother Russia: The Communist Left and Nationalist Right in the Struggle for Power, 1991–98." In Victoria E. Bonnell and George W. Breslauer, eds., *Russia in the New Century: Stability or Disorder?* Boulder, CO: Westview, 2001: 290–325.

Vulf, Martin. "Chem ekonomicheskaia reforma otlichaetsia ot revoliutsii." *Izvestiia (Financial Times/Izvestiia supplement)* 140, June 1992.

Walker, Edward W. *Dissolution: Sovereignty and the Breakup of the Soviet Union.* Boulder, CO: Rowman and Littlefield, 2003.

Walker, Edward W. "The New Russian Constitution and the Future of the Russian Federation." *The Harriman Institute Forum* 5, 10 (June 1992).

Walker, Edward W. "Politics of Blame and Presidential Powers in Russia's New Constitution." *East European Constitutional Review* 2, 4 (Fall 1993/Winter 1994): 116–19.

Wallace, Stuart. "Trans-Siberian Expects to Mine 280,000 Ounces of Gold by 2006." *Trans-Siberian Gold,* November 25, 2003. Online at www.trans-siberiangold.com. Site consulted March 2004.

Walsh, Conal. "Putin Turns Up Heat on Oligarchs." *The Observer,* November 9, 2003. Online at guardian.co.uk. Site consulted March 2004.

Wasserman, Danuta, and Airi Vdmik. "Perestroika in the Former USSR: History's Most Effective Suicide Prevention Programme for Men." In Danuta Wasserman, ed., *Suicide: An Unnecessary Death.* London: Martin Dunitz, 2001: 253–7.

Way, Lucan. "Pluralism by Default and the Sources of Political Liberalization in Weak States: The Case of the Former Soviet Union." Paper presented at the conference on "Democratization by Elections? The Dynamics of Electoral Authoritarianism," División de Estudios Políticos, CIDE, Mexico City, April 2004.

Way, Lucan. "Weak States and Pluralism: The Case of Moldova." *East European Politics and Societies* 17, 3 (Summer 2003): 454–82.

Weber, Max. *Economy and Society,* ed. Guenther Roth and Claus Wittich. Berkeley: University of California Press, 1978.

Weiner, Myron. "Empirical Democratic Theory." In Myron Weiner and Ergun Özbudun, eds., *Competitive Elections in Developing Countries.* Durham, NC: Duke University Press, 1987.

Weinthal, Erika, and Pauline Jones Luong. "Energy Wealth and Tax Reform in Russia and Kazakhstan." *Resources Policy* 27 (2001): 215–23.

Weir, Fred. "Kremlin Squeezes Political Parties." *Christian Science Monitor,* August 14, 2002.

References

Welsh, David. "Domestic Politics and Ethnic Conflict." In Michael E. Brown, ed., *Ethnic Conflict and International Security*. Princeton, NJ: Princeton University Press, 1993: 43–60.

White, Stephen, and Ian McAllister. "Putin and His Supporters." *Europe-Asia Studies* 55, 3 (May 2003): 383–99.

White, Stephen, Richard Rose, and Ian McAllister. *How Russia Votes*. Chatham, NJ: Chatham House, 1997.

Winiecki, Jan. "The Polish Generic Private Sector in Transition: Developments and Characteristics." *Europe-Asia Studies* 54, 1 (January 2002): 5–29.

Wishnevsky, Julia. "Russia on the Eve of the Parliamentary Election." *CSIS Post-Soviet Prospects* 3, 4 (May 1995). Online at csis.org/ruseura. Site consulted January 2004.

Woodruff, David. *Money Unmade: Barter and the Fate of Russian Capitalism*. Ithaca, NY: Cornell University Press, 2000.

Working, Russell. "Letter from Vladivostok: Election Graft a Grave Issue." *Moscow Times*, December 21, 1999[a].

Working, Russell. "Unity Beats Communists in Far East." *Vladivostok News*, December 24, 1999[b]. Online at vlad.tribnet.com/1999/current/text/upd4.html. Site consulted May 2004.

World Bank. *World Development Indicators 2001*. Washington, DC: The World Bank, 2001.

World Bank. *World Development Indicators 2002*. Washington, DC: The World Bank, 2002[a].

World Bank. *World Development Indicators 2003*. Washington, DC: The World Bank, 2003.

World Bank. *World Development Report 2002*. New York: Oxford University Press, 2002[b].

World Bank. *World Tables 1995*. Baltimore: Johns Hopkins University Press, 1995.

World Bank, Russia Country Department. "Russian Economic Report, February 2004." Online at worldbank.org.ru. Site consulted March 2004.

Wu, Yu-shan. "The ROC's Semi-presidentialism at Work: Unstable Compromise, Not Cohabitation." *Issues and Studies* 36, 5 (September–October 2000): 1–40.

Wyman, Matthew, Stephen White, and Sarah Oates, eds. *Elections and Voters in Post-Communist Russia*. Northampton, MA: Edward Elgar, 1998.

Yabolkova, Oksana. "Ministry Defends ARCSPO Overhaul." *Moscow Times*, September 3, 2003[a].

Yabolkova, Oksana. "Young Analyst Takes over ARCSPO." *Moscow Times*, September 12, 2003[b].

Yarlykapov, Akhmet. "Islamic Fundamentalism in the Northern Caucasus: Towards a Formulation of the Problem." *Caucasian Regional Studies* 4, 1 (1999). Online at poli.vub.ac.be/publi/crs/eng/0401-02.htm. Site consulted May 2004.

Yates, Douglas A. *The Rentier State in Africa: Oil Rent Dependency and Neocolonialism in the Republic of Gabon*. Trenton, NJ: Africa World Press, 1996.

Yegorov, Sergei. "Hospitals Trade Medical Care for Votes." *Gazeta.ru*, March 11, 2004. Online at gazeta.ru. Site consulted March 2004.

"Yukos Stake Sale." *Moscow Times*, August 29, 2002.

"Zashchita Iliumzhinova: Khod konem." *Novaia gazeta*, July 6–12, 1998.

Zaslavskaia, Tatiana. "Sotsial'naia struktura sovremennogo rossiiskogo obshchestva." *Ekonomicheskie i sotsial'nye peremeny: Monitoring obshchestvennogo mneniia* 6, 1995: 7–13.

Zaslavsky, Victor. "The Russian Working Class in Times of Transition." In Victoria E. Bonnell and George W. Breslauer, eds., *Russia in the New Century: Stability or Disorder?* Boulder, CO: Westview, 2001: 201–30.

Zimmerman, William. *The Russian People and Foreign Policy: Russian Elite and Mass Perspectives, 1993–2000.* Princeton, NJ: Princeton University Press, 2002.

Zolotov, Andrei. "Foreign Pastors Put on Blacklist." *Moscow Times*, July 23, 2002.

Zudin, Aleksei. "Oligarkhiia kak politicheskaia problema rossiiskogo postkommunizma." *Obshchestvennie nauki i sovremennost'* 1, 1999: 45–65.

Zueva, Elena. "Prilagatel'noe okazalos' somnitel'nym." *Rossiiskaia gazeta*, August 29, 2001.

Index

Index

Index

Index

Marx, Karl, 11, 157, 183, 184
Maslov, Viktor, 61
Mastruzzi, Massimo, 21–22
Matvienko, Valentina, 269
McFaul, Michael, 2, 3, 28
media in Russia, 30, 34–35, 47–48
    passim., 46, 60, 68–75, 187–188
  civil society and, 187–188
  Internet and, 69
  journalists, repression of, 60, 68–70
  Moscow Times, 34–35, 47–48 passim,
    73
  television and, 71–72, 73–74,
    187–188
Menon, Rajan, 115
methodology, 6–14, 20–23, 82–83
Mexico, 79
Migdal, Joel, 238–239, 240
Mikhailov, Evgenii, 59
Mill, John Stuart, 9, 184
Mironov, Sergei, 79, 268
modernization effect, 116, 123–127,
    138
  indicators of, 124–125
Moldova, 206–207, *see also*
    postcommunist region
Mongolia, 214, *see also* postcommunist
    region
monocracy, 20, 26–27
Moore, Barrington, 157, 183
Mordovia, 55
Morocco, 25
Moscow, 44
Moscow Times, 34–35, 47–48 passim,
    73
Motherland Party, 78
Motrich, Dmitrii, 69
Motrich, Lada, 69
Murashev, Arkadii, 44
Murmansk, 69
Murtazin, Irek, 43

Nadezhdin, Boris, 265
Narantsatsralt, Janlav, 235
Nasser, Gamal Abdul, 238

natural resource endowment, Russia
    and, 84, 114–128, 129–130,
    134–138, 247–248, 251, 254,
    258–261
  corruption and, 127–128,
    129–130, 134, 247, 259,
    260–261
  democratization and, 247–248, 254,
    258–261
  diversification and, 258–259
  Economic Freedom Index (EFI) and,
    135
  economic policy effect and,
    134–137
  political openness and, 115–118,
    135–136, 137–138
  postcommunist region, 117
  state control and, 260–261
  transfer pricing, 84
Nazarbaev, Nursultan, 244
Nazdratenko, Evgenii, 60, 62, 269,
    270
Nechiporenko, Taisiia, 39
Nemtsov, Boris, 235–236
neoliberalism, 140–141, 150–155, *see*
    also economic policy in Russia;
    shock therapy
  public welfare and, 151–155
Nietzsche, Friedrich, 184
Nikolaev, Mikhail, 64–65
Nilsen, Thomas, 44
Niyazov, Saparmurat, 186, 206
Nizhnii Novgorod, 56–57
North Ossetia, 63
NTV, 187–188, 271

O'Driscoll, Gerald, 135
oil and gas in Russia, *see* natural
    resource endowment, Russia and
oligarchy, 20, 25, 26, 29
  British empire and, 29
  South Africa and, 29
Organization for Security and
    Cooperation in Europe (OSCE),
    47–50, 80–81

Index

Other Books in the Series *(continued from page iii)*